A SHORT COURSE OF POLITICAL ECONOMY

by
L. Leontyev

PROGRESS PUBLISHERS
MOSCOW

Translated from the Russian
by DON DANEMANIS

Designed by V. DOBER

First   Printing   1968

Л. ЛЕОНТЬЕВ

КРАТКАЯ ПОЛИТИЧЕСКАЯ ЭКОНОМИЯ

На английском языке

Printed in the Union of Soviet Socialist Republics

CONTENTS

SOCIALISM AND COMMUNISM

4

Chapter I

WHAT IS POLITICAL ECONOMY?

Before taking up the study of any science, we should find out what it studies, what its subject-matter is. Astronomy, for example, studies the movement of the heavenly bodies, geology—the structure of the earth's crust, biology—the development of living organisms. What does political economy study?

Political economy is the science of the laws governing the production and exchange of the material means of subsistence in human society at the various stages of its development. It studies the social structure of production.

Natural and social sciences
The various sciences help people understand the world around them, which exists irrespective of the will and consciousness of people. People themselves are part of that world. Hence, the world embraces both nature and social life.

At every step people discover that each practical task demands of them some knowledge that is given by science. A metallurgist must know the chemical and technological processes at work in the blast or open-hearth furnace to smelt pig iron or steel. A machine-builder must know the laws of mechanics. The gardener understands that the success of his work depends on his knowledge and skilful application of the laws of botany, the laws of plant life.

The same applies to social activity. It, too, can be successful only if it relies on a precise knowledge and skilful application of the laws of social development. Otherwise it will result in failure and disappointment.

Every science deals with a definite field of natural or social phenomena. This field of phenomena is the subject-matter of a science.

Political economy is a social science. Social sciences study the various aspects of the life of human society. They elucidate the laws governing the development of definite spheres of social life.

Can there be a scientific knowledge of social life?

There are some who answer this question in the negative. Social development, they say, differs radically from natural development. In nature we are able to discern unalterable laws—identical conditions always produce identical results. But this, they say, does not apply to social life, where everything is accidental, spontaneous and unpredictable. Social development depends on the innumerable actions of people, on a medley of undefinable individual actions. Outstanding people—great thinkers, rulers, generals—carve history as they choose.

Is this correct? No, it is entirely wrong!

People do make history, and on the surface social development may appear to be a chain of accidents. But this does not mean that we cannot discover the genuine causes governing the actions of people, including those of outstanding individuals. A scientific analysis of social development demonstrates that in the seeming medley of events we can discern definite laws and that social life can be studied no less successfully than natural life.

Why then do some people deny that a scientific knowledge of social life can be gained?

The reason for this is not hard to see. In our time genuine social science leads to the conclusion that the doom of capitalism is sealed, and the triumph of communism inevitable. Small wonder, the ruling classes of the capitalist countries reject genuine social science. They recognise only a "science" that justifies their domination and defends their interests. Their "science" declares that the capitalist system is eternal. It also maintains that there are no laws of social development that impel the movement of society from the lowest to the highest forms.

Conversely, the working class is vitally interested in disclosing the laws of social development, in a genuine flourishing of social science. Marxism-Leninism is such a science, for it was the first to put the study of social life on a sound scientific basis.

The emergence of Marxist teaching was not accidental.

On the contrary, it resulted from the evolving requirements of the working-class struggle and absorbed the valuable experience of the working-class movement of all countries, having separated the flour from the bran. For the first time in the history of human thought, the theory of scientific communism disclosed the laws governing social development. The knowledge of these laws lent the working class invincible strength in the struggle against oppression and slavery, for freedom and a life worthy of man.

Marxism-Leninism proceeds from the assumption that human society, like nature, develops according to definite laws. These are objective laws, which means that they do not depend on the will and consciousness of people. Moreover, they themselves largely determine the consciousness, will and actions of the members of society.

We must not confuse social laws with laws enacted by legislative authority in all countries. The laws of social development are of an entirely different nature. They are conditioned by the whole system of social relations and, first and foremost, by the socio-economic system. Thus, in a capitalist country, the economic laws of capitalism operate irrespective of its constitutional regime, whether it is a monarchy or a republic. It is these laws that determine the development of industry and agriculture, the relations between classes and the nature of the class struggle. They govern the whole course of social development.

Social life is many-sided. Marxism has discovered that economic relations play a special role in the aggregate of social relations. They are basic and primary because they determine all other relations.

Material production —the basis of social life
The economic conditions of social life are determined primarily by material production.

People would not be able to live without food, clothing, shelter and other material means of subsistence. All of them are created by human labour.

The labour activities of people directed at creating the material means of subsistence are called production. People apply their labour to things found in nature and change them to make them suitable for their requirements. To build houses, for example, people first cut timber, produce bricks, cement, iron, concrete and other building materials.

To manufacture clothing they grow cotton, spin, weave and sew.

Along with labour in the diverse fields of material production, an important role is played in social life by the labour of people working in other fields of socially useful activity. This is the labour of teachers, doctors, scientists, artists, of those engaged in administration and the maintenance of law and order. This labour is also needed by society.

The modern scientific and technological revolution makes the labour of scientists and the activities of research institutions and establishments all-important. This applies not only to design offices, plant laboratories and specialised institutes, engaged in applied sciences, but also to research centres working on fundamental scientific problems. Without modern mathematics, for example, there would be no artificial earth's satellites and spaceships, no automatic machine-tools, automatic control systems, etc.

Production requires that there be: 1) human labour, 2) objects of labour and 3) instruments of labour.

Labour Ages of oppression and exploitation made people regard labour as a curse, "the curse of Adam".

In reality, however, labour is the main condition of man's existence. Generally, nature does not provide the means of subsistence—food, clothing, shelter, etc.—ready-made. People must apply their labour to change the things they find in nature into material means of subsistence.

Labour is the activity of people directed at adapting objects found in nature to the satisfaction of human wants.

It is through labour that man takes possession of the life-giving inexhaustible wealth of nature. The labour of innumerable generations enables man to master the forces of nature and to use them to his benefit.

Man develops his abilities through labour and only productive activity adds to people's knowledge and skills and advances science and culture. People's art and poetry, and the works of great artists have created immortal images glorifying the creative power of labour which transforms man from a pityful cringing worm into the ruler of nature.

Engels gave an excellent characteristic of labour when he said: "It is the prime basic condition for all human existence, and this to such an extent that, in a sense, we have to say that labour created man himself."[1]

In 1925, in the American town of Dayton, a young teacher by the name of Scopes was summoned for telling his pupils that man had descended from apes. The indictment read: if man descends from ape, where does God fit into the picture? Scopes was charged with committing a crime against religion.

Yet, the young teacher only repeated what had long since been irrefutably proved by science. The process of man's sublimation from the animal world embraces hundreds of millennia. Labour played the decisive role in that long process. Labour gradually perfected the organs, notably the hands, of our remote ancestors. It was through labour that articulate speech emerged and the human brain developed.

The genuine significance of labour, the true place of material production in social life were first disclosed by Marxism, the revolutionary world outlook of the working class. This discovery opened a new chapter in the development of human thought. It laid the foundation for scientific socialism. The irrefutable conclusion that labour will become the lord of the world follows from the proposition that labour is the maker of man's greatness.

One often reads of the "work" of ants, bees, spiders and beevers. Sometimes the "work" of the ant or beever is likened to that of man. However, the instinctive actions of animals have nothing in common with human labour.

Human labour has two distinctive features. First, human labour is an activity aimed at the achievement of a pre-set-aim. Secondly, it is indispensably connected with the production of instruments of labour.

An animal is only able to adjust itself to nature and to use what it finds in it. Man uses instruments to make nature serve his ends. Thanks to labour man begins to rule over nature. "This is the final, essential distinction between man and other animals," Engels wrote, "And once again it is labour that brings about this distinction."[2]

When people work they set certain parts of their bodies

---

[1] K. Marx and F. Engels, *Selected Works*, Vol. II, Moscow 1962, p. 80.
[2] Ibid., p. 89.

—their hands, legs, brain—in motion. In the process of labour people expend muscular, nervous and mental energy. In other words, they spend their labour power. Labour power is man's ability to work. Labour power in action is live human labour.

In the course of history man's ability to labour develops and his skills improve.

Objects of labour and instruments of labour

The things people act upon, i.e., everything upon which man's labour is used, are called objects of labour. Such objects can be things found in nature and things to which some labour has already been applied. In the latter case the objects of labour are called raw materials. Thus, every raw material is an object of labour but not every object of labour is a raw material.

The universal object of labour is the earth (the land and water) and all it contains. An old economist once remarked: labour is the father of all wealth, the land—its mother. Nature provides all the objects of labour and people only have to adapt them to their needs. Such, for instance, is the fish caught in the sea or ore extracted from the bowels of the earth.

Ore is the product of the labour of miners. But at an iron and steel works that very same ore is an object of labour, or a raw material. The steel produced at the works is an object of labour, but it is a raw material for the machine-builder. One and the same object of labour can undergo many stages of processing.

The instruments of labour are things man uses to act upon objects of labour. These are the things which man in the process of labour places between himself and the object he works on. Instruments of labour transfer man's action on to the objects of labour for the purpose of changing it.

The instruments of labour play a particularly important role in the development of material production. These are the means of production that in a sense are an extension of man's natural organs—his hands, legs, brain. Production of the instruments of labour is a distinctive feature of human labour. It was in this context that a writer called man an animal that produces instruments. In the course of history the instruments of labour developed a long way from the stone and stick of primeval man to modern sophisticated machines and mechanisms, electronic computers and control systems used in production, science and management.

In addition to the instruments of labour, the means of labour include also things used for the storage of objects of labour, such things as casks, pipes, all sorts of reservoirs, etc. Finally, in a wider sense, the means of labour are all the material conditions required in the process of labour. They first of all include the land with all the wealth it contains, and also production buildings, canals, roads, etc.

Means of production The objects of labour and instruments of labour together form the means of production. One and the same thing is often a product of one labour process and an instrument of labour in another. Whether a thing is a product of labour, raw material or instrument of labour depends on its role in the labour process.

Thus, for example, a loom is the product of labour of the workers of an engineering works but an instrument of labour for the workers of a textile mill. Livestock is the product of the labour of livestock breeders, but is an object of labour or a raw material to a meat-packing plant and an instrument of labour (draught animal) to the farmer.

The further society develops, the greater becomes the importance of the means of production, created by human labour. These means of production embody past labour. They are labour embodied in things. In political economy this labour is called embodied labour.

But any means of production are no more than a lifeless heap of scrap until people apply their labour to them. Hence, a condition essential to any production process is the marriage of the means of production to labour power, i.e., the connection of embodied and live labour.

Productive forces and relations of production The productive forces of society are the means of production and labour power in their interaction. Naturally, the decisive productive force of a society is man himself, his live labour power. It is the motive force of progress for it puts life into the means of production.

The productive forces grow and multiply with social development. The instruments of labour become ever more perfect. As science and technology progress, ever new materials are used in production. At the same time the skills of people improve and their production experience widens. The level of development of the productive forces is a yardstick for measuring man's mastery of nature. As time goes by man harnesses ever new forces of nature. Way back in the abyss of time, the discovery of fire was man's greatest victory over nature. In our time man has penetrated into the atom and is beginning to master outer space.

Man has never lived alone. People always formed groups, societies. Articulate speech could not have emerged without social life and social activity. Aristotle, the great ancient thinker, said that man was a social animal. Production has therefore a social character. The productive activities of people link them with an innumerable number of other people. At all stages of the historical development of society production is always social: it is always carried on jointly by more or less large societies, by groups of people.

"In production," Marx wrote, "men not only act on nature but also on one another. They produce only by co-operating in a certain way and mutually exchanging their activities. In order to produce, they enter into definite connections and relations with one another and only within these social connections and relations does their action on nature, does production, take place."[1]

The relations which arise among people in the process of production are called the relations of production or production relations.

Social system of production

Production differs much at different times and in different countries. This not only in the sense that, say, a hundred years ago there was even no thought of spaceships, electronic machines, man-made fibre, semiconductor devices, TV sets, planes, cars, power stations and many other things without which life would be inconceivable today. Today, too, there are highly developed industrial countries, such as the Soviet Union, the USA, many Central and West European countries along with economi-

---

[1] K. Marx and F. Engels, *Selected Works*, Vol. 1, Moscow 1962, p. 89.

cally less developed countries, like India, Indonesia and some African, Asian and Latin American countries.

The social aspect of production is also not identical everywhere. The social relations of people in the process of production are inseparably linked with their relations towards the means of production. The connection of the means of production with live labour power proceeds in a different way at different stages of social development. In capitalist society the working class is deprived of the means of production which belong to the bourgeoisie. Conversely, in socialist society the means of production are the common property of the working people. The question of who owns and controls the means of production is of decisive importance for characterising the social system of production.

The method by which live labour is combined with the means of production determines the class structure of society. Classes are large groups of people, differing as regards their place in social production, as regards their relation to the means of production. Thus, capitalist society, where the means of production belong to the bourgeoisie, appropriates the labour of the working class. In socialist society, where the means of production belong to society, there is no appropriation of other people's labour, no exploitation of man by man.

In every society the relations of production form a definite system. For example, under capitalism the relations between the bourgeoisie and the proletariat form the basis upon which are built all other production relations, those between the landowner and the peasant, between the different groups of the bourgeoisie, between large-scale and small-scale production, etc. The aggregate of production relations comprises the economic system (or economic structure) of society.

Mode of production Production does not exist outside of space and time. When we speak of production we always refer to a certain stage of social development. Definite productive forces and definite relations of production exist at every stage. Thus, for example, feudal relations ruled in the European countries in the Middle Ages and the productive forces were poorly developed. Production relations, taken in their connection and unity with the productive forces, are called the mode of production.

History knows five basic modes of production or five principal stages in socio-economic development. They are: primitive society, slavery, feudalism, capitalism and socialism which is the first phase of communism.

Exploitation of man by man

When the oppressed rose against their oppressors in ancient Rome, a champion of the ruling class thought up the following fable. Society, he said, is like a human body. The body has a brain to control all its parts, hands to carry out all work, and a stomach to digest food. Thus, he continued, in society too there must be, on the one hand, people who fulfil all sorts of work, and, on the other, those to whom all are subordinated and who use the fruits of other people's labour.

In reality, however, the history of mankind shows that for ages there was no division into classes, no class exploitation and oppression. The exploitation of man by man means that some people live at the expense of others: the exploiting class appropriates part of the product created by the direct producers. It is the product of labour exceeding the barest necessities for the subsistence of the working people—the so-called surplus product—that forms the unearned income of the exploiters.

Slavery, feudalism and capitalism are three consecutive stages in the economic enslavement of the working people. Common to all these modes of production is that the means of production and subsistence are, in one form or another, the property of the ruling class, which forces the working people to work for its benefit. These modes differ as regards the relations between the owners of the means of production and the mass of the working people who create all wealth. The relations between the exploiting class and the exploited class are the main production relation in each of these societies. Under the slave-owning system, this is the relation between the slave-owner and the slaves; under the feudal system, the relation between the feudal landowners and the serfs; under capitalism, the relation between the capitalists and the wage workers.

But exploitation is not eternal. The whole course of history proves that capitalism is the last social system based on exploitation. It will inevitably be destroyed by socialist revolution. This revolution overthrows the power of the bourgeoisie and establishes the power of the working class which, in alliance with all the working people, builds a new, socialist society.

Socialism is a system in which exploitation has been destroyed forever. In socialist society there are no classes of exploiters and exploited, pursuing opposed interests. Socialist society consists of friendly classes whose vital interests coincide, of workers and peasants with whom the people's, socialist intelligentsia is inseparably linked. The main production relation of socialist society is friendly co-operation and mutual assistance between workers free from exploitation.

In the course of history people have greatly increased their power over nature. But in countries where the exploitation of man by man still exists, the working masses are oppressed by the existing social relations. These relations prevent the bulk of the population of the capitalist countries from enjoying the benefits afforded by man's greater power over nature. Things are very different in the Soviet Union and other socialist countries. Here the fruits of progress belong to the people, every advance in man's rule over nature benefits the working people.

Economic laws

Political economy has the task of revealing the economic laws of social development.

Any science studying some sphere of nature or social life has the aim of disclosing the laws operating in that sphere. Scientifically interpreted, the term "law" implies the internal connection of phenomena, their essence. The internal connection of phenomena exists whether we like it or not. In other words, natural and social laws are of an objective nature, they do not depend on the will and consciousness of people. But people can discover these laws and make use of them.

A knowledge of the laws of nature gives people a powerful weapon for taming its blind forces, for using them to the benefit of man. Electric power in the form of lightning is one thing. That same power used by man in production, for illumination, etc., is quite another. A knowledge of the laws operating in social life supplies people with a basis for their practical activities.

Disclosing the economic laws of capitalism, political economy reveals the conditions for the existence of that society and the trends of its development. In this way political economy reveals the true basis of the class struggle in bourgeois society, proves the inevitability of the aggravation of class contradictions in that society and shows the working class the road to socialism.

Political economy teaches the working class in the capitalist countries to understand that only irreconcilable class struggle for the destruction of the capitalist system, for socialism, brings with it the liberation of the exploited masses. At the same time it explains the sense, significance and methods of the class struggle of the proletariat and its political and economic organisations fighting for its immediate demands against the onslaught of the capitalist monopolies on the elementary rights of the working people and on their living standard.

The laws governing the economic development of bourgeois society prove scientifically that the doom of capitalism and the triumph of communism are historically inevitable.

When a Marxist speaks of the historical inevitability of the replacement of capitalism by socialism, of the irrefutable supremacy of socialism over capitalism, he does not rely on blind faith or subjective wishes, but on an exact scientific knowledge of the objective laws of social development. This gives Marxism-Leninism, the only real science of the life and development of human society, enormous advantages over bourgeois science, which is unable to penetrate into the depth of social processes, disclose their nature, and determine the trends of social development.

Investigating the nature and content of the economic laws of socialism, political economy proves that the victory of socialism in its economic competition with capitalism is historically inevitable. Socialism is free from the faults of capitalism. In socialist society production serves not to enrich a hundful of exploiters but to satisfy social requirements, to advance the people's welfare. Socialist economy develops according to plan, knows no crises, no ruthless competition, unemployment, these destructive corollaries of capitalism. To use all the advantages of socialism to the full, the economy must be managed efficiently and rationally, and maximum results must be obtained at the minimum outlay. This, too, is taught by political economy and other economic sciences.

Socialism is built on a firm scientific basis. It opens up broad vistas for the utilisation of science in all practical fields. The political economy of socialism reveals the economic laws of the socialist mode of production. Society gets to know these laws and is guided by them in its many-sided practical activities concerned with economic development.

Socialist society develops its economy consciously, in a planned way, in the interests of the whole people, with the aim of promoting the progress toward communism. Communist society embodies the highest stage of balanced organisation of the whole public economy. Communism ensures the most effective and rational utilisation of the material wealth and labour resources for the satisfaction of the people's growing requirements.

Economic science elaborates the methods for the most advisable utilisation of the resources of socialist society. It serves as a sort of compass pointing to the most economical and effective way of business activity in individual enterprises, districts, and the country as a whole. It teaches to commensurate expenditure with returns, to strive for greater results at lower expenditure.

Economic science generalises the experience of millions, teaches to draw on advanced achievements, discloses the latent reserves in every enterprise, every district, in the economy as a whole. This makes economic science invaluable to socialist society.

Political economy—a historical science
Marx's and Engels's revolution in social science is justly compared with that effected by Darwinism in the science of organic nature.

Before the discoveries made by Darwin the world of living organisms was considered petrified and immutable. Darwin showed that incessant changes are at work in organic nature. The organic world is in a state of constant motion.

Marxism effected a similar revolution in social science. Marxism put a stop to the former view about the constancy, the immobility of society. Marxism demonstrated that society develops and that this advance conforms to definte laws. According to these laws some forms of society are replaced by others. Human history is based on the development of material production, the changes of the modes of production.

The development of the productive forces and the economic social system which derives from it determines the whole course of history. The socio-economic system forms the basis on which state institutions, juridical views, science and the arts develop. Disclosing the laws of production and distribution of the material wealth at the various stages of social development, political economy provides the key to an understanding of the whole complex process of historical development.

The growth of the productive forces extends man's power over nature and at the same time changes the production relations, the social system of production. One system of production relations existed in ancient times, another in the Middle Ages. The development of the productive forces makes old production relations obsolete and they must give way to new ones.

Does this mean that it is enough for the productive forces to develop to replace the existing production relations by others? No, it does not. The development of the productive forces prepares the conditions for such a replacement, but the old social system refuses to quit the stage voluntarily.

Throughout history social development proceeded in the following manner. The productive relations emerging at a definite level of the development of the productive forces promoted up to a certain time the further development of the latter. But, at a certain moment they become an obstacle to the further growth of the productive forces. Then the historical inevitability arises to remove the old production relations and to replace them by new ones. In a class-antagonistic society this replacement takes the form of a revolution. The ruling class out to maintain its power and wealth resists the revolution. The revolution is effected by the oppressed classes. It smashes the obsolete forms of social life and clears the road for the further growth of the productive forces.

There were many revolutions in history. But all revolutions of the past replaced one form of exploitation by another. The only exception is the socialist revolution which destroys all exploitation. For this reason there are no opposing classes in socialist society. Socialist production relations opened up unprecedented vistas for the development of the productive forces. As the productive forces grow, socialist production relations improve and gradually grow into communist relations of production.

Political economy studies the most important aspect of society's existence and advance—its economic life. Disclosing the laws governing social production, it provides the key to an understanding of the whole complex process of social development. Characterising the basic features of Marxist theory, Lenin pointed out that its economic teaching is the deepest, all-round, detailed confirmation of that theory. Lenin called this teaching the main content of Marxism as the theory of scientific socialism.

The class and party approach to political economy

Political economy deals with the burning problems of the class struggle. It studies the vital interests of the main classes of capitalist society. What is more, it poses and answers the question of the very existence of this society.

For that reason, political economy cannot be neutral in the class struggle. On the contrary, it is a class, a party science. All talk of a neutral or above-party political economy is no more than a guise for economists who, defending the interests of the moribund classes, prefer not to reveal their true face.

The exploiting classes defend their material interests and their rule with all the means at their disposal. In political economy the servants of the bourgeoisie have a dual aim: on the one hand, to whitewash and embellish capitalism, and, on the other, to blacken, and defame socialism, since socialism is a more progressive system than capitalism.

In the early stages of capitalist development the bourgeoisie fought obsolete feudal survivals. At that time the proletariat had not yet appeared in the arena of social struggle, and the bourgeoisie was still an ascending class. Its scientists advanced social science. But even then their class limitations prevented them from discovering the true laws of social development. They considered the bourgeois system an eternal and natural state of society.

After the bourgeoisie had come to power and the working class had appeared on the historical scene, bourgeois scientists became mere servants of the capitalists. Bourgeois political economy has adopted an unscientific stand, and turned into a defender of the capitalist system.

The only genuinely scientific political economy is that of the working class, created by its great teachers, Marx, Engels and Lenin, and being developed and enriched by all Marxist-Leninist parties in the world.

Marxist-Leninist political economy demonstrates that the relations and laws of capitalism are not eternal and immutable and that they do not apply to all societies. They emerge at a definite stage of social development and must inevitably disappear and be replaced by new, superior economic relations as society develops.

Having discovered the objective laws of social development, Marxism-Leninism has shown that the contradictions inherent in capitalism must reach a revolutionary bursting point and that society's transition to communism is a certainty. The development of world capitalism and the revolutionary struggle of the working class have fully confirmed the correctness of the Marxist-Leninist analysis of capitalism and of imperialism, its highest stage.

Marxist-Leninist political economy is not afraid of the truth; the proletariat is the most progressive social class and looks into the future with confidence. The proletariat's class interests coincide with the interests of progressive social development. The political economy of the working class conducts an irreconcilable struggle against bourgeois pseudo-science, which eulogises the decaying capitalist system and defames socialism.

Marxist-Leninist political economy endows the working class and all progressive social forces with the invaluable gift of scientific foresight, which is of enormous importance to successful practical action. It develops in connection with the general course of historical development, in close relation with practical tasks. The practice of socialist and communist construction in the socialist countries, the practice of the revolutionary struggle of the working class in the capitalist countries for its vital interests, for socialism, continuously enrich Marxist-Leninist political economy.

1. What is the role of material production and labour in social life?
2. What is understood by the terms productive forces and relations of production?
3. What do you know about the nature of economic laws?
4. What advantages does the study of political economy offer?

Chapter II

PRE-CAPITALIST MODES OF PRODUCTION

1. PRIMITIVE SOCIETY

The emergence of human society   The primeval epoch was a very long one. It lasted many hundred thousands of years and ended only six or seven thousand years ago. Primeval people had no written language and therefore left no written history behind. Scientific data on their life and their social relations are provided mainly by archaeological and ethnographical research.

Our planet, like the whole solar system, has existed for several thousand million years. Hundreds of millions of years were to pass before life evolved on it. But even after that it took a long time for man to sublimate from the animal kingdom.

Man's remote ancestors lived in herds; primeval men also lived in herds. In groups they searched the land for food, jointly they made instruments and jointly they used them. The thing that distinguished human society from the animal herd from the very moment of its emergence was labour, the production of instruments of labour. The herd of apes devoured all the fruit it could find and then hunger chased it to another place. Instinct enabled them to adjust themselves to nature passively, and no more. Human society, conversely, acts upon nature by its labour.

There is no impassable chasm dividing society from nature, as averred by the exploiting classes, who cannot get by without a "creator". The emergence of human society was one of the greatest revolutionary leaps. Nature abounds in such leaps, in spite of the fact that this is unscientifically denied by the opponents of revolution.

Primeval man was weak and help-
less in the face of nature. Danger
lurked with his every step. The
earth was inhabited by giant predators. People lived in
herds, which probably did not exceed several dozen: a large
number of people would not have been able to find enough
food to subsist. They lived on roots and fruit.

The first tools man used were stones and sticks. In a
way they were an artificial extension of their bodily
organs: stones—of the fist, sticks—of the extended arm.
These simple tools put more food within reach of people.
Simple hunting became possible.

People hunted only small animals and fled when they
were attacked by large predators. They hunted in groups.
The bag was eaten jointly. Food was scarce and there were
no stocks.

Primeval people constantly went half-hungry. In their
caves and pitiful huts, which barely protected them against
cold and bad weather, they covered themselves with the
pelts of animals they had killed.

With the passing of time they learned to make weapons
that were more effective than simple sticks and stones.
They learned to use cudgels, spears, knives, hooks, harpoons
of stone, bone and horns. These weapons enabled them to
hunt larger animals and to take up fishing.

The discovery of fire opened a new era in the life of
primeval men. At first they learned to use fire and then,
thousands of years later, to make it. People saw lightning
set fire to trees, watched forest fires, and the eruption of
volcanoes. Finding a fire they took pains to keep it burning
for it protected them against beasts of prey and could be
used to prepare food. Later, as their instruments of labour
improved, they noticed that fire could be obtained by striking a flint or by rubbing dry wood.

The discovery of fire made man the master over one of
the forces of nature. It was this discovery that separated
man irrevocably from the animal kingdom.

It took an extremely long time until the rough-hewn
stones became finely chiselled instruments. Stone, wood,
bone and horns remained the main materials for a long
time. It was only much later that people learned to make
tools of metal—first of metals found in nature, such as

copper, later bronze, and finally of iron. The whole long period prior to written history is divided into ages: the stone, bronze and iron ages. Each of the three "ages" lasted many centuries, while the stone age lasted tens of thousands of years.

Simple co-operation. Common labour and common property

The basic type of production relations in primeval society was simple co-operation: people worked jointly, fulfilled identical labour. Working jointly enabled them to carry out tasks during the hunt that were beyond the powers of one person.

There was no private property. Everything the primeval group had was common property. Common labour and common property were dictated by the then obtaining development of the productive forces. The food was divided evenly. There were hardly enough products of labour to satisfy the most essential requirement. If one person were to receive more than the common share, some other person would have to go hungry. Labour did not produce any surplus product, i.e., it produced nothing in excess of vital requirements. Therefore there simply could not arise conditions for some people to live at the expense of others. Exploitation was impossible, i.e., there could be no systematic appropriation of the fruits of other people's labour.

Division of labour. Emergence of crop and animal farming

The development of the instruments of labour wrought a gradual change in the organisation of labour. First to appear were the rudiments of a natural division of labour, i.e., a division of labour according to sex and age. The imperfection of weapons still prevented solitary hunting. Collective forms of hunting predominated: battue, beating, etc. But people had already begun to hunt large animals. Women were left behind to care for children, to look after the house, to prepare food. When the group moved from place to place the few belongings of the whole group were carried by women. The men had to have their hands free to hunt on the way.

The invention of the bow and arrow made hunting more rewarding. At the same time hunting and fishing were becoming more complicated trades. Women were fully isolated from these complicated methods of procuring food.

The division of labour between the sexes became permanent.

The further improvement in the methods of obtaining means of subsistence was connected with rudimentary crop and animal farming.

The observation that grain accidentally dropped takes roots and grows probably provided the impetus for taking up agriculture. For a long time people tilled the land with a simple stick, then with a stick having a bent tip—a hoe. Animal farming probably emerged in the same way. They first domesticated the young of killed animals, who instinctively followed people carrying the killed mother-animal away.

Tribal system As time passed by the primeval herd evolved into the tribal system. The tribe was a group of people connected by bonds of blood relationship. At first the group consisted of several dozen people. Everyone outside the group was considered a stranger. The tribe gradually increased and later reached several hundred people. At first women played the dominant role in the tribal community. Relationship was determined by the maternal line. This was the so-called matriarchy.

The dominant position of women at the initial stage of the tribal system was no accident. At that time the collection of food and hunting were supplemented by rudimentary crop and animal farming. Both these trades had not yet become the basic source of subsistence and were conducted by primitive methods. They were plied predominantly by women, who remained at home.

With the further development of the productive forces matriarchy gave way to patriarchy. The dominating role was assumed by men. Relationship was established according to the paternal line. Decisive for this change was the development of nomadic animal breeding. Giving bountiful fruits it pushed primeval crop framing into the background. But stock-breeding, like hunting, was a man's job. Developed agriculture (crop farming) was also becoming a man's job.

The legend of the "golden age" The heavy lot of the masses under the exploiting system became responsible for the highly embellished idea of the primeval era. There are legends about a "golden age" in the art of many peoples. This legend was passed on from generation to generation. Religion created the myth of Paradise lost, of a Garden of Eden from which man had been evicted for his sins.

In reality, however, primeval people lived a hard life. Nature's power over man was unlimited. It ruled the life and destiny of people. How terrible are the adversities, privations and horrors of the exploiting system, if even the primeval period of man's life has been endowed with the halo of a "golden age".

Primeval communism Marx, Engels and Lenin, the great teachers of the working class, called the social system of the primeval era "primeval communism". They disproved the fabrications of bourgeois lackeys about the eternity of private property with historical evidence. History demonstrates that people lived for hundreds of thousands of years without any private property. The absence of private property, the domination of common property and collective labour make it possible to regard primeval society as primeval communism.

At the same time the founders of scientific socialism emphasised the historical limitations of primeval communism. Lenin wrote that there had never been a golden age in the remote past of humanity, that primeval man had had to bear the crushing burden of the struggle against nature.

The system based on common labour, common property and equal consumption was the only possible system in the primeval era. As the productive forces developed, primeval man gradually freed himself from the unlimited domination by nature. At the same time the relations of production, based on the close cohesion of people in a collective, gradually deteriorated. People were to shoulder the yoke of class systems for many ages.

Social division of labour, emergence of barter, private property and classes As we saw, the initial division of labour was based on the natural distinction between the sexes and the age groups of people in a single community. Later, however, there emerged specialisation of different communities, and then individual members within the community began to specialise in different spheres of production. This social division of labour is not to be confused with the natural division of labour.

Tribes living in places with rich pastures took to stock-breeding. They gave up crop farming and hunting, but scored considerable success in stock-breeding and began to produce more meat, wool and milk.

The separation of stock-breeding from crop farming was the first great social division of labour. It gave an impetus to the emergence of barter, private property and classes, to the disintegration of patriarchy and the birth of class society.

The second major social division of labour, the separation of the trades from agriculture, created a wider basis for the exchange of products. The products of craftsmen were used fully or almost fully for exchange. This was how production for exchange originated.

In the early stages exchange was effected by the tribal chiefs—elders, patriarchs. With the development and expansion of exchange they began to regard public property as their own. Cattle was the principal object of barter and was, therefore, the first to become private property. Inequality as regards property emerged among the members of the community.

With the growth of the productive forces the labour used in stock-breeding or crop farming began to bring richer fruit. There emerged the possibility of obtaining surplus labour and surplus product, i.e., an excess of labour and products over and above the minimum required for the subsistence of the worker.

Formerly prisoners were killed or reprieved—there was nothing else that could be done with them. Now prisoners were made slaves. In addition to the division into rich and poor there emerged the division into masters and slaves. Slave labour widened the gap of inequality between people. Later rich nobles made slaves not only of prisoners but also of members of their community, who had fallen into poverty and debt.

Thus, the development of private property inevitably gave rise to the formation of classes. The primeval system was replaced by class society. From that time onwards the whole history of mankind became a history of class struggle.

2. THE SLAVE-OWNING SYSTEM

Slavery is the earliest and most undisguised form of exploitation. The later two forms of exploiting societies—feudalism and capitalism—are, to quote Marx, nothing but mitigated forms of slavery.

From patriarchal slavery to the slave-owning mode of production At first slavery was of a patriarchal nature. There were few slaves and their owners worked together with them. At that time slaves were basically helpers in the household, or domestic servants.

The master had unlimited power over his slaves but the sphere in which slave labour could be applied was very limited. Slave labour was used to satisfy the various wants and requirements of large patriarchal families.

Further development brought a radical change. The invention of iron smelting revolutionised production. The iron axe and iron-tipped hoe made it possible to cultivate large tracts of land. Small farmers could not cope with such a volume of land but slave-owners using slave labour could.

The development of stock-breeding took a similar turn. The herds of rich families grew quickly and additional hands were needed to look after them. This task too was solved by slave labour.

With the growth of the social division of labour and the development of exchange separate clans and tribes drew closer and formed unions. This changed tribal institutions. Elders and war leaders became counts and kings. Formerly they held authority as persons who had been elected by the tribe or the union of tribes. Now they began to use their power to defend the interest of the propertied élite to oppress their ruined fellow-tribesmen and to suppress the slaves. Armed detachments, courts, and punitive institutions also served the same purpose. This is how the state emerged, the ruling class's instrument of violence over the exploited masses.

Exploitation of slaves In the period of the full development of slavery, slave labour formed the basis of social existence. The number of slaves grew enormously. Their exploitation assumed a monstrous scale and forms.

Large enterprises shot up, using the labour of many hundreds, sometimes of thousands of slaves. Great numbers of slaves were used also as domestic servants, pandering to the whims of the slave-owners.

In the fields, gangs of slaves laboured from early in the morning till late at night to the crack of the whip. They lived in mud-huts that resembled caves of beasts rather than human dwellings. They were half-starved, were given food that was not always fit for animals. Slaves were often taken to work in irons to keep them from escaping. They were branded to make them easy to catch if they escaped. Many of them wore an irremovable iron collar on which their owner's name was engraved.

Slave labour was undisguised forced labour. Not only the means of production but also the workers were the property of the exploiting class. Slaves were bought and sold like cattle. The slave-owner could even kill his slave if he so desired. Slaves were treated worse than cattle. They were often cheaper than cattle. In Rome sick and old slaves nobody wanted to buy were taken to a remote island and left there to the mercy of fate.

Everything created by the labour of slaves belonged to the slave-owner. He supplied the slaves with the instruments and materials for production, and distributed work and the means of subsistence among them as he wished.

Requirements grew as exchange developed. The slave-owners intensified the exploitation of slaves. They appropriated not only the surplus but also a substantial share of the necessary labour of their slaves. They attempted to get more work from the slaves and a larger share of their product.

Technological stagnation In the slave-owning formation production techniques were extremely primitive and did not advance. For centuries the instruments of labour did not develop beyond the simple tools used by artisans.

Artisan slaves were often highly skilled, but their instruments of labour were primitive. People and animals were the only tractive force to be used in those days. The only instruments in addition to manual tools, were mechanical devices multiplying muscular power, such as levers, blocks, gears.

Grain was generally ground by hand. The water mill came to Rome only in the first century B.C., but even then it did not become popular: slaves or animals were used as before to turn the grind-stones. Even though ancient people knew of the action of steam, they did not know how to use it. A writer of that time describes the principle of a steam engine, but he describes it as a curiosity, as a thing that should "cause extreme amazement".

Slave labour was unproductive. A slave was not interested in the results of his labour. His position remained hopeless and oppression did not become less hard to bear no matter how hard he worked. The slave-owners were not particularly interested in raising labour productivity: they commanded an enormous free labour force.

Considered no more than a thing and treated like an animal, the slave generally expressed his protest and indignation by smashing the instruments of labour. That is why only the simplest and unproductive instruments were used. Slave labour was expended extremely unproductively. The ruling classes wallowed in luxury. Wastefulness was rampant.

Development of exchange and emergence of money

Under the slave-owning system the basic mass of products was produced not for exchange but for the direct consumption of the slave-owner, his numerous hangers-on and family. Gradually, however, exchange began to play a greater role.

In political economy the product manufactured not for direct consumption but for exchange, for sale, is termed a commodity. Production for exchange, for sale, is called commodity production. An economy that produces not for exchange but for consumption is known as a natural economy. In a natural economy the products of labour are used in the household in which they are produced.

At first exchange was purely accidental. Generally, it took the form of barter, of a direct exchange of one product of labour for another. A stock-breeders' community, for example, gave a sheep and received two bagfuls of grain in return. But, gradually exchange expanded and became regular.

It was then that the need for a special commodity arose, for one that could serve as a medium of exchange. Spontaneously, one commodity out of the mass of commodities was given preference over all others. It was willingly accepted in exchange for all other commodities. This was because it could be exchanged for any other commodity. It became the yardstick for the value of all other goods. Money is such a universal commodity. The appearance of money in turn furthered the growth of trade links, the development of commodity production.

Trade and usury
The development of handicrafts and the growth of exchange led to the foundation of towns. First towns were small and did not differ very much from the countryside. But gradually manufacture and trade concentrated in towns. The way of life and activities of the urban population began increasingly to differ from those of the rural population.

That is how the separation of town from countryside took place.

While exchange was still weakly developed, the producers—crop farmers, stock-breeders, artisans— exchanged their goods themselves. But the mass of the commodities exchanged grew steadily. At the same time there was an extension of the territorial limits within which the exchange was effected. Merchants appeared, who bought goods from the producers, took them to the market, sometimes quite remote from the place of manufacture, and sold them to consumers.

That is how trading capital originated.

The growth of production and exchange considerably increased the inequality as regards property. The rich now owned not only the mass of slaves but also large sums of money. The poor were forced more and more often to turn to them for loans. Usury brought great riches to few and bondage and ruin to many.

That is how usurious capital emerged.

The activities of trading and usurious capital undermined the foundation of the natural economy. The expansion of exchange wetted the appetites of the slave-owners. But slave-owning society made the workman (the producer) a thing. In these conditions, trading and usurious capital could not master production and effect a switch-over to wage labour. It, to use Marx's vivid expression, stuck to the mode of production based on slavery, bleeding it white to complete exhaustion.

Contradictions of the slave-owning system

Having achieved dominance, the slave-owning system could not ensure a substantial development of technology. At the same time it ruthlessly destroyed human labour power, the main productive force of society.

At large slave-owning enterprises there was much more joint labour than in the primeval era. Simple co-operation was used on a hitherto unprecedented scale. However, the slave-owning mode of production was unable to awaken the dormant forces of collective labour. This was because it did not create collectives but transformed the workman into a simple instrument, into a thing.

The slave-owning system educated a deep contempt for labour. Formerly, while there were patriarchal relations between the master and his slaves, both worked jointly in the field and at home. But as the slave-owning mode of production asserted itself things changed radically. The slave-owners withdrew more and more from the control of production. They passed those duties on to managers and supervisors, who for the most part were recruited from among the slaves. Physical labour came to be considered the lot of slaves, an occupation unworthy of free people. Contempt for productive labour became an obstacle to social development.

As the slave-owning mode of production developed small producers were ruined. Their households fell into decay because they were unable to cope with the fierce competition from large-scale production founded on slave labour. At the beginning of the first century A.D. the whole of Italy was divided into a comparatively small number of latifundia —enormous estates. Sheep farming had ousted crop farming, the fields had become pastures, the labour of free farmers—slave labour.

Ruined small producers were pushed out of the production process without any hope of ever returning to it. They turned into an idle crowd demanding bread and entertainment. The slave-owning state gave them handouts out of the surplus product created by slave labour.

In ancient Rome these people were called proletarians. The Roman proletariat was the exact opposite of the modern proletariat: in Rome the proletariat lived at the expense of society, under capitalism society lives at the expense of the proletariat.

The ruin of the peasantry undermined slave-owning Rome's military power. Soldiers for the Roman legions were recruited from among slaves and emancipated slaves. Defeats took the place of victories and dried the mainspring of the unending supply of slaves.

Downfall of the slave-owning system

As compared with the primeval era the slave-owning system was a step forward in human history. However, later that system became a fetter to the further development of the productive forces. Having become an obstacle to social development the slave-owning mode of production perished under the burden of the contradictions tearing it asunder.

Having achieved full domination, slavery became obsolescent. Commerce decayed, once rich lands lay in waste, the population declined, formerly flourishing trades were ruined.

Having become unprofitable slavery was doomed. But its poison continued to work in people's minds—free people despised productive labour. Rome, as pointed out by Engels, landed in a blind alley: slavery had become economically impossible, the labour of free people was held in moral contempt. The first could no longer, the second could not yet become the basic form of social production. Only a radical revolution could provide a way out of this quandary.

As slave-owning production declined, the struggle of the enslaved masses against the oppressors intensified. Uprisings of slaves intertwined with the struggle of the ruined small peasants against the rich slave-owning élite.

The slaves hated their oppressors, but they had no clear objectives. They dreamed about a restoration of the patriarchal system, which had become a thing of the irrevocable past. The slave uprisings therefore could not put an end to exploitation.

The feudal system replaced the slave-owning system. Feudal forms of exploitation opened up greater possibilities for the development of the social productive forces than the slave-owning system.

Slavery under capitalism
With the fall of the ancient world, the slave-owning system was no longer the dominant social system. However, slavery as such was not abolished.

It reappeared on a large scale at the dawn of capitalism. After the conquest of the Americas, at the end of the 16th century, Europeans introduced slavery there. The enslaved Indians quickly died out as a result of the back-breaking toil they were forced to do. Their uprisings were cruelly suppressed. "The only good Indian is a dead Indian", "witty" colonialists used to say.

Then African slaves were brought to the Americas. The slave trade came into being. It flourished in the 17th and 18th centuries. Enterprising adventurers organised the slave hunt in Africa.

The exploitation of Negro slaves in America became extremely brutal when the market for slave labour products, especially for cotton, expanded. The demand for cotton grew with the development of the textile industry in England and other European countries. Work on the cotton plantations of the slave-owners drove completely healthy people to an early grave after an average of seven years of work.

In the Civil War (1861-1865) the industrialy developed North defeated the slave-owning South. Juridically slavery was abolished. But Negroes continued to be the most oppressed part of the population.

Although slavery was abolished in America, it did not disappear from the capitalist world. Remnants of slavery remained in many colonies and semi-colonies. Only the abolition of colonialism proceeding in our time will eradicate the disgrace of slavery once and for all.

3. FEUDAL SYSTEM

Emergence of feudalism
The feudal system arose in Western Europe on the ruins of the Roman slave-owning system, on the one hand, and the disintegration of the tribal system of the Vandals, who pillaged Rome, on the other. Feudalism was the child of these two parents.

The Roman Empire fell at the end of the 15th century.

The tribes that conquered Rome seized a large part of its territory. At first the land became common property. Soon, however, the chieftains began to appropriate the people's property. Monarchic power emerged.

The kings distributed the land among their retinue, who at first received the land for lifelong tenure, later, however, it became their hereditary possession. Large plots went to the Church, which became a pillar supporting the monarchy. The king's body guards and servants, the princes of the Church and monasteries were all given huge estates.

Those given land were obliged to render military services to the king. The land was still worked by small producers, who were dependent on their new masters. The masters imposed manifold duties on the dependent peasants.

The plots of land distributed by the new owners were known as feuds (or fiefs), their owners as feudals. This is how feudalism got its name.

In Russia feudalism superseded the early form of slavery (patriarchal slavery). When agriculture became the principal occupation of the population, the land was considered "no-one's" or "god's". The land cleared of forest and tilled by peasants was the property of the peasant commune. Soon, however, the princes, like the kings in Western Europe, seized the land. They made large plots their property, and distributed large tracts of arable land among boyars (nobles) and monasteries.

From the 11th to 19th centuries, feudalism oppressed millions of peasants. After the formation of Muscovy (14th-15th centuries), the princes and tsars divided the land among their retinue.

At first the peasants were not attached to the land and were allowed to move from one landowner to another. But at the end of the 16th century this right was revoked and they were attached to the land and became serfs.

Domination of natural economy

Like the slave-owning economy, the feudal economy was mainly natural. The rule of natural economy was especially undivided during early feudalism.

The peasants produced predominantly for their own consumption and exchange was only accidental. The feudal lord also rarely resorted to trade: almost everything he needed for his upkeep and that of his family and retinue was produced by the labour of serfs. All sorts of artisans lived on the estates: blacksmiths, millers, bakers, joiners, harness-makers, etc.

Typical of the feudal system is a combination of agriculture—the main type of labour—and the domestic trades, playing a supplementary role. This combination formed the basis of the natural economy.

State of technology

Agronomical methods were primitive, especially at the beginning of the feudal period. In the 9th-10th centuries the long-term fallow system was still predominantly in use in Western Europe: a plot was sown for several years in succession and then left to "recuperate" for 20-25 years. Only one-fifth to one quarter of the available land was used under this system. Later the two-field system of agriculture was introduced. In the 11th century three-field rotation became widespread. It remained the dominant system of agriculture for many centuries.

Only primitive implements were used: spades, picks, wooden ploughs and sickles. There was little livestock because of frequent wars. The peasants often had to draw the plough themselves.

Yet, under feudalism the productive forces reached a higher level than they had under the slave-owning system.

Slowly but surely the methods of grain farming, market gardening, wine- and butter-making were improving. The methods of smelting and working iron were advancing and gradually iron ploughs, harrows and looms became more widespread. The development of the trades and the gradual improvement of the instruments used by artisans created conditions for the emergence at the end of the feudal era of capitalist manufactures.

Feudal exploitation

Feudal landownership was combined with direct rule over the people who in one form or another were attached to the land.

The land was the decisive means of production in those days. It was the property of the feudal lord. But the power of the lord was determined not so much by the size of his estate as by the number of dependent people.

The feudal system was based on the exploitation of peasants by the landowners. The latter appropriated the surplus product of the peasants' labour. The two main forms of feudal exploitation were corvée and rent in money or kind.

Corvée meant that the landowner appropriated the surplus labour of his serfs directly. Under the rent system he appropriated the product of that labour.

Under the corvée system the peasant worked part of the week (say, three days) with his own means of production (cattle, plough, etc.) on his plot, and the rest of the week (i.e., the remaining three days) with the same means on his master's fields.

Under the rent system the peasant was obliged to hand over regularly to the landowner a definite amount of grain, cattle and other agricultural products or a definite amount of money.

Thus, rent was paid either in kind or in cash. More often than not, in addition to the payment of rent, the serfs had to render various services on the landowner's estate.

The surplus product appropriated by the landowners is termed ground rent. The surplus product appropriated by the ruling class under feudalism is called feudal ground rent. The condition making possible its appropriation was feudal landownership, combined with direct rule over the serfs.

In its development, feudal (pre-capitalist) rent passed through three stages and correspondingly assumed three forms: 1) corvée, 2) rent in kind and 3) rent in cash.

A. Radishchev, a progressive Russian writer of the end of the 18th century, gave a vivid description of the life of serfs in tsarist Russia. He once met a peasant who was tilling the land on a Sunday. "Aren't the other days of the week enough?" the writer asked. The peasant replied that he was working the landowner's fields for six days a week.

Such cruel exploitation reduced the serfs to appalling poverty. Radishchev describes a hut without windows, the wind blowing through the many cracks in the walls; a stove without a chimney; a pot that hardly ever contains thin broth; bread consisting mainly of chaff.

Feudal slavery Lenin called feudal dependence "chattel slavery". From the day of his birth to his dying day the peasant was completely dependent on his lord and master. This dependence and lack of rights became particularly pronounced in the late stages of feudalism, when the oppression of the landowners became unbearable.

The landowners sold their serfs, lost them at cards, exchanged them for horses and dogs. The wealth of the landowner was measured by the size of his land, the number of "souls" (i.e., serfs). Under serfdom in Russia a peasant could be mortgaged like all other property.

A. Herzen, the outstanding Russian writer and democrat of the 19th century, bitterly styled serfs "baptised property". The landowners competed in thinking up way of torturing them. Particularly cruel was a certain Saltykova, who under the reign of Catherine II owned about 600 "souls" in Moscow, Kostroma and Vologda gubernias. She tortured 139 people to death.

There was little difference between the conditions of a serf and a slave. And yet, as distinct from the slave, the serf could (as Lenin emphasised) spend at least part of his time on his plot and did to some extent belong to himself. This opened up before society ways of development, inconceivable under slavery.

Possibilities of economic development in feudal society
All forms of feudal exploitation boiled down to the appropriation by the landowners of other people's labour or the product of that labour. But different forms of exploitation tended different possibilities for the economic development of society.

Under the corvée system, the peasant spent his surplus labour on the landowner's field under the supervision of the landowner or his manager. Paying rent, the peasant had to spend the surplus labour while working on his own plot.

Labour for himself and labour for the exploiter were no longer noticeably divided in space and time. On the face of it, the peasant could dispose of his working time at his discretion, but a considerable part of that time continued to be spent on the landowner.

Under the corvée system the serf was interested in raising labour productivity only during the time he was working on his plot. Under the rent system it was advantageous to him to raise the productivity of his entire labour.

The transition to rent in cash forced the peasant to sell

the product of his surplus labour on the market in order to be able to pay the rent to the landowner in cash. The peasant household thus became linked with the market. began to lose its former natural character, took to an ever growing extent to commodity production.

The development of exchange undermined the foundation of the feudal system and prepared its supersession by capitalism. It accelerated the stratification of the peasantry. Under natural economy stratification proceeded only within very narrow limits. With the transition to production for the market some peasants grew rich, but the bulk fell into poverty.

Medieval towns. The crafts

The fall of the ancient world meant the fall of towns. Many of them were destroyed and disappeared from the face of the earth forever. Others turned into large villages.

In the Middle Ages towns gradually began to revive. In the early stages of feudalism there was no big difference between town and country. The peasants produced a large part of the artisan articles they needed for themselves and for the landowner. In the towns the population not only plied the crafts and trade, but also worked the land. The medieval town, surrounded by fields and pastures, looked very much like a big village.

At first the artisans in towns worked according to orders. The feudal lord or peasant supplied the artisan with raw materials and the latter delivered the finished article. Generally, the artisan was paid in kind. The instruments of labour were extremely primitive and constituted the property of the artisan. His product hardly ever reached the market. At that stage the crafts were in stagnation, similar to small-scale peasant farming.

Gradually, however, the artisans were drawn into the commodity exchange. In addition to work according to orders, the artisans began to produce for the market. In a sense the artisans became the vehicle of commodity production, while the peasants continued to live under the natural economy.

As time went on the crafts became more and more profitable. The townspeople gradually gave up agriculture. The peasants began to buy manufactured articles from the townspeople. Thus evolved the final division between the crafts and agriculture, and between town and country.

The artisan, as distinct from the peasant, could not exist by consuming the products of his labour. He had to exchange his products for means of subsistence and for raw materials he needed to ply his trade. Therefore the development of the crafts was closely linked with the development of trade.

In the initial stages trade was carried on only in the products being supplied by artisans and serfs, and also in those brought from remote countries. But with the development of trade these sources became insufficient. Small-scale artisan production was unable to provide goods in large enough amounts. They hardly sufficed to satisfy local market requirements. The need for the expansion of production became acute.

Small-scale commodity production was unable to ensure the expansion of production. Its possibilities were far too limited. It became necessary to make the transition to large-scale production.

At the end of the 14th century in Italy, and in the 16th century in other countries, the first large enterprises came into being. These were capitalist manufactories. They were owned by capitalists and employed wage workers.

Capitalist relations thus matured in the womb of feudal society.

Downfall of the feudal system

As compared with the slave-owning system, feudalism was a step forward in social development. The productive forces were given some scope for development. However, their growth possibilities were limited.

Feudal relations in the countryside and guild limitations in town fettered technological progress. Long feudal wars, ravaging epidemics turned flourishing regions into deserts, decimated the population.

Feudalism gave birth to forces which subsequently strove to break out of the limits set by that system. The social division of labour grew, exchange expanded, production techniques improved slowly but surely, especially in the urban crafts. The natural economy was being undermined by the exchange, while growing exchange eroded the foundations of the feudal mode of production.

The feudal system fell under the pressure of the bourgeois elements that had matured in its womb, under the impact of the class struggle of the oppressed and cruelly exploited masses, who had realised that it was impossible to continue living in the old way.

Throughout the era of serfdom the peasants had struggled bitterly against the feudal lords and their system. The struggle of the serfs became particularly intense in the late feudal period, when the exploitation of serfs intensified to the utmost.

Peasant wars undermined the feudal system and led to its downfall. The struggle of the peasants against the landlords was used by the nascent bourgeoisie to hasten the downfall of the feudal system and to substitute capitalist exploitation for feudal exploitation. The peasants constituted the bulk of the insurgents in the bourgeois revolutions. Bourgeois revolutions overthrew the rule of the feudal lords and opened up wide vistas for the development of capitalism.

Feudal vestiges under capitalism

Having seized power from the feudal the bourgeoisie soon realised that it was threatened by the rising working class. The bourgeoisie then hurried to enter into an agreement with those who only yesterday were its enemies.

In most countries the ruling bourgeoisie left the system of feudal tenure intact. A handful of landowners continued to own an enormous portion of the land. The exploitation of the peasants by the landowners remained, changing only in form.

The residua of feudalism were particularly heavy in the economically backward countries. In the colonial and semi-colonial countries the people had to bear the double burden of feudal oppression and capitalist oppression. The colonialists were supported by the feudal lords and in their turn they supported the feudal lords in every way, saving them from the anger of the people.

In tsarist Russia capitalist relations intertwined with the many remnants of serfdom, the omnipotence of the landowners, the presence of a vast sea of landless and land-hungry peasants. Only the Great October Socialist Revolution, which put an end to the bourgeois system, swept away all the vestiges of the feudal system.

1. How did class society arise?
2. What is the essence of the slave-owning form of exploitation?
3. What are the distinctive features of the feudal mode of production?

THE CAPITALIST SYSTEM

Chapter III

CAPITALIST COMMODITY PRODUCTION

1. COMMODITY PRODUCTION UNDER THE DOMINATION OF PRIVATE PROPERTY

Conditions for the emergence of commodity production
In capitalist society, products are manufactured mostly for sale. A product manufactured for sale, for exchange, is called a commodity; an economy manufacturing products for exchange is called a commodity economy. An economy in which products are made for direct consumption and not for sale is called a natural economy.

Commodity economy emerged when the primeval system was disintegrating and private ownership of the means of production appeared. It existed under the slave-owning system and under feudalism; but it did not play a dominant role in those days. The serf gave a considerable part of the products of his labour to the landowner and received nothing in return. For a long time only a small share of the products was manufactured for sale on the market, the bulk was used in the household producing them.

Commodity production developed considerably when feudalism began to disintegrate. But it became dominant only under capitalism.

Capitalist enterprises produce their entire output for sale. As capitalism develops, small producers (the peasants) sell an ever increasing share of their output on the market. Almost all means of production and articles of consumption are bought and sold under capitalism. Thus commodity production becomes all-embracing, universal.

Commodity production is based on the social division of labour. The social division of labour means that individual members of society produce different products. Such a division of labour existed even before the emergence of commodity production. There were craftsmen in many primeval communities: a blacksmith, potter, miller, etc., who manufactured all sorts of implements and household articles for the community. The community, in turn, supported them for their work, supplied them with agricultural products.

For natural economy to become commodity production there must be in addition to the social division of labour also private ownership of the means of production. When the artisan becomes the private owner of his means of production he begins to sell the products of his labour.

Hence, the conditions for the emergence and development of commodity production are 1) the social division of labour and 2) private ownership in the means of production.

Simple and capitalist commodity production

When there were no large capitalist enterprises, production was conducted by small commodity producers—peasants and artisans. They were self-employed, hired no workers, owned simple and inexpensive instruments of labour. This economy of small commodity producers, exchanging the products of their labour, is known as simple commodity production.

Simple commodity production has an important feature in common with capitalist commodity production—both are based on private ownership of the means of production. But at the same time simple commodity production differs substantially from its capitalist counterpart.

Simple commodity production is based on the personal labour of small commodity producers. Capitalism is based on the labour of wage workers, who do not own any means of production and are subjected to exploitation by the capitalists, the big owners of the means of production.

Capitalism develops by ruining and subjugating small commodity producers and transforming many of them into wage workers. Simple commodity production inevitably gives rise to capitalism.

Dual nature of the commodity

Thus, the production of commodities, i.e., of articles designed for exchange, for sale, is dominant under capitalism. What are the properties of a commodity?

To be a commodity the product of labour must satisfy some human want; therein lies its utility. This property of the product of labour makes it a use value. The fact that meat and milk satisfy people's requirements for food makes these products of labour use values. A shirt, coat, shoes serve to satisfy the requirement of people for clothing and footwear, and this makes them use values too.

Many things that are not products of human labour have a use value, for example, the water of a spring and wild-growing fruit.

Products of labour satisfy definite human wants both in natural and in commodity economy. The bread a peasant produces for his own consumption satisfies his requirement for food and, hence, is a use value. The bread the peasant produces for sale has the same useful property: if for some reason bread were to lose this property (were to rot and become unfit for consumption) nobody would buy it. But by becoming a commodity bread acquires also another very important property: it can be exchanged for any other commodity.

Thus, a commodity is 1) an article that satisfies a definite human want and 2) an article that can be exchanged for another article.

Commodities are exchanged in definite proportions. Say, a bagfull of flour is exchanged for a pair of boots. A commodity can be exchanged in a definite quantitative relation for another commodity, i.e., it constitutes what is called an exchange value (or simply a value). This property is acquired by a product of labour when it becomes a commodity. Hence a commodity has two properties: it has a use value and value.

Labour as the basis of value For articles of different use values to be exchanged they must be commensurable. In fact, we only exchange articles because they have different use values. Nobody would be interested in exchanging a kilogram of bread for a kilogram of the same bread. Nobody would think of selling a pair of boots to buy for the money he received an identical pair of boots. Only articles satisfying different human wants are exchanged.

The quantitative relations in which commodities are exchanged fluctuate frequently. Some commodities become cheaper, others more expensive. Yet, no matter how great these fluctuations, a ton of copper, for example, is always more expensive than a ton of steel and is always cheaper than a ton of silver or, especially, of gold. Hence, there must be some more or less sound basis for the quantitative relations in which commodities are exchanged. What constitutes this basis?

Every quantitative comparison presupposes some common property in the articles being compared. One often compares entirely different things, but for such a comparison to be possible they must have something in common. It is also necessary that this common property be measurable. We can say, for example, that a steel sheet of a certain size weighs as much as two sacks of flour. The steel sheet and the two sacks of flour have something in common: their weight. This enables us to compare two different things like steel and flour.

If a bushel of grain is exchanged, for example, for ten horseshoes, this means that the two commodities have something in common. What is the thing they have in common? What is this common property that makes these two different commodities commensurable?

This property is not their weight, volume or hardness, for a bushel of grain and ten horseshoes have entirely different weights, volumes and other physical properties. It is also not the utility of the two commodities, for their utilities are also of an entirely different nature. Commodities having absolutely different use values possess only one common property, namely, they are products of human labour.

This property can be measured: labour is measured by the amount of time spent on the production of a given commodity. The amount of labour spent on the production of commodities determines the proportions in which one commodity is exchanged for another.

Thus, exchange relations of commodities are based on the labour spent on their production.

This is confirmed by many commonly-known facts. Many commodities which were once expensive have become much cheaper when better technology decreased the amount of labour needed for their production. Some 50 years ago, aluminium, for example, was dozens of times more expensive than silver. Now its price is a fraction of the price of silver. This is because the development of electrotechnics made it possible to produce aluminium with much less labour.

While exchange was comparatively rare, products were exchanged in accidental relations. But the position changed when a large share of the social product was manufactured for exchange. The relations that established themselves for the exchange of commodities began more and more frequently to correspond to the amount of labour expended on their production.

At the beginning of the past century in many European countries the bulk of the population still consisted of small commodity producers. In these conditions, when a farmer exchanged grain for horseshoes, he knew very well how much labour the blacksmith had expended on their manufacture. The farmer gave for the horseshoes an amount of grain which approximately embodied as much labour as that which had been expended on the manufacture of the horseshoes.

In turn, the village blacksmith and also the town artisan knew the conditions on the farm: more often than not he had a plot of land himself, a market garden and domestic cattle. In this way labour expended on the production of commodities was the only possible basis for their exchange.

The labour embodied in the commodity forms its value. The exchange of commodities according to value, i.e., in proportion to the amount of labour expended on their production is an economic law of commodity production.

Socially necessary labour time
The value of a commodity is determined by the amount of labour spent on its production. Yet how can we explain that identical commodities, on the production of which one producer spent more labour than others, still sell at the same price?

True, different commodity producers expend different amounts of labour on the production of identical commodities. This is because different manufacturers produce commodities under different conditions. Some have only simple instruments and manufacture commodities by manual methods, others use machinery. Some have less production experience, others have more.

But the consumer does not care how much labour has been expended by the individual commodity producer on the commodity. If the quality of the commodity is the same, the price should also be identical.

The value of a commodity does not depend on the amount of labour every individual commodity producer expends on its production in every individual case. The value of the commodity is determined by the amount of labour time necessary to produce a given commodity in conditions normal for the technological level of production in the given society and with the average level of skill and intensity of labour.

The average labour time required for the production of a commodity is called the socially necessary labour time. The socially necessary labour time determines the value of the commodity.

Dual nature of the labour embodied in a commodity As we already know the commodity is both a use value and a value. The labour embodied in the commodity, too, has a dual nature.

Labour is just as diversified as the use values it produces. The labour of the locksmith differs from that of a shoemaker, the labour of a miner from that of a tailor.

Different kinds of labour differ from each other as regards their purpose, their methods, their instruments, their objects, and also their results. A miner uses a coal cutter, makes it cut into the coal seam to obtain coal. A tailor uses a sewing-machine, scissors, needles, he cuts and sews cloth to produce garments.

Hence, every use value embodies a definite, concrete kind of labour: coal—the labour of a miner, garments—the labour of a tailor, steel—the labour of a steel founder.

But being exchanged all these different commodities are compared and commensurated. For example, a definite amount of coal costs as much as a pair of boots. In this commensuration the use values of the commodities are ignored because they are incomparable. Here we discover, as stated above, that different commodities have a common property, namely, that they are products of labour, are values.

Disregarding the use values of the commodities, we can also disregard the differences between the concrete types of labour of the commodity producers. Exchanging coal for boots we disregard the difference between the concrete labour of the miner and the concrete labour of the shoe-maker. Coal, boots and all other commodities are considered products of human labour in general.

Therefore, the labour embodied in the commodity is considered homogeneous, an expenditure of human labour power in general—abstract labour. As such the expenditure of labour power of different producers does not differ qualitatively but only quantitatively.

Hence, all labour of the commodity producer is, on the one hand, concrete labour creating use values as such and, on the other hand, the expenditure of labour in general, abstract labour, a share of the social labour, creating the value of the commodity as such.

Thus, the dual nature of the commodity is the inevitable consequence of the dual nature of the labour embodied in it.

Simple and complex labour
The value of a commodity is the expenditure of human labour in general. But the labour creating use values differs as regards skill.

An unskilled worker has no preliminary training. But, a steel founder, turner, weaver must receive preliminary training. In the first case we have to do with simple labour, in the second with complex labour.

A commodity may be the product of the most complex labour but its value equates it with the product of simple labour. The social process, to quote Marx, unfolding behind the backs of the producers, daily reduces all types of complex to simple labour. Complex labour is multiplied simple labour; in one hour of complex labour the producer creates a value that simple labour would require several hours to produce.

Contradiction of simple commodity production
When man makes a product for his own use he is in no way connected with society as a producer. But when he produces a commodity, this has to be a product to satisfy some definite want of other members of society.

In a society based on private property every single producer—the small artisan or the big capitalist—acts at his own risk. Every commodity producer is independent, production is his private business, his labour is private labour.

Yet, at the same time every commodity producer depends on many other commodity producers. To be able to live and do business he must exchange the commodities he produces, sell them in order to buy raw materials and instruments. and consumer goods for himself and his family. Individual commodity producers are linked among themselves and depend upon one another. This connection, however, is a spontaneous one, it is effected through the exchange of commodities.

The labour of an individual producer must comprise a definite share of the total labour being expended by society as a whole for the satisfaction of its requirements. It is the social labour embodied in the commodity that forms its value. The contradiction of simple commodity production lies in the contradiction between private and social labour. This contradiction develops further under capitalism.

Commodity fetishism The exchange of commodities reflects the relations between the people producing commodities. Hence, value expresses the social relation of production, the relation between people producing commodities.

However, this relation between people is manifested as a relation between things qua commodities, and the value of the commodity seems as much its natural property as, for example, its colour or its weight. One says, for instance, that a loaf of bread weighs so many grams and costs so much money.

At the lower stages of cultural development many peoples worshipped the sun, fire, various animals, ascribing to them miraculous powers. This is called fetishism.

Bourgeois society ascribes such miraculous powers to things qua commodities. The property which commodities possess only by virtue of a difinite system of social relations are regarded as their natural property. This is the fetishism of commodities typical of capitalist production. Fetishism conceals the essence of capitalist relations, their true nature, lends them a deceptive appearance.

2. MONEY UNDER CAPITALISM

Gold and its riddle   Saxon porcelain is famed throughout the world. Its excellent
qualities are commonly known. But few of those who
relish the elegant and noble forms of Saxon porcelain know
of the unusual fate of the person who invented this wonderful material. His name was Johann Friedrich Bettger
and he lived at the end of the 17th and the beginning of the
18th century. Bettger was a pharmacist at the court of the
Saxonian Kurfürst and of the Polish King August II. He
spent many years in the Meissen tower into which he had
been confined by his monarch.

What crime did Bettger commit to warrant so heavy a
punishment? The inventor of porcelain was not only a
pharmacist, he was also an alchemist. August II was constantly short of money: he was a spendthrift and constantly
conducted campaigns that swallowed a lot of funds. Bettger
undertook to create artificial gold but was unable to fulfil
his promise. He paid for this with many years of impris-
onment.

For more than a thousand years alchemists attempted to
transform all sorts of base metals into gold. We associate
the word "alchemist" with a person who having isolated
himself from the world around him conducts endless exper-
iments in search of the "philosopher's stone". That is how
people called the wonderful material that was supposed to
be capable of transforming base metals into gold. Throughout the Middle Ages alchemists tirelessly laboured to solve
this mystery, but in vain.

Later, when man learned more about nature the naive
belief in a "philosopher's stone" was discarded by science.

It also took a long time to solve another puzzle posed by
gold: why does this metal have such a miraculous power
in society, where private property dominates? "Gold is a
wonderful thing," Christophor Columbus wrote in 1503 from
the America he had discovered, "he who owns it is master
of all he desires. Gold can even unlock the doors of
Paradise."

Columbus who discovered America could not solve the
mystery of the magic power of gold. Before him and after
him many people mused over this mystery. What explains
the unlimited power of this yellow metal?

Why has gold for centuries and even for millennia been such a despot? Neither chemistry nor any of the natural sciences could give an answer to this question. It was explained by another science, by the science about human society.

The might of gold is connected with the role it plays in society where private property dominates. Under capitalism gold is the undivided ruler over people. Under that system factories, the land, machinery—in short, everything needed for production—can be bought and sold. The owners of factories exploit the working people. They receive enormous unearned incomes, live at the expense of other people's labour.

This explains the unquenchable thirst for gold. Gold enables people to become owners of enterprises in which other people's labour produces all the wealth in the world.

This puzzle of gold was solved by economic science. But it took a long time before it found the solution to that mystery. For a long time economists ascribed the role played by gold under the domination of private property to the natural properties of that metal. They could not imagine that there could be a social system different from the one under which they lived.

They, therefore, drew the conclusion that gold was money by its very nature, and that money in turn was capital by its very nature, i.e., that it was a means with the help of which some people could live at the expense of other people.

This delusion of the economists was dispelled only by the founders of Marxism. Marxism disclosed the important fact that capitalist production relations were always connected with things, displayed themselves as relations between things, assumed a thing-form.

It was thus that the mystery of gold was solved. Gold is not money by nature—it becomes money only in the course of social development. At earlier historical stages the role of money was played by cattle, salt, fur and other articles. Later, when socialism and communism will have triumphed all over the world, there will no longer be any need to use gold as money.

This is what Lenin meant when he wrote: "When we are victorious on a world scale I think we shall use gold for the purpose of building public lavatories in the streets of some of the largest cites of the world. This would be the most 'just' and most educational way of utilising gold for the benefit of those generations which have not forgotten how, for the sake of gold, ten million men were killed and thirty million maimed in the 'great war for freedom', the war of 1914-18, ... and how, for the sake of this same gold, they certainly intend to kill twenty million men and to maim sixty million in a [new] war. ...

"But however 'just', useful, or humane it would be to utilise gold for this purpose, we nevertheless say that we must work for another decade or two with the same intensity and ... in order to reach this stage. Meanwhile, we must save the gold in the RSFSR, sell it at the highest price, buy goods with it at the lowest price. When you live among wolves, you must howl like a wolf. ..."[1]

Essence of money As shown above, money is the result of the development of exchange. It appears long before commodity production becomes dominant. Developed commodity production is inconceivable without money. It is only money that makes possible the all-round social links that exist between isolated individual producers under commodity production.

The value of a commodity can be expressed only by comparing it with another commodity, by exchanging it for another commodity. Under developed commodity production goods are generally not exchanged directly. All commodities are expressed in a definite sum of money.

Every commodity must be exchanged for money, i.e., it must be sold. If a commodity cannot be sold that means that the labour of its producer has been wasted. That means that because of the anarchy of production he has wasted his labour and the means of production on the production of a commodity for which there is no social demand. If the commodity has to be sold at a lower price, that means that part of the labour of its producer has not been recognised by society. Thus, the emergence of money promotes the further growth and development of the contradictions inherent in the commodity.

With the emergence of money the world of commodities is split into two poles: on one pole are all ordinary commo-

---

[1] V. I. Lenin, *Collected Works*, Vol. 33, Moscow 1966, pp. 113-14

dities, on the other—the special commodity, playing the role of money. This commodity acquires special properties, it becomes a privileged commodity. Money is such a universal commodity. It is the universal equivalent.

Commodity exchange through the medium of money differs radically from simple commodity exchange (barter). In the case of direct commodity exchange every sale is at the same time a purchase. Every transaction is an isolated act. Take, for example, two hunters exchanging pelts for arrows. This exchange concerns only the two parties directly participating in the transaction.

Things are quite different when the exchange is effected through the medium of money. When the weaver sells his cloth and buys bread with the proceeds, he actually exchanges cloth for bread. But this exchange is effected with the help of money. To sell his material the weaver must find a person who has money, that is, a person who has sold his commodity at an earlier date.

Thus, the exchange with the help of money presupposes an all-round connection of the commodity producers and a constant intertwining of their transactions. At the same time exchange with the help of money makes it possible to separate sales from purchases in time. The producer can sell his commodity and keep the proceeds for some time.

But because of the close economic links between producers and their interdependence the large-scale sale of some commodities without a buying of others in exchange will cause a glut in the sale of some commodities, i.e., will lead to the emergence of a crises of overproduction for these commodities. The further development of commodity production and its transformation into capitalist production makes crises inevitable.

**Functions of money.
Measure of value**
In capitalist society money performs several functions. It serves as 1) a measure of value, 2) means of circulation, 3) means of accumulation, 4) means of payment, 5) universal money.

Every commodity is sold for a definite sum of money. This sum expresses the value of the commodity. The price of a commodity is the monetary expression of its value.

Before buying or selling a commodity it is essential to measure its value in money, i.e., to determine its price. The measurement of the commodity's value in terms of money is a precondition for any exchange of the commodity, for its purchase or sale. Money serves in these transactions as the measure of value.

To be a measure of value money must have value itself. At first a definite amount of the money-commodity served as measure of value. In Britain, for example, this unit is called the pound sterling to this day; once it corresponded to a pound of silver.

The money unit—first a measure of weight, later a coin— and its parts serve as a standard of price. When we say that a ton of pig iron is worth a gram of gold, and a ton of copper—five grams of gold (or that a ton of pig iron costs five dollars, and a ton of copper—twenty-five dollars), the standard of price is expressed in unit weights of gold or units of money.

Medium of circulation

After a commodity has been valued in terms of money the decisive moment sets in: it must be sold, that is, exchanged for money. The exchange of commodities through the medium of money is called the circulation of commodities.

Here money serves as the circulating medium. The circulation of commodities is indissolubly linked with the circulation of money, when a commodity passes from the seller to the buyer, money passes from the buyer to the seller.

To perform its function as a measure of value money should not necessarily be available in cash. We can evaluate all the wealth in the USSR without having a single ruble. When we say, for example, that during the year so many thousand million rubles' worth of commodities have been produced, we only imagine a definite sum of money.

But things are quite different when we have to do with money as the circulating medium. To perform this function money must be available in cash. We can imagine a million but cannot buy anything with that imaginary million. But with every coin we really possess we can buy a commodity of corresponding value.

For money to be a measure of value it must have a value itself. Conversely, to fulfil its function as the circulating medium, money does not necessarily have to possess value. The seller of a commodity accepts money in return for his commodity to be able in his turn to exchange it for another commodity, that is, to buy another commodity. As long as money serves as the means of circulating medium it does not lie long in the wallets of people; it continues its endless movement in a direction opposite to that of the movement of commodities. Being constantly in circulation it plays only a momentary role in individual purchase and sale transactions. This makes it possible for full-value money—gold—to be replaced in its function as the circulating medium by substitutes or representatives.

Notes (paper money, banknotes), silver and copper coins, etc., are such representatives of gold. These substitutes (tokens of value) either have no value of their own or have a much lower value than the one they represent. Just as the moon shines with the reflected light of the sun, so they reflect the value of genuine money, which is gold.

For the function of measure of value the amount of money is immaterial. But there must be a definite amount of money for the latter to perform the function of circulating medium.

For a commodity worth 1,000 rubles to be sold there must be a thousand rubles, not an arbitrary amount of money, but exactly a thousand. On the other hand, the thousand rubles that have been paid for the given commodity can subsequently serve as the circulating medium for other commodities having also a value of a thousand rubles.

Commodities are sold and bought in many places simultaneously. Therefore, the money supply needed at every given moment depends on the sum of prices of the circulating commodities. The sum of prices in its turn depends on the amount of available commodities and the price of every single commodity. The money supply required, for example, within the year depends not only on these two factors but also on the rate at which the money circulates. The higher the rate of money circulation, the smaller is the amount of money required, and vice versa.

Means of accumulation
Money is the representative of universal wealth. It can be transformed into any commodity at any time. Under capitalism it is difficult to convert commodities into money but not money into commodities. Therefore, money is used for accumulation and hoarding.

To play the role of a means of accumulation money must be money in the full sense of the word. It must possess a value of its own, as in the case of its function as a measure of value. But, at the same time it must always be available in cash, in its genuine form. Thus, it must also possess the property characteristic of the circulating medium.

Means of payment Commodities are often bought and sold on credit. The buyer receives the commodity but pays the seller only after the expiration of a definite time. Here money plays the role of a means of payment.

This function of money reflects the expansion of exchange. The links between individual commodity producers become more intimate and their interdependence grows. The buyer becomes a debtor, the seller a creditor. When the term of payment is due and the debtor must obtain the money he owes, no matter what the cost, he must sell his commodity to be able to pay the debt.

What will happen if he does not find a buyer and is unable to pay his debt? This will harm not only his own business but also that of the creditor, who will not be refunded the amount he had granted on credit.

Universal money Finally, money plays the role of universal money. In the turnover between different countries gold is essentially a commodity like any other. However, the characteristic difference is that this commodity is accepted by everybody and refused by none. Therefore, in trade between countries gold serves as money.

Gold and paper money In the capitalist countries the volume of commodities to be produced and placed on the market cannot be estimated in advance. The amount of money needed for circulation cannot, therefore, be fixed in a balanced way. It depends on spontaneous market fluctuations.

When gold coins serve as money their number is easily adjusted to the demands of trade. Let us suppose that the production of commodities has been curtailed, trade has diminished and that there is too much money. Commodity prices begin to grow and much less commodities can be bought for the same amount of money. In that case it will be more profitable for the owners of gold coins to sell these coins as gold for the manufacture of ornaments or to hoard it. Part of the gold coins will be melted down or hoarded, the amount of money will diminish, and it will once again be brought in conformity with market requirements.

In the capitalist countries paper tokens are used instead of gold coins to make purchases and payments. When these paper tokens are issued by banks in limited quantities necessary for circulation, their amount is adapted spontaneously to the requirements of commodity circulation. Such paper money is called bank-notes.

Things are different when the capitalist countries issue large amounts of paper tokens to cover their expenditure. In that case the amount of paper tokens issued does not depend on the need for the circulating medium. Such paper tokens, as distinct from bank-notes, are called paper money.

Inflation and its consequences for the working people

Paper money may depreciate. This depreciation takes place when paper money is issued in excessive quantities or when commodity circulation diminishes.

Suppose the amount of paper money issued is twice as great as is needed. In that case the buyer will be able to purchase only half the amount of commodities with every paper mark or paper franc. The money has depreciated to half its former value. This depreciation of money owing to its excessive issue is called inflation. The depreciation of money lowers the living standards of the working people in the bourgeois countries. The factory and office workers receive the same or slightly higher wages than they did before, while the commodity prices rise at a rapid pace.

The exploiting classes and the bourgeois governments defending their interests often readily resort to inflation to lower the living standards of the population and to intensify the exploitation of the working people.

3. LAW OF VALUE IN CAPITALIST PRODUCTION

How the law of value operates

In capitalist society based on private property the law of value, like other economic laws, acts as a blind force. It operates through the medium of competition, a most violent struggle of one and all.

Anarchy of production reigns in a society consisting of independent commodity producers. Literally, the word anarchy implies absence of government. Anarchy of production means unplanned production scattered among disunited commodity producers.

We have already seen that the value of a commodity is determined by the amount of socially necessary labour expended on its production. This does not mean, however, that every commodity is actually exchanged in full conformity with its value. The value of a commodity is expressed in its price, i.e., in a definite sum of money. But the prices of commodities fluctuate constantly depending on market conditions and the changing relation of supply and demand.

When there are more commodities on the market than can be bought by consumers, their prices drop; conversely, when there is not enough of a commodity and the demand for it is high, its price rises. For this reason the price of a commodity does not always coincide with its value. Value is the point about which prices fluctuate. The prices of commodities deviate now upward, now downward from their value. These deviations may be very considerable.

These price fluctuations show individual private producers whether or not the commodities they produce are needed at the given moment. If the price, say, of boots has dropped below their value, this means that more boots have been produced than is required on the market. That drop in the price of boots will make a number of boot-makers take up production of other commodities. This will decrease the amount of boots offered on the market. If, however, the price of boots rises to a figure exceeding its value, profitable market conditions will draw new boot-makers into the production of boots, and after some time the supply of this commodity will grow on the market.

Every commodity producer works blindly, at random, without a plan. While the commodity he produces meets a ready sale, he strives to produce as much of it as possible. But when he discovers that his commodity is not at all marketable or can be sold only at low, unprofitable prices, the producer is compelled to curtail production or stop it completely and to take up the manufacture of some other commodity.

Hence, under the rule of private property, deviations of the prices of commodities from their value cannot be regarded as the result of some failure to take into account the operation of the law of value. On the contrary, constant fluctuations of prices around value are the only possible mode in which the law of value can operate in capitalist economy. It is, thus, among innumerable fluctuations, that the division of social labour between the various branches of production proceeds, without which no society could exist.

As a result of the universal distribution of commodity production under capitalism, production is no longer in the hands of small commodity producers but in those of the capitalists. Hundreds and thousands of workers toil in capitalist enterprises. They produce huge amounts of the most diverse commodities, which are often sold in the remotest corners of the globe. Under these conditions, the anarchy of production manifests itself in full measure. It is part and parcel of capitalism and makes itself felt with particularly destructive force during crises.

Role of the law of value in the emergence and development of capitalism

Under private ownership of the means of production the law of value inevitably leads to the emergence and development of capitalist relations.

The fact that the value of commodities is determined by the socially necessary labour time has important consequences for commodity producers. Individual producers are not equally efficient. One may spend 20 hours to make a pair of boots, the other only 12 hours. But boots are sold on the market at a value determined by the socially necessary labour time which, let us assume, is 15 hours.

The producer who expends more labour on the production of the commodity than is required by average social conditions realises for his commodity a sum of money embodying only part of the time he has spent. Conversely, he who produces the commodity at a labour expenditure lower than the socially necessary labour time has an advantage over the former.

As a result the exchange is profitable for one and unprofitable for the other. Every producer seeks to use better equipment to decrease the labour time spent on the production of a commodity. This promises him more profitable conditions for the sale of his commodities. A fierce competitive struggle for more advantageous production conditions and for a more profitable exchange of commodities invariably breaks out among individual producers. As a result of this struggle some producers are ruined, others get rich. The latter expand production, hire workers, buy new machinery and become capitalists. The mass of small producers run into debt, find themselves dependent on the rich, are brought to ruin and pushed into the ranks of the proletariat.

The exchange of commodities in accordance with the law of value results in a stratification of producers. Technical innovations lower the socially necessary labour time required for the production of commodities. Technological progress ruins small producers—artisans, craftsmen—who cannot keep pace with large enterprises. Under private ownership in the means of production, commodity production inevitably leads to capitalism.

REVISION QUESTIONS

1. What are the conditions for the emergence of commodity production?
2. What are the main properties of a commodity?
3. What determines the value of a commodity?
4. What is the essence of money and what are its main functions?
5. What is the role played by the law of value in the emergence and development of capitalism?

Chapter IV

THE ESSENCE OF CAPITALIST EXPLOITATION

1. CAPITAL AND WAGE LABOUR

**Growth
of money capital**

Richard Price, a British theologian and economist, computed in the early period of capitalism that if a single penny had been deposited in the first year A.D. at compound interest, it would, by the beginning of the capitalist era, have become a ball of gold of a size exceeding that of our planet many times over.

This speculation is interesting in that it clearly characterises the idea of capitalist exploitation. In bourgeois society unearned income is received not only by the proprietor of industrial or trading enterprises. Under capitalism a growing number of parasites receive huge incomes without moving a finger to earn them, receive them only because they own large capital, large sums of money. The owners of money capital invest money to make it grow. How does that money grow? Money is not a plant that grows under the rays of the sun. And really the growth of money has nothing to do with the growth we observe in nature. Money can grow only under a social system that enables the capitalists to appropriate the unpaid labour of the workers.

**Conditions
for the emergence
of capitalism**

How did capitalism emerge? The bourgeoisie and its servants disseminate the following fable. In the days of yore, they say, there lived on earth people with different inclinations. Some were industrious and thrifty, others lazy and wasteful. The former gradually obtained enormous wealth, the latter remained indigent. Thus, they say, emerged the division into rich and poor, into capitalists and workers.

There is not one iota of truth in these inventions. In reality, capitalism superseded feudalism, also an exploiting system. The initial source for the development of capitalism was small commodity production with its competition, which brings ruin to some and riches to others.

Two main conditions are necessary for capitalism to emerge: first, the accumulation of wealth in the hands of a few and, second, the creation of a mass of destitute pepole, who are personally free but have neither means of production nor means of subsistence and are therefore compelled to sell themselves into the bondage of capitalists.

Once capitalism has emerged the division of society into opposing classes is ensured by the economic laws of that system: the capitalists continue to possess enormous wealth, the working class, as hitherto, is deprived of everything. The existence of capitalist owners and propertyless proletarians is a sine qua non of capitalist production. The creation of the historical preconditions of capitalism is a process called the primitive accumulation of capital.

Primitive accumulation of capital   During the feudal epoch, prior to the emergence of capitalism, production was conducted by small landtillers and artisans. Agriculture was the principal occupation and the land—the basic means of production. The peasants were attached to the land and exploited by the landowners. The simple implements—the hoe, the sickle, a small number of cattle—were the property of the peasants.

Feudalism was based on the exploitation of small producers, personally dependent, but owning means of production, notably land. To make him a wage worker, the producer had first of all to be freed from direct personal dependence. To be thrown into capitalist bondage he had first to be relieved of serfdom.

The lackeys of the bourgeoisie speak only of this aspect of capitalist development. They laud capitalism for having destroyed feudal laws and declare the bourgeois system a kingdom of freedom and justice. But they deliberately refuse to look at the other side of the coin.

The producer becomes a wage worker only when he is "freed" of all conditions for production, when he is deprived of the possibility to work independently. Capitalism presupposes that the producer is divorced from the means of production which he possessed under feudalism.

It was this separation of the immediate producers from the means of production—the expropriation of the peasants from the land—that lay at the root of the whole process of primitive accumulation. At the time when feudalism was disintegrating, feudal laws were abrogated in one country after another but, together with the liberation of the peasants from feudal dependence there was another, no less important, "liberation": the peasants were "liberated" of the land on which they lived and which they tilled. The peasants were left (in most cases they had to pay a compensation) only part of the land that had sustained them. "Surplus" hands left the villages and joined the army of wage workers placed at the disposal of capital. Such, in brief outline, was the process that created free working hands for emergent capitalism. In different countries it took a different course but its main trend and content was the same everywhere.

Those same methods of violence and robbery that transformed peasants into landless and homeless proletarians resulted in the concentration of huge tracts of lands in the hands of a small number of persons.

But this was not enough for the emergence of capitalist production. In addition, enormous wealth in the form of money had to be concentrated in the hands of few, money which could at any time be exchanged, be converted into any means of production and used to create conditions of production.

The concentration of wealth in the hands of a few individuals was given great impetus in the era of great geographical discoveries (15th-16th centuries). The discovery of America was followed by the emigration to that continent of people in quest of easy gain. Their number increased particularly when gold and silver deposits were found in America. The European states equipped expeditions which destroyed and looted flourishing countries, whose misfortune it was that precious metals had been discovered on their territory.

Colonial trade was one of the most important channels for the primitive accumulation of capital. The Dutch, British, French and others established East India companies for exploiting the trade with then rich India. These companies were supported by the respective governments. They were granted the monopoly of trade in colonial goods.

The looting of rich overseas countries was one of the most prolific sources for the primitive accumulation of capital in Europe, notably in Britain. For centuries the British, and later the French bourgeoisie, accumulated uncountable wealth through looting foreign lands and practising bloody brigandage in the colonies. Everywhere the state authorities fostered the formation of huge fortunes in the hands of a few people.

Private ownership in the means of production

Speaking on Red Square in Moscow in May 1919 Lenin said: "Our grandchildren will examine the documents and other relics of the epoch of the capitalist system with amazement. It will be difficult for them to picture to themselves how the trade in articles of primary necessity could remain in private hands, how factories could belong to individuals, how some men could exploit others, how it was possible for those who did not work to exist."[1]

Half a century has passed since these words were spoken. A generation has grown up which can imagine the capitalist system only with difficulty. It looks with amazement at the morals and manners in the capitalist countries.

Capitalism is based on private property. However, it is not only the existence of private property that matters. Of prime importance is the fact that under that system the means of production are private property, that is everything man needs to work: the land, machinery, instruments, raw materials, etc. Important is also the fact that under capitalism the bulk of the means of production are the private property of a few people—the capitalists and landowners. The bulk of the population, the working people, own no means of production and are forced to become hired workers of the owners of factories, mines, the land.

In the capitalist countries there are also small craftsmen and peasants who till their small plots with simple implements. These small producers cannot compete with big

---

[1] V. I. Lenin, *Collected Works*, Vol. 29, Moscow 1965, p. 330.

owners and suffer almost the same oppression from the big capitalists and landowners as the wage workers.

The big owners of the means of production, who possess enormous wealth, comprise a small minority, while people who have no property, or hardly any, comprise the bulk of the population in the capitalist countries. It is because all social wealth, all means of production are the private property of a few people that the mass of the propertyless workmen are compelled to work for the capitalists.

What is capital? A bourgeois economist answered this question as follows. "In the first stone which ... [the savage] flings at the wild animal he pursues, in the first stick that he seizes to strike down the fruit which hangs above his reach, we see the appropriation of one article for the purpose of aiding in the acquisition of another, and thus discover the origin of capital."[1]

This definition of capital is very convenient for the bourgeoisie. Its aim is to make people believe that capital has always existed and will always continue to exist.

If every instrument of labour were capital, people, obviously, could not live without capital: for instruments of labour were and will always be necessary. Accepting this definition we should regard even a monkey, who smashes a coco-nut with a stone, as a capitalist.

However, this explanation is incorrect from beginning to end. The stone and the stick are instruments of labour but are not means of exploitation per se. Under simple commodity production the owner of commodities sells his goods, which are not a use value to him, in order to purchase another commodity which is a use value. The purpose of this exchange is obvious: it serves to satisfy the requirements of commodity owners.

The capitalist pursues quite a different aim in investing his money. His aim is to make a profit. The capitalist owning a definite amount of money strives to increase that amount, i.e., to make a profit. The amount of money initially invested by the capitalist grows in the process of capitalist production.

Capital is not a thing but a definite social relation. It is a social relation between the class owning the means of

---

[1] K. Marx, *Capital*, Vol. 1, Moscow 1965, p. 184.

production and the class deprived of these means and therefore compelled to submit to exploitation. Things— buildings, machinery, raw materials, finished articles—are not capital per se. But a definite social system turns these things into means of exploitation, i.e., capital.

Means of production are not capital in themselves. They become capital, i.e., means of squeezing unpaid labour out of workers only under definite social relations, namely, when two opposing classes emerge in society—the class of private owners of the means of production and the class of propertyless wage workers—the proletarians. These social relations are not eternal. On the contrary, they emerge at a definite stage of social development and are abolished at another, later stage of development.

The Great October Socialist Revolution in Russia and later the triumph of socialist revolutions in a number of other countries proved in practice that the means of production cease to be a means of exploitation when the power of the bourgeoisie is overthrown and private ownership in the means of production is abolished.

Labour power as a commodity

Under the rule of private capitalist property the only thing owned by the bulk of the people is their ability to work, their labour power.

Man possesses labour power under any social system. But it is only under capitalism that labour power turns into a commodity, i.e., into an object of purchase and sale. When the capitalist hires workers, he buys a definite commodity, the only commodity the workers possess and are able to sell. This commodity is labour power. Capitalism is commodity production at the highest stage of its development, in which labour power, too, is a commodity.

Labour power becomes a commodity only under definite social conditions. It cannot be a commodity under the slave-owning system. Under that system the slave himself is a commodity, not his labour power. The slave is not free, he is the property of the slave-owner. Since he is not his own master he cannot sell his labour power. The same can be said of the peasant, who is a serf of the landowner. He is not free either, for he is the property (not complete) of the landowner. For that reason he, too, cannot sell his labour power.

An independent peasant or artisan, owning means of production, does not sell his labour power—he uses it on his own farm or in his workshop. Things change when the peasant is driven from his land and when the artisan is ruined and deprived of his instruments and raw materials. The only thing left to them is to sell their labour power in order to subsist.

After the abolition of capitalism labour power is no longer a commodity. In socialist society the means of production are socialist property. The working people here do not sell their labour power. They use it in enterprises which are public property.

Specific features of the commodity "labour power" When a worker goes to work at a capitalist enterprise he does not sell his labour power forever, but for a certain period—a day, a week, a month. In return he receives daily, weekly, monthly wages.

Like every other commodity, labour power has a definite value. We have already learned that the value of a commodity is determined by the amount of socially necessary labour required for its production. What then is the value of the commodity sold by the worker—his labour power?

Man can work only if he maintains his life: eats, dresses, is provided with shelter, i.e., satisfies his essential needs. The satisfaction of the vital needs of the worker is necessary to maintain his labour power in a condition in which it is able to act.

But all the objects serving to satisfy man's needs— bread, meat, clothes, housing, etc.—are commodities under capitalism. A definite amount of labour has been spent on their production, the amount that constitutes the value of these commodities.

Thus, the value of the commodity labour power is equal to the value of the commodities needed by the worker to maintain his life and to regenerate his ability to work. In other words, the value of labour power is the value of the means of subsistence needed to support the life of its owner.

Capital needs a constant influx of labour power. For this reason the worker must be given the opportunity to support not only himself but also his family. The capitalists need not only unskilled but also skilled workers, able to operate sophisticated machinery. Therefore, the value of labour power includes also some expenditure on training the growing generation of workers.

That is how things stand with commodity labour power. Having become a commodity, labour power has also a use value. What makes labour power a use value to the capitalist buying it? It is a use value because he makes the workman work, and because the workman's labour creates a value which is greater than that of the commodity labour power. This feature of the commodity labour power is the key to an understanding of the mechanism of capitalist exploitation.

2. PRODUCTION OF SURPLUS VALUE

The worker's surplus labour— the source of the capitalist's wealth Taking up business the capitalist buys a factory or builds one, i.e., pays for the building of the factory premises, acquires all the needed means of production: machines and equipment, raw and other materials, fuel. But all these things remain dead and unproductive until live human labour is applied to them.

The capitalist then hires workers, who put the machines in operation and turn the raw materials into finished goods, into commodities. The factory-owner sells these commodities and buys raw and other materials, pays the workers, etc., with the proceeds.

What is the value of the newly-produced commodity?

This value includes, first and foremost, the value of the commodities consumed in its production: raw materials have been processed, fuel has been burned and machinery worn. Let us assume that the value of these commodities is 200,000 working hours, or $400,000 in terms of money.

The value of the newly-produced commodity also includes the new value created by the labour of the workers at the relevant factory. Let us assume that 200 persons worked 100 days at the factory for eight hours a day. During that time they created a new value amounting to 160,000 working hours or $320,000.

Hence, the full value of the newly-produced commodity amounts to 360,000 working hours or $720,000 in terms of money.

Thus, the value of the commodity includes, first, the value of the materials consumed, and the value of the equipment worn and, secondly, the value created by the labour spent by the workers on the production of that commodity. Let us now see how much the commodity costs the capitalist.

The industrialist paid $400,000, i.e., a sum corresponding to 200,000 working hours, for the machines and materials needed for production. In addition to these 200,000 working hours the value of the new commodity includes 160,000 working hours spent by hired workers at the capitalist's factory. The workers' labour created a new value equal to $320,000.

Did the capitalist pay the workers an amount equal to all this value or not? The answer to this question solves the mystery of capitalist exploitation.

Capitalism presupposes a comparatively high level of labour productivity. At this level the daily labour of the worker produces considerably more products than are necessary for his subsistence. That is why the value produced by the worker's labour and the value of his labour power are of a different magnitude. The magnitude of the former is much bigger than that of the latter.

The difference between these two magnitudes is an essential condition for the exploitation of labour by capital. For the difference between the value of the labour power and the value of the articles produced by the worker's labour is appropriated wholly by the capitalist.

The capitalist pays the workers only for the value of their labour power. Let us assume that the means of subsistence the worker needs to satisfy his essential wants cost $8 a day. In that case the entrepreneur pays 200 workers the sum of $160,000 for 100 days.

The capitalist receives $720,000 for the commodity produced at his factory during that 100-day period. His expenditure on the production of the commodity comprises $400,000 plus $160,000, i.e., $560,000. The difference of $160,000 is the increment to his capital.

In our example every worker worked daily for eight hours and created 16 dollars' worth of new value. The capitalist paid the worker $8 for his eight-hour working day, i.e., he paid him only for the value of the labour power, or in other words, for the value created during 4 hours of work. Hence, the worker worked 4 hours to compensate for the value of his labour power and another 4 hours, free of charge, for the capitalist's benefit.

This shows that the labour the worker spends at a capitalist factory can be divided into two parts. During one part of the working day he produces the value that equals the value of his labour power. This is necessary labour. During the other part of the working day he produces the value that is appropriated by the capitalist without compensation to the worker. This is surplus labour.

This shows that the surplus labour of the worker is the source of the capitalist's wealth. In fact, it is the source of all unearned incomes in bourgeois society: the profits of industrialists and merchants, the dividens of share-holders, the interest of usurers and bankers, the ground rent of landowners, etc.

Surplus value   The value created by the surplus labour of the worker is surplus value. Surplus value is created by the unpaid labour of workers.

The appropriation by the capitalists of the surplus value created by the wage workers' labour—such is the essence of capitalist exploitation. The production of surplus value and its appropriation by the capitalist is the motive force of the capitalist mode of production.

Surplus labour existed even before capitalism. All exploitation of man by man consists in the appropriation by the exploiting class of the surplus labour of the exploited class.

However, under slavery and serfdom, when natural economy was predominant, the appropriation of surplus labour was limited. The slave-owner and the feudal lord squeezed from the slaves and serfs they were exploiting as much labour as they needed to satisfy their wants and whims.

The capitalist, on the other hand, transforms the product of the workers' surplus labour into cash. This money can again be used as additional capital to produce more surplus value.

73

The greed for surplus labour therefore knows no limits under capitalism. The capitalists do not shrink from using all and every means to intensify the exploitation of their wage slaves. Capital, as Marx said, exhibits a truly wolfish greed for surplus labour.

In his *Capital* Marx quotes the words of a British trade union functionary of the middle of the last century, which strikingly characterise the insatiable greed for profit inherent in the very nature of capital. He wrote:

"Capital is said... to fly turbulence and strive, and to be timid, which is very true; but this is very incompletely stating the question. Capital eschews no profit, or very small profit, just as Nature was formerly said to abhor a vacuum. With adequate profit, capital is very bold. A certain 10 per cent will ensure its employment anywhere; 20 per cent certain will produce eagerness; 50 per cent, positive audacity; 100 per cent will make it ready to trample on all human laws; 300 per cent, and there is not a crime at which it will scruple, nor a risk it will not run, even to the chance of its owner being hanged."[1]

Constant and variable capital

The various elements of capital play different parts in the production of surplus value. The entrepreneur transforms one part of his capital into means of production: factory buildings, machinery and plant, raw materials and fuel. The value of all these items spent on the production of the commodity is included in the value of the finished product without any change in its magnitude. Since the magnitude of the value of this part of the capital does not change it is called constant capital. Constant capital is designated by the letter c.

The entrepreneur uses the other part of his capital to hire workers, i.e., to purchase labour power. By their labour the workers create a new value. This value, as we have already shown, exceeds the value of the labour power, i.e., the magnitude of the value of the part of the capital spent on the hiring of workers changes (grows) in the process of capitalist production; that is why the part of the capital used to buy labour power is called variable capital. Variable capital is designated by the letter v.

---

[1] K. Marx. *Capital*, Vol. 1, Moscow 1965, p. 760.

The labour process under capitalism is notable for two important features. First, the worker labours under the command of the capitalist who decides what should be produced, in what sequence and by what method. Secondly, the capitalist owns not only the worker's labour but also the product of his labour. This transforms the worker's labour under capitalism into forced labour, makes it a repellent burden.

The labour the worker expends at the capitalist enterprise on the production of commodities has a dual nature. It produces, on the one hand, definite use values and, on the other, value containing surplus value.

The capitalist is not interested in the use value of the commodities being produced at his enterprise but only in their value, since the latter contains the surplus value produced by the workers' unpaid labour. The capitalist does not set himself the aim of satisfying social wants but of acquiring surplus value—profit.

The value of a commodity produced at a capitalist enterprise is composed of two parts. First, a certain amount of raw materials, fuel, etc., was spent on the production of the given commodity. The value of these materials and the wear of the machinery are included in the value of the finished product. Secondly, in addition to all this, a certain amount of labour was expended on the manufacture of the commodity. The value produced by the labour is also included in the value of the finished product.

Hence, the labour of the worker at a capitalist enterprise has a twofold nature. First, it transfers to the product the value of the consumed means of production, i.e., the value of the constant capital. Secondly, it creates new value, which compensates for the value of the variable capital and in addition contains a definite surplus, the surplus value.

Labour performs its first function as concrete labour. Thus, for example, the value of the flax, spindles, etc., can be transferred to the finished product—yarn—only by the labour of a spinner, and not by the labour of a tailor or a blacksmith. Its second function labour performs as abstract labour creating value.

There is a tangible difference between the two aspects of the labour process under capitalism. Let us assume that the spinner's labour productivity has grown 100 per cent, and that he consequently transfers to the product during his 10-hour working day twice as big a value as before. However the total new value he creates corresponds as hitherto to ten hours of work.

Thus, the difference between concrete and abstract labour is also apparent when we consider the capitalist mode of production as the difference between constant and variable capital, remembering that the latter helps to lay bare the essence of capitalist exploitation.

The aim of capitalist production is the creation of surplus value. The creation of use values is only a means for the achievement of that aim, since the use value is in a sense the bearer of value and because the latter cannot exist without the former. It will be shown further in the book that the development of capitalism inevitably creates a contradiction between the aim—the production of surplus value—and the means by which this aim is achieved—the production of use values.

Rate of exploitation

How intense is capitalist exploitation? An idea of this can be gained by the proportion in which the working day is divided into surplus and necessary labour time. The rate of the exploitation of labour by capital increases when the surplus labour time grows, while the necessary labour time contracts.

The surplus (unpaid) labour is embodied in the surplus value, while the necessary (paid) labour corresponds to the variable capital. The ratio of the surplus value to the variable capital is called the rate of surplus value. This rate is an indicator of the rate of exploitation of the worker by the capitalist.

In our example the rate of surplus value is:

$$\frac{160,000 \text{ dollars' worth of surplus value,}}{160,000 \text{ dollars' worth of variable capital}} \text{ i.e., 100 per cent.}$$

Surplus value is designated by the letter m. Hence the rate of surplus value is $\frac{m}{v}$.

In the capitalist industry of tsarist Russia in 1908, 2,254,000 workers received wages amounting to 555,700,000 rubles, an average wage of 246 rubles a year. At the same time the profits of the capitalists amounted to 568,700,000 rubles, which means that every worker gave the capitalist a profit of 252 rubles a year.

This computation, Lenin pointed out, shows that the worker laboured the smaller part of the working day for his own benefit, and the larger part—for that of the capitalist. The rate of surplus value was over 100 per cent.

The rate of surplus value grows with the development of capitalism. In the capitalist countries today it is 200, 300 per cent and sometimes even higher.

Two ways of raising the rate of exploitation In the pursuit of higher profits the capitalists strive to raise the share of surplus labour they squeeze from the workers in every possible way. They achieve their aim by two methods.

First, they extend the working day. An extension of the working day increases the amount of surplus labour squeezed from every worker. If the capitalist could he would compel the workers to labour 24 hours a day. However, this is impossible: the worker needs time to rest, sleep, eat, otherwise he will be unable to work. Besides, the workers increashingly resist the capitalists' move to extend the working day.

For this reason the capitalists resort to the second method of increasing their profits. They introduce new machinery, apply all sorts of inventions, use higher technique. Higher technique requires much less labour to produce the workers' means of subsistence than before. Thus, the value of the workers' means of subsistence drops as technology improves.

This means that the worker compensates the money he has been paid for his labour power in less time than before. Therefore the capitalist appropriates a much greater amount of the unpaid labour of the worker even without extending the working day, i.e., the rate of the worker's exploitation rises.

Striving for higher profits the capitalists raise the intensity of the workers' labour in every way. This means that the worker has to spend more energy per hour or per day than he did before, that he has to work more intensively. If, for example, the worker formerly produced 100 articles a day, he now has to produce 150, 180, 200 articles with the same machinery for the same pay.

In this way the capitalists increase the surplus value and, hence, their profits. Higher labour intensity at capitalist factories leads to an increase in the number of accidents and industrial injuries, to a greater incidence of occupational disease among the workers, to a premature loss of their ability to work and to premature old age.

Capitalism and technological progress

In search of profits the capitalists have remoulded the whole system of social production. Instead of the former small-scale production based on manual labour, they have created large-scale industry based on machine production. Factories mushroomed everywhere, ruining and ousting the small producers. The invention and utilisation of machinery was instrumental in spreading the capitalist mode of production all over the world.

Capitalist machine industry first emerged and developed in Britain. Within a short time (the last third of the 18th and the early 19th centuries) a great many machines appeared in Britain and changed the country's face beyond recognition. Once an agricultural country, Britain turned into an industrial power. Large industrial centres sprang into being all over the country. A numerous industrial proletariat developed. Soon large-scale machine industry spread from country to country.

Do the capitalists always strive to introduce new machinery in their factories? No, they do not, not unless it increases their profits. A machine is profitable to the capitalist only if the expenditure connected with its use is smaller than the wages of the workers replaced by the machine. That means that the lower the wages the less interested are the capitalists in introducing machinery.

Under capitalism up-to-date technology in some branches lives side by side with backward technology in other branches. It is often profitable for the capitalist to have workers perform some jobs at their homes. Women and children work at home all day long. Their wages are so low that it costs him less to pay for their work at home than he would have to pay for mounting additional machine-tools at the factory.

In pre-revolutionary Russia a large group of workers were employed as burlaks. The burlaks walked in a long line along the river bank towing heavily loaded barges. The pay for this extremely exhausting labour was miserable but there was no other occupation for the ruined peasants.

It might be thought that in the machine age such an absurd waste of human power was conceivable only in backward Russia. However, this is not so. Marx in his *Capital* tells that in the mid-19th century there were cases in Britain when women were employed to tow barges along canals. This was more profitable to the capitalists than to use horses or machines for that purpose.

Capitalist utilisation of machinery and the working class

The capitalist introduces new machines only to shorten the part of the working day during which the worker labours for himself, so as to lengthen the other part of the working day during which he produces surplus value for the capitalist.

At an early stage of capitalist development the workers were bitterly opposed to the introduction of machinery. Machines deprived the mass of the workers engaged in manual labour of their daily bread and condemned them to starvation.

At first the spontaneous protest of workers found expression in their desire to smash machines, to sweep them from the face of the earth. A wide movement of "machine-destroyers" developed at the beginning of the 19th century in Britain, where machines were first introduced. Similar movements emerged later in other countries, where the development of capitalist machine industry brought ruin and poverty to the working masses.

But the naive protest of the unfortunate and desperate people could not stop the triumphant march of machine industry. When the workers change over from scattered spontaneous protests to a conscious struggle for their vital interests, they are fully aware that it is not the machinery per se that is their enemy but the capitalist system, under which it is used. The baneful consequences for the working class are not brought about by the machines themselves but by their capitalist utilisation.

In socialist society the machine is the faithful helper of man, serves as a means of lightening his labour. Under socialism the utilisation of machinery multiplies the country's wealth and raises the material and cultural level of the working people. Capitalism, on the other hand, makes the machine a terrible competitor of the worker, depriving him of his daily bread.

The machine is intended to lighten labour. Under capitalism, however, it increases the intensity of labour to the utmost. This has a disastrous effect on the worker, wears out his organism, reduces his ability to work, makes him an early invalid.

The machine per se is a faithful helper of man in his struggle for the mastery over the forces of nature. Under capitalism, however, it is a terrible weapon used by the exploiters in their struggle against the exploited. With the help of machinery the capitalists worsen the conditions of labour and try to break the resistance of the workers against increasing exploitation.

In raising labour productivity the machine multiplies social wealth. But under capitalism all the fruits yielded by growing labour productivity are reaped by the capitalists, who use machinery to make the worker a pauper.

Thus, the utilisation of machinery under capitalism contains deep contradictions. These contradictions cannot be resolved so long as the capitalist system continues to exist.

Is it the fault of the knife? Champions of the bourgeois system cannot think of any other way of using machinery except in the capitalist way. They call everybody who reveals the contradictions inherent in the capitalist utilisation of machinery an enemy of social progress. Exposing these lackeys of the bourgeoisie, Marx showed that in their views they resembled the cutthroat in Dickens' *Oliver Twist* who addressed the court in the following words:

"Gentlemen of the jury, no doubt the throat of this commercial traveller has been cut. But that is not my fault, it is the fault of the knife. Must we, for such a temporary inconvenience, abolish the use of the knife? Only consider! Where would agriculture and trade be without the knife? Is it not as salutary in surgery, as it is knowing in anatomy? And in addition a willing help at the festive board? If you abolish the knife—you hurl us back into the depth of barbarism."[1]

The capitalists and their hangers-on, hearing of the innumerable calamities resulting from the capitalist machine industry, argue like this cutthroat. "Do you expect us to do without machines because of such 'a temporary inconvenience'?" they say. However, class-conscious workers fighting for their rights and interests are not against technological progress but are all for it. They understand that the fight should not be directed against machinery—such a fight is not only purposeless but also reactionary, for the wheel of history cannot be turned back from machine production to manual labour. The fight should be directed against capitalist exploitation, which gives all the fruit of technological progress to the non-working classes, condemning the creators of all social wealth—the working masses—to a miserable subsistence.

Wages under capitalism conceal exploitation

As we have seen above, the labour of the wage worker at the capitalist enterprise consists of two parts: paid and unpaid labour. When the entrepreneur pays the worker his wages, the worker does not see that his wages compensate for only part of his labour, the other part being appropriated gratis by the capitalist. The payment of wages is always effected in a form creating the semblance that the worker is paid for his entire labour.

Actually the capitalist does not pay the worker for all the value he produces, but only for part of it. Is the worker able to find out how great is the value he creates every day for his boss? At the factory the working time is not divided to show that the worker compensates for his wages and works for the sole benefit of his boss during the rest of the time.

The buyer of a commodity can use it only after he has paid its price. The capitalist, however, buying the commodity—labour power—pays the worker only after he has used his labour.

Wages are calculated in two ways. In some cases they are calculated in accordance with the length of working time:

---

[1] K. Marx. *Capital*, Vol. 1, Moscow 1965, p. 442.

hours or weeks; this is called time wages. In other cases wages are calculated in accordance with the quantity of products made; this is called piece wages. But in both cases a false impression is created that the worker does not sell his labour power, but his labour, that he is paid for the whole of the labour power he expends.

Wages under capitalism conceal the division of labour time into necessary and surplus. The form of wages does not reveal that the capitalist pays the worker for only part of his labour and appropriates his surplus labour free of charge. Capitalist exploitation is camouflaged.

Thus wages conceal the exploitation of the worker by the capitalist, create a semblance of full reward for his labour. This plays an important role in the life of capitalist society. These false impressions continue to grip the minds of the workers until they manage to free themselves from the ideological influence of the bourgeoisie: the press, church, science, etc., all of which serve to engrave this illusion on the minds of the working people.

Wages and the economic position of the proletariat

Capitalists strive to lower wages to a minimum. It is commonly known that the prices of commodities fluctuate, now rising above, now falling below their value. But as distinct from the prices of other commodities, wages, i.e., the price of labour power, tend to fall below their value.

The capitalists have devised numerous methods of picking the worker's pocket, of reducing his real earnings, but they all come to one and the same result: the worker is compelled to economise on food, clothing, housing.

The workers in the capitalist countries suffer most from the rising cost of living. The sum of money the worker gets from selling his labour power—the nominal wages—is one thing; the amount and the quality of foodstuffs, clothing, household goods, etc., the worker can buy for the money he earns is quite another. The amount of means of subsistence the worker is able to buy for his money determines his real wages. As the cost of living rises, as taxes grow, real wages drop and the conditions of the working class worsen.

In the capitalist countries there are many categories of low-paid workers and even whole branches of production in which wages are low. This applies, first and foremost, to agriculture and also to some industries, the textile industry, for example. Women draw lower wages than men. In some cases the wages of women are only half of those paid to men.

According to official US data, 35 million people live in poverty in that country. The US Government has declared poverty a "national calamity" and has hypocritically declared "war on poverty". However, in reality only second-rate measures are taken under this demagogic slogan, which do not exert a tangible influence on the disastrous position of millions of people.

Racial discrimination In the colonial and dependent countries European workers get 10 to 13 times more than native workers for the same work. Because of discrimination on racial and national grounds considerable sections of the working people are barred from skilled labour and are the first to get the sack.

The native population in the colonies and dependent countries works predominantly as coal miners, stevedores, farm hands on the most difficult and low-paid jobs. They are barred from education.

In the USA 15 million American Negroes are deprived of civil rights and are subjected to cruel exploitation. The vast majority of Negroes take on such low-paid work as stevedores, domestic servants, dish washers, laundrymen, etc.

In the USA many institutions and organisations refuse to employ Negroes. When Negroes are hired they are used only for auxiliary, unskilled jobs.

Wage slavery In capitalist society wage labour is essentially wage slavery. A Roman slave was fettered by chains, while a wage labourer, to use Marx's expression, is tied by invisible threads to his owner. The whip of the overseer is successfully replaced by the fine book. The inexorable laws of the capitalist mode of production fetter the worker effectively to the chariot of capital.

Capitalist exploitation is camouflaged by illusions created by its specific features, by its distinction from the old forms of exploitation. The bourgeoisie skillfully exploits the illusions created by the outward form of wage labour to make its slaves work with an expenditure of physical and mental labour that was unprecedented under slavery and under feudalism. Capitalism has invented a multitude of artful methods and systems, from "participation in profits" to "social partnership", and all sorts of "people's capitalism" theories which simultaneously camouflage and intensify the threat of starvation.

These false theories are used by the advocates of capitalism to keep the working masses in spiritual bondage. The champions of the outmoded system maintain that capitalism has changed its nature and essence, that there has been a "democratisation of capital".

They attempt to impress upon the working people that they are able to do away with privation and attain better living conditions under capitalism. They picture capitalism as a social system that provides "equal opportunities" to everybody. These assertions are a downright lie.

In reality capitalism dooms the bulk of the population, the working people, to poverty and hunger, privation and suffering.

Uncertainty of the future, insecurity of existence, constantly worsening living conditions—such is the lot of millions of working people under capitalism.

The development of capitalism worsens the conditions of the working people and multiplies the wealth of the bourgeoisie. Year in, year out the exploiting classes concentrate ever greater riches in their hands. At the same time the conditions of the working class and of all working people keep deteriorating.

The mechanics of capitalist society is such that the workers constantly remain propertyless proletarians, whose only way out is to sell their labour power. The capitalist, on the other hand, remains the owner of capital, accruing continuously owing to surplus value.

The humiliating position of labour and the working people in the society based on exploitation produces a corresponding attitude towards labour, distorted views on labour. The slave-owner considered labour an occupation below the dignity of a free person, the contemptible lot of slaves. The feudal lord saw the decisive superiority of "blue blood" in the fact that it freed the nobility of the need to work, shifting the burden of labour to the shoulders of the "common" people. The bourgeois hypocritically exalts labour, but only the labour of others, the labour of the people who are the source of his enrichment. He himself builds his welfare on unearned incomes.

Under all forms of exploiting society, labour is regarded as a misfortune, a punishment inflicted upon man for his sins. The exploitation of man by man makes labour a heavy burden, a curse.

Capitalism—a dirty word Capitalism still rules in most countries. Hundreds of millions of people live under its rule. Modern capitalism causes suffering to the popular masses, dooms them to ruin and to fear of the future, to exploitation and oppression. The danger of bloody wars is always imminent as long as capitalism exists. These wars take a heavy toll of human lives. They also destroy huge material and cultural values, created by the labour of the people throughout the ages.

Recently an American newspaper offered a large prize to anyone who could think up a successful term to replace the name "capitalism". Explaining its offer, the newspaper wrote that the word "capitalism" was no longer of any use—the masses are dissatisfied with it, it has become almost a dirty word.

True, the capitalist system has been condemned by millions of people in all countries. Even the faithful servants of the bourgeoisie are compelled to admit this. But it is not the word "capitalism" but the essence of the social system, designated by this word, that rouses the indignation of the people.

Modern defenders of the exploiting system try to substitute the word "capitalism" by all sorts of hazy expressions. They call capitalism "the system of free enterprise", the "system of private initiative", etc. But although they can invent any amount of names for the capitalist order, this will not help them to whitewash its essence.

Hypocritical talk about freedom and equality under capitalism The bourgeoisie and its lackeys extol the capitalist system as embodying freedom and equality. Events, however, nail the lie at every step.

Formally, according to the laws of bourgeois countries, workers are "free". The capitalist does not have the right to buy and sell workers. In actual fact, however, the capitalist has unlimited power over wage workers: he can condemn them to starvation. The worker can leave the enterprise in question, but he can do no more than change one particular yoke for an equally heavy one, for he has to enter the employ of another capitalist who will exploit him as ruthlessly as his former employer.

Thus under capitalism "freedom" is the complete and unrestricted freedom for the capitalist to exploit workers, and the "freedom" for the workers to sell themselves into bondage to capitalists.

Equally untrue is all talk about "equality" under capitalism. Bourgeois revolutions proclaimed the equality of all citizens before the law. However, it is easy to see that there is no, nor can there be, genuine equality of people in conditions of exploitation. What equality can there be between the exploiter and the exploited, between the rich and the poor, between the oppressor and the oppressed?

The bourgeoisie and its lackeys try in every way to picture capital as wealth earned through personal effort. In a thousand ways they repeat the stupid legends about rich people who began their careers without a penny and acquired riches only thanks to their thrift, love of labour and enterprise. They try by all means to make the working people believe that they have the opportunity of becoming rich, of becoming capitalists. In reality, however, from among the people beginning life as wage workers only one in many thousands becomes a petty shop-keeper, and only one in a million—a capitalist, and this generally as a result of guile and, more often than not, of crime.

Basic contradiction of capitalism

The contradictions of capitalism are inherent in the commodity, in the conditions of commodity production under the domination of private ownership in the means of production. Already under simple commodity production there is a contradiction between private and social labour. Under capitalism, this contradiction turns into that between the social nature of production and the private capitalist form of appropriation of the fruits of production.

With the development of modern machine industry, production becomes increasingly social. Hundreds and thousands of people are employed in every enterprise. There are close links between individual enterprises. Hence, hundreds of thousands and millions of people are interconnected in the production process. But the product of this social production instead of being placed at the disposal of all of society is appropriated by a handful of private owners. Capital organises the labour of hundreds and thousands of workers in every enterprise separately, while unco-ordinated anarchical production carried on by private industrialists rules social production as a whole.

This is the basic contradiction of capitalism, which finds expression in the anarchy of production, in effective demand lagging behind growing production, in the class struggle between the working class and the capitalists.

Significance of the theory of surplus value Exploitation is camouflaged under capitalism. Only Marxist political economy revealed the essence of the exploitation of labour by capital. The mystery of capitalist exploitation is disclosed in the theory of surplus value evolved by Marx.

The theory of surplus value teaches the working class and all the working people in the capitalist countries to see the genuine causes of their oppression, poverty and privations. It shows that the oppression and privations of the workers and of all working people are not accidental, are not due to the arbitrary rule of individual capitalists, but spring from the whole system of capitalism, from the very essence of capitalist production relations.

Defenders of capitalism strive to deny that the working class is exploited by the capitalist class. They refer to the fact that in their purchase and sale transactions, the worker and the capitalist are formally equal commodity-owners. Marxism revealed that this formal equality serves as a guise for the system of wage slavery, that it conceals monstrous factual inequality.

The purchase and sale of labour power is only the introduction to the process of capitalist production. It is in the very process of production that the true nature of relations between the capitalist and the worker is revealed. They are the relations between the exploiter and the exploited. The theory of surplus value throws a spot-light on the class relations between the proletariat and the bourgeoisie. It shows how the hire of workers, the purchase and sale of labour power, camouflages the enslavement of millions of wage workers by a handful of factory and landowners.

The theory of surplus value reveals the essence of capitalist exploitation. Lenin called the theory of surplus value the corner-stone of Marx's economic theory. It lays bare the roots of class contradictions and class struggle in capitalist society.

3. DEVELOPMENT OF CAPITALISM AND CONDITION OF THE WORKING MASSES

Growing wealth of the capitalists. Accumulation of capital

It seems at first sight that the capitalist can do with his surplus value as he pleases. There really are bourgeois who spend their profits in the most imprudent way. Generally, however, the capitalist always uses part of his profit to expand production. Of course, there are no written laws forcing him to do this, but there are other motives that compel the capitalist to act in this manner, namely, competition and the greed for profit.

Capital is insatiable in its greed for profit. No matter how rich an entrepreneur, no matter how large his profits, he wants to be richer still.

In capitalist society *homo homini lupus est*. Every entrepreneur does his utmost to throttle his competitors, to get the edge on them in the competitive struggle, to take over their enterprises, to clear for himself the road to market domination, to multiply his wealth. If the capitalist does not want to go under in this fight with no holds barred of each against his neighbour, he has to add a large share of his profits to his capital, to invest it in production.

The addition of a part of the surplus value to the capital is called the accumulation of capital. Accumulating every year part of the surplus value, the capitalist becomes the owner of a steadily growing capital. If the enterprise of a capitalist was originally valued at, say, $1,000,000, by accumulating $50,000-100,000 a year he increases his capital over a ten-year period by 50 or 100 per cent and becomes the owner of a capital of $1,500,000 to $2,000,000.

Capital also grows in another way. In the system ruled by the quest for profits the strong strangles the weak, the large capitalist swallows up his small and weaker competitors. Buying up the enterprises of his ruined competitors for a song, or grabbing them as payment for their debts, the large industrialist increases his capital. Thus capital grows as a result of the struggle, bringing victory to few and ruin to many as a result of several sums of capital merging into one.

Large-scale production is more profitable than small-scale production. The former makes it possible to use machinery on a wide scale. It can raise the productivity of labour to a far higher level than small-scale production. For this reason large-scale industry consistently ousts artisans. Among the capitalists themselves there proceeds a constant struggle resulting in the ruination of the owners of small enterprises and bringing victory to the owners of big enterprises, employing vast numbers of workers. The larger the enterprise, the larger the mass of surplus value appropriated by its owner, and, hence, the quicker the accumulation of capital.

As a result huge sums of capital become the property of a very small number of tycoons. This handful of millionaires and multimillionaires owns huge fortunes and decides the fate of tens and hundreds of thousands of people. The mass of wealth produced by the labour of the working class and concentrated in the hands of a small group of capitalist magnates grows with every passing decade. At the same time, those who create all the good things of life and feed and clothe the world are forced to go through ever greater hardships.

If the capitalist did not appropriate the unpaid labour of workers his capital would melt in a few years. He spends enormous sums on himself every year, and after a while his capital would be eaten up completely. Actually, however, capital does not decrease but grows all the time.

The secret of this mystery lies in the appropriation of the unpaid labour of the working class. No matter what the initial source of capital, after a while it turns into the accumulated unpaid labour of others.

Accumulation of capital and the working class

Accumulation of capital has very important consequences for the working class. Expanding production, the capitalists introduce machinery requiring a smaller amount of live labour. This changes the relation between the two parts of capital—constant and variable capital. Constant capital grows much quicker than variable capital.

The workers ousted by machinery, the defenders of the bourgeoisie contend, can easily find employment because production expands steadily. Actually, however, production expands slower than workers are ousted by machinery. Besides, production expands irregularly: some industries expand and hire new workers, others contract and dismiss their workers.

Thus the course of capitalist production ensures the entrepreneur with a constant reserve of working hands. But this in itself is not enough. Under capitalism there are also other inexhaustible sources for supplementing the army of the unemployed. There is a steady influx of free working hands from the countryside. Agriculture does not provide the means of subsistence for hundreds of thousands of landless and land-hungry peasants. They are compelled to abandon their miserable farms and to move to towns in search of work, landing right in front of the gates of capitalist factories.

Furthermore, there is a multitude of artisans, small tradesmen, owners of small workshops, etc. No matter how hard they cling to their small enterprises, their independence is always threatened. Competition with big factories, the high cost of living and heavy taxes ruin them and push them into the ranks of the unemployed.

The universal law of capitalist accumulation

When a capitalist installs new equipment he strives to raise the profitability of his enterprise. Technological innovations lower the value of the workers' means of subsistence: less amount of labour is needed for their production than before. The worker compensates the value of his labour power by fewer hours' work.

Whereas the working day was formerly divided into 5 hours of necessary and 5 hours of surplus labour, the development of technology has divided it into 4 hours of necessary and 6 hours of surplus labour time, then into 3 and 7 hours respectively, etc. This means that while the duration of the working day is unchanged the capitalist appropriates a larger amount of the workers' unpaid labour, a larger amount of surplus value.

Hence, accumulation of capital goes hand in hand with the steady rise in the rate of the exploitation of workers by capitalists. The greater the social wealth under capitalism, the larger the army of unemployed, condemned to poverty and hunger. Accumulation of wealth at one pole of society is at the same time accumulation of misery, agony of toil, insecurity at the opposite pole, i.e., on the side of the class that produces all the wealth of society.

Such is the law of capitalist accumulation discovered by Karl Marx.

Relative and absolute deterioration of the working class's position

The growing rate of exploitation of labour by capital means that the working class is receiving an ever smaller share of the wealth it produces.

The total sum of values produced during a definite period, say, over a year, in a country is called the national income of that country. In the capitalist countries the share of the working class in the national income is systematically decreasing. At the same time the share in the national income appropriated by the bourgeoisie and its hangers-on grows constantly.

For example, in the United States the working people received 54 per cent of the national income before the Second World War, and only 42 per cent after the war. In Britain the share of the working people in the national income decreased from 45 to 40 per cent during that time. The share of the exploiting classes in the national income of the USA and Britain is steadily growing. What is lost by the proletariat is gained by the bourgeoisie.

Therein lies the relative deterioration of the working class's position. It is called relative because there is a change in the relation between the incomes of the working people and those of the non-working classes, the relation between the living standard of the working class and that of the bourgeoisie. The exceedingly low living standard of the working class lives side by side with wanton waste of the bourgeoisie.

Thus, American newspapers report on rich people who pay $1,500 for a tie. For millions of low-paid American working people this is a year's income. There was a report about a multimillionaire, who to amuse his guests had adorned the trees in his garden with fruit of gold. On the estate of another capitalist snow-white sheets with his coat of arms embroidered on them were spread in the stable for horses to sleep on. In American newspapers there was an advertisement offering for sale an out-of-town estate with a two-mile-long private beach, a summer theatre, four gardens, one of which is a copy of the famous Versailles Park.

Defenders of the bourgeois system assert that the position of the working class improves with the development of capitalism. Look, they say, did any generation in the past have so powerful a technology? Have there ever been such railways, ocean liners, cities with millions of inhabitants, factories employing thousands of people? Has the workman ever used such sophisticated, highly productive machinery? From this they draw the conclusion that the development of the capitalist system has raised the material welfare of society.

However, the defenders of the bourgeoisie lauding the progress achieved under capitalism do not say the whole truth. They tell only part truths, and part truths are worse than bare-faced lies.

Undeniably, during the 150-200 years of its domination, capitalism has developed powerful productive forces. As regards the mastery over nature, society has during that time greatly advanced in comparison with all former epochs.

But this is only one aspect of the matter. The other aspect is that the greater power of man over the forces of nature has been achieved at the price of the enslavement, oppression and ruthless exploitation of many generations of working people. Capitalism has created a powerful technology, but it has built it literally on the bones and blood of hundreds of millions of people.

Capitalism is responsible, not only for the relative but sometimes also for the absolute deterioration of the working class's position, i.e., it worsens its living and working conditions. This means that workers have to eat worse and dress worse, live in slums and go without bare necessities.

In the face of these facts the champions of capitalism are sometimes forced to admit that there is a relative worsening of the working class's conditions, but they furiously deny that there is an absolute deterioration. Do not, they ask, the workers of the second half of the 20th century enjoy many benefits inconceivable a hundred and even fifty years ago? This is usually followed by a reference to bicycles, motor cycles, cars, radios and TV sets, washing machines, refrigerators, etc., invented comparatively recently.

They try to confuse the question of the working class's position under capitalism by such references. They ignore a thing every rational person understands, namely, that the requirements of people are not immutable.

The improvement of technology, the development of the productive forces and the growth of social wealth evolve ever new requirements with all members of society, including, of course, the working masses.

The requirements of the working class grow with the progress of historical development. But in capitalist conditions it is becoming increasingly difficult for the working class to satisfy its normal requirements.

The position of the working class deteriorates because an enormous tax burden is placed on its shoulders. High rents and all sorts of deductions from their wages decrease the real incomes of the working people. Labour is becoming more back-breaking and industrial injuries distressingly frequent. It is only through its stubborn struggle that the working class counteracts the capitalist's desire to reduce their living standard to an absolute minimum.

In recent years consumer credit has become widespread in the capitalist countries. Many working people, especially those in the higher-paid bracket, buy furniture and other consumer durables, sometimes even motor cars, small houses or flats on credit.

The champions of the bourgeoisie maintain that such purchases indicate an improvement of the working class's conditions. Actually, however, consumer credit is but another form of additional exploitation of the working people. Buying things on credit they have to pay for them 15 to 25 per cent more than they would have had to pay in cash. Besides, the capitalists charge extremely high interest rates (from 6 to 12 per cent a year) for goods sold on credit. Finally, if the buyer fails to pay his regular installment, and this is frequent because of unemployment, sickness or other reasons, the articles bought on credit have to be returned to the seller and the buyer's investment is lost.

Unemployment— the proletariat's scourge

Capitalism cannot exist without an army of unemployed. This army supplies the capitalist with free working hands whenever market conditions warrant an expansion of production. Bourgeois politicians frankly admit that unemployment is essential to the capitalist system. In a talk with a correspondent, ex-President Harry Truman said that a certain number of unemployed, say 3 to 5 million people, was admissible. It was good, he said, when some people were looking for work, this was healthy for the economic organism.

The capitalist big wigs and their servants say that millions of unemployed are essential for "a healthy economic organism". It is easy to see that the capitalists favour unemployment because it is a powerful weapon against the working class. Always and everywhere the capitalist uses unemployment to exert pressure on his workers, to worsen their living and working conditions and to raise his profits in that way.

Unemployment is a scourge to the working class. The inevitability of unemployment under capitalism brings insecurity, constant uncertainty about the future to all wage workers. The worker's life is of no value to the capitalist. There are many willing to take the place of a worker leaving the ranks. At capitalist factories many healthy people quickly become invalids, grow old prematurely. The high pace of work there, the unbearable duration of the working day and industrial injuries are responsible for it.

In the dependent countries and colonies unemployment runs into many millions.

Unemployment affects also the conditions of employed workers. The large number of unemployed makes their jobs unstable, makes them uncertain of the future. They have work today but no security that they will have it tomorrow. This position is not the result of accidental causes but of the economic laws of the capitalist mode of production.

Through their long persistent struggle the workers of the developed capitalist countries have succeeded in shortening the working day. But labour has become very intensive and the worker has to spend more energy in an hour than he did in two hours before. Under capitalism the excessive labour of one part of the working class is concomitant with the forced idleness—full or partial—of its other part.

In the USA, for example, during the whole post-war period over 20 per cent of the working people worked more than 48 hours a week, while a large part of them worked even over 50 hours. At the same time about 10 to 15 per cent are compelled to work only part of the week—from 1 to 34 hours, with a corresponding decrease in wages, while millions of workers are fully unemployed.

The bourgeoisie conceals the proportions unemployment has reached. It likes to count money but it does not like to count the lives it has wasted. An American scholar said there were exact statistical data on the number of pigs reared every year and on the amount of wheat harvested, but nobody bothered to find out how many workers had no work. Official statistics deliberately understate unemployment figures.

In a number of capitalist countries bourgeois statistics list as unemployed only those "fortunate" few who receive miserable unemployment relief or handouts from private philanthropists. There is not a single country in which those who look for work for the first time—the growing working-class generation—are included. Official data do not include the unemployed who have succeeded in securing temporary jobs. In the USA, for example, even workers employed for one hour a week and those who have no work but have been promised to be given some within a month are also not considered unemployed. Obviously, therefore, the figures on the size of unemployment, which are now and then published by the official bodies in the bourgeois countries, reflect only a small part of the real unemployment figure.

In modern bourgeois society mass unemployment has become a normal state of affairs. In the USA, the main capitalist country, even according to the deliberately understated official statistics, the unemployment figure has for many years now never dropped below 3 to 4 million. According to official statistics, in 1964 the number of unemployed in the USA was 3.9 million people, or 5 per cent of the total labour force. But, according to trade union data, another 2.5 million of partly employed, i.e., those compelled to work only part of the working day, and many millions of concealed unemployed, i.e., those who have despaired of ever receiving work and therefore do not go to the labour exchange, should be added to the 3.9 million of fully unemployed workers. Thus, not 5 but 9 per cent of the total labour force is deprived of the chance to work.

Aggravation of class contradictions With the development of capitalism society is divided more and more sharply into two hostile camps, into two opposing classes: the proletariat and the bourgeoisie. All wealth and power is concentrated in the hands of the bourgeoisie : it owns nearly all the means of production and therefore appropriates the product of social labour. The bourgeoisie holds power but it cannot exist without the working class. The capitalist could not thrive if workers did not operate the machines at his factories. Having produced incalculable wealth for the capitalists, the working class remains a poor and oppressed class.

At the present time the number of wage workers, employed at factories and offices, comprises about 200 million people in the economically developed capitalist countries. In the European capitalist countries there are about 100 million factory and office workers, in North America about 70 million, in Japan about 25 million, in Australia and New Zealand about 4 million. In the economically less developed countries of the capitalist world there are about 170 million factory and office workers; some 90-95 million in Asia, about 40 million in Latin America and about 20 million in Africa.

The bourgeoisie and the proletariat are the two main classes in capitalist society. In addition to these classes there are other classes and intermediate strata in nearly all capitalist countries. In most capitalist countries the peasantry constitutes a particularly large part of the population. The development of capitalism, however, inevitably leads to the impoverishment and ruin of the bulk of the rural workers subjected to exploitation by the capitalists, landowners and rich peasants.

The spread of large-scale production is attended by growing class contradictions both in town and country. The intermediate layer is being eroded. There proceeds an increasing stratification of the petty bourgeoisie: few become capitalists, while many thousands are pushed into the ranks of the working class. The development of large-scale capitalist production inevitably polarises society: a few bourgeois grow rich, while want and privations become the lot of the mass of working people.

A writer once remarked: if a rich man ate a chicken and a poor man ate nothing, both "ate half a chicken on an average". This ironical remark illustrates the method by which modern bourgeois economists embellish dire capitalist reality. They are very fond of "averages", which conceal the true state of affairs.

They add the high salaries of the directors of capitalist firms and the wages of workers and fabricate an "average earning", which considerably exceeds the true level of workers' wages. In other cases they compute "average" indices for the peasant households, which conceal the enormous difference between the levels of the rich households of the kulaks and the beggarly households of the poor peasants.

The development of capitalism widens the gulf dividing the bourgeoisie, on one side, and the working masses of town and country, on the other. The capitalist system has created a large-scale industry with modern equipment, means of transport and communications, has opened up rich deposits hidden in the bowels of the earth. During the past 150-200 years or so man has greatly extended his power over nature. But this success in mastering the forces of nature has exacted a heavy toll from the people, has been paid for by the sweat and blood of many generations of workers. The growth of man's power over nature has intensified the exploitation of man by man.

Was Marx right? The slave-like, humiliating position of the workman under capitalism has been vividly described by Marx:

"He works in order to live. He does not even reckon labour as part of his life, it is rather a sacrifice of his life. It is a commodity which he has made over to another. Hence, also, the product of his activity is not the object of his activity. What he produces for himself is not the silk that he weaves, not the gold that he draws from the mine, not the palace that he builds. What he produces for himself is *wages*, and silk, gold, palace resolve themselves for him into a definite quantity of the means of subsistence, perhaps into a cotton jacket, some copper coins and a lodging in a cellar. And the worker, who for twelve hours weaves, spins, drills, turns, builds, shovels, breaks stones, carries loads, etc.—does he consider this twelve hours' weaving, spinning, drilling, turning, building, shovelling, stone breaking as a manifestation of his life, as life? On the contrary, life begins for him where this activity ceases, at table, in the public house, in bed. The twelve hours' labour, on the other hand, has no meaning for him as weaving, spinning, drilling, etc., but as *earnings*, which bring him to the table, to the public house, into bed. If the silk worm were to spin in order to continue its existence as a caterpillar, it would be a complete wage worker."[1]

But, the reader may object, Marx wrote this in the middle of the 19th century, over a hundred years ago. Has nothing changed since then?

There is no doubt, much has changed over the last 100 years in the capitalist countries. The tenacious struggle of the working class of the developed capitalist countries for its vital interests has not been in vain. During the past decades the success achieved in the construction of a new life in the Soviet Union and other socialist countries has inspired the workers in the capitalist countries, has made them resist the exploiters even more stiffly and has forced the bourgeoisie to make concessions time and again. In the old capitalist countries the working day is no longer 12 hours, as it was a hundred years ago, it is now 8 hours in most of

---

[1] K. Marx and F. Engels, *Selected Works*, Vol. I, Moscow 1962, pp. 82-83.

them. In the economically less developed countries, especially those still languishing under colonialism, workers still labour for 12 and more hours.

However, in spite of the concessions the working class has wrested from the bourgeoisie, the essence of the capitalist system has not changed. Like in Marx's time, that system is based on exploitation of labour by capital. The gulf between labour and capital has not disappeared but, on the contrary, has widened enormously. The development of capitalism leads to the enrichment of small groups of the bourgeoisie, while the bulk of the population is proletarianised, i.e., is transformed into destitute, poor people living on the sale of their labour power.

This shows that Marx's characteristic of wage labour is no less true today than it was in his days. Moreover, in present-day conditions it is applicable to wider masses of the working people than it was in the past century.

Two nations   The exploitation of man by man means that the handful comprising the rich élite of society lives at the expense of the labour of the unfortunate majority. This state of affairs continues to exist in our time in the part of the globe still living under capitalism.

A pamphlet that appeared several years ago in Britain contained the admission that both in economic and social respects there continue to be "two nations" in Britain. The property of half of the people consists almost exclusively of personal things and domestic belongings while one per cent of the population owns about half of all the private property in the country.

An article in an American magazine said that the United States, like any other capitalist country, consists essentially of two nations. One comprises those who work but do not live, the other those who live but do not work.

Under capitalism, rich idlers lead a parasitical life at the expense of other people's labour. But side by side with it there is the compulsory idleness of millions of people. The bourgeois system deprives them of the chance to work, dooms them to lasting unemployment. The mechanism of the capitalist system is such that from time to time most able-bodied people become "redundant".

7*

They become redundant not because society overproduces foodstuffs, clothing, housing, etc. On the contrary, the working masses are in dire need of the most essential means of subsistence, while the unemployed are half-starved, and often have no shelter. Under capitalism, production is carried on not for the purpose of satisfying the requirements of the people, but to make profits. Therefore, entrepreneurs reduce production when they find it profitable, deprive people of work and doom machinery and plant to idleness.

The bourgeois state

The bourgeoisie has created an enormous apparatus of violence and deceit to keep the people in subjection. The bourgeois state, irrespective of its form, is an instrument of domination, relying on the police, gendarmery, troops, courts and gaols.

Bourgeois ideologists try to deny the class character of the capitalist state. The state, they say, stands above classes. It serves the whole population. Does not the state plan and provide facilities and amenities in towns, does it not fight epidemics, does it not introduce compulsory education in schools? On this basis they conclude that the modern bourgeois state is a "welfare state".

This statement has nothing in common with reality. In actual fact all the activities of the bourgeois state serve the interests of the capitalists. The class nature of the bourgeois state becomes clearly evident, when the authorities send troops against striking workers, imprison fighters for the working people's cause. A closer look shows that in other cases too the bourgeois state acts in the interests of the capitalists.

Take compulsory education, for example. At the present level of technology, illiterate workers are not needed by the industrialists. Typical in this respect is the fact that in 1960 the Federation of British Industries asked the government to extend the term of general universal education at schools, since young people did not know mathematics and English well enough to meet the demands of modern technology. The same applies to the care shown for the public health service: the authorities show concern for public health because the spread of mass diseases would harm the capitalist economy, the rule of the bourgeoisie.

Continuing to proclaim liberty and equality, the bourgeoisie of our days destroys the democratic rights the people have won by their long and tenacious struggle. The bourgeoisie violates the laws it has enacted when this serves to perpetuate and intensify exploitation.

Economic and political struggle of the proletariat

At first the capitalist entrepreneurs had to do with a disunited mass of workers. Nothing limited the arbitrary rule of the capitalists. There was nothing to stop them from worsening working conditions. If a worker did not consent to the conditions, the capitalist could easily find a substitute. But the workers inevitably came to realise the community of their interests. They began to unite into trade unions. The entrepreneurs no longer faced individual proletarians but an organisation of proletarians. The capitalists in their turn formed entrepreneurs' unions. They bribe the most complaisant trade union leaders, hire strike-breakers. They use the police, troops, courts and gaols in their struggle against the class organisations of the proletariat.

In the developed capitalist countries the working class increasingly resists all attempts by the capitalists to lower its living standard. By its stubborn struggle for many years it wrests certain concessions from the capitalists. But the gains of the proletariat are constantly threatened. The capitalists try to use every favourable situation to go back on the concessions they were forced to make, to deprive the workers of their former gains.

When the working people are unable to put up a sufficiently strong resistance against the exploiters, they are condemned to extreme poverty. This is the case notably in the colonial and dependent countries. Capitalism has brought the peoples of those countries untold sufferings.

The economic struggle of the proletariat is of great importance. The trade unions are able to resist the onslaught of the industrialists successfully if their leadership is efficient, if it relies on correct class positions. The trade unions are also a school of class struggle for the mass of the workers.

While admitting the importance of economic struggle, Marx always emphasised that this struggle was directed only against the consequences of capitalism, but not against the root cause of the oppression and poverty of the proletariat. The root cause is the capitalist system itself. The proletariat cannot do away with the growing exploitation by the capitalists exclusively through the economic struggle of the trade union organisations. To achieve this it must lead a stubborn political struggle. Only by overthrowing the power of the bourgeoisie does the proletariat destroy class exploitation, the source of its poverty and privations.

The workers cannot get rid of exploitation while capitalism continues to exist. The proletariat therefore struggles for the overthrow of the bourgeois system, for the abolition of capitalist slavery, for the creation of a new, socialist society. To achieve this the working class must have a militant political organisation. The proletarian revolutionary party is such an organisation, armed with a knowledge of the laws of social development, and able to lead the workers and all working people in the struggle for the destruction of the system of capitalist exploitation and for its replacement by a new system—communism. The Marxist-Leninst Party, the vanguard of the working class, heads the revolutionary struggle of the proletariat, rallies all the working people oppressed by capitalism around itself and directs their struggle towards the achievement of the great aim— the triumph of communism.

The proletariat— the grave-digger of capitalism

The whole course of historical development prepares the proletariat for its great historical role— that of the grave-digger of the bourgeois system and the builder of a new, socialist society.

Capitalism unites the workers by their joint labour. Life itself, the conditions obtaining in capitalist society, make the workers unite in the struggle against their exploiters. At every step the workers convince themselves that in bourgeois society they are condemned to back-breaking, forced labour, to unemployment and hunger, to lack of rights and poverty.

As capitalism develops, the proletariat's ranks swell, supplemented by ruined small producers—peasants and artisans. The workers become increasingly aware of the essence of capitalist slavery, and this strengthens their determination to struggle for their vital interest. The working class becomes a force able to rally around itself all working people and to lead them in the decisive battle for the overthrow of capitalism and the revolutionary reorganisation of society along socialist lines.

The proletariat is the most advanced class in capitalist society. It is deprived of the means of production. In this it differs from the peasants, who run their small farms on the basis of private property. The proletariat is in no way interested in perpetuating private property. Only the proletariat fights consistently and to the end for the abolition of all exploitation, for socialism. The proletariat creates enormous wealth by its labour: factories, railways, houses and public buildings. United at large factories, trained by the harsh capitalist labour discipline, the proletariat assimilates urban culture.

In addition to being the only force able to overthrow capitalism, the proletariat is by its very nature capable of building a new society free from the exploitation of man by man. Decades of strike action, revolutionary struggle and class battles have tempered the proletariat and made it grow into the genuine leader of all working masses. Only under the leadership of the working class can the other strata of the exploited population free themselves from the capitalist yoke and embark on the road to a free life worthy of man.

Marxist political economy teaches the proletariat of the capitalist countries to understand that only the irreconcilable class struggle for the overthow of the capitalist system and the building of socialism can liberate the exploited masses. At the same time it explains the meaning, importance and methods of the proletariat's class struggle and its political and economic organisations for their immediate demands, against the onslaught of the capitalist monopolies on the elementary rights of the working people and on their living standard.

A hundred years ago Marx regarded the victory of the British working class in the struggle for a legislative limitation of the working day as an open capitulation of the bourgeoisie's political economy to the political economy of the working class, as a triumph of the political economy of labour over the political economy of property. At that time it was a question of passing a law to limit the working day to ten hours. Since then the political economy of the working class has scored enormous victories over bourgeois political economy. The rule of the bourgeoisie has once and for all been overthrown on a territory where over one-third of the world's population live, while in the remaining part of the world the bankruptcy and doom of the capitalist system is becoming more and more evident at every new turn of history.

REVISION QUESTIONS

1. What are the features of commodity labour power?
2. Where and how is surplus value created?
3. What is the main contradiction of capitalism?
4. How does the position of the working masses change with the development of capitalism?
5. What is the historical mission of the working class?

Chapter V

DISTRIBUTION OF SURPLUS VALUE AMONG THE VARIOUS GROUPS OF EXPLOITERS

The surplus value created by the labour of the wage workers is the source of all unearned incomes in bourgeois society. Surplus value is distributed between the various groups of exploiters as a result of the operation of spontaneous economic laws of capitalism, through incessant struggle and cutthroat competition.

1. PROFIT OF INDUSTRIAL CAPITALISTS

Value of the commodity and its production costs The value of the commodity manufactured at a capitalist enterprise consists of two elements. First, it is the value transferred from the means of production (part of the value of the machinery, the value of the raw materials, fuel, etc.), and, secondly, the value newly created by the labour of the workers.

The capitalist does not spend his labour on the manufacture of commodities, he spends only his capital for that purpose. He is interested mainly in this expenditure. It also consists of two elements. First, it is the expenditure of constant capital (which includes part of the value of the machinery, the value of the raw materials, fuel, etc.) and, secondly, the expenditure of variable capital (the wages of the workers). The capitalist production costs of commodities consists of these two elements.

Let us compare the value of the commodity with its production costs. The first component part of the value of the commodity coincides with the same part of the production costs. As regards the second component, in the value of the commodity it is the value newly added by the labour of the worker, whereas in the production costs it is the value of the labour power.

But the value of the labour power, as we have shown

above, is smaller than the value created by the labour of the workers. The value created by the workers' labour embodies: 1) compensation for the value of the labour power and 2) the surplus value.

Hence, the capitalist's costs of production of the commodity are lower than their value, or the real production costs. The cost of the commodity to the capitalist is measured by capital expenditure; the real cost of the commodity—by labour expenditure.

The surplus value is the difference between the labour expenditure and the capital expenditure on the production of any commodity, the difference between the capitalist production costs and the actual costs of production. It is the part of the commodity's value that did not cost the capitalist anything. The capitalist appropriates this part of the commodity's value free of charge, through the exploitation of the workers.

Capitalist profit When the capitalist sells the commodity he recovers not only the production costs but also gains a surplus value. In other words, it is not the capital outlay but the labour outlay that he puts into his pocket.

It follows that the capitalist can sell the commodity profitably even when he sells it at a price that is below its value. If the selling price of the commodity is higher than its production costs but lower than its value, the industrialist still gains some of the surplus value embodied in the commodity.

When the capitalist sells the commodity that has been produced at his enterprise, the surplus value is a certain surplus over and above the costs of production. It is the difference between what the capitalist has received from the sale of the commodity and the production costs of the commodity. This surplus is calculated in relation to the whole capital invested in the enterprise. The surplus value computed in relation to the whole capital is the profit.

One might get the wrong impression that profit is created by the entire capital—variable and constant—and that all parts of capital are a source of profit in equal measure.

We have seen above that the form of wages conceals exploitation, creates the false impression that the worker is paid for all of his labour. The form of profit conceals the relations of exploitation to an even greater extent, also creating an illusion that profit is created by capital itself and not by the workers' labour.

Thus, the forms of capitalist relations camouflage their real content.

Rate of profit

We have mentioned above that the rate of surplus value is the percentage ratio of the surplus value squeezed from the workers to the variable capital. The percentage ratio of the mass of the surplus value to the whole capital is the rate of profit.

Let us take, for example, a capital of $300,000 and assume that the constant capital is equal to $285,000 and the variable capital is $15,000. Let the surplus value be equal to $45,000. In that case the rate of surplus value will comprise $\frac{45}{15}$ or 300 per cent. The rate of profit will be $\frac{45}{300}$ or 15 per cent.

Since the whole capital is bigger than its variable part, the rate of profit is lower than the rate of surplus value. At an identical rate of surplus value, the rate of profit is the lower the smaller is the variable and the larger is the constant capital. It is the rate of profit and not the rate of surplus value that shows how profitable a given enterprise is to the capitalist.

Levelling of the rate of profit

Capitalist economy consists of an enormous number of factories in diverse branches of industry. Capital of different size is invested in different enterprises. But in addition to size, their capital also differs as regards organic composition.

The organic composition of capital is the ratio of the constant to the variable capital ($c:v$).

In enterprises where many workers are employed, and where the expenditure on buildings, machinery and plant, raw materials, etc., is small the organic composition of capital is low. Conversely, the composition of capital is high in enterprises where most of the labour is automated and mechanised, or where very expensive raw materials are processed and relatively little money is spent on the purchase of labour power.

Competition between capitalists results in a levelling of profits on equal sums of capital.

Let us assume for the sake of simplification that there

are only three sectors in a country, which have a capital of identical size but of a different organic composition. The size of capital in each sector is equal to 100 million (dollars, pounds sterling, or any other currency). In the first sector the total capital consists of 70 million constant capital and 30 million variable capital; in the second of 80 and 20 million respectively, and in the third of 90 million and 10 million respectively. Let the rate of surplus value in all three sectors be 100 per cent.

In that case the surplus value squeezed from the workers in each of the three sections will be equal to the variable capital, i.e., 30 million surplus value will be produced in the first sector, 20 million in the second and 10 million in the third.

If the commodities are sold at their value the capitalist in the first sector will make a profit of 30 million, the one in the second 20 million and the one in the third 10 million. But the overall size of the capital is identical in all three sectors. Such a distribution of profits is advantageous for the capitalists in the first sector but entirely unfavourable for those in the third. The capital from the third sector will therefore flow into the first sector. Competition between the capitalists will compel those in the first sector to lower the prices of their commodities. At the same time it will enable the capitalists of the third sector to raise the prices of their commodities to a figure that will make the profit in all three sectors approximately equal.

The course taken by the levelling of the rate of profit can be seen from the table below:

Sectors	Constant capital	Variable capital	Surplus value	Value of commodities produced	Price of commodities	Rate of profit, per cent
I	70	30	30	130	120	20
II	80	20	20	120	120	20
III	90	10	10	110	120	20
Total . . .	240	60	60	360	360	20

Thus, competition between capitalists results in the domination of the law of the average rate of profit.

Like all laws of capitalism it establishes itself through innumerable deviations.

Price of production   In our example commodities produced in all three sectors are sold at 120. At the same time the value of the commodities in the first sector is 130, in the second—120, and in the third—110. Thus the prices of commodities differ from their value. The price of all three commodities is made up by adding the average profit (20) to the production costs—(100). The price equal to the costs of production plus the average profit is called the price of production.

In capitalist society commodities are sold not at their value but at the prices of production. This does not mean, however, that the law of value ceases to operate in capitalist conditions. On the contrary, it holds good in full measure.

The price of production is nothing but a modified form of value. This can be seen from the following.

First, while some industrialists sell their commodities above value and others below, on the scale of society as a whole the sum of prices of production is equal to the sum of the values of the commodities. Thus, all capitalists taken together obtain the full value for their commodities. Secondly, the profits of the whole class of capitalists are equal to the surplus value created by the whole unpaid labour of the proletariat. Thirdly, the drop in the value of commodities entails a drop in their prices of production. Conversely, a growth in their value leads to an increase in the prices of production of commodities.

The levelling of the rate of profit means that part of the surplus value produced by workers in the sectors in which the organic composition of capital is low flows into the sectors with a high organic composition of capital. Hence, the workers are exploited not only by the capitalists who employ them but also by the capitalist class as a whole. Only the struggle against the capitalist class as a whole, for the destruction of the bourgeois system, enables the working class to abolish exploitation.

Tendency to a lower rate of profit   The organic composition of capital grows with the development of capitalism. Every time an entrepreneur, replacing workers by a machine, makes production cheaper, expands the sale of his commodities and boosts his profits. The mass of raw materials, machinery and equipment in enterprises increases and the part of the capital intended to pay for embodied labour rises, while the variable capital intended to pay for live labour increases at a much slower rate.

Let us return to our former example. The total sum of capital is made up of 240 million (dollars, pounds sterling, etc.—it does not matter which) constant capital and 60 million variable capital. At a rate of surplus value of 100 per cent, the surplus value amounts to 60 million, which means that the rate of profit in our example is 20 per cent.

Let us assume that after ten years of accumulation the total sum of capital has grown from 300 to 500 million. At the same time, owing to technological progress, the organic composition of capital has grown and these 500 million now consist of 425 million constant and 75 million variable capital.

In that case, at an equal rate of surplus value (100 per cent), 75 million surplus value will be produced. The rate of profit will equal: $\frac{75}{500} = 15$ per cent. In other words, at an unchanged rate of surplus value the mass of profit will increase (75 instead of 60) while the rate of profit will fall (15 per cent instead of 20).

Thus, the increase in the organic composition of capital engenders a tendency for the average rate of profit to fall. Like all laws of the capitalist mode of production, this tendency establishes itself through a maze of deviations.

A number of factors oppose the tendency to a lower average rate of profit. They obstruct this tendency, retard the decrease of the rate and partly paralyse it. First among these obstructive factors is the intensification of the working class's exploitation. The rate of surplus value grows as capitalism develops. Furthermore, the value of every machine, of every piece of equipment, drops with an increase in labour productivity. These are but some of the factors containing the falling rate of profit.

The sinking rate of profit does not at all mean that there is a decrease in the mass of profit, i.e., the sum total of the surplus value squeezed from the working class. The same reason that is responsible for the falling of the rate of profit

—rising labour productivity—makes for the growth of the mass of profit.

The tendency of the rate of profit to fall exacerbates the contradictions of capitalism.

The capitalists strive to counteract this tendency by intensifying the exploitation of workers. This aggravates the contradictions between the proletariat and the bourgeoisie.

The tendency to a lower rate of profit also intensifies the struggle within the bourgeoisie itself. Striving for a higher rate of profit the capitalists export their capital to other countries where labour power is cheaper and the organic composition of capital is lower than in the countries with highly developed industry.

To maintain prices at a high level industrialists unite in all sorts of associations. They strive to raise their profits that way and to prevent the rate of profit from falling.

The contradictions engendered by the tendency of the rate of profit to fall become particularly acute during crises.

2. TRADING CAPITAL AND LOAN CAPITAL

Trading capital and trading profit The surplus value created by the workers' labour is appropriated primarily by the industrial capitalist. He shares his profits with the owners of trading and loan capital.

These are the oldest representatives of capital. Merchants and usurers existed even under the slave-owning and feudal systems. Trading and usurious capital played an important role in the process of primitive accumulation, prepared the ground for capitalist production.

In pre-capitalist times the surplus product created by the labour of the slave, the serf or the artisan was the source of profit for merchants and usurers. The merchant and usurer either pumped this surplus product directly out of the small producers or appropriated part of the product received by the slave-owner or the feudal lord as a result of their exploitation of slaves or serfs.

Under capitalism the merchant and usurer continue to exploit and ruin the small producer—the peasant and the artisan. But the main source of their profits is the surplus value squeezed by the industrialists from the wage workers.

Commodities produced at a capitalist enterprise must be

sold to buy new means of production and to hire workers so as to continue production. But trade also requires capital. If the industrialist were to sell his commodity to the consumer himself, he would have to spend a certain part of his capital on equipping trading premises, on hiring the sales staff, etc. Delegating all these functions to the merchant, he shares with him some of his profit. He sells him commodities at the factory price, which is lower than the price of production.

Trading profit is therefore part of the surplus value which the industrialist concedes to the merchant. Spending a certain amount of capital, the merchant must receive on this capital a profit of the usual size. It would be unprofitable to engage in trade if trading profits were below the usual average rate.

Commodity exchange and speculation

Under capitalism the prices of many commodities fluctuate under the influence of many factors. It is very difficult and often even impossible to foresee all these factors. Thus, if there are prospects for a rich harvest, grain prices drop at the beginning of summer; if the harvest prospects deteriorate later, grain prices shoot up.

This opens up the possibility for speculative trade. Commodity exchanges are centres of such trade. Large-scale trade in uniform commodities (grain, cotton, metals, etc.) is concentrated at these exchanges.

On commodity exchanges, transactions are concluded for a definite period: the seller undertakes to deliver to the buyer a fixed amount of the commodity of a given type at a stipulated time. Many of the transactions on these exchanges are performed in expectation of price fluctuations and, hence, of deriving speculative profits.

Loan capital

The capitalist does not have to spend the proceeds from the sale of his commodity immediately. He may have at his disposal money he does not need for the time being.

Thus, every capitalist has at certain times a surplus of money capital for which he cannot find immediate application. This is idle capital, i.e., capital that does not produce profit. At other times the capitalist is short of money, for example, when he has to buy new equipment. To ensure the uninterrupted operation of his enterprise the capitalist must have reserves to use when he is short of money, but which lie idle at other times.

Since there are many capitalists, it often happens that when one of them has a temporary surplus of money capital, another experiences a temporary shortage of money. Competition compels the capitalist to see to it that every part of his capital gives a profit. The capitalist therefore lends his free money.

Being able to receive money on loan, the industrial capitalist does not have to keep substantial sums of money idle. He can use a loan to expand production, to increase the number of workers he exploits and, hence, to obtain more surplus value.

The industrialist pays the moneylender part of the surplus value as a reward for the money capital placed at his disposal. This part of the surplus value is called interest. Loan capital is capital yielding an interest. Usurious capital was the forerunner of loan capital, which operated long before the emergence of capitalist production, i.e., under the slave-owning and feudal systems.

Interest and its rate   Capital in the function of loan capital is a commodity and therefore has a price. The price of capital is the interest, i.e., the sum of money being paid for the use of a capital of a definite size over a definite period. If $3 are charged for the loan of $100 for a year this means that the rate of interest (or simply the interest) is 3 per cent.

Banks charge different interest rates for different transactions. They naturally pay less for deposits (passive operations) than they charge for loans (active transactions). They also charge different interest for loans, depending on the time-limit for which the loan is granted, and on other conditions. Banks likewise pay different interest on deposits. The difference in terms of deposits—primarily the difference between demand and time deposits—gives rise to a difference in rates of interest.

The rate of interest fluctuates frequently. Like in other business transactions, the price in the given case depends mainly on demand and supply.

If the supply of money is greater than the demand for it. the rate of interest drops, and vice versa. Under normal conditions the rate of interest is limited by the rate of average profit. In exceptional cases, however, when, for example, the capitalists are faced with bankruptcy, the rate of interest may rise above the average rate of profit.

The interest yielded by loan capital is part of the surplus value. In this case the source of surplus value is extremely well camouflaged and the deceptive outward appearance of capitalist relations reaches its apogee.

The fact that loan capital brings in an income in the form of interest seems just as natural as a pear-tree yielding pears. Money itself is the source of income. This, according to Marx, is the extreme form of the mystification of capital.

Banks as dealers in capital

The movement of loan capital is effected by banks. On the one hand, they collect all idle capital, and, on the other, place money capital at the temporary disposal of capitalists in need of it.

Banks originated before the capitalist mode of production. But it is only under capitalism that they have developed fully and become widespread.

Initially the banks were mainly intermediaries in the settlement of accounts. Entrepreneurs usually keep their money in a bank. The bank makes payments according to their orders. In view of this the banks collect all sorts of money incomes and lend them out to capitalists. The money of industrialists and merchants flows to banks, and also the money savings of the working people, which reach banks mainly through savings accounts. Finally, a growing part of bank deposits is formed of the moneys of capitalists who prefer interest on capital to the risk and trouble of running a business.

Generally, at every given moment only a small number of depositors apply to a bank for a refund of their deposits. The withdrawal of money is generally compensated by the influx of new deposits. The bank is therefore able to pay back deposits to all those who demand it even though it keeps only a comparatively small amount of money. The bank places the bulk of the money capital at the disposal of capitalists in the form of loans.

The picture changes radically in the event of upheavals: during crises, wars, etc. The mass of depositors wish to withdraw their deposits. If the bank was unable to prepare for this rush and to collect a sufficient amount of money in its safes by borrowing from other banks or the govern-ment, it goes bankrupt and declares that it is unable to pay back deposits. The bankruptcy of a bank results in the ruin of many capitalists, the loss of the savings of the petty bourgeoisie, etc. Bankruptcies deepen a crisis.

The industrialist pays the bank a certain compensation for the loan he receives. If he takes $1,000 at the beginning of the year, he has to return $1,030 at the end of the year, which means that the bank charges an annual interest of 3 per cent.

In that case the bank pays the owners of the money (the depositors) a smaller interest, say, 2 per cent. This means that of the $30 received by the bank from the industrialist, it has to pay $20 to the money owners. Hence the income of the bank is $10.

This transaction reminds one of an ordinary business deal in which a merchant buys a commodity for $20 and sells it for $30. The only difference is that the commodity bought and sold by the bank is not an ordinary commodity, but a special one. This commodity is a sum of money that has turned into capital and is used as capital.

Thus, the bank deals in capital. Capital has become a commodity and serves as an object of purchase and sale transactions.

Joint-stock companies Some enterprises, for example, the building of railways, demand huge capital outlays. Joint-stock companies are set up to raise large sums of capital for such purposes.

Joint-stock companies existed as early as the 17th cen-tury but became widespread only in the second half of the 19th century. In modern capitalist countries the bulk of large enterprises are joint-stock companies.

A joint-stock company is an enterprise whose capital is owned by many. Every owner holds a definite number of shares. A share is a certificate confirming that its holder has invested in the enterprise a certain amount of money, say 1,000 dollars, marks, etc.

Formally the joint-stock company is governed by the general meeting of shareholders. It appoints the board of directors and other officials, hears and confirms reports on the work of the company and decides important issues.

But at the shareholders' meeting each share has a vote

and the true owners of the company are the big shareholders, i.e., those who own a large stock of shares.

Myth about the democratisation of capital Defenders of capitalism allege that the spread of joint-stock companies results in a democratisation of capital. In this connection they lavishly praise the issue of small shares, i.e., shares of a comparatively small denomination.

Every factory or office worker, they say, can afford to buy such shares, and this enables the working people to become full-fledged co-owners of enterprises. According to them this means that capital is dispersed, that it assumes the character of "people's" capital.

In reality, however, even in the USA, the richest capitalist country, nine-tenths of the population own no shares. The shareholders are the big, medium and partly petty bourgeoisie, highly-paid officials, office workers, people of free professions and a small part of skilled workers. Only a few dozen out of a thousand workers own shares, and only a few people in a thousand farmers and agricultural workers have them. What is most important is that the working people own only a negligible portion of the shares in the country. The family of the multimillionaire Du Pont owns ten times more shares than all American workers taken together.

The small shareholders have no influence in the company. One big shareholder owning, for example, a million dollars' worth of shares has more votes than 9,999 small shareholders, each of whom owns 100 dollars' worth of shares.

The joint-stock form of enterprises does not in the least mean that there is a democratisation of capital. On the contrary, it enables large capital to subject and use to its ends the accumulations of small and medium capitalists and a certain portion of the savings of the upper echelons of the factory and office workers. The joint-stock form of enterprises greatly promotes the growth of capital and the amalgamation of production.

Dividends. Quotations A share entitles its owner to a part of the profits of the enterprise. Let us assume that the total share capital of a company is $1,000,000, divided into a thousand shares of $1,000 each. Let us further assume that the enterprise has made a profit of $250,000. The board decides to leave $100,000 as reserve capital and to distribute the remaining sum among the shareholders. This means that every share will yield its owner an income of $150.

The income received by the shareholder is called the dividend. In the above case the dividend will be $\frac{150}{1,000}$ or 15 per cent.

Shares are bought and sold on the stock exchange. The price at which a share is sold is called its quotation.

Instead of buying shares, the capitalist could deposit all his money in a bank. In that case he would receive an interest of 3 per cent on his $1,000, i.e., $30. However, the owner of the money is not content with such an income. He prefers to buy shares, for even though this is connected with some risk, it promises a greater return.

If a money-owner wants to buy shares of an enterprise paying a dividend of 15 per cent, the holders of these shares will be unwilling to part with them at their nominal price (i.e., at the price stated on the shares).

A share of a thousand dollars yielded a dividend of $150. The prospective buyer of this share will have to pay more than a thousand dollars for it. The upper limit to which this share can rise is, perhaps, $5,000; by depositing this sum in a bank, its owner can get the same $150 in the form of interest.

Fictitious capital When an enterprise belongs to a single owner, his capital—say, a million dollars—takes the form of factory buildings, machinery, reserve stocks. raw materials, finished products, and a certain sum of money, which is kept in the safe of the enterprise or in the owner's current account in a bank.

What happens when an enterprise of a single owner is transformed into a joint-stock company? Suppose a thousand shares of $1,000 each are issued. As a result of this operation the capital of the enterprise doubles, as it were.

The factory buildings, stores, machinery—all remain as they were. They constitute the actually existing capital of a million dollars. In addition to it, there emerges a million dollars' worth of securities. These are the shares distributed among various holders.

This issue of shares introduces a double count. The same

capital exists, first, as the enterprise, machinery, stocks of raw materials, etc., and, secondly, as securities.

In reality the issue of shares has not added a cent to the initial capital. But it does seem as if new capital has appeared, that the capital has doubled.

Shares are no more than a reflection of the actually existing capital of an enterprise, but at the same time they exist independently of the enterprise: they are bought and sold, deposited, etc.

This new capital existing in the form of securities is called fictitious capital. In addition to shares, fictitious capital may take the form of bonds. These are promissory notes issued by enterprises or the bourgeois state floating a loan on definite conditions.

During crises and other upheavals, fictitious capital depreciates at a catastrophic speed. The depreciation of fictitious capital exercises a far-reaching effect on the whole economy because this capital is linked by thousands of threads—through banks, the monetary system, etc.—with actual production and circulation.

Stock exchange For various reasons the quotations of shares fluctuate constantly. Nobody knows beforehand how great will be the dividend yielded by a share. The quotations of the war industry shares rise when the arms race intensifies. The shares of locomotive-building, rail-rolling mills go up if a long railway is to be built. Transactions with securities are performed at the stock exchange. The stock exchange is a market where shares and bonds are bought and sold. It is a centre for speculation in securities.

Big capitalists and banks play a decisive role at the stock exchange. When there is a speculative rise in quotations they skim the cream, and when there is a stock exchange crash, small shareholders and small speculators are ruined en masse.

Separation of the ownership of capital from capital investment At the dawn of capitalist production the capitalist was both the owner and the manager of the enterprise. The spread of credit and especially of joint-stock companies brought about a different state of affairs.

The distinguishing feature of loan capital is that it

is used in production not by its owner. The ownership of capital is thus separated from capital investment.

The capitalist becomes an owner who has nothing whatever to do with production. Production is run by hired servants of capital—by managers and directors. With the development of capitalism a growing number of people derive huge profits from capital without lifting a finger to earn them.

The separation of the ownership of capital from capital investment strikingly demonstrates that the capitalist ownership of property is unnecessary for production, and that this ownership is of a parasitical nature.

3. GROUND RENT UNDER CAPITALISM

Private ownership in the land and capitalist rent

In nearly all capitalist countries there are vestiges of feudalism. The most important one of them is private ownership in the land.

Land is the basic condition for agricultural production. Under capitalism an enormous area of land is in the hands of big landowners. The landowner uses his right of property to exact a toll from society. This toll is capitalist ground rent.

Capitalist ground rent differs substantially from its precapitalist counterpart. Under feudalism the landowning class appropriated the whole surplus social product in the form of rent. Under capitalism the landowners appropriate only part of the surplus social product, only part of the surplus value.

The theory of rent proceeds from the following propositions. The landowner leases land. The lessee is the capitalist who runs the farm with the help of hired workers. The unpaid labour of the hired workers produces surplus value.

This surplus value goes first and foremost to the capitalist lessee. He keeps part of it—the profit on his capital. The other part, a certain surplus profit, he is forced to pay to the landowner as ground rent.

The landowner frequently does not lease his land but hires workers himself to run the farm. In that case the rent and profit is appropriated by a single person. In addition, a great role is played by the rent collected from the peasants.

But to understand these complex relations we must first of all gain a better understanding of the essence of capitalist ground rent.

A distinction should be made between differential and absolute rent. Let us first discuss differential rent.

Differential rent Individual tracts of land differ as regards their fertility. With the same labour expenditure, a more fertile plot will yield a more abundant harvest.

The distance of the tract from towns, rivers, the sea or railways is also crucial. The owner of a farm occupying a more favourable situation saves a lot of money on the transportation of his products.

Let us consider three plots of different fertility. The lessee of each spends on workers' wages, the purchase of seed and the maintenance of cattle, etc., say, $1,000 a year. Let us further assume that the average profit is 20 per cent.

Owing to the different fertility the harvest will amount to 100 centners of wheat on the first farm, 120 on the second and 150 on the third. The price of production is the same on all of them, i.e., $1,200 (the production cost plus the average profit). In that case the price per centner will be $12 on the first farm, $10 on the second and $8 on the third.

The market takes no account of the different fertility of the plots. The price per centner of grain is the same, no matter where it was grown. Normally, the market needs the grain from all three plots. What will be the market price per centner?

If the price were to be $8, the lessees of the first and the second plot would not be able to recoup their outlay, let alone make the average profit. In that case they would transfer their capital into industry or other economic branches.

If the price were to be $10, the lessee of the first plot would only recover his expenditure but would not make the average profit and would therefore reinvest his money in industry.

Hence the market price must be $12, i.e., must equal the price of production of the least fertile plot. And since society needs the products of all three plots, it is exactly this price that is established on the market.

Difference in the situation of plots are no less important than differences in their fertility. The tenant of the remotest plot spends more on the production and delivery to the market of one centner of grain than does the tenant of a plot located closer to the market.

In industry the price of production is determined by average production conditions. If an enterprise is run according to obsolete methods, it spends more labour per unit of commodity but realises from the sale of the finished product only the price determined by the average level of technical development.

The price of production of agricultural products forms in a different way. It is determined by the conditions of production on the worst of the cultivated plots. The land area is limited. For this reason it is impossible arbitrarily to set up a desired number of equally good plots, as distinct from industry, where an enterprise can be equipped with any number of perfect machines. The surplus profit due to the expenditure of capital on a better plot of land or the more productive use of capital forms the differential rent.

But, to return to our example, let us assume that the market price of wheat is $12 a centner.

The tenant of the first (worst) plot will get $1,200 for his harvest of 100 centners. This will equal his production outlay ($1,000) plus the average profit (200).

The tenant of the second plot will get $1,440 for his 120 centners. He will make $240 over and above the production outlay and average profit.

The tenant of the third plot will receive $1,800 for his 150 centners, i.e., will make $600 over and above the production outlay and average profit.

Naturally, the tenants of the second and third plots would be only too happy to pocket the surplus. But there is competition between capitalists. Any number of capitalists is willing to return the surplus over the average profit to the landowner as rent, keeping the average profit. The surplus over and above the average profit is therefore collected by the landowners as differential rent. The surplus yielded by the outlay of capital on better soil forms the differential rent.

The surplus over and above the average profit received from better plots of land arises irrespective of the system of landownership. But private ownership in the land enables the landowner to appropriate this surplus in the form of differential rent.

This surplus profit, like all surplus value in general, is created by labour alone. On more fertile plots labour is more productive than on less fertile ones. The difference in fertility is responsible for the difference in labour productivity.

Under capitalism one gets the false impression that rent is a product of the land and not of labour, since it is appropriated by the landowner. Actually, however, the only source of rent is surplus labour, surplus value.

Absolute rent   In addition to differential rent the landowner receives absolute rent.

Let us once again remember our example. No surplus profit forms on the first, the worst, plot of land. We assumed that the tenant of that plot sells wheat at a price which is made up of his outlay plus the average profit, i.e., at the price of production.

But the owner of the plot will not allow the tenant to use it free of charge. Hence, the tenant of the worst plot must make a certain surplus over and above the average profit when he sells his wheat to pay the landowner for the right to invest his capital in the land. This means that the market price of agricultural products must be higher than the price of production on the worst plot of land.

Agricultural products are therefore sold at prices that are higher than the price of production. The surplus thus received goes to the landowner. This is the absolute ground rent.

As distinct from differential rent, absolute ground rent is the result of private landownership. Without private ownership in the land there could be no absolute rent.

Differential rent is the result of a single market price. Matters stand differently with absolute rent: it is itself responsible for higher market prices of agricultural products. Like differential rent, absolute rent is part of surplus value.

The toll paid   Ground rent is a toll that society
to parasitic landowners   under capitalism is compelled to
pay to the class of landowners. This toll increases with the development of capitalism.

Yet, the landowner is an absolutely unnecessary figure for capitalist production. His income is of a purely parasitic nature.

The existence of differential rent deprives society of all advantages connected with the natural fertility of the soil, and gives these advantages to the landowners. Absolute rent makes agricultural products—foodstuffs for the workers and raw materials for industry—more expensive. If there were no absolute rent these products would be sold at the prices of production. Hence, because of absolute rent, they are sold at prices above the prices of production.

Rent through exploitation of the peasants

Frequently land is leased from the landowners not by capitalist entrepreneurs but by small farmers. They cultivate the land by their own labour and do not hire working hands. Where then does the rent come from, since there is no hired labour to produce surplus value?

Here the source of ground rent is the exploitation of the peasants by the landowner. The peasant gives part of the products of his labour to the landowner. Marx wrote that under capitalism the exploitation of the peasants differs from the exploitation of the factory proletariat in form only.

Very often the part given to the landowner is so large that the peasant has to lead a half-hungry existence in spite of his back-breaking labour. This applies particularly where there is a heavy residuum of feudal times and where vestiges of pre-capitalist rent are added to the capitalist rent collected by the landowner from the tenant.

This was the case, for example, in tsarist Russia. The landowners bled the land-hungry peasants white. The landowner collected rent as a downright payment and in addition demanded all sorts of labour rent and payments in kind.

Price of land

Being private property, land can be bought and sold. If we leave out of account all sorts of installations and improvements (buildings, water-supply, irrigation systems, etc.), the land as such does not have and cannot have any value, since it is not a product of human labour. But even though land has no value it always has a price under capitalism.

This price is not a monetary expression of value. It expresses something different. Land has a price because the landowners have turned it into their private property.

The price of land depends on the size of the annual income it yields. The price of a plot of land is expressed in a sum of money, which, if deposited in a bank at the existing rate of interest, would give an income equal to the rent from the given plot. This calculation is called capitalisation.

The price of land is nothing else but capitalised rent. For this reason the price of a plot of land is the higher the greater is the rent and the lower is the rate of interest. In buying land, the buyer actually pays the landowner ground rent for a number of years in advance.

The lie about the "law of diminishing returns" The advocates of capitalism attempt to explain away the high cost of living caused by the payment of rent to the landowners by references to "natural laws". They declare that agriculture is affected by the law of "diminishing returns".

This "law", they say, is a natural law and in no way depends on the social system. They say that every subsequent amount of labour applied to the soil bears less fruit than the preceding one.

This invention of the "law of diminishing returns" is intended to whitewash capitalism and to relieve it of the responsibility for the poverty of the working people. Capitalism, say its advocates, is not guilty of the privations suffered by the popular masses. These privations, they allege, are due to the fact that the population grows at a faster rate than the production of agricultural products. On this basis the most shameless lackeys of the bourgeoisie even laud wars and epidemics, which decimate the population.

The misanthropic "law of diminishing returns" is nothing but pure invention. It leaves out the most important consideration, namely, the technological level of production, the state of the productive forces. The defenders of the notorious law proceed from the false assumption that technology in agricultural production is as a rule at a standstill and that changes are the exception. But the point is that additional labour applied in crop farming is generally connected with technological advance, with the introduction of new and better methods of agricultural production.

Lenin compared the advocates of the "law of diminishing returns" with people who say that as a rule trains stand at stations, and move only as an exception.

Distribution of land in the capitalist countries

In the capitalist countries the large mass of small peasants owns less land than a handful of big landowners. In pre-revolutionary Russia the bulk of the land was owned by big landowners, the tsar's family, monasteries and kulaks (rich farmers). There were about 30,000 big landowners in Russia owning 500 dessiatines each. They held about 70,000,000 dessiatines of land.

Ten million of the poorest peasant farms also had about 70,000,000 dessiatines. Large estates averaged 2,300 dessiatines each, while a peasant household held 7 dessiatines of land. Thus, one estate was as large as about 330 poor peasant farms.

There was a sea of land-hungry and landless peasants in Russia. Only the Great October Socialist Revolution evicted the parasites from the land and gave the land to the working peasantry.

In modern bourgeois countries the land is concentrated mainly in the hands of big landowners. This leads to the oppression and impoverishment of the peasantry.

Separation of agricultural production from landownership

The development of capitalism leads to an ever greater separation of agricultural production from the ownership of land. The owner does not till the land but only appropriates the ground rent.

Capitalism, Marx wrote, carries landownership to an absurdity. It is clear that agricultural production can be carried on without private landownership.

The separation of agricultural production from landownership proceeds in two forms.

First, in the form of leases. The farm is run by the tenant, while the land belongs to the landowner. Leasing of land thrives in all capitalist countries. The working peasants have to lease land from the landowner on the most onerous terms.

Secondly, in the form of mortgages. Mortgage loans are credits secured by a mortgage on real property. When a landholder needs money for some urgent payments (for example, to pay his taxes), he applies to a bank for a loan. Often a small peasant applies for a loan to buy a new plot of land. The bank grants the loan by taking a mortgage on that plot of land as security for this loan.

If the loan is not repaid in time the bank takes possession of the plot. To all intents and purposes, the bank becomes the owner of the plot even earlier, for the debtor peasant gives his income from the land as interest to the bank. This means that the rent is received not by the peasant, who formally owns the land, but by the bank. Mortgages mean the most merciless exploitation of the mass of peasantry.

Community of interests of the working class and the working peasantry in the struggle against exploitation

Capitalism condemns not only the working class to insecurity but also the bulk of the peasantry. The peasants are cruelly exploited by the landowners and capitalists. The development of capitalism is attended by the stratification of the peasantry. The small top echelon in the countryside—the kulaks—get rich by ruthlessly exploiting the working peasantry. As a result, many peasants are ruined, sell their miserable farm and become farmhands or go to the towns in search of work. The great intermediate section of the middle peasantry lives in conditions of instability and uncertainty.

In agriculture, as in industry, large-scale production has enormous advantages over small-scale production. Machinery and other technical improvements can be used in large-scale production, while small-scale production cannot afford them. In many bourgeois countries a large part of the land belongs to landowners who fleece the peasants. Every tax increase, every drop in the prices of agricultural products jeopardises the further existence of a multitude of small peasant households. The peasants incur debts and are victimised by usurers and banks. Even though peasants work their fingers to the bone to maintain their seeming economic independence, a great many small farms are ruined and their owners become either wage workers at industrial enterprises or farmhands. The farm-hands receive miserable pay for their labour and the length of their working day is decided arbitrarily by the boss—the big agricultural capitalist or the kulak.

Thus, under capitalism the mass of the working peasants suffers cruelly from exploitation. On this basis there arises a community of interests between the working class and the peasantry in the struggle against the exploiters—the capitalists and the landowners. The leadership in that struggle belongs to the proletariat as the most progressive social class.

Growing antithesis between town and country Long before the emergence of capitalism, trades were separated from agriculture. That was a large step forward in the social division of labour. In pre-capitalist societies, however, farming was predominantly natural. The level of technical equipment in trades was not much higher than in agriculture. Agriculture was the dominating branch of production.

The situation changed radically with the emergence and development of capitalism. Formerly shoes, clothing and all sorts of domestic articles were made by the peasant's family or by peasant-artisans. Capitalism creates a textile and shoe industry, and factory-made goods oust home-made articles because they are both cheaper and better. Commodity production becomes dominant. The transition to machine industry brings about the complete separation of industry from agriculture.

Capitalism separates ever new sectors of industry from agriculture and the distinction between industry and agriculture, between town and country, becomes ever deeper. The capitalist town ruthlessly exploits the countryside.

Technological advances—new methods of production, new improvements and machinery—are introduced in industry. Until recently agriculture was based on backward equipment and manual labour even in the most developed capitalist countries. Machinery and advanced agricultural techniques were widely introduced in the agriculture of the advanced countries only after the Second World War. This transition from manual labour to modern machine production is attended by the ruination and liquidation of the millions of peasant households which are being swallowed up by large-scale capitalist enterprises. In the economically underdeveloped countries, however, agriculture still remains at an extremely low technical level.

Ground rent serves to pump enormous funds into the pockets of the big landowners. The mass of surplus value being produced in the countryside is appropriated by them. They spend these funds in a parasitic way.

Even when the farmer buys land he is no better off. He has to spend a large part of his funds on the purchase of land and little is left to buy machinery, implements, etc. This is one of the main reasons for the ruin of the peasants.

Capitalism bursts the narrow confines of the natural economy but at the same time dooms the broad masses of the rural population to more ruthless exploitation. Even in the most developed capitalist countries the bulk of the peasantry is cut off from urban culture.

The antithesis between town and country is one of the deepest contradictions of the capitalist system.

REVISION QUESTIONS

1. How is the surplus value divided among the exploiters?
2. What is the source of commercial profits, interest on loans and ground rent?
3. What can you say of the role played by the private ownership of land?
4. Where do the interests of the various groups of exploiters coincide and where do they differ?

Chapter VI

CAPITALIST REPRODUCTION AND ECONOMIC CRISES

1. SIMPLE AND EXTENDED CAPITALIST REPRODUCTION

**Production
and reproduction**
The mass of commodities being produced in a country is in constant movement. Various products are produced, used up and reproduced. Just as society cannot stop consuming, it cannot stop producing. This constant renewal, this uninterrupted repetition of production is called reproduction. Reproduction is a necessary condition for society to exist under any social system. If society were to produce year in year, out the same amount of products, this would be simple reproduction.

Before the emergence of capitalism the development of the productive forces proceeded slowly. The volume of social production changed little from year to year and from decade to decade. To all intents and purposes reproduction was simple.

With the transition to capitalism the formerly virtually stagnant state of social production gave way to rapid development of the productive forces. What is characteristic of capitalism as a social system is not simple but extended reproduction, i.e., a yearly increase in the output of products.

Any society reproduces not only the mass of products but also the social relations of production. If production has a capitalist form, reproduction too assumes this form. This means that capitalist relations of production, notably those between the capitalists and workers, are being reproduced every year.

**The social product
and national income**
A country's social product is the total output of the country over a stated period, say a year.

The social product is made up of two parts. One part compensates for the means of production used up during the year: the raw materials, fuel, machinery, etc. These expenditures must be replaced for production to be continuously renewed, i.e., to make reproduction possible. The other part of the social product is the value newly created during the year. This is the country's national income.

In capitalist society this income is national only by name. The bulk is appropriated by the capitalists. What is left goes to the working class as wages. The share of the national income remaining in the hands of the capitalists is spent, first, on their personal consumption, on the satisfaction of their various whims, the maintenance of servants, etc., and secondly, on accumulations with a view to enlarge capital and expand production.

A large part of the national income is appropriated by the bourgeois state. State budget allocations are spent mainly on the maintenance of the state apparatus, which is an instrument of violence the exploiters use against the exploited, on the arms race, on assistance to capitalist firms experiencing financial difficulties, etc.

For production to expand part of the national income must be used to set up new enterprises, to enlarge productive capacities in existing factories and to hire additional contingents of workers. In capitalist society all questions connected with the extension of production are solved by private owners—capitalists. They dispose of the part of the national income going to accumulation. Thus, society's most important task, the increase in the volume of the output, depends on the arbitrary decisions of the capitalists.

Contradictions of capitalist reproduction

Every capitalist taking up production buys means of production and labour power. After the process of production is completed, the capital of the industrialist, which has been increased by the surplus labour of workers, takes the form of a definite amount of finished products—commodities. The capitalist sells these commodities and realises a definite sum of money. He then buys new means of production and hires workers with this money and the process of production is renewed.

Hence, every capital passes through a cycle known as the circulation of capital. For reproduction to take place there must be a constant circulation of capital.

But in bourgeois society there are many capitalists and many sums of capital. It is therefore necessary that the whole mass of capital should be able to circulate. In other words, all capitalists must be able to sell the goods made at their factories.

The actions of the individual capitalists, and hence the movements of the various sums of capital are closely interlinked. This multilateral link of the individual enterprises and the individual sums of capital makes itself felt on the market where the capitalists sell commodities produced at their factories.

In their circulation the individual sums of capital are interlinked and this circulation comprises the movement of social capital as a whole. Hence, social capital is the entire mass of individual sums of capital in their interrelation and interdependence.

Social capital is not just a simple arithmetical sum of all individual sums of capital. In the social capital the individual sums of capital are interconnected. While each one is independent of the other, yet they all depend on each other. This contradiction becomes manifest when the finished product is sold, in the course of the reproduction of the total social capital.

In the course of capitalist reproduction there is not only a constant renewal of the relations of exploitation of labour by capital but these relations assume a wider scale. More and more workers are brought under the yoke of capitalist exploitation, and the rate of their exploitation is steadily rising. Thus, capitalist reproduction is always linked with a growth of class contradictions in bourgeois society.

The problem of realisation The annual product of a country consists of many different commodities. As regards their material form the whole mass of diverse commodities is divided into two major groups: 1) means of production and 2) means of consumption.

Correspondingly, production is divided into two major groups: 1) the production of the means of production and 2) the production of articles of consumption.

In the final analysis all products of human labour serve to satisfy diverse requirements of individuals and social groups. The only difference is that some products serve this purpose directly (articles of consumption), while the others serve for the production of articles of consumption (means of production). The material form of every product predetermines its further role in the reproduction process.

When they sell the produced mass of commodities the capitalists must realise its value so as to be able to continue production. We already know that the value of the individual commodity manufactured at a capitalist enterprise consists of 1) the fixed (constant) capital, 2) the variable capital and 3) the surplus value.

These three parts make up the value of the whole annual product of capitalist society. The division of the annual product according to value predetermines diverse roles to its various parts in future.

In the process of realisation every part of the annual product must be exchanged in a way enabling it to play in future the role assigned to it both as regards material form and value. This calls for a definite quantitative correlation between the separate parts of social production—both in value and in physical form. This constitutes the problem of realisation of the social product.

Conditions of realisation under simple and extended reproduction

For the sake of simplification let us assume that the whole economy of a country is conducted along capitalist lines. In that case simple reproduction will proceed as follows.

The whole mass of commodities produced within the year by the first group of enterprises, i.e., by the enterprises manufacturing means of production must be equal to the mass of the means of production consumed during the year at enterprises of both groups. For example, if 200 million tons of coal are burned during the year, the annual coal production must also constitute 200 million tons. If 100,000 lathes are worn out during the year, an equal number must be produced during that period.

Let us now turn to the second group of enterprises, i.e., to those manufacturing articles of consumption. The whole mass of the commodities produced by that group must be equal in value to the income of all the workers and capitalists of both groups of enterprises. For all the produced articles of consumption must be consumed by the capitalists and workers, since according to our presupposition there are no other classes in the country. But the capitalists and the workers are able to consume only as much as they are able to buy for their income: the surplus value appropriated by the capitalists and the wages paid to the workers.

Thus, an essential condition of simple reproduction is that the sum of the variable capital and the surplus value of the first group should be equal to the fixed capital of the second group.

Let us now take a look at the conditions of realisation under extended reproduction.

Extended reproduction involves accumulation. To increase production the existing enterprises must be expanded or new ones built. In either case this means that a certain amount of new means of production must be put into operation. These means of production must be manufactured during the preceding period.

Hence the annual finished product of the first group of enterprises, producing means of production, must contain a certain surplus over and above the amount needed for simple reproduction. This means that the sum of the variable capital and the surplus value of the first group must be greater than the fixed capital of the second group.

Such are the conditions essential for the realisation of commodities under simple and extended capitalist reproduction. For reproduction to pursue its unhindered course there must constantly be a complex correspondence between the individual branches.

But the movement of capitalist production proceeds spontaneously, through uninterrupted fluctuations and deviations, through the constant violation of the ratios that must exist between individual enterprises and groups of enterprises. The complexity of the process of capitalist reproduction interferes with its normal course. For this reason the course of capitalist reproduction is inevitably interrupted by periodical economic crises (i.e., crises recurring at regular intervals).

2. ECONOMIC CRISES UNDER CAPITALISM

Want and surplus In the capitalist part of the world changes in the economic climate affect the lives of millions of people. Economic life under capitalism constantly fluctuates and changes even sharper and more unexpectedly than the caprices of the weather. There are many indicators that are considered barometers of the economic climate: the state of the stock exchange, price fluctuations, changes in commodity stocks at warehouses, the movement of orders at enterprises, etc. There are institutes engaged in forecasting the economic climate. Alas, these forecasts are often even less reliable than weather forecasts. Frequently the forecasters predict a cloudless sky when a storm, an economic crisis, is in the offing.

Why are the forecasts of the economic climate so unreliable? The fault lies not only with the imperfect methods used for its observation and study. Most important is the fact that this climate does not depend on the people's will. If it were within the power of the capitalists, they would gladly banish crises from the economy, but they cannot and that is the whole trouble.

A book describing the life of miners in the USA contains the following conversation. A miner's son asks his mother:

"Ma, why don't you light the stove, Ma, it's cold."

"We have no coal. Your pa has no job and we have no money for coal."

"Why has he no job, ah, Ma?"

"Because there is too much coal."

The family of the miner freezes because too much coal has been mined. Millions of working people, among them many peasants, starve because too much grain has been harvested. The country has sufficient means of production, articles of consumption and workers but the factory chimneys do not smoke, locomotives stand idle, standing grain rots, warehouses are filled to bursting while workers are forced to unemployment and their families go hungry. Such are the conditions during crises of overproduction.

An American newspaper published the following calculation. In 1934, the year following the destructive 1929-33 crisis, about 2,400,000 people starved to death in the capitalist countries. In the same year over a million carloads of grain, 267,000 carloads of coffee, 258,000 tons of sugar, 26,000 tons of rice, 25,000 tons of meat and many other products were deliberately destroyed.

**Epidemics
of overproduction**
Society went through many upheavals and catastrophes before the capitalist system emerged and asserted itself. But then the causes of these catastrophes were natural and social disasters: floods, droughts, devastating wars and epidemics.

Such calamities often turned flourishing countries into barren deserts or heaps of rubble. A sharp decrease in production followed, the fruits of the labour of many generations were destroyed, the people were condemned to extreme poverty and hunger.

But only capitalism has given rise to crises of overproduction and to cruel deprivations of the working masses as a result of the production of "an excess" of commodities.

However, is an excess of coal, grain, clothes and housing really being produced? Of course not. The requirement in grain, coal, clothes is enormous. But the working people have to go without even the bare necessities because their pockets are empty.

That means that too many commodities are produced not as compared with the actual requirements of the majority of the working people but as compared with their purchasing power. Capitalism does not worry about satisfying the requirements of the working people. The capitalists are interested only in selling their commodities at a price that will ensure a sufficiently high profit. But during crises they are deprived of this possibility. The sharp discrepancy between the mass of the commodities produced at capitalist enterprises and the effective demand of the population leads to economic crises of overproduction.

During the 1929-33 crisis in the United States wheat and maize were used for heating instead of coal. Millions of pigs were destroyed. A large portion of the cotton harvest was left in the fields to rot. In Brazil millions of bags of coffee were thrown into the sea. In Denmark herds of cattle were destroyed, in France and Italy—thousands of tons of fruit.

**Inevitability of crises
under capitalism**
Economic crises of overproduction are caused by the basic contradiction of capitalism. This, as we saw above (see Chapter IV), is the contradiction between the social character of production and the private capitalist form of appropriation of the fruits of production.

With the development of modern industry production has acquired a social character. Hundreds and thousands of people are employed at every enterprise. There are close links between enterprises. Hence, hundreds of thousands and millions of people are closely interlinked in the production process, but the product of this social production is not placed at the disposal of society as a whole, but is appropriated by a small group of private owners.

The basic contradiction of capitalism leads to anarchy of production and the limited consumption of the masses, owing to the exploitation of labour by capital.

Capitalism is a social system in which anarchy of production reigns supreme. All capitalists strive to make a high profit. Everyone seeks to lay his hands on the largest possible amount of profit, to encroach upon the interests of his rival or even to remove him, if possible. It is the survival of the fittest as in the animal kingdom. Everything is decided by those who can subject the others and to enforce their domination. Anarchy of production is a law of capitalism.

Typical of capitalism is the conflict between two important conditions of production: between the means of production concentrated in the hands of the capitalists, and the workers who are deprived of everything but their labour power. This conflict rises quickly to the surface during crises of overproduction, when a vicious circle forms: on the one hand, there is a surplus of means of production and products, on the other—a surplus of the labour force, masses of unemployed deprived of the means of subsistence.

The anarchy of capitalist production and the exploitation of labour by capital make the economic crises of overproduction, that shake the capitalist countries periodically, inevitable.

Capitalist production does not pursue the aim of satisfying social needs but of deriving profits at the expense of the workers' unpaid labour. In the final count, however, even under capitalism production is connected with consumption and depends on it. The consumption level of the working masses is limited because of their exploitation by the capitalists. The growth of capitalist production leads to an intensification of exploitation. This involves a relative decrease in the effective demand of the bulk of the population and hence a decrease in commodity sales.

An expansion of production results in a temporary increase in the sales of means of production. The more production expands, the more machinery, building materials, raw materials and fuel are needed. The enterprises using these means of production put out an ever increasing mass of consumer articles. At a certain moment it becomes difficult to sell the rapidly growing amount of consumer articles because the hand-to-mouth existence led by the masses prevents consumption from rising, i.e., production expands without a corresponding expansion of consumption. Sales, therefore, inevitably run up against the wall of the limited consumption of the working masses.

The capitalist cycle and its phases Crises of overproduction emerged together with capitalist large-scale industry. In the course of 150 years they have shaken the bourgeois world every few years. They repeat themselves with a certain regularity. Capitalist industry goes through a definite cycle between two consecutive crises.

On the eve of a crisis production reaches its top level. There is already overproduction even though it is not yet apparent. Frequently, but not always, financial collapse is the first indication of imminent break-down. Brokers, bankers, speculators panic. A feverish hunt for money begins. Creditors demand the payment of debts. Depositors rush to the banks. A great number of small and medium and some large enterprises go bankrupt.

The crisis continues. Warehouses are packed with goods which cannot be sold. Many enterprises close down. Workers are given the sack and unemployment grows. Wholesale prices drop, sometimes even retail prices sink, but the demand does not grow. Surviving enterprises have to curtail or even to stop production for the time being.

A period of stagnation (depression) sets in. Industry marks time.

This state of affairs makes the capitalists intensify the exploitation of workers, lower their wages and make them work harder. At the same time the capitalists strive to make production cheaper by introducing all sorts of technical improvements and to make it profitable even in conditions of decreased demand. Enterprises are re-equipped and there is an extensive renewal of fixed capital.

The demand for means of production rises. There is a change from stagnation to revival. Many of the weaker enterprises have gone to ruin. The surviving enterprises renew production and expand. Every industrialist attempts to recoup the losses he incurred during the crisis. Production regains its former level.

Gradually production outstrips its former level and a boom sets in. Production expands without due regard for effective demand. Owing to the contradiction between the social character of production and the private capitalist form of appropriation this demand is limited, and after some time increased production inevitably comes in conflict with the narrow confines of the market. A new crisis breaks out and the cycle repeats.

Economic crises in modern times

As stated above, crises have been capitalism's faithful companion throughout its existence. In modern times, when the world is split into two systems—socialism and capitalism—the bourgeois system has lost its former stability. Capitalist reproduction proceeds at a time when its contradictions and difficulties have grown immeasurably.

After the First World War and the victory of the socialist revolution in Russia the contradictions of the capitalist system made crises more frequent and disastrous. In 1920-21 an economic crisis played havoc with the majority of the capitalist countries. In 1924, and again in 1927, the USA experienced great difficulties in selling its output. In Germany economic conditions deteriorated rapidly in 1926. British industry stagnated during the whole period between the two world wars.

The deepest and most crushing of all crises ever to have hit the capitalist economy broke out in 1929. The crisis embraced all capitalist countries and raged for four years, leaving a deep scar in the consciousness of the peoples of the capitalist world. The memory of the "great depression" —that is how the bourgeois science and press christened the 1929-33 crisis—still haunts the minds of millions of people.

The crisis led to a drop of production in the whole capitalist world by 44 per cent, in some countries by 50 per cent. As regards the level of production the capitalist countries were thrown back by 25-40 years. The number of unemployed in the leading capitalist countries reached 30 to 40 million. The earnings of workers decreased sharply. Great numbers of peasants were ruined. Millions of families experienced hunger and want.

At a time when there was a shortage of everything the capitalists, being unable to sell their commodities, destroyed the fruits of the people's labour. The production apparatus was also destroyed: blast furnaces were dismantled, mines flooded, fruit trees cut down, crops burned, etc.

A cruel economic war broke out on the world market. The world trade turnover sank to one-third of its former volume.

The capitalists found a way out of the crisis by intensifying the exploitation of the working class, by further ruining the peasantry. This hastened the maturity of the next crisis of overproduction, which began in the second half of 1937. The number of unemployed in the capitalist countries, which had dropped from 30 million in 1933 to 14 million in 1937, rose again to 18 million in 1938.

The thirties of this century were marked by large-scale unemployment, a drop in the living standard of the working class and intelligentsia and the ruin of peasants.

After the Second World War the triumph of socialism in a large group of European and Asian countries and the collapse of the colonial system further contracted capitalism's sphere of domination. The difficulties of capitalist reproduction multiplied. At the same time the successes of socialism throw the danger of acute crises and mass unemployment under bourgeois rule into bold relief. The ruling classes have grounds to fear that a crisis resembling the catastrophe of the thirties may wreck capitalism through the action of the working class and all working people. This makes the bourgeois states direct their policy to preventing especially sharp and deep disturbances in reproduction so as to safeguard the rule of the capitalist class as a whole. Hence, the extensive militarisation of the economy and all sorts of assistance to the monopolies by the bourgeois governments which command large economic resources.

The advocates of the bourgeoisie spread the lie far and wide that the arms race gives employment to the working people and obviates crises. Events have belied what they have said. The arms race is headed by the USA. But it is exactly that country that has become the centre of economic slumps and crashes, of mass unemployment and under-capacity production at enterprises. In the USA economic crises of overproduction have become increasingly frequent. During the post-war period the US economy experienced four crises: in 1948-49, 1953-54, 1957-58 and 1960-61.

The economic upheavals in the USA affected the whole capitalist world. The US crisis in 1958 had far-reaching side-effects on the West European economy. Production was reduced and unemployment shot up in a number of West European countries. The difficulties of reproduction in-crease periodically in all capitalist countries and this leads to a sharp decrease in the industrial production growth rates and sometimes even to a drop in the volume of output. Stagnation sets in in various industries and is observed in some economic regions for a lengthy period, while produc-tion is greatly curtailed in others and workers are losing their jobs. The ruthless struggle on world capitalist markets brew frequent balance of payments crises, which in turn lead to cuts in production. State budget deficits grow and the state national debt increases in many countries.

3. CRISES AND THE POSITION OF THE WORKING PEOPLE

Consequences of crises for the working class
Crises reveal the deep-rooted contradictions of capitalism. Dur-ing crises the fruits of the labour of millions of people are destroyed, while most people are unable to satisfy their essential requirements. The pro-ductive forces of society are being wasted. Equipment stands idle, machine-tools rust and factory buildings de-teriorate. The labour force, society's main productive force, is wasted most of all. Hundreds of thousands and millions of workers are thrown out into the street.

Millions of people are doomed to protracted unemploy-ment. The cream of the working class has to lead a pur-poseless existence. They lose the skills they acquired during years of strenuous work. Workers, having reached a cer-tain age, have to give up the hope of ever returning to the bench. The growing generation of the working class is barred from production. Highly skilled people, trained in educational institutions, cannot apply the knowledge they have acquired. There is also unemployment among the intelligentsia.

The capitalists use crises and unemployment to lower wages and worsen labour conditions. During crises it is much more difficult for the working class and its trade unions to fight the actions of the capitalists directed at lowering the living standard of the working people. Crises therefore not only bring down enormous want on the unemployed but also deteriorate the position of the working class as a whole.

Crises aggravate class contradictions by ruining small producers and making wage labour more dependent on the capitalists. Crises make many workers who formerly were not enemies of capitalism or regarded it with indifference join the active struggle against bourgeois domination.

Crises and the aggravation of the contradictions of capitalism

Crises devastate the economy and obliterate the fruits of the labour of millions of people. This strikingly illustrates the inability of capitalism to cope with the forces it has brought into being. The anarchic nature of capitalist production becomes abundantly evident.

"The crisis shows," Lenin wrote, "that modern society could produce immeasurably more goods for the improvement of the living conditions of the entire working people, if the land, factories, machines, etc., had not been seized by a handful of private owners, who extract millions of profits out of the poverty of the people."[1]

Defenders of the bourgeois system attempt to gloss over the true nature and the causes of crises. Trying to conceal the inevitability of crises under capitalism they assert that these are a result of accidental causes, which according to them can be obviated even under the capitalist system of economy. The ultimate cause of crises, they declare, is an accidental disturbance in the proportionality between the branches of production, or "underconsumption", and they

---

[1] V. I. Lenin, *Collected Works*, Vol. 5, Moscow 1961, p. 92.

recommend such means as the arms race and war to do away with it.

Actually both the lack of proportionality in production and "underconsumption" are not accidental under capitalism, but are inevitable because they are products of the basic contradiction of capitalism, which cannot be abolished as long as that system continues to exist. In the intervals between crises bourgeois politicians, scholars and businessmen often shout from the rooftops that an end has come to all crises, that capitalism has entered the road of crisesfree development. The facts invariably reveal that these statements are as unsound as are all the remedies for curing capitalism of its ills.

Other advocates of capitalism assure us that crises are inevitable under any social system. This malicious fabrication is fully exposed by the fact that in the Soviet Union and in other Asian and European socialist countries economic crises have disappeared after the capitalist system was abolished. The aim of socialist production is the satisfaction of the people's material and cultural requirements. All branches of the economy in socialist society develop rapidly in order to achieve this aim. Socialist enterprises, which are based on public ownership of the means of production work to satisfy the constantly growing requirements of the economy and of all the working people. Since these requirements constantly grow, socialist enterprises must continuously expand and improve production, manufacture better products at lower prices, etc.

Economic crises of overproduction are essential concommitants of capitalism. Capitalists and capitalist states are unable to abolish crises until the reason causing them continues to exist. This reason is capitalism itself, its main contradiction between the social character of production and the private capitalist form of appropriation.

REVISION QUESTIONS

1. What is simple and what is extended reproduction?
2. Why is capitalist reproduction contradictory?
3. Why are economic crises inevitable under capitalism?
4. How do crises affect the conditions of the working people?

Chapter VII

BASIC FEATURES OF IMPERIALISM

1. TRANSITION TO IMPERIALISM

Lenin's scientific theory of imperialism

For a time capitalism developed along an ascending line. The bourgeoisie created powerful productive forces on the bones of many generations of the working people. By the last third of the past century capitalism reached the peak of its development. After that bourgeois society began to decline. The capitalism of free competition was superseded by monopoly capitalism—imperialism. This is the highest and last stage of capitalism. It assumed its final shape by the end of the 19th and the beginning of the 20th century.

Lenin made a Marxist analysis of monopoly capitalism. He revealed the economic and political essence of imperialism and showed the working class the road leading to the triumph of socialism.

Lenin showed that imperialism is a special stage of capitalism—its highest and last stage. In some respects the monopoly stage of capitalism differs radically from the preceding pre-monopoly stage. Lenin described the main economic features of imperialism as follows: first, concentration of production and capital has reached such a high degree that the resultant monopolies have begun to play the decisive role in the economy; second, there has been a coalescence of monopoly banking capital and monopoly industrial capital and a formation on this basis of finance capital and a finance oligarchy; third, the export of capital, as distinct from the export of commodities, has acquired special importance; fourth, international monopolistic unions of capitalists have been set up, which divide the world; fifth, the territorial division of the world among the largest capitalist powers has been completed.

Imperialism is the inevitable upshot of capitalist development. The transition from pre-monopoly capitalism to imperialism was prepared by the whole development of capitalism, its productive forces and relations of production and its insoluble contradictions.

Concentration of production and capital

The development of technology made the advantages of large-scale production over small-scale production ever greater. Free competition led invariably to the victory of large enterprises over small ones, to the ruin of small and medium enterprises and to their being taken over by large ones. Thus proceeded the concentration of production and its concentration at large enterprises. More and more workers are employed at these enterprises. They process a huge mass of raw materials and produce the bulk of the industrial output.

At present the biggest enterprises, employing 1,000 and more workers, account for only a negligible share (one or two per cent) of the total number of enterprises in the capitalist countries. But they employ about one-third of all the factory and office workers in the manufacturing industry in the USA, 34.5 per cent in Britain, and 41 per cent in West Germany. Similar conditions prevail in other capitalist countries.

Parallel to the concentration of production, we observe a concentration of capital, i.e., the concentration of an ever larger mass of capital in the hands of few. The spread of joint-stock companies is a powerful lever promoting the concentration of capital. These companies concentrate huge sums of capital which were formerly scattered among many owners. These sums serve to organise giant enterprises owned by a handful of the biggest capitalists.

By the end of the 19th and the beginning of the 20th century joint-stock companies began to predominate. At present nine-tenths of the US industrial output is produced by corporations (the American for joint-stock companies). Similar conditions prevail in other capitalist countries.

Fifty-five of the 500 biggest US corporations had a turnover of over $1,000 million in 1964. In the rest of the capitalist world only 21 out of the 200 biggest companies had such a turnover.

The predominant role of industrial giants The concentration of production and capital in the leading capitalist countries led to a rapid growth of a small number of large and very large enterprises, in comparison with which the hundreds of thousands of small enterprises play a negligible role.

At the present time 500 of the largest US companies account for over 50 per cent of the total output of the US manufacturing industry and over 70 per cent of the profits being made by all industrial companies. In Britain 180 large companies employing together one-third of all industrial workers, produce about two-fifths of the total industrial output.

In all capitalist countries the concentration proceeds most rapidly in all branches of heavy industry and also in the new industries which began to mushroom in the imperialist era, viz., mining, metallurgy, the electrical industry, engineering and the chemical industry. Conversely, a number of light industries lag behind as regards the degree of concentration. There still are many small enterprises in the garment, tobacco, footwear, toy and other industries with a comparatively low technical level, which still exist mainly by virtue of the high-level labour exploitation in them.

Tsarist Russia's industry was distinguished by an extremely high concentration of production. Enormous masses of workers were concentrated in big and giant enterprises. This contributed to the strength of the organisation and the power of the working class.

Thus, under imperialism a handful of industrial giants outplay all others in the capitalist economy.

Emergence and development of monopolies The concentration of production and capital prepares the ground for the emergence and growth of monopoly associations. At a certain stage of its development concentration leads directly to monopoly.

What is a monopoly? There are different kinds of monopolies. A monopoly can be considered an agreement, union or association among capitalists. An individual big enterprise can also be a monopoly. But no matter how different the monopolies, they all pursue a single aim, which is to dominate production and the market and to use this domination to reap super-high profits.

While production in each branch is divided up among hundreds and thousands of independent small and medium enterprises, it is difficult to establish a monopoly. The situation changes with the concentration of production and capital. As a result of the concentration in a branch only several dozen big enterprises remain in it. It is much easier for them to enter into an agreement than it would be for hundreds of medium or thousands of small enterprises.

At the same time it is exactly the large size of enterprises that drives their owners towards an agreement among themselves. Competition between large enterprises is extremely intense and costs them a lot of money. Every big enterprise has to spend large capital on buildings, structures, giant machinery. It is almost impossible to use this capital for the production of other goods when prices for the main product are unfavourable. This makes the withdrawal of capital from these branches extremely difficult.

By the beginning of the 20th century the monopolies began to hold a dominant position in the economies of the capitalist countries. The capitalism of free competition had been superseded by monopoly capitalism—imperialism.

Monopoly domination —the essence of imperialism

Lenin said that if it were necessary to give the shortest definition of imperialism, it could be called the monopoly stage of capitalism.

Monopoly domination is imperialism's main economic feature. The economic essence of imperialism lies in the supersession of free competition by monopoly domination.

Monopolies rule undividedly in all capitalist countries. They are omnipotent in production, trade and credits. The monopolies, like octopuses, have spread their tentacles over every corner of capitalist economic and political life.

The domination of monopolies, their size and importance in the economies of capitalist countries have grown immeasurably within a few decades. The production of a number of key commodities is now controlled by a single monopoly. "Big twos", "big threes", "big fours", etc., dominate the production of other commodities.

In the USA and West Germany five monopolies account for 60 per cent of the total steel output. The United States Steel alone produces 25 per cent of the steel in the USA. Nine firms in Britain produce some 75 per cent of the country's steel. In France all ferrous metallurgy is controlled by five companies. In the USA the bulk of the aluminium is produced by three companies, in France 80 per cent of all aluminium is produced by a single firm.

Four big monopolies control the US motor industry. The two biggest—General Motors and Ford Motor—account for 80 per cent of the total production. In Britain three companies dominate the motor industry, in France—four, in West Germany—five.

At the end of 1964 a hundred of the biggest capitalist companies had a capital of $183,000 million. Their enterprises employed 9.7 million people. Oil, chemical, electrotechnical, motor, engineering, and military concerns are the biggest. The US General Motors trust is the biggest monopoly in the capitalist world. In 1964 its sales turnover comprised about $17,000 million, its capital over $11,000 million, its profits $1,700 million. General Motors employs over 660,000 people.

Main forms of monopoly
The simplest form of monopoly is short-term price agreements. The agreement obliges the participants to maintain sales prices stipulated in the agreement during the period of its validity. Such short-term agreements are generally unstable. They fall to pieces when market conditions change.

Monopoly agreements on prices and sales conditions called cartels and syndicates are far more widespread. Cartel is a French word; syndicate—a word of Greek origin. Both these words mean agreement, union.

The members of a cartel divide the sales market among themselves and are obliged not to lower commodity prices below a certain stipulated level. It often happens that a cartel fixes a certain sales quota for each participant. A violation of that quota entails the payment of a fine into the common fund. The individual firms joining a cartel keep their independence in production and trade.

Enterprises belonging to a syndicate lose their commercial independence but produce commodities independently and keep their juridical autonomy. The sale of goods, sometimes also the purchase of raw materials, passes into the hands of the syndicate's office.

Trusts are the highest form of monopoly associations. When it enters a trust the enterprise completely loses not only its commercial independence but also the control over its production activities. Formerly independent enterprises fully merge into a single enterprise. The management of all business passes into the hands of the trust's administration. The former owners of the enterprises become shareholders of the trust, and receive dividends according to the number of shares they hold. A trust often closes part of the enterprises under its control and concentrates production at the factories working most profitably.

Concerns are the largest monopoly associations. Large concerns embrace dozens, sometimes hundreds of enterprises in different industries and also trading firms, banks, transport companies, etc. The group dominating the concern controls enormous sums of capital.

Thus, there are many different forms of monopolies in the capitalist economy, from short-term agreements to giant associations embracing a multitude of different enterprises.

Monopolies and competition Monopolies are the direct opposite of free competition, which prevailed during the pre-monopoly stage of capitalism. At the same time the domination of monopolies does not abolish competition. On the contrary, it becomes even more violent and destructive.

Even in the most advanced capitalist countries premonopoly and even pre-capitalist forms of economy exist side by side with the monopolies. In the less developed countries the share of these forms of economy is even higher.

In the capitalist world peasants account for a considerable part of the population and there are numerous layers of artisans working in small workshops. Side by side with the monopolies there are independent enterprises, which consider it unprofitable to join monopoly unions.

Thus monopolies do not embrace all social production. Lenin called imperialism a sort of superstructure on the old capitalism. He pointed out that "pure" imperialism, divorced from the main foundation of capitalism, did not exist anywhere and never would.

Yet, the monopolies dominate because they control all the commanding heights of the economy.

Under these conditions a violent struggle is waged between the monopolies and non-monopoly enterprises (outsiders), betweeen monopolies within the same branch, between monopolies within different branches, and finally within monopoly unions. The oppression and arbitrariness of the monopolies make competition—a war of everybody against everybody—ruthless and ruinous.

This is no longer the former competition of many disjointed and comparatively small enterprises. This is a merciless struggle waged by a small number of powerful predators. They use every means, including direct violence, bribery and blackmail and intricate financial machinations, to gain their ends.

The bourgeoisie always prided itself on "free competition", asserting its indispensability in the development of initiative and enterprise. Competition in the imperialist stage, Lenin said, is the brutal suppression of the enterprise, energy, initiative of the masses, and the population as a whole, and degrades into financial fraud and despotism. The combination of monopoly and competition generates deep contradictions and adds fuel to the anarchical flame typical of the capitalist system.

Legend about "organised capitalism" The monopoly champions depict monopoly rule as a replacement of the anarchy of production by "organised capitalism". They maintain that monopoly domination eliminates competition, crises and doctors other ills of the bourgeois system.

At every step however the facts disprove the "organised capitalism" theory. Actually monopoly rule makes the competitive struggle even more desperate and ruthless, since it is being waged by powerful enterprises controlling huge sums of capital. Far from disappearing, the anarchy of production grows and the economy is threatened with chaos.

2. FINANCE CAPITAL AND THE FINANCE OLIGARCHY

The formation of banking monopolies The changed role of banks must be taken into account to understand the effective power of the monopolies.

Like in industry, free competition inevitably leads to concentration also in banking. Small banks are ruined and taken over by their more powerful competitors. Others, while formally keeping their independence, actually fall under domination of their stronger competitors. A merger and an interlinking of banks takes place.

The number of banks decreases but their size and the volume of their transactions grow. A small number of the biggest banks comes to the fore in each country. They accumulate huge sums of free money resources.

Like in industry, concentration in banking leads to the formation of monopolies. The leading role in the banking business passes to a small number of the biggest banks. Competition no longer takes place between hundreds of disjointed banks but between large unions of banking capital.

Naturally, it becomes a matter of growing interest for these unions to enter into a monopoly agreement, to bring about a union of banks. Large financial transactions—the floating of government loans, the foundation of big joint-stock companies—are more and more frequently carried out not by a single bank but by several leading banks, which have entered into an agreement.

In the USA the share of the four biggest New York banks in the sum total of deposits has grown from 1/5 in 1900 to 3/5 in 1955. Wall Street, the New York street housing the biggest banks, is the financial heart of the USA. In Britain the five biggest banks account for close on 4/5 of the bank balances of all banks put together. In West Germany the dominant position is held by three banks, which have concentrated in their hands 3/5 of the sum total deposits on the balance of all of the country's credit banks.

Banks and industry The concentration of industry and banking, the formation of industrial and banking monopolies incur a substantial change in the interrelations between banks and industry.

Initially banks were intermediaries in payments. But as capitalism developed the credit activities of banks extended and they became merchants in capital. Banks granted the capitalists short-term loans when they were short of cash.

The picture changed radically as capitalist production further developed and the mass of deposits in the banks grew. The amount of money concentrated in the banks was enormous, and not all of it could find application in short-term crediting.

The banks therefore began to look for other fields of application for the money resources they had accumulated. They formed closer links with industry—began to issue loans for long terms. This naturally changed the interrelations between banks and industry.

Acquiring shares and bonds in various companies the banks became co-owners of industrial, trading and transport enterprises. In their turn, industrial monopolies hold shares in the banks connected with them.

Finance capital and the finance oligarchy

This gives rise to a "personal union" of the heads of banking and industrial monopolies. Bank directors are on the administrative bodies of industrial enterprises. At the same time industrial monopolies have their representatives on the boards of banks. The same people head the largest monopoly associations in banking, industry, trade and in the most diverse branches of the capitalist economy.

There is an ever greater coalescence of banking and industrial capital. The joint capital of banking and industrial monopolies is called finance capital.

The coalescence of banking capital and the industrial monopolies is one of the distinguishing features of imperialism, the monopoly stage of capitalism. It is for this reason that imperialism is called the epoch of finance capital.

The growth of monopolies and finance capital places the keys of a country's economic life into the hands of a few of the biggest bankers and monopolist-industrialists. The destiny of any capitalist country is determined by a small number of big business tycoons, by the omnipotent finance oligarchy (the Greek word oligarchia means "rule by few").

The élite of the US big bourgeoisie, a mere one per cent of the population, owned 21 per cent of the private wealth in the country in 1949, and already 28 per cent in 1961. This élite holds more than 75 per cent of the total shares. In Britain one per cent of the population own 35 per cent of the country's private wealth.

Uncrowned kings of capital
The United States of America is a republic. Yet there are more kings in that republic than in all monarchies taken together. There are oil and steel kings, chemistry and aluminium kings, railway, motor-car, coal, newspaper kings, banking dynasties and even pork stew and chewing-gum kings.

These monarchs consider themselves the Lord's anointed. The American kings are the anointed of a lord more powerful than the gods of any religion. They are the anointed of god-capital. Even in their wildest dreams the crowned kings of the past and present never dreamed of as much wealth and power as these uncrowned kings possess.

The Rockefeller family consists of five brothers and an uncle. They are among the richest people in the USA and in the whole capitalist world. The Rockefellers are the oil kings. In the early sixties they controlled one-third of all known reserves and a quarter of the production, transportation and processing of oil in the capitalist world. They own oilfields in the USA, Venezuela, Iran and the countries of the Arab East. They run various mining enterprises, banks, railway companies, insurance companies and a multitude of other enterprises. In recent years the Rockefeller group has extended its control over new rapidly growing industries: the chemical, electrical, aircraft-missile and atomic. The power of the Rockefellers extends over enterprises the value of which exceeds $60,000 million.

The powerful house of Morgans competes with the Rockefellers. They are the steel kings. Their domain embraces banks and insurance companies, transport, municipal and many other enterprises. In recent years the Morgans have also begun to exert influence on the oil, chemical and electronic industries. This group controls enterprises in dozens of capitalist countries, including Britain, France, and West Germany.

The Rockefeller and Morgan empires are the most powerful financial groups in the USA. Together with six other big financial groupings they control banking, industrial, insurance, transport and other enterprises valued at over $218,000 million. This is more than 25 per cent of the total funds owned by all US corporations.

The anointed of the god-capital are the undivided rulers also in all other bourgeois countries. In West Germany the owners of the biggest concerns, those that placed Hitler in power, rule undividedly and their power has grown in recent times.

Thus, in West Germany, the number of joint-stock companies decreased by 56.5 per cent as compared with prewar, while the sum total of their capital doubled. In 1962, 200 big companies owned 85 per cent of the total share capital in the country.

The entire West German economy is in the hands of a small number of capitalist magnates. More than 110,000 people work at the giant Krupp concern, and its yearly turnover exceeds 5,000 million marks. It is owned by Alfred Krupp von Bohlen und Halbach. Owning a wealth of 5,000 to 6,000 million marks, Krupp is one of the ten richest people on earth. Uncounted wealth is concentrated in the hands of other West German capitalist magnates: the heirs of Thyssen, Haniel, Flick and Sons, and others.

Banker today—minister tomorrow

The finance oligarchy is closely interlinked with the bourgeois state apparatus. Big bankers and industrialists often hold leading government posts. But even if they do not participate openly in governments, the capitalist magnates exert a decisive influence on the composition of the government élite and direct its activities.

They actually dismiss and appoint the government. They use state power to ensure their high monopoly profits, to maintain their rule, while highly placed government leaders obtain well-paid positions in banks and concerns upon retiring.

This creates a condition which is best described as: banker today—minister tomorrow, and minister today—banker tomorrow.

A small handful of the biggest businessmen, having control over thousands of millions, are the initiators of the aggressive policies, invasions, the arms race, the preparation of new wars. The finance oligarchy controls the bourgeois press, science and art. It bribes the top civil servants and MPs, moulds "public opinion" to suit its interests and controls the whole apparatus poisoning the minds of the masses.

3. THE STRUGGLE FOR WORLD DOMINATION

The export of capital The export of commodities was typical of pre-monopoly capitalism with its free competition. Under imperialism and monopoly rule the export of commodities grows enormously. Typical of imperialism, however, is the export of capital.

In the advanced countries the accumulation of capital assumes a gigantic scale under monopoly rule. On the eve of the First World War about 75 per cent of the world's industrial production and about four-fifth of the securities were concentrated in the four biggest capitalist countries: the USA, Britain, France and Germany. Thus a small number of wealthy countries possessed large sums of capital and held a monopoly of "surplus capital".

Capital becomes "surplus" mainly for two reasons.

First, the low living standard of the masses impedes the further growth of production. Secondly, the development of the different economic branches grows still more unevenly. If capitalism could raise the backward branches of the economy and the living standard of the masses there would be no surplus capital. But, Lenin said, in that case capitalism would stop being capitalism, for both uneven development and the low living standard of the masses are the basic, inevitable conditions and prerequisites of the bourgeois mode of production.

"Surplus" capital is exported, predominantly to backward countries. In those countries there is little capital, land is comparatively inexpensive, wages are low and raw materials cheap. This is where capital yields a high rate of profit.

The champions of the bourgeoisie try to picture the export of capital by the imperialist powers as a boon to the poor and backward countries. Investing their capital the rich countries, they say, help the poor countries develop their industry, build railways and advance along the road to progress.

Actually, however, the export of capital serves as a means of subjugating some countries to others thus founding the system of imperialist oppression. The countries importing capital become dependent on the imperialist powers. By exporting capital the finance oligarchy of a few developed capitalist countries fetters the backward countries economically.

Fettering terms are imposed on the countries forced to import capital. The monopolists exporting capital dictate them their conditions. They obtain concessions on profitable terms, seize valuable raw material sources and the sales market.

The export of capital is a means of expanding the export of commodities. Generally, the purchase of goods in the creditor country is made a condition of the loan. The imperialist countries are particularly eager to grant loans for the purchase of armaments.

All imperialist states export capital. One of the most important consequences of the export of capital is the intensification of inter-imperialist competition, growing contradictions between them and the struggle for spheres of influence.

As a result of the export of capital the few richest capitalist countries turn into usurers as regards their economic relations with all other countries. A stream of surplus value—interest on loans and the profits of enterprises in foreign countries—flows steadily to the usurer countries. The income from exported capital is a major source of enrichment for the monopolies in the main capitalist countries.

Distinguishing features of the export of capital in modern times At present when the peoples of the newly-free developing countries strive to abolish the heavy after-effects of colonial oppression, foreign monopolies use their capital investments in those countries to perpetuate their economic domination.

Under the guise of "economic aid", the imperialist states seize important branches of the economies in the developing countries. The export of capital is used for attempts to lock the newly-free peoples once again in the chains of colonial slavery, by transforming their political independence into a cloak for the rule of foreign monopolies. Foreign capital in the young sovereign states gives all-out support to the reactionary forces there, organises plots and subversions in order to reinstate colonial oppression in new forms.

At the same time in modern conditions there has been a substantial increase in the export of capital from some advanced capitalist countries to other advanced capitalist countries. There has been a particularly high increase in the export of capital by the US monopolies to Canada and the West European countries. US monopolies establish their branches in Britain, West Germany, France and other West European countries. Capitalising on the lower wage level of the West European workers as compared with their US counterparts, the US monopolies seize markets and push back their competitors. In turn the capital of a number of West European countries is exported beyond the ocean, where it is invested in spheres in which West European firms hold definite advantages. The export of capital from some advanced capitalist countries to others inevitably aggravates the competitive struggle between the monopolies of different countries and inflames imperialist contradictions.

International monopolies The export of capital typical of the imperialist era has given rise to the emergence and world-wide activity of international monopolies. Having assured their predominance in the economic life of the leading countries, the monopolies strive first and foremost for the undivided domination of the home market. But they do not confine themselves to this. The scale of production of the monopoly giants often exceeds the volume of the domestic market. The biggest monopolies concentrate a substantial share of the world output of definite commodities in their hands. The struggle between them becomes particularly acute and destructive. As the biggest monopolies continue to grow they spare no effort to try to divide the world market. This leads to the formation of international monopolies—agreements of the monopolists of a number of countries on the division of the world market.

The rise of international monopolies dates back to the sixties and eighties of the 19th century. During the first decade of the 20th century powerful monopoly organisations emerged in the advanced industrial countries, which began to influence the world market.

Defenders of capitalism attempt to paint the international monopolies, which are the source of the most acute conflicts, as an instrument of peace. They assert that international monopoly agreements are able to eliminate the contradictions between imperialist powers in a peaceful way. Such assertions are anything but the truth.

In reality the international agreements of monopolists are extremely unstable. They are hotbeds of violent conflict. The world market is divided up among the international monopolies in accordance with their strength. Each one of them constantly struggles to increase its share, to expand the sphere of monopoly exploitation. The strength of the monopolies of different countries changes incessantly. These changes entail a violent struggle for the redivision of markets. This struggle is waged by various groups and supported by their states.

In the period between the two world wars international monopolies spread far and wide. Their importance in world politics grew enormously. They played a baneful role in the preparation of the Second World War by the forces of world imperialism.

US, British and French monopolies were closely linked with the German magnates who midwived Hitler and his fascist gang to power. The plots of the monopolists underlay the policy of "appeasement" and encouragement of the fascist aggressors, which the Western powers conducted and which led to the outbreak of the Second World War.

Territorial division of the world and the struggle for its redivision
Under imperialism the largest monopolies divide the world among themselves economically, while the imperialist powers complete the territorial division of the world.

In the 1870s the colonial possessions of the European countries embraced only a comparatively small part of overseas territories. In 1876 only one-tenth of Africa's territory had been colonised by the European powers. About 50 per cent of the Asian mainland and of Polynesia had not yet been seized by the capitalist states. Vast territories had not yet fallen under the domination of the capitalist powers.

During the last two decades of the 19th century the map of the world changed radically.

In the wake of Britain, the oldest colonial power, all other advanced capitalist countries began to seize territories. From 1876 to 1914 the great powers seized 25 million square kilometres, a territory twice the area of the whole of Europe. Practically all of Africa, a large part of Asia and Latin America became colonies and semi-colonies of a few imperialist countries—Britain, France, the USA, Germany and Japan—and of the smaller predators—Belgium, the Netherlands, Portugal and Spain.

By the beginning of the First World War about 600 million out of the world population of 1,700 million lived in colonies, and only 350 million in the metropolitan countries. The greater part of the colonies belonged to the great powers. On the eve of the First World War they ruled over three quarters of the colonial world and over the absolute majority of the colonial peoples. The division of the world was completed, free lands were no longer available. Territory could be acquired only by taking it away from some other colonial predator. The question of a redivision of an already divided world had been placed on the agenda.

Imperialism's aggressive nature The struggle for the redivision of the already divided world is one of the distinguishing features of the monopoly stage of capitalism. The struggle of the imperialists for the redivision of the world ultimately becomes a struggle for world domination. It leads to bloody, devastating wars. The First World War (1914-1918) was a war for such a redivision.

Monopoly capital strives to expand, i.e., to extend the sphere of its domination, to seize foreign territories and enslave their peoples. The expansion of the monopolies inevitably becomes a cause of sharp conflicts between the imperialist powers. These conflicts are fraught with the danger of armed conflicts. At the same time the expansionist aspirations of the monopolies are a mortal danger to the peoples of the less developed countries.

After the First World War the aggressive forces of the international monopolies gave birth to fascism—the open terroristic dictatorship of the most reactionary and aggressive circles of finance capital. A wave of fascist coups swept Europe at a time when the 1929-33 crisis threatened the further existence of the capitalist system. Imperialists the world over, notably the US monopolists, supported German and Italian fascism as their shock troops in the struggle against the forces of democracy and socialism.

As the internal contradictions in the capitalist countries reached a breaking point, the imperialist bourgeoisie became more and more involved in external adventures and plunged mankind into the Second World War, which ended in the rout of the fascist aggressors.

After the rout of the fascist aggressors the USA became the stronghold of world reaction and imperialist aggression. American imperialists in collusion with their West European partners, notably with the West German revanchist-militarists, have ever since the Second World War acted as a world gendarme and launched one military adventure after another. The aggressive actions of US imperialists—the Korean war of the fifties, the present war in Vietnam, the provocations against the Cuban people, the subversive activities against a number of countries of the Arab East, Africa and Latin America—imperil the world with a new war and pollute the international climate.

American imperialism, having set up a de facto colonial empire, has become the world's biggest exploiter. US monopoly capital fights all democratic and progressive movements of today. It supports decrepit anti-popular regimes throughout the world, knocks together aggressive military blocs, obstinately conducts the cold war policy, so polluting the international atmosphere. The glaring contradictions of modern capitalism multiply imperialist recklessness and threaten the peoples, the cause of peace and social progress. Ever more frequently the imperialists seek a way out of their troubles through military provocations, all sorts of blocs and direct military intervention. All peace-loving forces able to rebuff the aggressive plans and actions of imperialism must consolidate to prevent further aggravation of international tension.

4. THE COLONIAL SYSTEM OF IMPERIALISM

What is colonialism? Hundreds of millions of people in Asia, Africa and Latin America know no word more hateful than colonialism. Colonialism is the system of exploitation, oppression and violence imperialism has set up in the colonial and dependent countries.

Colonialism has condemned many peoples with an ancient culture to economic backwardness and extreme poverty. For two centuries India languished under British rule. Semi-colonial dependence was China's lasting curse. The peoples of the Arab East and Africa, Latin America and South-East Asia had to bear the yoke of ruthless colonial exploitation fettering their development. Colonialism brought hunger to countries with inexhaustible natural riches and an industrious population.

Seizure of colonies The means by which the colonies were seized by the capitalist countries was described by a bourgeois politician in the following words: "First missionaries, then merchants, and finally gunboats."

Missionaries generally were the first scouts of the notorious capitalist civilisation. They came to "save the souls" of the native population. They were followed by traders, who cheated, gave the trusting natives alcohol or worthless trinkets in exchange for valuable products (precious metals, ivory, fur, cotton, coffee), or simply robbed them. They were followed by armies which subjected the country to the new ruler—capital.

The new rulers imposed heavy taxes on the people whose land they had seized. Sailors, soldiers and all sorts of adventurers brought syphilis and other diseases to the colonies, which spread like a wildfire. Alcohol was the only commodity abundantly supplied to the colonies. Disease and drunkenness became responsible for the catastrophic eclipse of entire nations. Such is the picture of the "boon" capitalism brought to many peoples.

Imperialism's colonial policy Colonies existed before imperialism and even before capitalism. But the importance of colonies grew enormously during the monopoly stage of capitalism.

First, imperialism's colonial policy is indissolubly bound

with the rule of the monopolies in the countries that enslaved the colonies and semi-colonies. Monopoly rule substantially changed the role of the colonies. The monopolies of each industrial country keep foreign competitors from the domestic market. Under these conditions there is an increasing need for sales markets and raw material sources and also for spheres of profitable capital investments. The exploitation of the colonies and dependent countries is an important source of monopoly superprofits.

Secondly, imperialism's colonial policy is a struggle for a redivision of the already divided world. A handful of imperialist countries holds a monopoly on colonial possessions. The struggle for colonies intensifies to the utmost.

By the beginning of the First World War imperialism's colonial system, to use Lenin's definition, meant the looting of about a thousand million of the world's population by a handful of big powers. The colonial powers became the full-fledged owners of countries with a population that was many times larger than that of the oppressor countries. On the eve of the Second World War there were 47 million people in Britain but 480 million in her colonies, 42 million in France and 70 in her colonies, 9 million in the Netherlands and about 70 million in her colonies, 8 million people in Belgium and about 14 million in her colonies.

Some British colonies were inhabited by settlers who had emigrated from the metropolitan country, had cruelly enslaved the native population and exterminated a large portion of it. These colonies later became capitalist states dependent to a larger or smaller extent on Britain and the United States (Canada, Australia, New Zealand).

However, the bulk of the colonial and dependent peoples of Asia and the Pacific Ocean, Africa and Latin America were fettered in the chains of merciless exploitation and unbearable oppression by the imperialists.

Imperialism's colonial system doomed the peoples of whole continents to economic and cultural backwardness, to a sub-human existence. The colonialists' looting led to hunger which decimated the population. National oppression, racial discrimination, lack of rights, epidemics, an unprecedented growth of crime, sowing of enmity in keeping with the "divide and rule" principle—such are the "benefits" the colonialists brought to the colonial people.

The capitalist world economic system

Capitalism created the world market at the dawn of its existence. Commodities produced in capitalist enterprises found their way to the most remote corners of the globe. At the monopoly stage of capitalism the economic links between the various countries grew enormously. These links entangled the whole world. The spread of capitalism throughout the globe gave rise to the emergence of the capitalist world economy.

This system is founded on relations of domination and subordination. The imperialist powers established their rule over the greater part of humanity.

The economic laws of capitalism lead to the accumulation of wealth by a small group of capitalists and to the increasing poverty of the broad masses of working people. These same laws are widening the gulf between a handful of European and US monopolies from the hundreds of millions living in the countries enslaved by them.

The defenders of capitalism are fond of speaking about the benefits the highly developed bourgeois countries have allegedly brought to the peoples of the dependent countries. The relations between the metropolitan countries and the colonies are pictured as an "alliance". In reality this is an alliance between the rider and the horse. Talk about the blessings the colonialists have bestowed upon the enslaved peoples is as stale a tale as that about capitalists bestowing blessings upon the workers.

The colonial system of imperialism is indissolubly connected with the unprecedented intensification of national oppression and racial discrimination. The imperialists established regimes in the colonies and semi-colonies in which people from the metropolitan country—civil servants, military, merchants, fortune-seekers, all sorts of adventurers—enjoy the rights of people of a "superior race" who could treat the native population as they saw fit. At its monopoly stage capitalism became the greatest oppressor of the nations.

Exploitation of the colonies—the source of monopoly superprofits

Colonial exploitation became one of the mainstays of the imperialist economy. Colonies became the well from which imperialism drew enormous wealth.

The monopolies receive a lavish tribute from the enslaved peoples of the colonial and dependent countries as profits from capital investments, transport, insurance and financial transactions.

On the eve of the Second World War the annual tribute British imperialism exacted from India amounted to £150-180 million.

The colonies were the most reliable and profitable sales market for the monopolies.

In the free competition stage of capitalism commodities were sold more or less without restrictions not only in the colonies but also in other capitalist countries. Under monopoly domination the domestic market of every industrial country is ruled exclusively by the monopolies of that country.

At the same time the growing scale of production and the limitations imposed on the domestic market by the low purchasing power of the masses make it necessary to acquire foreign sales markets. Foreign competition in the colonies is discouraged by establishing high customs duties; and this enables the monopolies to sell their commodities at inflated prices.

Under imperialism the importance of the colonies as raw material sources has grown enormously. The capitalist countries receive a number of key raw materials—non-ferrous metals, oil, rubber, cotton, coffee, cocoa and others—largely or almost exclusively from the less developed countries.

The colonies are particularly important for the monopolies as a sales market and raw material source under the system of unequivalent exchange. Unequivalent exchange means that one capitalist country systematically sells another country (generally a colony or a semi-colony) its commodities at highly inflated prices and buys from it commodities at extremely low prices.

Unequivalent exchange has become a means of fleecing the colonies and dependent countries. It was and continues to be one of the most important sources of monopoly super-profits. The monopolies engaged in colonial trade (the purchase of raw materials and the sale of industrial goods) made profits amounting to several hundred per cent. They became the rulers over entire countries, disposing of the lives and property of scores of millions of people.

The colonies have been a very reliable field for capital investments. The political and economic domination of the monopolies in the colonies guaranteed high profits on invested capital. Colonial rule ensured a complete and undivided monopoly of capital investments, cheap labour power and raw materials.

Cheap labour power meant that the metropolitan countries could import from the colonies and dependent countries hundreds of thousands of workers, breaking their backs for pittances.

The colonial powers received enormous profits from their possessions in the form of all sorts of taxes and excises, kept an army of civil servants and policemen in those countries at the expense of their peoples.

Colonialism— the cause of the developing countries' economic backwardness

Imperialism made the colonies and dependent countries agrarian and raw material appendages of the metropolitan countries. The ruling monopolies only tolerated the development of the branches of production ensuring deliveries of raw materials and foodstuffs, of the extractive industries, the cultivation of marketable crops and their primary processing.

As a result the economies of the colonies and semi-colonies acquired a one-sided and subordinated nature. The economies of many dependent countries specialised in the production of one or two products, 100 per cent of which were exported: cotton, oil, coffee, rubber, sugar, etc.

The one-sided development of agriculture (its single-crop system) made whole countries fully dependent on the monopolies purchasing raw materials. The bulk of the colonial and dependent countries enjoyed favourable natural conditions for agricultural production, but because of their one-crop economy were compelled to import foodstuffs for their population.

Africa accounts for one-fifth of the world's agricultural

land mass. At the same time its share in the production of grain is exceedingly small—only 7 per cent of the world's barley, less than 4 per cen of the maize, 2 per cent of the wheat and less than 1.5 per cent of the rice and only 0.5 per cent of the world's oats.

In their quest for superprofits the monopolies were compelled to build railways, enterprises for the extraction of minerals and for the primary processing of raw materials in the colonies and semi-colonies. But imperialist rule arrested the advancement of the productive forces in the colonies. It deprived the oppressed peoples of the conditions needed for independent economic development.

Capital flowing into the colonies was used to deepen their economic dependence. The dominating monopolies strove to prevent the development of the production of means of production. They refused to grant the colonies and dependent countries credits for these purposes and did not sell them the necessary equipment. The industrialisation of the colonies was incompatible with their subjugation to the imperialist powers.

There is no or almost no heavy industry in the economically less developed Latin American and African countries, and in some Asian and Middle East countries. Even in the countries where industry is comparatively better developed, for example, in the Latin American countries, only the extractive and light industries (cotton, tanning and food industries) are growing.

Africa possesses enormous mineral wealth. It can be justifiably called the world's great storehouse. It produces 96 per cent of the total diamonds in the capitalist world, 71 per cent of cobalt, 60 per cent of gold, 42 per cent of phosphorites, 24 per cent of copper and 21 per cent of manganese, but the African peoples live in extreme poverty because of their terrible economic backwardness.

All African countries put together with a population of over 200 million smelt only 1.2 million tons of steel a year, while Belgium with a population of 8.7 million smelts 5 million tons a year. This is much more than in the developing countries, the population of which reaches 1,000 million. Under British rule the per capita consumption of steel in India was 2 kilograms a year as against 220 kilograms in Britain.

Even the textile industry in the colonial and dependent countries remains underdeveloped and backward. In India, in colonial times, there were only 9.7 million spindles as compared with 41.1 million in Britain, whose population is 1/8 of that of India; in Latin America there are only 4.4 million spindles as against 281 million in the USA.

Colonial exploitation of the working masses The countries enslaved by imperialism remain agrarian throughout the period of colonial oppression. The main source of subsistence of the majority of their population is agriculture, cramped in semi-feudal fetters.

The land is concentrated in the hands of feudal lords and usurers. Besides, huge tracts of land are seized by foreign monopolies.

Imperialists have set up a plantation economy in a number of colonies and dependent countries. Plantations are large agricultural enterprises owned by the colonialists and producing vegetable raw materials (cotton, rubber, jute, sizal, coffee, etc.). They are based on the slave- or semi-slave labour of the natives deprived of any rights.

Small peasant farming generally predominates in the most densely populated dependent countries. Big landowners lease out small plots to peasants on the most onerous terms. The peasants, oppressed by both the landowners and usurers, are able to afford only the most primitive implements. This exhausts the soil to the extreme. In the countries enslaved by imperialism agriculture tends to decay.

A large portion of the scanty product of the peasants' backbreaking labour is appropriated by the exploiters: landowners, usurers, wholesalers, tax collectors, etc. They appropriate not only the product of the peasant's surplus labour but also a considerable part of the product produced by the necessary labour, leaving him an income that more often than not fails to provide even a half-hungry existence.

Semi-feudal forms of exploitation predominate also in the industry of the colonial and dependent countries. To the working class colonialism means a complete lack of political rights and monstrous exploitation.

The cheap labour power, the almost gratis labour of the colonial slaves are responsible for the low technical level at the industrial enterprises and plantations. At the low level of technology, the enormous profits of the monopolies are based on the extremely high rate of surplus value. Mass unemployment and the widespread application of undisguised slave labour hampered the struggle of the workers for their vital rights.

In the colonies the working day lasted 14, 16 and more hours. There was no social legislation. As a rule, there was also no labour protection of any sort at factories and transport enterprises.

The wages of colonial workers are far below the subsistence level. Native workers receive only a fraction of the wages paid to workers in the metropolitan country doing the same job.

In the clutches of poverty and hunger The low economic development level and the high degree of exploitation brought the colonial peoples poverty and hunger and pushed them to the verge of extinction.

According to UN data, the per capita income of two-thirds of the world's population barely reaches $41 a year. This is from one-tenth to one-fifteenth of the incomes in the metropolitan countries. Hundreds of millions of people, living in wretched poverty are deprived of medical services. In the USA there is one doctor to every 800 people, in France one per 900, in West Germany one per 700, in many of the former colonial countries only one doctor to 40,000-70,000 people.

One of the most horrible aftermaths of colonial oppression is the high rate of infant mortality. In the advanced capitalist countries 20 to 30 infants in 1,000 die before the age of one, in some newly free countries—over 100. The average life span in the advanced capitalist countries ranges from 63 to 74 years in a number of former colonial countries from 35 to 43 years.

Every year millions of people in the colonial and dependent countries die of hunger, scores of millions lead a half-starved existence. In Africa 57 per cent of the native population dies under the age of 15. In Brazil, Argentina, Chile and other South American countries about 60 million people are permanently undernourished.

The colonial peoples have long
since been fighting their foreign
enslavers. They often rose in insur-
rections which were cruelly put
down by the colonialists.

Under imperialism the liberation struggle of the colonial
and dependent countries assumed an unprecedented scale.
One of the basic characteristics of imperialism, Lenin said,
is that it accelerates the development of capitalism in the
most backward countries and thus extends and intensifies
the struggle against national oppression. The national
liberation movement in the colonies draws the vast majority of the world population, subjected by the finance
oligarchies of a handful of the biggest capitalist powers,
into the anti-imperialist struggle.

Imperialism is the common enemy of the proletariat in
the advanced capitalist countries and of the oppressed
peoples in the colonies. This means that the struggle of
the working class for socialism and the national liberation
movement of the colonial peoples can and must be merged
into a common struggle against imperialism.

The national liberation movement in the colonies and
the struggle of the proletariat and all working people
against the capitalist system of exploitation are based on
identical laws of social development. The growing national
liberation struggle of the oppressed peoples in the colonies
and dependent countries undermines the foundations of
imperialism, heralding its collapse.

The peoples of the colonial world, who are ruthlessly
exploited by the monopolists of the imperialist powers, rise
up in arms against foreign oppression, for freedom and
independence. The national liberation struggle in the colonies and dependent countries weakens capitalism's positions throughout the world.

The triumph of the socialist revolution in the USSR has
boosted the national liberation movement in the colonial
and dependent countries. The weakening of the colonial
powers as a result of the First and particularly of the Second World War has created favourable conditions for the
liberation struggle of the colonial peoples. The emergence
and development of the socialist world system, the growing
might and prestige of the socialist countries and the rad-

ical change in the relation of forces between socialism and capitalism have enabled the peoples enslaved by imperialism to smash colonialism once and for all, to win freedom and independence and to embark on the road of non-capitalist development, which opens up wide prospects for the achievement of rapid economic and social progress.

Political economy proves scientifically that the peoples of the economically less developed countries are able to throw off the heavy burden of poverty, backwardness and slavery only by waging a resolute and irreconcilable struggle against all vestiges of colonialism, fighting for national sovereignty and radical socio-economic reforms.

The objective laws of social development make the complete collapse of the colonial system, which has become a disgrace to humanity, inevitable. All attempts by colonialists to perpetuate their rule by means of new methods of violence and deceit are invariably abortive.

REVISION QUESTIONS

1. What are the main economic symptoms of imperialism?
2. What is the role of the finance oligarchy in modern capitalism?
3. Why do the imperialists fight for world domination?
4. What is the importance of the struggle of the colonial and dependent countries for political and economic independence?

Chapter VIII

IMPERIALISM'S PLACE IN HISTORY. GENERAL CRISIS OF CAPITALISM

1. IMPERIALISM—A SPECIAL STAGE OF CAPITALISM

Imperialism is a special stage of capitalism. It has three distinguishing features. Imperialism is, first, monopoly capitalism; secondly, parasitic, or decaying capitalism; and thirdly, moribund capitalism. Imperialism is the eve of the socialist revolution. Such is its historical place with respect to capitalism in general.

Monopoly capitalism The domination of the monopolies involves an enormous growth in the socialisation of production. Many thousands of people work in enterprises belonging to monopolies. The monopolies merge many enterprises into one. They assume control over sales markets, raw material sources, inventions and improvements. Big banks control virtually all the money resources of society.

The high degree of socialisation of production shows that the material preconditions for a socialist transformation of society are already there. But the enormous progress in the socialisation of production serves the mercenary interests of a handful of monopolists. The popular masses receive no perceptible benefits from the enormous development of the productive forces. Moreover, their exploitation gets fiercer.

Thus, imperialism, being monopoly capitalism, is a new stage in the development of the basic contradiction of capitalism—the contradiction between the social character of production and the private capitalist form of appropriation. The socialisation of production by the monopolies goes hand in hand with an aggravation of the competitive struggle between them. Attempts to do away with competition, to unite production on a national scale inevitably end in failure so long as the means of production remain the property of capitalists.

Imperialism and technological progress

Monopoly rule tends to arrest technological progress and to result in technological stagnation. Since the monopolies are able to dictate the prices for their output and to keep them artificially on a high level they are not always interested in introducing technological innovations.

However, the tendency of the monopolies to slow down technological progress clashes with an opposing tendency— that of applying technological improvements. In that struggle the upper hand is taken now by one, now by the other tendency. As a whole, capitalism grows quicker than it did before, but this growth is extremely uneven and is paralleled by stagnation in some industries and some countries.

The struggle of the two tendencies is typical of the monopoly stage of capitalism as a whole. However, it takes different forms at the different stages of monopoly capitalism's development.

The tendency towards technological stagnation is expressed with particular force in the first stages of monopoly capitalism. At that time pre-monopoly forms were still widespread. In the competitive struggle against the technologically far less equipped non-monopoly enterprises, the monopolies often delayed technological progress in order to avoid a depreciation of the enormous sums of capital invested in outmoded equipment.

This state of affairs has changed substantially at the present stage, when the monopolies have tightened their grasp on the economy. Competition is now the realm of giant monopolies, which in their struggle, naturally, do not neglect such a mighty weapon as technological progress. The scientific and technological revolution makes the monopolists improve production so as not to lag behind their competitors. At the present rate of technological development backwardness would endanger the further existence even of the largest firms. The large scale of research in the capitalist countries is attributable to this.

The lion's share of the work is financed by the government while its results are placed at the disposal of the monopolies. Research has progressed at a particularly high rate in the USA. At the end of the Second World War less than 2,000 million dollars were spent on research in the USA, of which 44 per cent were financed by the government. By 1962-63 the total expenditure had grown to 16,000 million dollars, the government's share to 64 per cent.

The competitive struggle on the world capitalist market is an important stimulus raising the technological level of production. The intensification of the struggle for foreign markets makes the monopolies apply serious efforts to avoid any lagging behind their competitors and to outstrip them, if possible.

The new situation in the world which compels the capitalist countries to compete economically with the socialist system plays an even greater role in that respect. Economic growth rates are extremely important in that competition. The rulers of monopoly capital and the governments serving their interests spare no effort to achieve higher growth rates. The existence of the world socialist system is a factor that must be taken into account if an understanding is to be gained of the concrete situation in which the struggle between the two tendencies in technological progress develops under modern capitalism.

The intensification today of the working class's struggle for its rights and economic interests also exerts a major influence on the course taken by the two vying tendencies. The fight of the working class for an improvement of its position stimulates an introduction of technological improvements, for, obviously, the lower the wages the less the capitalists are interested in raising the technological level of production but the higher the wages the more interested are they in introducing new equipment, in saving live labour. This shows that the struggle of the working class for its economic interests far from arresting technological progress as alleged by its enemies, promotes the growth of the productive forces.

Parasitism and decay of capitalism

Imperialism is parasitical or decaying capitalism. Like an overripe fruit that has not been harvested capitalism decays and disintegrates.

The decay of capitalism condemns the working masses in town and country to the most wretched privations. Capitalism treats human labour power, society's main productive force, in a predatory way. The exploitation of the proletariat intensifies and this adds to the insecurity of the working people's existence.

The decay of capitalism progresses with the spread of parasitism. The layer of rentiers, people who live in idleness on the income from securities, has grown enormously. These are the owners of shares, bonds of state loans, etc., who live by "clipping" coupons. The bulk of the bourgeoisie has dissociated itself from the process of production. The management of enterprises has passed into the hands of hired executives.

Not only a great number of people have made idleness their profession, but whole countries have become rentiers. Investing a large share of their wealth abroad, they are the centres of the financial exploitation of the capitalist world: the export of capital ensures them a steady influx of tribute from abroad.

The non-productive consumption of the people's labour and of its fruits is also growing. The branches and the number of people employed in rendering personal services to the propertied classes are increasing. Whole countries, like Switzerland, and vast areas (in the South of France, Italy, Austria, and partly in Britain) have become places where the international bourgeoisie dissipates its unearned incomes.

Militarism, growing at a monstrous rate, consumes an ever greater share of the people's income in the capitalist countries. All imperialist countries participate in the arms race. The preparation for aggressive wars swallows huge funds.

State-monopoly capitalism The exacerbation of the main contradiction of capitalism leads to the direct intervention of the bourgeois state in the economy in the interests of the finance oligarchy and to the growth of monopoly capitalism into state-monopoly capitalism.

Lenin noted that the First World War and the resultant dislocation forced all countries to switch from monopoly capitalism to state-monopoly capitalism.

The growth of state-monopoly capitalism continued also after the end of the First World War: during the period between the two world wars, during the Second World War and after it.

In times of war or crises the government helps the monopolies overcome difficulties they themselves would be unable to cope with. In wartime the government builds enterprises which the monopolies do not consider sufficiently profitable. It often happens that they are later sold to private monopolies for a song. During crises the state saves the monopolies from collapse by issuing them loans and direct financial aid from the Treasury.

The bourgeois state nationalises enterprises and even whole branches in the interests of the capitalist monopolies. In a number of cases the state buys from the monopolies obsolescent, unprofitable enterprises and spends huge sums on re-equipping them. In this way state monopolies emerge in addition to private monopolies.

State and private monopolies merge. The activities of the state monopolies are subordinated to the interests of private monopolies. State monopolies supply the private monopolies with electric power, fuel and metal at reduced rates. State railways transport the freight of private monopolies at lower tariffs. The losses are covered by taxes levied on the working people.

In the interests of the monopolies the bourgeois state carries out measures to regulate the economy: distributes raw material and fuel, provides labour power, and finances and credits production. The regulating bodies are generally under the complete control of the monopolists and their representatives. The state places extremely profitable orders with the biggest monopolies. Particularly profitable are arms orders, both during wars and during war preparations.

The growth of monopoly capitalism into state-monopoly capitalism tightens finance capital's oppressive grip and its rule over the lives of the peoples. Dominant monopoly capital and the state administrative machinery become closely interlinked. The state has become a committee for the management of the business of the monopoly bourgeoisie. It administers the dictatorship of a handful of monopolists who use state power and its apparatus to perpetuate the bourgeois system, for their superprofits, domination of markets, and redivision of the world.

State-monopoly capitalism unites the power of the

monopolies with the power of the state in a single mechanism for the purpose of enriching the monopolies, suppressing the labour movement and the national liberation struggle, safeguarding the capitalist system and unleashing aggressive wars.

The anti-popular nature of state-monopoly capitalism
Defenders of the monopolies assert that the intervention of the bourgeois state in the economy is able to solve the contradictions of capitalism. The reformist lackeys of the bourgeoisie depict state-monopoly capitalism as a new social system devoid of the sores and ills of capitalism, as socialism. They aver that capitalism has changed its nature, that it has become "planned", "regulated", "people's" capitalism.

Such assertions have nothing to do with reality. State-monopoly capitalism does not change the nature of the bourgeois system. Profits through the exploitation of the working class and the broad working masses continue to be the aim of production. The gulf between labour and capital, between the majority of the nation and the monopolists, is deepening. Competition becomes more intense, the anarchy of production grows. This aggravates the general chaos and disorganisation of the capitalist system as a whole.

Trying to remove the threat of economic crises the bourgeois state spends enormous sums to give the economy artificial respiration. The money flowing from the Treasury into the safes of the monopolies are exacted from the population. This reduces the effective demand of the population. The expansion of military production reduces the output of production for peaceful purposes.

The facts have refuted the inventions about "people's" capitalism. The defenders of the monopolies and their reformist lackeys maintain that in bourgeois society the state is a supra-class and extra-class body which takes care of the people's interests. In reality, however, the bourgeois state serves wholly the interests of the finance oligarchy. Both in its domestic and in its foreign policy it fulfils the will of the ruling monopoly groups.

Thus, the development of state-monopoly capitalism not only fails to solve the contradictions and conflicts of bourgeois society but on the contrary aggravates them.

Instead of strengthening capitalism, as the bourgeoisie expects, it knocks a few more bricks out of its foundations.

Material preparation of socialism

The intervention of the bourgeois state in the economy gives the monopolies fabulous profits. At the same time it leads to a further socialisation of production.

State-monopoly capitalism is the highest stage of the socialisation of production under capitalism when the means of production continue to be privately owned. In this sense Lenin considered state-monopoly capitalism the complete material preparation for socialism, its eve.

Events show, however, that material preconditions in themselves are not enough for a transition from capitalism to socialism. The presence of the material prerequisites of socialism indicates that the socialist revolution can and should be urgently effected. In these conditions the political consciousness and cohesion of the masses in their struggle to curb monopoly power, abolish its domination and establish socialism is crucial.

The transition of separate enterprises and even whole branches into the hands of the bourgeois state—bourgeois nationalisation—is not a socialist measure since on a social scale the means of production continue to be the property of the capitalists. At private, like at state enterprises, labour continues to be exploited by capital. But under certain conditions the working class can use even bourgeois nationalisation as a weapon in the struggle against monopoly arbitrary rule. For this reason the bourgeoisie often opposes nationalisation, while the working class supports it.

Demanding the nationalisation of factories and banks the working class wants the management of the nationalised enterprises to be handed over to the true representatives of the people. In this way the working class strives to isolate the exploiter monopolists, to consolidate the broadest masses of the working people in the attack on the monopoly yoke.

Economic programming and planning

The intervention of the bourgeois state in the economy intensified after the Second World War and state-monopoly economic regulation assumed an even wider scale, particularly in the early sixties. In a number of countries (France, Italy, the Netherlands, Japan and other countries) the government bodies representing the interests of the leading monopoly capital groups began to work out economic programmes or plans for a number of years. Such programmes have the objective of establishing a definite economic growth rate, strengthening the positions of domestic monopolies in the competitive struggle on the world market, promoting the further concentration and monopolisation of the economy, improving the economic structure by developing the most profitable branches.

By economic programming and planning the monopoly bourgeoisie want to influence the spontaneous course of capitalist reproduction, to use the economic laws of capitalism in its economic and political interests. The monopolists hope that economic programming and planning will improve the capitalist economic mechanism, take the edge off social conflicts, overcome the difficulties posed by the modern scientific and technological revolution. Leading bourgeois groups believe that economic programming and planning will prove an effective means of economically competing with socialism.

Economic programming and planning emerged because the development of state-monopoly capitalism provided the bourgeois state with levers enabling it to exercise a serious influence on the country's economic life. These are the nationalisation of enterprises and whole branches, the growth of the state budgets, amounting in many cases to about 25 to 33 per cent of the national income, the taxation policy and the credit system. In a number of countries state finance accounts for a large share of the capital investments. The militarisation of the economy and the arms race are cardinal factors in strengthening state-monopoly capitalism.

Yet, there can be no genuine economic planning under capitalism, which is based on the domination of private ownership of the means of production. Economic programmes and plans being drawn up by the bourgeois governments exert a definite influence on the course of reproduction but are unable to abolish its laws operating spontaneously. The aims stipulated in the programmes and plans are achieved only to a very limited extent, and the mechanism of capitalist reproduction often plays havoc with the programmes.

At the same time the fact that economic programming

and planning have been introduced shows that modern capitalism is ripe for socialist reorganisation, that the material prerequisites for the socialist revolution have matured. The working class and its vanguard—the Marxist-Leninist parties—are advancing a democratic alternative to the economic management by and in the interests of a handful of finance oligarchy groupings within the framework of state-monopoly capitalism. This alternative provides for the destruction of the omnipotence of the monopolies, for the democratisation of the political and economic systems, for state regulation of the economy in the vital interests of the people.

The democratic alternative is a set of demands and measures designed to mobilise the powers and activity of the working class and of its allies for a consistent struggle against monopoly rule. It proposes to enhance the political role and influence of the working class, and thus to transform economic programming into a means of realising the vital tasks of social progress, of bringing about a democratisation not only of the political but also the economic structure of society by limiting the power of monopoly capital, and of democratising the management of the state sector of the economy and satisfying the lawful interests of the working class and all working people.

Intensification of political reaction
The fact that reaction is rampant in all spheres of social life strikingly demonstrates the decay and parasitism of capitalism. Free competition was consistent with bourgeois democracy. Monopoly entails political reaction all along the line. Finance capital strives for uncurbed domination.

The bourgeoisie attempts to deprive the people even of the limited bourgeois democratic rights and freedoms they have won as a result of the stubborn struggle of many generations. In its attempt to mask its rule, the bourgeoisie continues to shout slogans of liberty and equality, while it tramples underfoot even the laws of its own making. The state of monopoly capital limits voting rights, falsifies elections and persecutes workers' organisations. The monopolies keep gangs of cut-throats, who are paid to take savage reprisals against the activists of the working-class movement, against strike leaders.

The intensification of the bourgeoisie's reactionary policy stiffens the resistance of the popular masses, headed by the working class. This, Lenin pointed out, deepens the antagonism between imperialism, which denies democracy, and the masses, who strive for democracy.

The emergence of a handful of rich imperialist countries, which profit by looting the colonies and weak nations, is another very important feature of imperialism. While this looting of the colonies and dependencies prevents to some degree the emergence of strong revolutionary movements in the countries profiting by it, because the bourgeoisie divides a share of its spoils among a certain section of the population, it facilitates the emergence of such movements in the countries being looted and threatened with division and strangulation by the imperialists. Such was the position of Russia in 1917.

Moribund capitalism Imperialism is moribund capitalism. It is the final stage of capitalism, when the bourgeois system disintegrates under the impact of the contradictions tearing it apart.

Monopoly rule makes the existence of the broad mass of the working people ever more insecure. The tighter grip of exploitation enhances the resentment of the working class and steels its resolve to destroy capitalist slavery. The colonial peoples being exploited by the monopolists of the imperialist powers rise against the foreign yoke, fight for freedom and independence. The struggle of the imperialist powers for sales markets, spheres for profitable capital investments and raw materials, in short, the struggle for world domination becomes desperate.

Imperialism, moribund capitalism, is characterised by an unprecedented aggravation of the contradiction between the productive forces and the capitalist relations of production. The latter have long since become fetters for society's productive forces. This contradiction is the cause of all conflicts and clashes in the imperialist epoch.

Imperialism—the eve of the socialist revolution As we said above, imperialism is moribund capitalism. This does not mean, however, that it dies of its own accord. The historically predetermined supercession of capitalism by socialism is a result of the persistent revolutionary struggle of the proletariat, rallying the broad mass of the working people around itself.

Having defined imperialism as moribund capitalism, Lenin showed that imperialism was the eve of the proletariat's socialist revolution. The bourgeois system has exhausted its historically progressive role and become a monstrous obstacle on the road to the further development of society. The world capitalist system as a whole is ripe for the socialist revolution.

The law of uneven development
The conditions in which the struggle of the working class for socialism proceeds have changed substantially in the monopoly stage of capitalism. This change is a result of the operation of the law of the uneven development of the capitalist countries in the imperialist period.

Private ownership of the means of production and the anarchy of production prevent an even development of individual enterprises and branches and even of different countries. Some countries outstrip others in their development.

The uneven development of separate countries intensifies sharply in the imperialist period. The unprecedented technological advance has enabled the young countries rapidly to catch up and even outstrip their old competitors. Countries which embarked on the road of capitalist development later than others were able to use the fruits of technological progress, to use up-to-date equipment and machinery and to profit from improved technology. Concurrently, monopoly rule is marked by a tendency towards parasitism, decay and technological stagnation. This explains the rapid development of some countries and the retarded growth of others. The export of capital aggravates this uneven development too.

The division of the world into spheres of influence ruled by the imperialist groups and powers is already complete. There are no "free" territories left. The capitalists divide the world, as Lenin said, "according to capital", "according to power". But the power of individual countries changes with economic and political development.

The changed relation of forces between the powers runs up against the old distribution of colonies and spheres of influence. While imperialism ruled undividedly throughout the world, the struggle for the redivision of the already divided world inevitably led to bloody, devastating wars between imperialist groups.

The uneven political development of the capitalist countries in the imperialist epoch is closely linked with their uneven economic development. A tendency to enhance the reign of reaction can be observed in all capitalist countries in the imperialist period. However, the relation between the class forces and the conditions for the working-class struggle differ from country to country. The political consciousness and revolutionary determination of the proletariat and its relations with the mass of the peasants and other working sections of the population develop differently in different countries.

The unevenness of the economic and political development of the capitalist countries in the imperialist period is responsible for the uneven maturing of the economic and political preconditions for the socialist revolution. A socialist revolution takes place in the countries where the situation particularly favours the victory of the proletariat.

Possibility of socialism triumphing at first in a single country

The period during which imperialism ruled on a world scale has been characterised by Marxism-Leninism as the epoch of imperialism, wars and proletarian revolutions. Creatively developing Marxism, Lenin showed that the revolutionary collapse of capitalism does not proceed simultaneously throughout the world. Because of the uneven economic and political development of capitalism in the imperialist period the socialist revolution is accomplished in different countries at different times.

Socialism triumphs first in a single capitalist country. Gradually other countries fall away from capitalism and embark on the road to socialism. During the imperialist epoch socialist and capitalist countries co-exist. The peaceful coexistence of countries with different social systems is historically inevitable during that epoch.

Lenin's teaching that the socialist revolution can triumph in individual countries has opened up new revolutionary vistas to the proletariat and has given it the courage to storm bourgeois positions in their countries. It became a manual to action in the greatest revolution ever—the Great October Socialist Revolution in Russia. The break-away from capitalism of a number of countries and their first steps along the socialist path after the Second World War are again sure confirmation of Lenin's theory of the socialist revolution.

2. GENERAL CRISIS OF CAPITALISM

Emergence of the general crisis of capitalism

The revolutionary transition from capitalism to socialism is the result of a law-governed social process. The rule of capital could not have been overthrown if the whole course of economic development had not led up to it. No power could destroy capitalism, Lenin said, if it had not been undermined and eroded by history.

The substitution of the outmoded social system by the new and superior system inevitably embraces a lengthy period. This period is one of struggle between the new and the old, the nascent and moribund social orders. It is the period of the general crisis of capitalism. The collapse of capitalism develops during a long period of world history.

The First World War and the Great October Socialist Revolution ushered in the general crisis of capitalism. The socialist revolution in Russia was the first break-through in the imperialist front. It shook the foundation of the world capitalist system and threatened its further existence.

The socialist revolution in Russia, Lenin pointed out, marked the beginning of the world socialist revolution. Further historical development led to the collapse of capitalism in a number of other European and Asian countries and to their embarkation on the socialist road. Socialism transcended the borders of a single country and became a world system. Capitalism was unable to halt this epoch-making process. By now more than one-third of the world population has thrown off the capitalist yoke once and for all and the foundations of bourgeois rule are tottering in the rest of the world.

**The split
of the world into
two systems** Russia's break-away from capitalism meant that the capitalist system was no longer the only world-wide economic system. The undivided rule of the capitalist system in the world was past history. In addition to capitalism a socialist economic system had emerged and begun to grow. The world had been split into two systems.

Socialism and capitalism are not only different but also opposing social systems. The contradiction between the two systems is mankind's main contradiction today.

The struggle between the two systems—moribund capitalism and triumphant socialism—has become the decisive factor in world history. The powerful advance of socialism brings out the disintegration of capitalism in bold relief.

The simultaneous existence of the two systems incurs competition between them. This competition embraces the economy, politics, culture and all other spheres of social life. There is not a single sphere in modern society which is not affected by this great historical competition. The competition of the two social systems constantly demonstrates the supremacy of socialism over capitalism and is a pointer to the main trend of historical development.

**Stages of
the general crisis
of capitalism** The general crisis of capitalism passes through a number of stages in its development.

The first stage embraces the period from the beginning of the general crisis of capitalism to the Second World War.

The second stage was ushered in by the Second World War and by its consequences—the break-away of a large group of European and Asian countries from the capitalist system.

The third stage set in as a result of the enormous growth of the socialist forces and the weakening of the forces of imperialism in the course of the peaceful economic competition. The most crucial single feature of the third stage is that it developed not in connection with world war.

Since the outbreak of the general crisis of capitalism the world political map has radically changed. In 1919 the socialist countries occupied 16 per cent of the world's area and embraced 7.8 per cent of the world's population. In

183

1964 they occupied 26 per cent of that area with 34.6 per cent of the world's population. The big imperialist powers (the USA, Britain, the Federal Republic of Germany, France, Japan, Italy) and their colonies covered 44.5 per cent of the world's area in 1919 and had 48.1 per cent of the world's population. In 1964 the figures were 10.6 per cent and 16.2 per cent respectively. In 1919 all colonies, semi-colonies and dominions covered as much as 77.2 per cent of the world with 69.2 per cent of its population, but only 6.8 per cent and 1.4 per cent respectively in 1964. The colonial and semi-colonial countries who had gained independence since 1919 (excluding the socialist countries) occupied in 1964 56.4 per cent of the world's surface and embraced 42.6 per cent of its population.

The main content of the modern epoch The main content of the modern epoch is the transition from capitalism to socialism and its underlying trend is for the socialist world to expand and for the capitalist world to shrink. The laws of imperialism no longer reign supreme throughout the world. New laws of social development inherent in the socialist system have emerged and consolidated and are exercising an ever greater impact on social development.

Our epoch, the Programme of the Communist Party of the Soviet Union says, whose main content is the transition from capitalism to socialism, is an epoch of struggle between the two opposing social systems, an epoch of socialist and national liberation revolutions, of the breakdown of imperialism and the abolition of the colonial system, an epoch of the transition of more and more peoples to the socialist path, of the triumph of socialism and communism on a world-wide scale.

Thus, the modern epoch of world development is determined by three basic processes.

This is, first, the emergence and the consolidation of the new system in the countries in which the socialist revolution has triumphed;

second, the collapse of colonialism under the impact of the national liberation movement of the peoples oppressed by imperialism;

third, the exacerbation of all internal and external contradictions in the capitalist countries, the maturing of prerequisites for the triumph of the socialist revolution in them.

The highest of these three processes is the growth of the forces of socialism. It exerts a decisive influence on all other processes. The epoch of the general crisis of capitalism is the epoch of the struggle between two systems—the socialist and the capitalist. The forces of socialism are steadily growing. More and more countries are breaking away from capitalism. The relation of forces between imperialism and socialism changes in favour of socialism.

Colonialism collapses because the positions of imperialism in the colonial and dependent countries are undermined, the enslaved peoples of the less developed countries gain independence and expel the imperialists.

The aggravation of the contradictions of imperialism shows that that system has entered the period of decline and destruction. The irreversible process of decay infects the whole body of capitalism: its economic and state system, its politics and ideology.

The increasing internal instability of the capitalist economy can be seen from capitalism's growing inability to use the productive forces of society to the full. It is displayed also by the more and more frequent economic recessions and the symptoms of stagnation discernible in a number of countries, the undercapacity operation of factories and chronical unemployment. The development of state-monopoly capitalism and the growth of militarism have further aggravated the contradictions of imperialism.

As capitalism progressively disintegrates the struggle between labour and capital unavoidably gets hotter. The contradictions between the imperialist powers are also deepening. The bourgeoisie strengthens political reaction all along the line and rejects bourgeois democracy. In some countries it establishes fascist tyrannies.

Emergence of the world socialist system and its transformation into the decisive factor of world development

For close on three decades the Soviet Union built socialism in capitalist encirclement. The rout of the fascist aggressors in the Second World War promoted the break-away of a number of European and Asian countries from the capitalist system.

The socialist revolutions in these countries inflicted another heavy blow on imperialism. The revolutions in a number of European and Asian countries, the Programme of the CPSU says, have been the most important events in world history since October 1917. The triumph of the socialist revolution in these countries made socialism a world system. In our time there are two world systems—the socialist and the capitalist.

International reactionaries resorted to armed intervention against the young Soviet Republic in an attempt to counter the first break-through in the world imperialist front ushered in by the October Revolution in Russia. But imperialism could not resort to this measure after the second break-through effected by the people's democratic revolutions in a number of European and Asian countries.

The reason for this was the existence of a powerful socialist country—the Soviet Union. With all its economic and political might the Soviet Union resolutely supported the young socialist countries that emerged after the Second World War.

The emergence and consolidation of the world socialist system have substantially changed the relation of forces between socialism and capitalism in the world today. Over a thousand million people live under socialism. This is over one-third of the world population.

The world community of socialist countries is a powerful stronghold of the world's progressive forces. Its strength grows every year. No powers in the world can restore capitalism in the countries that have broken away from the capitalist system.

Socialism's development into a world system has convincingly proved capitalism's inevitable doom. A new stage has set in in the struggle between the two social systems, the struggle which is the main feature of the general crisis of capitalism. The main contradiction of the modern epoch—the contradiction between growing socialism and dying capitalism—has reached a higher stage.

Competition between the two systems made massive strides when it became a competition of world systems. The socialist system has proved its superiority over the capitalist system over an entire historical period. The decisive supremacy of the world socialist system over the world capitalist system is becoming apparent.

To an ever greater extent the world socialist system is becoming the decisive factor of social development. The relation of forces between socialism and capitalism continuously changes in favour of socialism, to the detriment of capitalism.

The unparalleled successes of socialism have enabled the Soviet Union to enter a new historical stage of development, the period of building the material and technical basis of communism. The European and Asian socialist countries too have scored enormous successes in their peaceful economic and cultural development. The foundations of socialism are being laid in these countries, while in some of them full-scale socialist construction is already underway. Co-operation between the socialist countries in the economic, political and cultural fields is ever expanding.

All these changes are inseparably interlinked and interdependent. They amount to a single process of steady development and rapid growth of the world socialist system, which progresses confidently towards the decisive victory in its economic competition with capitalism. The world socialist system exercises a growing influence on world social development in the interests of peace, democracy and socialism.

At present it is not imperialism but socialism that determines the main trend of world development. The world socialist system, the forces struggling against imperialism and fighting for the socialist reorganisation of society, determine in our time the main content, main trend and main features of mankind's historical development.

Crisis of colonialism

The crisis of the imperialist colonial system broke out in the first stage of the general crisis of capitalism. This crisis emerged under the direct influence of the October Socialist Revolution in Russia.

The emergence of socialism marked the advent of the era of liberation of the oppressed peoples. The October Revolution weakened world capitalism and inflicted a crushing blow on the imperialist system. It struck a blow at the rear of imperialism and undermined its rule in the colonial world.

Imperialist rule in the colonies, formerly more or less

stable, had come to an end. The struggle of the oppressed peoples against colonialism acquired an unprecedented scale. In many cases this struggle was headed by the working class led by the Communist Party.

Relying on the backing of the Soviet Union some economically underdeveloped countries succeeded in dismissing their imperialist masters and in defending their independence against imperialist encroachments (Afghanistan, Turkey, Iran). Helped by the Soviet people, Mongolia gained independence and embarked on the road of socialist development, bypassing capitalism. The imperialists were still able to maintain their rule in most colonial and dependent countries, yet their savage reprisals were unable to throttle the national liberation movement. The movement began to embrace ever broader masses of the people, who united in the fight for liberation, against imperialism and feudalism. The great sacrifices made in the liberation struggle have not been in vain.

Disintegration of the colonial system   The Second World War exposed the vices of colonialism. The national liberation movement of the oppressed peoples gained impetus during the war years. The rout of the fascist aggressors created favourable conditions for the success of that struggle.

The national liberation movement of the peoples enslaved by the imperialists moved into a new stage. The proletariat and its Communist Parties began to play a greater role. This exerted an enormous influence on the national liberation struggle against imperialism. In some countries a united national democratic front was formed. The working class and the peasantry in the anti-imperialist and anti-feudal struggle strengthened their alliance. The powerful upsurge of the national liberation movement in the colonial and dependent countries led to the disintegration of imperialism's colonial system.

The existence of the socialist countries constrained the aggressive forces of imperialism, and facilitated the struggle of the colonial and semi-colonial countries for the conquest and consolidation of their independence.

More than 50 per cent of the world population broke free of colonial and semi-colonial oppression after the Second World War.

In the new period in world history predicted by Lenin, the peoples who had long been prevented by the colonialists from advancing along the road of progress, began to participate actively in shaping the future of the whole world. As a result of the disintegration of the colonial system of imperialism international affairs are no longer relations between states inhabited predominantly by peoples of the white race, and are now increasingly becoming genuine world relations. The ex-colonial peoples have become makers of a new life, a revolutionary force smashing imperialism.

The disintegration of the colonial system of imperialism takes a variety of forms. Having evicted the imperialists and their henchmen, the Chinese people took the socialist road. This road was taken also by the peoples of the Korean People's Democratic Republic and the Democratic Republic of Vietnam. Some less developed countries, which have thrown off the colonial yoke and gained political independence, have not yet succeeded in breaking away from the world capitalist economy.

At the present stage of the general crisis of capitalism the colonial system of imperialism has disintegrated to an extent that sets the task of abolishing it completely. The colonial system has to all intents and purposes collapsed under the powerful blows of the national liberation movement.

Following the Second World War more than 60 sovereign states rose on the ruins of the colonial empires. Most of them won political independence after 1955. The bulk of the Asian and African peoples have thrown off the colonial yoke.

The triumph of the people's revolution in Cuba was a break-through in the US colonial front in Latin America. The Cuban people, defending their independence, embarked on the road of socialist development. The example of revolutionary Cuba inspires all Latin American peoples in the struggle against the oppression by US monopoly capital, for freedom and independence.

The peoples still languishing under colonialism are waging a stubborn battle against their oppressors. The walls of colonialism's last strongholds are shaking. The sixties of the 20th century will go down in history as the years of the colonial system's final collapse.

Struggle to overcome the aftermaths of colonialism The liquidation of colonialism is a result of the long and stubborn liberation struggle of the peoples enslaved by imperialism. They have always had the support of the socialist countries and of all progressive forces. The conquest of political independence allots to the peoples of the economically less developed countries imposing tasks. To consolidate their political independence they must achieve economic independence from foreign capital. Only this will enable them to do away with their grim heritage.

This heritage includes: extraordinary technological and economic backwardness; outmoded forms of social life which were artificially maintained by the colonialists; an extraordinarily low level of labour productivity and national income; extreme poverty of the population which was doomed to hunger and extinction. So long as the peoples in the less developed countries remain economically dependent on imperialism they will continue to be objects of semi-colonial exploitation.

The peoples who have freed themselves from the colonialist yoke must choose what road of development to embark upon. The capitalist road means deepening social inequality, suffering and privations and perpetual poverty and backwardness. Socialism will boost their economy and culture, giving the people genuine freedom and happiness.

Practice has convinced the peoples of the newly-free countries that the best way to overcome their age-old backwardness and poverty is to embark on the non-capitalist road of development. Only this break-away will rid them of exploitation and improve their conditions. In a number of countries—the UAR, Algeria, Mali, Guinea, the Congo (Brazzaville), Burma—far-reaching social reforms are being introduced to abolish the domination of foreign monopolies, to develop the state sector in the economy and to improve the living conditions of the people.

Neo-colonialism The imperialists with the USA as their ring-leader attempt to prevent the national and social renascence of the Asian, African and Latin American peoples.

Using a blend of violence and deceit the imperialist predators resort to new forms of colonialism. They try to enslave the peoples of the economically less developed countries by drawing them into aggressive military blocs, rendering them "aid" on exorbitant terms. In this way they attempt to cling to their old positions and to seize new ones.

The imperialists use the intricate social and class situation in the newly-free countries, their economic hardships, and the domination of foreign monopolies still persisting in many of them, to gain their ends. The newly-free countries have become an arena of combat between the progressive patriotic forces and reactionary circles, who overtly or covertly form alliances with imperialism. The relation of forces in the world today and the powerful support given to them by the world socialist system enable the ex-colonial peoples to frustrate the plans of the colonial powers.

3. EXACERBATION OF THE CONTRADICTIONS OF WORLD CAPITALISM

Growing instability of the capitalist system The break-away of a number of countries from the capitalist system has greatly increased the breach in the imperialist front and contracted the sphere of capitalist domination. The embarkation of the colonial peoples on the road of independent development has undermined the system of colonial exploitation and brought about a further very substantial limitation of its sphere of activity. All this added to the range and depth of the contradictions inherent in the capitalist system.

Even in the first stage of the general crisis of capitalism the decay and internal instability of capitalism gained momentum.

Imperialism tends to impede the development of society's productive forces. In the first stage, the inability of the bourgeoisie to use productive forces to the full was strikingly reflected in the systematic under-capacity production of factories and mass unemployment. Soaring exploitation of the working masses made effective demand fall increasingly short of commodity supply. Tsarist Russia, until then an object of exploitation, dropped out of the sphere of world capitalism. As a result of all this a substantial part of the production apparatus was doomed to idleness and enterprises began to work below capacity.

In the USA, Britain, Germany, France and other capitalist countries, industry ran during the whole inter-war period at an average of 50 to 66 per cent capacity. In other words, with the same productive apparatus the factories of the capitalist world could have produced from 50 to 100 per cent more goods than they actually did. During economic crises the equipment utilisation rate was even lower.

Chronical mass unemployment was an inevitable consequence of the under-capacity operation of factories. Between 1921 and 1936 the number of fully unemployed averaged 1.7 million people a year in Britain. This means that for 16 years one out of seven workers in Britain was unemployed. Between 1929 and 1933 one out of four workers was unemployed in Germany, while in 1936 every sixth worker was redundant in the USA.

After the Second World War the economic growth rates in the main capitalist countries were higher than they had been in the inter-war period. Yet, the capitalist economy continues to be unstable. In many countries there is growing inflation, booms alternate with depressions, the state debts grow enormously and financial difficulties multiply.

Militarisation of the economy and its consequences The development of state-monopoly capitalism goes hand in hand with an unprecedented growth of militarism.

An ever-growing share of the national income—from one quarter to one-third—is distributed through the state budget. The share of direct and indirect budget expenditure on the arms race is always multiplying.

The dominant monopolies and the imperialist governments carrying out their will attempt to stop the inevitable collapse of the capitalist system by force of arms. Militarism increasingly erodes all aspects of the life of the capitalist countries. In 1949 the USA knocked together the aggressive North Atlantic Treaty Organisation (NATO). During its existence the expenditure on the creation and improvement of that bloc's war machine amounted to over $1,000,000 million. War expenditure swallows the lion's share of the state budget funds. In the USA in the 1938/39 fiscal year direct military expenditure amounted to $1,000 million, reaching $55,000 million in 1964/65. The arms race also involves enormous expenditure on atomic energy research, on military and economic "aid" to other countries, which are accomplices or instruments of the US imperialist aggressive actions. At present more than 75 per cent of the expenditure in the US federal budget is in one way or another channelled towards military needs.

Individual groups of the monopoly bourgeoisie reap superprofits militarising the economy. But this policy tends to drain the economy, to sap the population's financial strength by taxation, inflation and higher living costs. Imperialist military build-up threatens mankind with loss of life and destruction on an unprecedented scale.

Increasingly uneven development of the capitalist countries and changes in the relation of forces within the imperialist camp Immediately after the end of the First World War a bitter struggle broke out between the imperialist powers over the division of the spoils of war. The danger of a new war emerged and began to grow. More and more conflicts and clashes played havoc inside the capitalist camp.

The development of the capitalist countries became ever more uneven and erratic.

The defeat in the war weakened Germany considerably, and this had a telling effect on the country's economy in the early post-war years. But the economic basis of German imperialism had not been shattered. In their blind hatred of the Soviet Union the monopolists of the victor-countries and notably the US finance magnates granted the German trusts huge loans and credits. In less than a decade German industry again took second place in the capitalist world.

The relation of economic forces between the USA and Britain also underwent a substantial change. The war enriched the US monopolies. In 1925 US industry produced as much as Britain, France and Germany put together. In 1929 US industrial output exceeded the 1913 level by 70 per cent, while its British counterpart barely reached the pre-war level.

As a result of the war Britain lost a large part of her capital investments abroad. New York usurped London's place as the main financial centre of the capitalist world.

The Second World War which was an upshot of the uneven development of capitalism further aggravated this unevenness. Three out of the six big imperialist powers—Germany, Japan and Italy—suffered military defeat. France was considerably weakened. Britain suffered heavy losses. The US monopolies used this weakening of their West European competitors to seize the main raw material sources, sales markets and spheres of capital investment.

The economic centre, and with it the political and military centre of imperialism, shifted from Europe to the USA.

The relation of forces between the imperialist powers changed in favour of the USA to the detriment of the European capitalist countries. In 1943 the output of US industry exceeded the 1939 level 2.2 times. In the main West European capitalist countries, which had seriously suffered from the war, industrial output had shrunk considerably towards the end of the war.

As a result the share of the USA in the sum total industrial output of the capitalist world grew considerably over the pre-war level. Later, however, the European capitalist countries not only regained their pre-war level but even topped it. This applied particularly to the defeated countries—West Germany, Japan and Italy. The US share in the capitalist world industrial output fell from 53.9 per cent in 1948 to 44.7 per cent in 1960; in exports, from 33 per cent in 1947 to 17.5 per cent in 1964. As a result the USA was pushed back to approximately the same place it had held among the capitalist countries before the war. In recent years the roles of the various countries underwent a further change. US economic growth rates increased, while those of the West European countries and Japan dropped.

American imperialism continues to be the principal economic, financial and military force in the imperialist camp. At the present time too the US economic potential is much higher than that of any other capitalist country. A maze of acute imperialist contradictions have arisen out of this.

The sharp narrowing of the sphere of imperialist domination has made the market problem extremely acute. Holding back the industrial development of the less developed countries and intensifying the exploitation of the working people, imperialism is unable to solve this problem. The capitalist countries are at each other's throats for sales markets, spheres of profitable capital application and raw material sources. In the attempt to solve the market problem, the capitalist countries set up state monopoly organisations under the "integration" slogan.

The European Economic Community (the Common Market) is such an organisation. This bloc was set up in 1957 by the monopolies of six West European countries—the Federal Republic of Germany, France, Italy, Belgium, the Netherlands and Luxemburg. Lowering and then abolishing customs duties within the Common Market goes hand in hand with the setting up of high customs barriers for trade with countries outside the bloc. The creation of the Common Market brings with it an increase in monopoly profits, greater oppression by the monopolies, a more intense exploitation of the working class, and accelerates the ruination of the bulk of the peasantry. The bosses of the Common Market strive jointly to exploit and fetter the less developed countries, especially the young African states, by neo-colonialist methods.

These closed economic blocs are actually new forms of the redivision of the capitalist world market. They do not remove the contradictions between states; instead they are an arena where the participants fight it out. The growing instability of the capitalist economy and the intensification of the struggle between the monopolists tend to undermine the economic and political blocs of the imperialist states.

Growing exploitation of the working masses

The deepening of the general crisis of capitalism intensifies the exploitation and insecurity of the working masses, notably of the working class. The arms race is financed mainly through the tax burden on the people's shoulders. In all imperialist countries the cost of living is rising, the gap between the nominal and real wage is widening, the real incomes of the mass of the working peasants are dropping. The main contradiction of capitalist society—the antagonism between labour and capital—is growing ever more acute. The real incomes of a considerable portion of the working people remain low even though there is a certain increase in nominal (monetary) wages. The increase in the nominal wages is more often than not eaten up by inflated prices, and the high cost of living. The benefit from the increase in labour productivity resulting from rapid technological progress is reaped wholly by the monopolies. In West Germany, for example, between 1950 and 1960, twenty million factory and office workers collected a total of 46,500 million marks as wages, while the fifty biggest concerns netted a profit of 44,600 million marks. Between 1952 and 1960 the incomes of Japanese capitalists rose by 350 per cent, while total wages rose only by 120 per cent.

During the Second World War scores of millions of people were enlisted in armies or engaged in the production of weapons. Unemployment was temporarily put by the board. In these conditions the defenders of the bourgeois system began to allege that capitalism could provide full employment. But these promises turned out to be nothing but eyewash. According to official statistics there are now no less than 7 million fully unemployed in the capitalist countries. An enormous mass of people who work only part-time should be added to this figure.

Capitalist economy is unable to use the productive forces rationally, and notably society's main productive force—the working class. Unemployment inevitably worsens the conditions of the broad mass of the working people.

Bourgeois and revisionist attempts to dress up modern capitalism as a "welfare state", are at odds with reality. In actual fact, modern capitalism is a world of glaring contrasts. Capitalism dooms millions of working people to insecurity and to all sorts of deprivations.

After a stubborn struggle, the working class of a number of economically advanced capitalist countries has succeeded in wresting certain social insurance benefits from the bourgeoisie. In many countries, however, there is hardly any social insurance, in others, none at all. Thus, for example, the pension age is far above sixty, while the average life-span of workers is below that age. In many countries there is no social insurance for temporary disablement. Apart from this a considerable part of social insurance expenditure is paid for by additional deductions from the workers' wages.

Intensification of the class struggle The working class of the capitalist countries counters worsening conditions by intensifying the class struggle against its exploiters.

The strike movement breaks out on an enormous scale. The number of strikes and strikers shot up after the Second World War. While 80.8 million workers came out in about 177,400 strikes between 1919 and 1939, between 1946 and 1966 there were 222.6 million people in 247,400 strikes. During the past decade the number of strikers doubled and now hits a total of 55 to 57 million a year with many strikes growing into political ones.

The workers are resorting to the time-tested strike in order to defend their economic interests and also to resist the anti-popular policy of the monopolies, rampant reaction and military preparations.

As the class struggle in the capitalist countries intensifies the socio-economic and political demands of the working class assume a wider scope. In a number of countries the working class demands ever more insistently that it be allowed to participate in the control over the activities of enterprises, that the key branches of economy be nationalised and the omnipotence of the monopolies restricted. The attack launched by the working class and the people in general on imperialist aggression, the threat of war posed by imperialist ventures, is drawing more and more support. The bourgeoisie attempts to counter this struggle by applying more and more cruel repressions. However, the organisation and cohesion of the working masses grows in spite of them.

The anti-popular omnipotence of monopolies is becoming more and more apparent. The development of capitalism and the growing proletarianisation of the working masses are concurrent processes. The mass of peasants and urban small producers are faced with the inexorable threat of ruination and pauperism. Formerly independent small industrial and trading enterprises become fully dependent on the monopolies. The monopolies' grip is becoming more and more difficult to bear by all sections of the people. The working masses are rallying around the working class. Overcoming the resistance of the monopolies, waging difficult class battles, the proletariat wins over the bulk of the peasants and white-collar workers. The consolidation of the masses promotes their struggle for the revolutionary transformation of society along socialist lines.

In the modern epoch, when the positions of imperialism have weakened and the relation of forces between socialism and capitalism in the world is constantly changing in favour of socialism and to the detriment of capitalism, the significance of the struggle for democracy and against reaction has grown enormously. In the new historical conditions the struggle for democracy is an integral part of the struggle for socialism, and does not stave off the socialist revolution but draws it nearer. In many bourgeois countries the working class is able to ensure that measures be carried out which transcend ordinary reforms and are therefore crucial for the working class and for its further struggle for socialism even before capitalism has been overthrown.

Fighting for democracy, against the omnipotence of monopolies the working class masses all progressive, democratic forces in a powerful anti-monopoly front. In the interests of the majority of the people the working class fights against the preparations for a new world war, local wars and the onslaught of fascist reaction and upholds the use of the economy for peaceful purposes, for a nationwide programme of peace, national independence, democratic rights and the raising of people's living standard. The working class stands for extensive nationalisation in the people's interests and for control to be exercised by parliament, the trade unions and other democratic and representative bodies over nationalised branches and the whole economic activity of the state.

Capitalism—a historically doomed system

Thus, the general crisis of capitalism deepens as a result of the growth of the forces of socialism, the disintegration of the colonial system and the aggravation of the internal social contradictions of bourgeois society.

The capitalist economy is growing increasingly unstable.

The contradictions of capitalism accumulate and set the stage for new upheavals. The conflict between society's productive forces striving for progress and capitalist relations of production rages and heralds the historical doom of the outmoded bourgeois system.

The aggressive forces of imperialism look for a way out by preparing for a new world war. The main source of war danger is the aggressive course steered by US ruling circles conspiring for the world domination of the American monopolies.

This does not mean, however, that new war is inevitable. Imperialism no longer holds sway over the majority of mankind. The sphere of its domination is steadily shrinking. The relation of forces between the two systems—the socialist and the capitalist—is such that capitalism can no longer count on gaining the upper hand over socialism. In a number of key branches of science and technology socialism has already outstripped capitalism, giving the peace-loving peoples powerful material means with which to curb imperialist aggression.

The peaceful policy of the Soviet Union and other socialist countries has the unanimous support of the vast majority of mankind. The consolidation of all forces fighting for peace is able to bridle the aggressive circles planning a new war. The forces of peace with the socialist countries as their main stronghold have strength enough to force the imperialists to scrap their war plans and to make them adopt a policy of peaceful coexistence between the two systems.

Capitalism has become a monstrous obstacle to human development. Ours is an age of rocketing productive forces and the unprecedented development of science and technology. And if it has not yet put an end to the poverty of hundreds of millions of people nor created an abundance of material and spiritual wealth for the whole population of our planet, capitalism is to blame. The Programme of the CPSU points out that "the growing conflict between productive forces and production relations demands imperatively that mankind should break the decayed capitalist shell, release the powerful productive forces created by man and use them for the good of society as a whole".

This task is being solved by the socialist revolution.

1. Why is imperialism the final stage of capitalism?
2. What is the essence of state-monopoly capitalism and what is its role?
3. What are the distinctive features of the modern stage of the general crisis of capitalism?
4. How is the deepening of the contradictions of world capitalism manifested?

SOCIALISM AND COMMUNISM

Chapter IX

THE PERIOD OF TRANSITION FROM CAPITALISM TO SOCIALISM

1. THE NEED FOR A TRANSITION PERIOD

Specifics of the emergence of the socialist mode of production

It is said that capitalism emerges, whereas socialism is built. This is not a play of words, it is a plain fact.

In the preceding chapters we have seen how capitalism emerged. The first large capitalist enterprises, the manufactories, were set up in feudal times. Manufactories were built to make profits. Their owners did not even think of replacing the existing system by a new, a different one. This shows that capitalism emerges spontaneously, that it is not set up according to a conscious plan. Slavery and feudalism, the exploiting systems preceding capitalism, also emerged spontaneously.

The socialist mode of production is born in quite a different way. The working class aims at replacing capitalism by socialism and communism. It realises this by the socialist revolution and the building of a new society.

The socialist revolution is the most radical revolutionary upheaval in the history of mankind. It differs fundamentally from all other revolutions.

All previous revolutions replaced one form of private ownership of the means of production by another form of such ownership. The socialist revolution abolishes private ownership of the means of production and makes them socialist property.

All previous revolutions substituted one form of exploitation for another. The socialist revolution abolishes all exploitation of man by man. The emancipation of labour from the exploiters' yoke, the destruction of the economic slavery of the working masses, puts an end to the exploiting classes and to their parasitism and to contempt for labour and false moral values.

No preceding revolution abolished the anarchy of social production. Only socialism introduces a planned organisation of social production. The national economy based on public ownership develops according to plan.

There can be no socialism while the bourgeoisie controls the state. This is because the means of production belong to the capitalists, while under socialism there must be public ownership of these means. The building of socialism begins only after state power passes from the hands of the bourgeoisie into those of the working class.

The socialist revolution effects this transition. Having seized state power, the working class takes the means of production from the bourgeoisie and makes them public property. Only then are capitalist relations of production replaced by socialist relations of production.

It is therefore clear, that unlike capitalism and all the preceding forms of society, socialism cannot emerge spontaneously. It is set up by the conscious action of the popular masses, headed by the working class. For this reason the building of socialism can begin only after state power has passed from the bourgeoisie to the worknig class, which rallies the broadest sections of the working people around itself.

Role of the proletarian dictatorship in the creation of a socialist economy The socialist transformation of society requires a revolutionary transition period. In different countries this period may have specific features of its own and may vary in duration. But always and everywhere the transition period begins with the triumph of the socialist revolution.

The socialist revolution may take a variety of forms. In some conditions it takes the form of an armed uprising, in others it may win by peaceful means. But in all events the socialist revolution invariably leads to a transfer of the state power from the hands of the bourgeois minority to those of the working class, which is leading the broad masses, the bulk of the population.

"Between capitalist and communist society," Marx said,

"lies the period of the revolutionary transformation of the one into the other. There corresponds to this also a political transition period in which the state can be nothing but *the revolutionary dictatorship of the proletariat.*"

Let us now establish why the state power must be held by the working class during the transition period. The working class is the only class in bourgeois society that is not connected with the private ownership of the means of production in any of its forms. Under capitalism the proletariat is deprived of that ownership. It is therefore able to head the transition from capitalism to socialism, a transition that brings about a complete break-away from private ownership and its replacement by public ownership. The working class is schooled by labour and struggle that tempers, consolidates and organises it. Marxism-Leninism, the proletariat's world outlook, is the most advanced scientific theory in that it discloses the laws of social development. The socialist transformation of society cannot be achieved without dictatorship of the working class. This does not mean, however, that the building of socialism is only the working class's affair.

In the course of the socialist reorganisation of society the working people as a whole realise that their vital interests coincide with those of the working class. This is instrumental in creating an invincible alliance between the working class and the non-proletarian working masses, first and foremost the peasantry, in the interests of the building of socialism and its further development towards communism. The alliance of the workers and peasants is the supreme principle of proletarian dictatorship. This alliance, in which the leadership belongs to the working class, was an essential condition for socialism in our country to be built. The experience of all socialist revolutions shows that in every country that has broken away from capitalism and embarked on the socialist road of development, the alliance between the working class and the peasantry has been an essential element in the successful struggle for socialism. This is a special sort of alliance for it aims not at maintaining class distinctions but eliminating them.

The dictatorship of the proletariat, the Programme of the CPSU says, is a dictatorship of the vast majority over the minority; it is directed against the exploiters, the oppression of peoples and nations and at the abolition of all exploitation of man by man. The proletarian dictatorship expresses not only the interests of the working class but also those of all working people; it is guided primarily not by violence, but by creation, building a new, socialist society and defending its achievements against the enemies of socialism.

The dictatorship of the working class, led by the Marxist-Leninist party, heads the working masses and organises them to battle against the forces and traditions of the old society. Crushing the resistance of exploiters, defending the country against hostile action from outside, the proletarian dictatorship organises and heads the building of a new, socialist economy. In the course of this economic construction the old bourgeois relations of production are destroyed and new, socialist relations of production are created. The new productive forces needed for building and developing the socialist mode of production are created in the process of this construction.

The Great October Socialist Revolution was mankind's first step along the formerly unexplored road to socialism. The Soviet people were assigned the task of blazing the trail to socialism. Soviet power was the first form of state power under the triumphant dictatorship of the working class evolved by history.

After the Soviet Union had smashed fascism in the Second World War, people's democratic revolutions, which paved the way for socialism, triumphed in a large group of European and Asian countries.

Maintaining that all peoples would inevitably approach socialism, Lenin correctly foresaw that the transition to socialism would differ from country to country, would be distinguished by certain specific features and that different forms of proletarian dictatorship would evolve.

In addition to the Soviet form of the reorganisation of society along socialist lines there is now another form—people's democracy—which has been comprehensively tested by practice and has proved its worth. This form of political organisation is a development of the socialist revolution in modern historical conditions, which are characterised by a weakening of imperialism and a change in the relation of forces in favour of socialism. It is also a reflection of the historically evolved conditions in definite countries.

The leading role of the Communist Party in socialist construction

The proletarian dictatorship is the main condition for the building of socialism, while the leading role of the Communist Party is an earnest of its success.

The Communist Party is the vanguard of the working class and of all the working people armed with Marxist-Leninist theory. The leadership of the Communist Party guarantees that the proletarian dictatorship follows a correct, scientifically-based course in the solution of the complex tasks of socialist construction both in the transition period and also during the subsequent development of socialist society along the road of communism.

Consistently conducting a class-oriented, proletarian policy, the Communst Party is closely linked with the non-Party popular masses. The leadership of the Communist Party ensures that the broad mass of the working people actively participate in the organisation of socialist economy.

The strength of the Communist Party lies in its cohesion and in its devotion to the cause of the working class, the cause of socialism. The leadership by the Communist Party is essential to ensure a unity of will and action in the struggle against the enemies of socialism and in the building of socialist society.

The experience of socialist construction in the Soviet Union and other countries has fully endorsed the Marxist-Leninist teaching on the decisive role of the Communist Party in the building and development of socialist society. Events have shown that only a party faithful to the revolutionary ideas of Marxism-Leninsm is able to organise the whole people and lead them onwards to the victory of socialism.

Socio-economic sectors and classes during the transition period

Taking up the socialist transformation of society the dictatorship of the working class first and foremost socialises the basic means of production, belonging to the capitalists and landowners. Taking over large-scale industry and transport, the banks and foreign trade it assumes command of the key positions in the economy. This inaugurates the socialist sector which assumes the leading position in the economy of the transition period. However, for some time it is not the only sector and not even the predominant one.

In the first years of Soviet power, Lenin pointed out, there were five different socio-economic sectors in Soviet economy:

1) the patriarchal peasant economy;
2) small-scale commodity production;
3) private capitalism;
4) state capitalism;
5) socialism.

The patriarchal peasant economy, the small peasant households, conducted mainly a natural economy, producing their products mainly for personal consumption.

Small-scale commodity production took in mainly the households of the middle peasants. They produced the bulk of the marketable grain. This sector included also self-employed artisans who did not employ wage labour.

Private capitalism was represented by the most numerous of the exploiting classes, by the rich peasants, the kulaks, and by the owners of small industrial enterprises, which employed hired labour, and by the merchants.

State capitalism existed mainly in the form of concessions granted to foreign capitalists and of enterprises, mines, forest lots and land leased to foreigners. State capitalism did not take root in the Soviet Union and played only a minor role in the economy.

The socialist sector was represented by the factories, transport facilities, means of communications, banks that had passed into the hands of the state and state farms. In agriculture there were also collective farms. For a number of years, however, they were only small islands in the sea of individual peasant farms.

In the other European and Asian socialist countries the economy of the transition period also has a multi-sectoral nature. The number of sectors and the importance of each depend on the level of economic development and on the historically-matured features in the relevant country.

The main forms of social economy in the transition period are: socialism, small commodity production and capitalism. To them correspond the main three class forces, namely, the working class, the peasantry and the bourgeoisie. Small commodity production is a hotbed of capitalism and constantly evolves capitalist elements.

During the transition period a struggle takes place between the working class and the bourgeoisie. The working class strives to liberate the mass of the peasants from the influence of the bourgeoisie. It forms a firm, inviolable alliance with the peasantry in the struggle against the bourgeoisie and capitalism and for the building of socialist society.

The transition period is a period of struggle between vanquished, but as yet not destroyed capitalism and nascent, but at first still weak, socialism. This is a life and death struggle, for it decides "who will beat whom".

The historical experience of the Soviet Union and of other socialist countries shows that this struggle assumes different forms. However, the development of the multisectoral economy always ends in the victory of socialism in all economic branches.

Main tasks of the transition period After the victory of the revolution and the take-over of the commanding heights, the socialist state is faced by enormous tasks. Its chief problem is the transformation of the multi-sectoral economy of the transition period into the socialist system of economy.

The economic policy the proletarian dictatorship pursues serves to solve this task. It embraces the sum total of economic measures taken by the socialist state, which is guided in its action by the economic laws of socialism.

The deep scientific basis of the policies of the proletarian dictatorship for the whole period of the transition from capitalism to socialism was compiled by Lenin. Lenin's plan for the building of socialist society embraces three basic links. These are the industrialisation of the country, the co-operation of farming and the cultural revolution. These transformations create the material and technical basis of socialism and ensure the complete victory of socialist production relations in the whole economy.

These main tasks in the transitional period face all countries embarking on the road to socialism. The magnitude of each task and the concrete methods for its implementation depend on historical features and on the level of each country's development.

2. LENIN'S PLAN FOR THE BUILDING OF SOCIALISM AND ITS IMPLEMENTATION

Socialist industrialisation in the USSR On the eve of the October Revolution Lenin aimed at first achieving political power and then, relying on it, overtaking and outstripping the advanced capitalist countries economically. Later, under Soviet power, this task came to be known as the main economic task of the USSR.

To build socialism in the USSR it was essential first to do away with its technical and economic backwardness and to exceed the development of productive forces in the capitalist countries. A powerful socialist industry had therefore to be set up and the country to be industrialised on socialist lines. Lenin emphasised that only a large-scale machine industry, able also to reorganise agriculture, could become the material basis of socialism.

The development of the productive forces involves the expansion of the productive apparatus of all branches of the national economy, its improvement through the introduction of new up-to-date machinery. Up-to-date machines, lathes, tools, instruments are manufactured by the engineering industry. The development of engineering is therefore the decisive condition for the technical re-equipment of all the branches of the economy—of industry, agriculture and transport. For this reason engineering is justly considered the backbone of industrialisation.

There must be metal, fuel, electric power, chemical products and building materials to produce machinery and equipment. This makes metallurgy, fuel extraction (coal, oil and gas), the chemical, power and building materials (cement, reinforced concrete, etc.) industries crucial. All these branches plus engineering comprise heavy industry. The growth of heavy industry serves as a basis for the successful development of agriculture, the steady increase in the output of consumer goods and the systematic rise in living standards.

Industrialisation is essential to ensure the economic independence of a country and to strengthen its defence potential. The growth of large-scale industry is vital for the consolidation of the dictatorship of the working class, is an earnest of its triumph over capitalist elements, is necessary to strengthen the working class's leadership of the millions of peasants.

The course steered towards the socialist industrialisation of the country was the basis of the general line taken by the Communist Party, aimed at building socialist society in the USSR.

The domestic and international situation made it essential to carry out the socialist industrialisation of the USSR as quickly as possible. The then prevailing petty peasant economy in the country was a basis more suitable for capitalism than for communism. The alternative was either to put the whole economy including agriculture on a basis of advanced technology and to introduce large-scale machine production, or to return to capitalism. Not only the triumph of socialism in the USSR but also the further independence of the country depended on the high rate of industrialisation.

The industrialisation of an enormous country in an historically short period involved many difficulties. The building of large modern enterprises generally takes several years. During that time large funds have to be invested and it is only later that the new enterprises justify themselves when they become operational. Industrialisation therefore makes it necessary to withdraw large material resources from the national economy for a lengthy period.

The industrialisation of the USSR was carried out without any assistance from abroad, it had to rely exclusively on domestic savings and accumulations. Thanks to the Soviet system the country did not have to pay interest on loans to foreign and domestic usurers, the fruits of the labour of workers and peasants were not wasted on capitalists, landowners, exploiter states, and material values were not destroyed by anarchy of production and crises. The Soviet Government initiated a consistent struggle for a rise in labour productivity and a lowering of costs, the observance of a strict regime of economy in expenditure and a drive for labour discipline. The funds thus accumulated were used by the Soviet Government for the industrialisation of the country.

The Soviet Union succeeded in building a large-scale machine industry even as a result of the first three five-year plans (1929-41). The Soviet Union attained the first place in Europe and the second in the world (after the USA) in industrial output. The country had become economically independent of the capitalist countries. The defence potential of the Soviet Union had grown immeasurably. The industrialisation of the USSR was a major feat of the working class and the whole people, who spared neither efforts nor means and consciously made sacrifices to pull the country out of its backwardness.

Socialist reorganisation of agriculture—the most difficult task after the working class seizes political power The socialist reorganisation of agriculture must be achieved before socialist society can be built. After the seizure of power the working class is inevitably faced with the task of solving the age-old peasant question. The peasantry is not homogeneous. At one end of the stick there are the poor peasants, the natural allies of the working class, on the other, the rural bourgeoisie, the kulaks. Middle peasants make up the bulk of the peasantry.

Lenin maintained that the policy concerning the middle peasants to be conducted by the working class after smashing the bourgeoisie should distinguish between the two motives in the mind of the peasant who is a worker and at the same time a proprietor of the land he tills. Lenin wrote that this distinction was the very essence of socialism.

The task of the working class is to draw the mass of the working peasantry into socialist construction by transforming small individual peasant farms into large-scale collective socialist enterprises. Only through an amalgamation of small individual farms into large collective farms is it possible to extract the roots of capitalism which continue to exist while there is small-scale production. For the bulk of the peasants only this is able to open up the road that is to lead them out of poverty and a miserable existence to highly productive labour and a prosperous and cultural life.

The socialist transformation of small scattered peasant farming is the most difficult task of the socialist revolution after the seizure of power by the working class. The fate of socialism in the USSR hinged largely on the solution of this vital question. The solution of this task is equally important to all other countries building socialism.

The socialist transformation of agriculture is being carried out as planned by Lenin. Lenin's co-operative plan is modelled on the following lines: the socialist state sets up a powerful industry which supplies agriculture with modern machinery. Gradually the peasants are instructed in the habits of collective labour—first through the organisation of the simplest forms of supply and marketing co-operatives. After all the necessary conditions have been prepared a transition is made from scattered individual farming to large socialist producer co-operatives—collective farms. The main condition for this transition is the leadership of the working class and the development of large-scale socialist industry able to re-equip agriculture technically.

The socialist state organises large socialist farming enterprises. It sets up state agricultural enterprises—in the USSR these are state farms, in other socialist countries—government farms, people's estates. The state also helps to set up co-operative enterprises in agriculture: in the USSR these are collective farms, in other socialist countries producer co-operatives of various types. The socialist state gives them every possible material assistance. By example the peasant masses are convinced of the advantages of large-scale socialist production.

Lenin wrote that the transfer of the peasants from individual to collective farming should be voluntary, that they should assure themselves in practice of the advantages collective farming has over individual farming. The principle of voluntariness rejects all coercion with respect to the working peasantry and is one of the highest principles of transition to collective farming. The leading and organisational role of the Communist Party and the socialist state combined with strict observance of the principle of voluntariness in uniting the peasants in collective farms is an earnest of success of the socialist reorganisation of agriculture. Lenin's co-operative plan is a genuine solution of the age-old peasant question.

In the Soviet Union the first major successes of socialist industrialisation cleared the path for the transition to large-scale agricultural production. The countryside began to receive new equipment, including tractors, complex farming machinery, etc. A network of state farms and machine-and-tractor stations was organised. The state farms convincingly proved the advantages of large-scale mechanised production in agriculture. The state-owned machine-and-tractor stations were an important means of collectivising agriculture and assisting the collective farms.

Under the leadership of the Communist Party and with the all-out assistance of the working class, Soviet peasantry embarked on the road to socialism. Millions of small peasant farms united voluntarily in collective farms.

The collectivisation of agriculture freed the countryside once and for all from kulak hegemony, class stratification, ruination and destitution. The division into poor and middle peasants disappeared in the collective farms. The countryside stopped supplying the town with hundreds of thousands of unfortunate people in search of work. This blocked one of the main channels swelling unemployment which by 1931 had been wiped out in the USSR.

The socialist reorganisation of the countryside makes the social form of agriculture identical with that of industry.

One of the features of socialist agriculture is that it uses scientific achievements in the interests of the masses. The laws of agricultural science are followed more closely, correct crop rotation is introduced, the quality of seed and animal strains is improved. The greater mechanisation of agricultural work leads to the emergence of professions formerly unknown in the countryside, for example, of tractor and combine operators, mechanics and drivers, agronomists and animal specialists.

With the triumph of socialist production relations in the countryside and with the progress in the technical re-equipment of crop and animal farming, and finally with the electrification of the countryside, agricultural labour draws closer to industrial labour. The farm products—wheat and cotton, milk and meat—embody not only the labour of the collective farmers but also the labour of workers—tractor-builders, oilmen, chemists and railway-workers.

The victory of socialism in the countryside tends to eliminate the age-old distinction between town and country and creates conditions for the further rapprochement of industry and agriculture.

The cultural revolution

The socialist transformation of society presupposes not only the creation of large-scale machine industry and large-scale socialist production in agriculture but also a deep revolution in culture.

The building of socialism requires that there be a cultural surge forward among the broad masses of the population. Large-scale socialist production, which is using the latest achievement of science and engineering, must have skilled workers, engineers and technicians. The rapid development of industry and agriculture and constant technical progress in all branches of the economy are inconceivable without a high level of scientific development.

The cultural revolution is instrumental in expanding the socialist economy and is economically crucial because it changes people, the main productive force of society.

The cultural revolution means first and foremost the rapid eradication of ignorance, the legacy of capitalism. In a short time the general educational level of the population soars. Compulsory universal education is introduced, the level depending on the concrete conditions in each country. Closer links are established between school and everyday life, practice and production.

The cultural revolution also means that the most favourable opportunities are created for the political, technical and cultural education of the working masses. Millions of workers and peasants systematically improve their knowledge, both general and special. This is achieved by the organisation of a wide network of extra-mural courses, schools for grown-ups, all sorts of cultural and educational institutions—lecture centres, libraries and clubs.

Last but not least, the cultural revolution is responsible for the rapid growth of higher and secondary special education. The new intelligentsia, evolving from the working people, is closely linked with the mass of the workers and peasants and devotedly serves the cause of socialism.

The implementation of the cultural revolution, the rise in the general educational, cultural and technical level of the people creates favourable conditions for drawing all the working people into active participation in the management of social life. The activity of the working class, peasantry and intelligentsia develops and they begin to participate more widely in the management of enterprises, institutions and the economy as a whole.

The socialist transformation of society firmly establishes the dominance of the only scientific and advanced philosophy—Marxism-Leninism. This ideology is incompatible with superstition and all sorts of obscurantism. Marxist-Leninist ideology is the key to massive, rapid scientific achievement, the revelation of all the secrets of nature and the successful harnessing of its inexhaustible forces.

Socialism makes science flourish and allots it a greater role in social life. Socialist culture, genuinely popular in character, flourishes vigorously. All the peoples of the socialist countries participate in the development of the new culture national in form and socialist in content.

As a result of the cultural revolution millions of people who had formerly been barred from education became active participants in cultural development. All the sources of culture and science are accessible to the working masses. Socialism gives the working masses material security, ensures a steady growth of their living standard and shorter working hours. All this opens up unprecedented possibilities for the all-round development of society's spiritual life, the flourishing of science, technology, the arts, and the efflorescence of the people's talents and abilities.

Thus, the socialist transformation of society tends to eliminate the distinction between physical and mental labour. Socialism creates the conditions that are needed steadily to diminish the distinctions between them.

General laws and features of the building of socialist economy in different countries

The experience of the Soviet Union and other socialist countries demonstrates that the building of socialist economy is based on general regularities which apply in all countries. First among them is the need for a socialist revolution in one form or another. It leads to the transition of state power into the hands of the working class, which leads the mass of the people, the bulk of the population. The socialist state is the main instrument for the socialist transformation of society and for the building of socialist economy. It organises and consolidates the masses, effects the planned leadership of economic and cultural development and safeguards the people's revolutionary gains. In the socialist state the working class fulfils its historical mission of building the new society in close alliance with the non-proletarian working masses, notably with the peasantry.

The building of socialist economy presupposes the implementation of fundamental socio-economic reforms, the nationalisation of the basic means of production, the abolition of all exploitation, the replacement of anarchic production for the sake of capitalist profits by planned production designed to satisfy the needs of society and of its every member. The transition from capitalism to socialism ensures a rapid development of the productive forces and higher economic growth rates as compared with the country's capitalist past.

In applying the general principles of the building of socialist economy the Marxist-Leninist parties take into account the concrete features prevailing in each country. The conditions depending on the country's historical development and its political and economic structure, the class composition of the population and the relation of the class forces—all this determines the forms taken by the socialist revolution, the dictatorship of the proletariat, the methods by which the main socialist reforms are carried out. Natural conditions also exercise an influence on the nature and direction of the development of the productive forces, promote the establishment and growth of definite branches of production.

3. TRIUMPH OF SOCIALISM IN THE USSR

Undivided rule of the socialist system of economy The socialist industrialisation, the collectivisation of farming and the cultural revolution bring about radical changes in the multi-sectoral economy of the transition period and the establishment of socialist economy.

The rapid growth of the productive forces leads to the creation of the material and technical basis of socialism and simultaneously the production relations undergo fundamental changes. The socialist sector grows bigger and stronger. The small commodity sector is reorganised along socialist lines. Capitalist elements are systematically ousted and then eliminated completely. These processes lead to the complete victory of socialism in the whole economy and to the undivided rule of the socialist system in all the economic spheres.

The building of socialist society eliminates the dominance of private property once and for all, does away with this source splitting society into hostile classes. Socialist ownership of the means of production becomes the unshakeable economic basis of society.

Socialism solves the greatest social problem—it does away with the exploiting classes and with the causes giving rise to exploitation of man by man. The enemies of the working class slander the socialist revolution alleging that it destroys the non-working classes physically. In actual fact the socialist reorganisation of society eliminates the exploiting classes only in the economic sense for it destroys the conditions under which some classes are able to live at the expense of other classes. The bulk of the people who formerly belonged to the non-working classes join in the labour activities of society.

The building up of socialism signifies the establishment of the broadest democracy. Socialist democracy includes political freedoms and social rights: the freedom of speech and of the press, the right of assembly, to elect and be elected, the right to work, rest and leisure, education, social security in old age and in the event of illness and incapacity. Socialism means equal rights for all citizens, irrespective of race or nationality, equal rights for women and men in all spheres of state, economic and cultural life. As distinct from bourgeois democracy, socialist democracy not only declares the rights of the people but also ensures the conditions for their implementation.

Socialist society ensures the genuine freedom of the individual. The highest manifestation of this freedom is the liberation of man from exploitation, the establishment of social justice.

Socialist society was built for the first time in history in the Soviet Union. The multi-sectoral economy of the transition period gave way to socialist economy. The question of "who will beat whom" had been solved in favour of socialism. Having completed the building of socialism the Soviet Union began to develop further in the direction of communism.

In the Soviet Union the tasks of the transition period from capitalism to socialism were fulfilled within approximately two decades. It takes the People's Democracies which rely on the help from the Soviet Union and on the mutual assistance within the world socialist system even less time to implement these tasks.

Radical changes in the class structure of society The victory of socialism leads to radical changes in the class structure of society. As a result of the elimination of the exploiting classes socialist society consists of two friendly classes—the working class and the peasantry. The intelligentsia works hand in hand with the working class and the peasantry in socialist society. At the same time the character of the working class, peasantry and intelligentsia has changed profoundly.

Under socialism the working class is no longer deprived of the means of production. This class plays the leading role in society. The life and labour of the peasants is no longer based on petty individual farming and backward equipment but on collective labour, collective ownership of the means of production and on up-to-date equipment.

The fundamental distinction between the working class and the peasantry has been eliminated since the socialist economy has become the source of subsistence for both classes. The common nature of the two forms of socialist property draws the working class and the collective farmers together, strengthens their alliance and makes their friendship invincible.

There has also been a fundamental change in the composition of the intelligentsia and in the nature of its activities. Its vast majority consists of people of working-class or peasant origin. The socialist intelligentsia is closely linked with the people and serves the cause of socialism. Together with the workers and peasants it actively participates in the building of socialism and communism.

The distinctions between the working class and the peasantry and also those between these two classes and the intelligentsia fade in socialist society. Their working and living conditions gradually begin to resemble each other. The community of fundamental interests has established an invincible socio-political and ideological unity of the people.

The triumph of socialism puts an end to all the social oppression and enslavement there is under capitalism including, of course, national oppression and the inequality of women.

Socialism not only proclaims the equality of nations but also creates the economic conditions to ensure this equality. All racial and national discrimination has been abolished in socialist society. The backward borderlands, inhabited by the formerly oppressed nations, reach within a short time the economic level of the more advanced parts of the country.

Socialism frees women of all limitations in their rights and offers them equal opportunities with men. Women, who under capitalism are paid less than men, receive the same wages as men under socialism.

The complete and final victory of socialism in the USSR Even during the first stages of socialist construction Lenin said that the Soviet country had everything required for building a complete socialist society. The Communist Party, implementing Lenin's plan of socialist construction, led the Soviet people onto socialism's complete victory.

But, having achieved the full victory of socialism, the Soviet people could not consider this victory complete until the Soviet Union remained the only socialist country in the world. It was encircled by capitalist countries which were superior to it economically and militarily. Under these conditions the Soviet people could not consider that they were fully safeguarded against military intervention and a forceful restoration of capitalism by world imperialism.

Now the world situation has changed radically. There is now a steadily growing world socialist system. Now we no longer speak about the capitalist encirclement of our country. Of course, like any other socialist country, the Soviet Union is not guaranteed against the possibility of aggression from the imperialist countries. But the relation of the forces in the world today is such that the Soviet Union, and all socialist countries are able to repulse the attack of any enemy. There are no forces in the world that could restore capitalism in our country or could crush the community of socialist countries.

This means that socialism has triumphed fully and irrevocably.

The stability of the socialist achievements within the world socialist system

While the Soviet Union was the only socialist country in the world there was only one country with a socialist economy, but the spread of socialism beyond the limits of the Soviet Union and the establishment of socialist economy in several countries made it a world system. The formation of the world socialist system is the main result of society's progressive development in the present epoch.

Within the framework of the world socialist system the socio-economic possibilities for a restitution of capitalism have been abolished not only in the Soviet Union but also in other socialist countries. In the People's Democracies firm foundations have been laid for the building of socialist society, and most of them are completing the building of these foundations. In all socialist countries far-reaching socio-economic reforms have been carried out which have brought profound changes in the class structure of society. The bulk of the population has firmly placed its trust in the socialist system.

As regards the danger of an attack from without, the existence of the world socialist community of countries, their unity and solidarity are a reliable defence against any imperialist aggression. Owing to the change in the relation of forces between socialism and capitalism in favour of socialism and to the detriment of capitalism, all aggressive ventures of imperialism with respect to any country of the world socialist system must end in failure.

1. Why is a transition period from capitalism to socialism necessary?
2. What are the main forms of social economy in the transition period?
3. What is the role of the proletarian dictatorship in the building of socialist society?
4. What is the essence of Lenin's plan for the building of socialism and how is it implemented in the Soviet Union?

Chapter X

SOCIALIST ECONOMIC SYSTEM

1. PUBLIC OWNERSHIP OF THE MEANS OF PRODUCTION. THE NATURE OF LABOUR UNDER SOCIALISM

Dominance of public, socialist property Every mode of production has a specific form of ownership of the means of production. Public ownership of the means of production rules undividedly under socialism.

The public ownership of the means of production becomes dominant as a result of the abolition of the private ownership of the means of production. The socialist revolution adopts a different approach to two types of private property: the private property of the capitalists and landowners, which serves as a basis for the exploitation of the proletariat and the peasantry and that of small producers, notably of the peasants, which serves as the basis of small commodity production and is based on their personal labour. Therefore, the public ownership of the means of production emerges in two different ways.

The socialist state carries out the expropriation of the expropriators forecast by the founders of scientific communism. It confiscates the land of the landowners, the factories, railways and banks of the capitalists and makes them national wealth. Depending on the concrete conditions in each individual country in which the revolution proceeds, the socialist state either confiscates the property of the capitalists and landowners without compensation or pays them some sort of compensation. This is generally carried out in a comparatively short time.

The socialist state adopts quite a different approach with respect to the property of the small farmers—it transforms scattered small-scale production in agriculture into aggregated large-scale socialist production. The socialist property of producer collectives, collective farms, forms through the voluntary union of peasant farms and the socialisation of their means of production. The carrying out of this task takes a longer time.

Two forms of public, socialist property

As a result of the two ways in which socialist property emerges, there are two forms of this property in socialist society.

This is, first and foremost, state property, belonging to the people as a whole, and secondly, co-operative and collective farm property. According to the Constitution in the Soviet Union state property, i.e., the property of the whole people, comprises the land and all the wealth therein, the water, forests, factories, mines, railway, water and air transport, banks, communications, state farms, public services and the main housing facilities in towns and industrial centres. Co-operative and collective farm property includes commonly-owned enterprises in collective farms and co-operative organisations with their live and dead stock, the output of collective farms and co-operative organisations and also their public buildings.

Both forms are variants of public, socialist property. The differences between them are determined by the difference in the paths they travelled toward their formation, by the specific way in which the workers and the collective farmers advance toward socialism and communism.

State property is the property of the whole people as represented by the socialist state. Co-operative and collective farm property is the property of groups of working people. In state enterprises all the means of production are socialised. In collective farms—which are artels as regards their organisational form—only the main, decisive means of production are socialised: the joint production is conducted on land which is owned by the state and is given to the collective farmers for use in perpetuity. Production is carried on with tractors and other equipment belonging to the collective farm, which owns also the bulk of the cattle on the farm. At the same time some means of production (productive cattle to the extent stipulated in the Rules of Agricultural Artel, the implements needed by the collective farmers to cultivate their individual subsidiary plots) remain the personal property of the collective farmers.

Thus, the difference between the two forms of socialist property is mainly a difference in the degree to which the means of production are socialised.

State property which is the property of the whole people plays the leading role in the economy. Co-operative and collective farm property can emerge only when state property has become predominant. Both forms of socialised, socialist property develop in close interaction.

Collective farm property is not immutable. As a result of progressive development it changed as compared with the initial collectivisation period, both in quantitative and in qualitative respects. At the close of the twenties and in the early thirties collective farm property was the simple sum of the socialised means of production of the peasant households—horses, ploughs, hoes, etc. The gradual development of the collective farms' commonly-owned economy enlarged their property enormously. It multiplied through collective labour of the farmers with the active participation of the working class and the whole Soviet people, and now has a huge arsenal of modern, highly-productive means of production at its disposal.

Two types of socialist enterprises
The presence of two forms of socialist property determines the existence of two types of socialist enterprises. These are, first, state enterprises: factories, mines, railways, state farms, trading enterprises, banks and communal enterprises, and secondly, the enterprises which represent collective farm and co-operative property: collective farms, producer artels and consumer co-operatives, chief among which are the collective farms.

Collective farms and state enterprises belong to the same type since both are socialist forms of economy. Yet, there are certain distinctions between the two. These are distinctions as regards the management of enterprises, the disposal of the finished product and the different method by which workers and collective farmers receive their incomes.

In state enterprises the manager is appointed by the state, he is vested with authority by it and is responsible to it for the fulfilment of plans. In the collective farm the supreme body of management is the general meeting of the collective farmers which elects the board and the chairman of the collective farm.

The output of state enterprises belongs fully to the state. It is sold at prices fixed by the state. The output of a collective farm remains the property of that collective farm. Having fulfilled their obligations to the state as regards the sale to it of the amount and variety of output provided in the plan, the collective farms dispose of the rest as they please, setting up funds in accordance with the decisions of the general meeting of the collective farmers, selling part of it on the market, etc.

Workers and collective farmers are paid in accordance with the quantity and quality of their labour. But the remuneration of factory and office workers comes out of the wage fund of the state, while that of the collective farmers comes from the income of their collective farm. As distinct from the worker, the collective farmer receives his wages not only in money but also in kind—part of the output of his collective farm.

The collective farmer is entitled to an individual subsidiary plot, productive cattle, fowl and minor farming implements. The plot serves as an auxiliary source for satisfying the personal requirements of the artel members for vegetables, milk, etc. The size of the individual subsidiary plot and the number of cattle are limited by the Rules of the Agricultural Artels.

The collective farmer is allowed to sell on the market the products from the commonly-owned sector he receives as pay in kind and also the products from his subsidiary plot. These sales are not a source of capitalist accumulation: the proceeds cannot be used for the purchase of means of production with which to exploit other people's labour, they can only be used to satisfy the personal requirements of the collective farmer.

While there are distinctions between state enterprises and collective farms, both are socialist enterprises and this is of decisive importance. The means of production are socialised in both. This precludes any exploitation of man by man. Labour is collective and is paid for in accordance with its quantity and quality. The aim of production is to satisfy the requirements of the members of society.

The setting up and consolidation of the collective farm system is one of the Soviet people's greatest achievements. The collective farm system fully corresponds to the level and to the requirements of the development of the productive forces in the countryside. If the management is efficient it ensures the effective application of powerful equipment and of scientific achievements, as well as the rational employment of labour resources. The agricultural artel harmoniously combines the personal interests of its members with social, public interests. "By virtue of the social form of its economy—its organisational structure, and its democratic groundwork—which will develop more and more," says the Programme of the CPSU, "the collective farm ensures that production is run by the collective farm members themselves, that their creative initiative is enhanced and that the collective farmers are educated in the communist spirit."

The strongest point of the collective farm is its democratic organisation, which ensures the wide participation of the collective farmers in the artel's affairs. The profoundly democratic nature of the collective farm tends to develop mass initiative aimed at boosting production. The collective farm is a school of communism for the peasantry. Its task is to develop the creative initiative and enterprise of the collective farmers, to strengthen democracy in them.

Personal property under socialism

In socialist society not only the means of production but also the products of labour are public property. However, the part of the social product being distributed among the members of society—the consumer articles—become their personal property.

Socialism does not belittle the human personality nor personal requirements and does not equalise people in poverty as its enemies assert. On the contrary, for the first time in history, it creates the conditions for the all-round satisfaction of the working people's diverse requirements. Collective labour and the public ownership of the means of production are instrumental in raising the material welfare of the working people and in fostering culture, which has now been placed within their reach.

While socialist society safeguards and defends the people's earned incomes, it does not tolerate people who attempt to live at the expense of other people's labour.

Equality of workers with respect to the means of production

The means of production are the joint property of socialist society, which consists of the labouring people in town and country. In socialist society there is not and cannot exist a state of affairs in which any class is deprived of means of production. Socialism therefore ensures the equality of all workers with respect to the means of production. The equality of the working people with respect to the means of production means that they have equal rights to work with these publicly owned means and that they are recompensed for their work in accordance with the socialist principle, in accordance with the quantity and quality of the labour expended by each worker. Exploitation of man by man is impossible because the means of production cannot be made private property.

The above clearly shows that under socialism means of production are not capital, i.e., not a means of exploitation. We speak and write about capital investments, capital construction, etc., but this does not mean capital in the politico-economic sense, i.e., is not applied to means of production, which serve as a means of exploitation. Under capital investments we understand the utilisation of the accumulated means for the building or expansion of enterprises, the building of housing, of roads, etc., i.e., for an increase in social wealth.

The bourgeoisie and its defenders maintain that private property is the foundation of personal freedom. But under capitalism the majority of the population has no property and to them the capitalist ownership of the means of production means not freedom but enslavement. Even to small producers property is a chain fettering them to monopoly bourgeoisie. Conversely, to big capital private property gives the freedom to exploit the mass of the working people, to profit from their labour. The experience of the Soviet Union and of the whole world socialist system demonstrates that it is not private but public property that frees man from all kinds of social dependence and provides every opportunity for the unhindered development of the individual.

Fundamental changes in the position of the working people in production For production to be carried out under any social system, there must be two elements: labour power and means of production. It is also necessary that these two elements be wedded. The way in which they interact differs in the different societies. For centuries the means of production belonged to the exploiting classes and opposed the working people as a foreign and hostile force. The worker employed in a capitalist factory sees that the machinery, raw materials, and finished output belong not to him but to the capitalist. The capitalist derives all the benefits from production.

The replacement of private by public ownership of the means of production fundamentally changes the way in which labour power interacts with the means of production. It now rests on a new and higher basis, which is large-scale production based on public ownership of the means of production, applying the achievements of modern science and technology, and united on a social scale.

The changes in social life under socialism have fundamentally altered the position labour holds in society and the attitude of people towards it. In socialist society labour is not a heavy yoke to be borne and endured. It has become free labour, all the fruits of which are reaped by the society of free working people.

This, naturally teaches people to regard work as a prime duty to society. "The awareness that they work for themselves," the Programme of the CPSU notes, "and their society and not for exploiters inspires the working people with labour enthusiasm; it encourages their effort for innovation, their creative initiative, and mass socialist emulation. Socialism is creative effort by the working masses. The growing activity of the people in the building of a new life is a law of the socialist epoch."

Socialist production relations and their role in the development of the productive forces Public ownership of the means of production gives rise to a new type of production relations, which are superior to those of capitalism. In socialist production relations there is no exploitation of man by man. These are relations of equal and free members of society, relations of mutual assistance and friendly competition in joint labour. They are truly humane relations differing entirely from the relations of exploitation and ruthless competition under capitalism.

The socialist revolution removes the contradiction between the productive forces and the relations of production prevailing under capitalism by establishing public ownership of the means of production. We said above that the main contradiction of capitalism is the contradiction between the social nature of production and the private capitalist form of appropriation. This contradiction cannot be removed until capitalism continues to exist. It is abolished only under socialism—the society that establishes the public ownership of the means of production that corresponds to social production.

Socialist production relations provide an enormous scope for the development of the productive forces. This refers notably to the main productive force of society—to the working masses. The liberation from exploitation makes the working people feel responsible about production. Those who create all material and spiritual wealth are vitally interested in the successes and the flourishing development of the socialist economy.

Everything hampering the full development of the creative activity and energy, talents and abilities of the broad mass of the working people has been removed.

Socialist production relations make it possible for the first time in history to utilise all productive resources of society, both the material and human resources, in the most expedient and rational way. The anarchy of production has been abolished and society is able to ensure the planned and proportional development of the economy. Socialism is free of such ulcers of capitalism as devastating economic crises of overproduction, unemployment, destructive competition. A steady and rapid growth of production and a rational distribution of the productive forces are typical of socialism.

Socialism creates conditions which ensure that the productive forces grow quicker than they did under capitalism. It clears the way for the rapid development of technology and accelerated technological progress, creates the conditions for a much quicker rise in labour productivity. The production growth rates in all the countries of the world socialist system exceed the production growth rates in the capitalist countries.

Yet, there are also internal contradictions under socialism. The nature of these contradictions differs from the nature of the contradictions in any other form of society.

Lenin pointed out that while contradictions remained under communism, antagonisms would disappear. An antagonism is an irreconcilable contradiction, one that can be solved only by a revolution. Such is the antagonism between the productive forces and the relations of production in bourgeois society, which is destroyed only by a revolutionary elimination of capitalist production relations. Such is the antagonism between the bourgeoisie and the proletariat, which disappears only as a result of the revolution which overthrows the rule of the bourgeoisie and does away with the exploiting classes.

The internal contradictions of socialist society are of quite a different nature. These contradictions do not have an antagonistic nature. They are solved in the course of the successful work of developing and consolidating the productive forces and production relations, in the course of the advance of socialist society to the highest phase of communism.

Under socialism progressive social development proceeds through the emergence, development and solution of contradictions. But this development through contradictions does not have a destructive effect on the productive forces. On the contrary it results in the rapid and powerful growth of these forces.

Under socialist production relations the steady satisfaction of the growing requirements of society as a whole and of its every member is a powerful driving force in the development of production. The ensuing growth in requirements in turn calls for a further increase in the scale of production, for a further growth of society's productive forces. In this way the production relations of socialism stimulate the rapid growth of the productive forces.

The advantages of the socialist economic system cannot be realised spontaneously, automatically. They are realised through the purposeful activity of the builders of socialism and communism, in the struggle between the new and the old, by surmounting newly-arising economic difficulties and residua of capitalism in the various fields of social life.

Material and technical basis of socialism Every social system has its material and technical basis. The material and technical basis of this or that society embraces first and foremost its productive apparatus. This is the total technical equipment provided to labour. This includes machinery, plant, instruments, production structures, etc. The level of the productive apparatus is indissolubly bound with the level of the human labour force, and also with a definite system of production relations. A major role in the creation and development of society's material and technical basis is played by the production of objects of labour—raw and other materials, fuel and power.

Marx defined the material basis of capitalism as large-scale machine industry based on hired labour. In other words, the material basis of capitalism is machine production operating under the domination of capitalist production relations and developing according to the economic laws of capitalism.

After the overthrow of capitalism the creation and development of the material and technical basis of socialism becomes the most important task in the building of the new society. The material and technical basis of socialism is large-scale machine production in industry, agriculture, building, transport and the other sectors of the economy. In other words, the material and technical basis of socialism is all-round developed machine production operating under the domination of socialist production relations and developing according to the economic laws of socialism.

As the material and technical basis of socialism grows and improves it turns into the material and technical basis of communism.

The prerequisites for the creation of the material and technical basis of socialism emerge under capitalism, which evolves a large-scale machine industry. But the material and technical basis of socialism itself is created after the triumph of the socialist revolution. It is the result of the socialist industrialisation of the country, of the collectivisation of agriculture and its technical re-equipment, and also of the cultural revolution which is of enormous importance to the development of material production.

The experience of all socialist countries confirms that the creation of the material and technical basis of socialism in the form of a modern large-scale machine industry, capable also of transforming agriculture, is the main condition for building socialist society.

The material and technical basis of socialism was created in the Soviet Union during the five-year plans for the country's economic development. The first five-year plan, adopted by the 15th Party Congress, mapped out a programme covering the period from 1928 to 1932. It was followed by the second (1933-37) and the third, which was interrupted in 1941 by Germany's invasion of the Soviet Union.

Even the initial five-year plans proved enormously successful in the creation of the material and technical basis of socialism. At the beginning of the first five-year plan, in 1928, the Soviet Union produced 5,000 million kwh of electric power, 4.3 million tons of steel, 11.6 million tons of oil, 300 million cubic metres of gas, 35.5 million tons of coal, 1.8 million tons of cement, 2,000 metal-cutting lathes, 800 motor cars, 1,300 tractors, 0.14 million tons of mineral fertilisers (in conventional units).

On the eve of the war, in 1940, the Soviet Union produced 48,300 million kwh of electric power, 18.3 million tons of steel, 31.1 million tons of oil, 3,400 million cubic metres of gas, 166 million tons of coal, 58,400 metal-cutting lathes, 145,000 motor cars, 31,600 tractors, 3.2 million tons of mineral fertilisers (in conventional units).

The war against Germany inflicted enormous losses. More than 20 million lives were lost and about 30 per cent of the national wealth was destroyed. On a large part of the European territory of the USSR thousands of towns and villages, tens of thousands of factories, mines, collective farms, state farms, schools, and houses lay in ruins.

But the Soviet people rehabilitated the war-devastated economy in an extremely short time and rapidly advanced the entire country's economy. During the post-war five-year plans—the fourth, fifth, sixth—and the seven-year plan (1959-65) the material and technical basis of socialism expanded and consolidated, the economic potential of the country grew enormously and the production of the basic types of industrial output soared. In 1965 the Soviet Union produced 507,000 million kwh of electric power, 91 million tons of steels, 243 million tons of oil, 129,000 million cubic metres of gas, 578 million tons of coal, 72.4 million tons of cement, 185,000 metal-cutting lathes, 616,000 motor cars, 355,000 tractors, 31.3 million tons of mineral fertilisers (in conventional units).

Thus, the output of electric power had during the five-year plan periods grown 101 times, steel and oil production—21 times, coal mining—16 times, cement—39 times, the output of metal-cutting lathes—93 times. There was also an appreciable increase in the output of consumer goods: textiles—3 times, leather footwear—8.4 times, granulated sugar—7 times. The average yearly volume of agricultural production increased by almost 2.5 times.

Technological progress in socialist society

Socialism accelerates technological progress. Under capitalism new equipment may not be introduced even if the employment of this equipment would save social labour. It is introduced only when this results in a saving of production costs to the capitalist. It often happens that the introduction of equipment would be profitable for society as a whole but unprofitable for the capitalist.

In the socialist economic system new equipment is introduced whenever it is profitable to society and when it saves and facilitates labour. The wide utilisation of new equipment under socialism lightens the labour of workers, reduces working hours and multiplies the social wealth. Technological progress leads to a growth in labour productivity, which in turn steadily advances the living standard of the people. Under socialism all the working people are therefore vitally interested in improving technology. They participate actively in the work of furthering technological progress and the improvement in the organisation of production.

Does this mean that socialist society is able to use any amount of equipment it pleases? Of course not. The mass of equipment that can be put into action depends on the level of social wealth. The possibilities for technological progress depend on the scale of production, the level of development of science and engineering, the funds society can afford to use for extended reproduction.

At the present level of social wealth the further growth rate depends largely on a rational utilisation of the material and labour resources. The rate at which the productive forces develop depends on most expedient capital investment channelling, the effectiveness of social production. The capacity for quick production growth rates inherent in the socialist economy is not realised automatically but through a perpetual struggle for the utilisation of the advantages of socialism.

2. ECONOMIC LAWS OF SOCIALISM

Specifics of the operation of the economic laws of socialism
With the transition from capitalism to socialism the economic laws of socialism replace the economic laws of capitalism.

Like the economic laws of all other societies, the economic laws of socialism too have an objective nature. This means that they express the inner connections of phenomena, which exist independently of the will and consciousness of people. But at the same time the economic laws of socialism differ substantially from those laws of all preceding forms of society.

Engels wrote that the difference between them can be likened to that existing between the destructive force of lightning and electricity, which submissively operates in the telegraph or in a lamp, between a conflagration and a fire benefiting man. This comparison vividly shows the essence of that difference. Both lightning and the electric power in a lamp are caused by an identical natural force. But lightning strikes man spontaneously and he is unable to control it. On the other hand, the natural force operating in an electric lamp has been understood and harnessed by man and is used by him deliberately.

The economic laws of capitalism and of all former social formations operate spontaneously. Just as the force of lightning, they are beyond people's control. Even when scientists revealed the nature of lightning it still remained an alien force. The same applies to the economic laws of capitalism. Under the rule of private ownership of the means of production people are deprived of the chance to use economic laws of social development consciously. Even after their nature has been revealed, these laws, like the unharnessed forces of nature, operate blindly, violently and destructively.

Socialism, based on public ownership of the means of production integrates the national economy into a single whole. National economic development becomes a sphere of conscious and purposive activity to a no less degree than is human labour in a single enterprise.

Under socialism people learn to understand the objective economic laws, to master them and to use them for practical economic development in the interests of all of society. Society, as represented by the socialist state, uses the economic laws of socialism scientifically. It harnesses them, just as the power of electricity in an electric lamp is harnessed.

In the course of socialist construction society gains an ever deeper knowledge of the economic laws of that system and masters them ever more successfully. This task is fulfilled by the Communist Party, which is armed with the knowledge of Marxist-Leninist theory. While fulfilling practical tasks, the Marxist-Leninist party concurrently develops revolutionary theory.

The Communist Party proceeds from the assumption that to build the socialist economy on a scientific foundation means to base it on the objective economic laws of socialism revealed by science, on a sober appraisal of the objective situation, the ability to learn from one's own experience and from that of others and the improvement of the means and methods of economic management.

Accumulation of practical experience and its scientific generalisation make it possible to put the economic laws of socialism to better use. In its turn the correct application of these laws ensures the successful implementation of practical tasks, while their violation impedes the fulfilment of these tasks.

Socialism and communism emerge and develop as a result of the operation of the economic laws of social development, which exist irrespective of the will and consciousness of people. At the same time socialism and communism emerge and develop as a result of the conscious activity of millions of working people.

The aim of socialist production.
The basic economic law of socialism

The transition from capitalism to socialism fundamentally changes the aim of production. Under capitalism the direct aim of production is to obtain profit through the exploitation of hired labour. The search for profit is the only force impelling the development of production. Capitalism is founded on the exploitation of hired labour by capital.

In socialist society there are no capitalists and no exploitation of man by man. Jointly owning the means of production, the working people produce with the aim of satisfying the requirements of society and all its members. The aim of socialism is the ever fuller satisfaction of the growing material and cultural requirements of the people through the constant development and improvement of social production. Therein lies the source of the enormous power of socialist economy, the source of the inexhaustible creative power of free socialist labour.

In this way socialism effects the transition from anarchic production, the aim of which is profit, to planned production with the aim of satisfying social requirements. Even before the establishment of Soviet power, Lenin wrote that the socialist revolution, replacing private ownership of the means of production by public ownership, introduces a planned organisation of social production to ensure the welfare and comprehensive development of all members of society.

Socialist society continuously expands and improves production in order to raise the material welfare and cultural level of the working people. This in essence constitutes the basic economic law of socialism. The constant growth and systematic improvement of socialist production which is a condition for the ever fuller satisfaction of the people's requirements forms the basis of socialist society's movement towards communism.

Socialism radically changes the conditions which determine the living standard of the working masses. The economic laws of capitalism limit the satisfaction of the vital requirements of the people. The capitalists strive to cut the earnings of the working people in order to raise their profits. For this reason the working class is able to ensure a certain improvement of its economic position only through stubborn class struggle against the capitalists.

In socialist society the improvement of the working people's living standard depends only on the level achieved by social production, on the growth in labour productivity and the volume of produced output. The more material wealth produced by society, the higher is the living standard of the people.

The socialist revolution ensures the working masses a higher living standard. The people's power reduces the working day and improves the housing conditions of the working people. It adopts a series of measures which first rapidly decrease, and then eliminate unemployment. Socialism paves the way for the prosperous and cultured life of the peasant masses.

But the socialist transformation of society takes on gigantic tasks. The solution of these tasks, especially in countries with a backward economy, calls for enormous efforts from the whole people. The only way to ensure a steady advance in the living standard of the working people is to expand the productive forces as quickly as possible. This involves expanding old and building new enterprises in industry, agriculture and other sectors, a steady rise in labour productivity, technological progress and better economic organisation at all levels.

The enemies of the working people make a lot of fuss about the fact that there still is no material abundance in the socialist countries. They intentionally gloss over the true causes of the difficulties socialist construction in the USSR and other socialist countries have to overcome. These causes are the former economic backwardness of Russia and other socialist countries, the hostile actions of the imperialists, the ruinous wars the Soviet Union has had to bear.

The principles of economic management worked out by the Communist Party provide for a combination of centralised management with an extension of the rights of Union republics, an enhancement of economic methods in economic management, a fundamental improvement in planning, an extension of the economic independence and initiative of enterprises, an increased material interest in the results of their activities.

3. ECONOMIC ROLE OF THE SOCIALIST STATE

The socialist state organises the creativity of the popular masses

In socialist economy which is based on the conscious application of the objective economic laws of social development, the state plays a fundamentally different role from the state in capitalist economy, which is governed by economic laws operating spontaneously.

The socialist revolution evolves a state of a new type unprecedented in the history of mankind. This state faces tasks that have never been faced by any government before —the tasks of destroying the old, outmoded capitalist economic system and setting up new forms of social economy, and building the socialist economic system.

The socialist state has real possibilities for the successful implementation of these tasks. Abolishing exploitation, the socialist state transforms the popular masses into conscious makers of history—this is the source of its creative power. It becomes the organiser of the masses, directs their endeavours to the accomplishment of the great tasks of social transformation.

The socialist state works out long-term and current economic plans through its planning and administrative bodies and organises fulfilment and overfulfilment of these plans. It appoints its representatives to manage individual enterprises, groups of enterprises, branches of the economy, determines the forms and principles governing the remuneration of the labour of factory and office workers, conducts a definite price policy on the output of industry and agriculture and establishes transport tariffs. The state budget, being the main financial plan of the socialist economy, is crucial to the whole economic life of society

The state monopoly of foreign trade serves as a barrier against foreign capital, stops it from penetrating the socialist countries with the aim of exploitation.

Another extremely important function of the socialist

state is the distribution of the social product. The state ensures the normal replacement of the expended means of production in all the spheres of the economy and distributes the national income to achieve a steady advance in the people's welfare and the steady growth and improvement of production on the basis of the most up-to-date equipment.

Socialist society lives and develops at a time when the aggressive forces of imperialism still continue to exist in the capitalist countries. This means that the socialist state has to organise and maintain the country's defence potential. The most important task of all socialist states is to strengthen the unity and cohesion of the world socialist system.

The scientific basis of the socialist state's economic policy The economic policy of the socialist state, like its policy in general, develops on the basis of Marxist-Leninist theory, which reveals the objective laws of social development in general, and the objective economic laws of socialism in particular.

Economic policy justifiably holds a central place in the comprehensive activities of the socialist state. It is directed to the development of the productive forces and relations of production of socialist society. It has the aim of ensuring not only the present but also the future of the Soviet people. The far-sighted economic policy of the socialist state ensures that the progress today lays the foundation for even more impressive progress in future, taking care not to sacrifice ultimate aims for the sake of achieving current aims and vice versa. It is with this in view that the fundamental problems of economic development are decided, problems including the economic development rates for the economy as a whole and for its individual sectors, the establishment of proportions in social production, the direction of technological progress and ways of advancing living standards.

The interests of the people and the policy of the socialist state which expresses these interests coincide fully with the objective trends of social development. Owing to the objective laws of social development triumphant socialism progresses towards communism and the Communist Party and the Soviet state pursue a policy aimed at propelling the country most successfully along the road to communism.

The whole policy of the socialist state, Lenin wrote, must be based on the unshakeable alliance of the working class and peasantry. This alliance consolidates as the socialist economy grows and becomes a mighty force. At all stages of economic construction the Communist Party takes full account of the specifics of the path along which the peasant masses advance towards socialism. It ensures this advance by combining the public interests of large-scale socialist collective farm production with the satisfaction of the personal interests of the collective farmers by ensuring the steady growth of the material interest of the farmers in the flourishing of the collective farm economy. The economic policy of the Party and the state, all the economic measures of the Soviet Government constantly strengthen the alliance of the working class and peasantry in the interests of communist construction.

Leninist principles in socialist economic management Lenin emphasised that the chief task of the triumphant working class in the socialist revolution was to regulate the new intricate and subtle organisational relations which govern the planned production and distribution of products needed for the existence of millions of people. After the political victory over the bourgeoisie has been achieved and consolidated, Lenin wrote, a similar victory must be achieved in the organisation of the economy.

The management of the socialist economy is called upon to ensure the smooth and precise functioning of the whole economic organism. The task is to ensure that the whole complex economy should work with the accuracy of a clockwork. As the socialist economy grows quantitatively and qualitatively the mutual links and dependencies grow more complex both within separate enterprises and between enterprises, branches, and economic districts. In these conditions the organisation of the country's economic management acquires growing importance.

Improving the methods of economic management the Communist Party relies on the principles of socialist management worked out by Lenin. Practice has brilliantly proved the strength and viability of these principles, which develop and grow richer as the socialist economy expands, as its development possibilities increase, and as its tasks become more intricate.

The management of socialist economy is based on the Leninist principle of democratic centralism. This principle demands strict one-man management in all the links of the production process and at the same time the enlistment of the broad mass of factory and office workers in economic management. It ensures the maximum scope for the creative energy and initiative of the broad mass of the working people and a unity of purpose and will without which there could be no normal functioning of large-scale production, of the modern highly developed economic organism.

The steady growth and expansion of the democratic basis of economic management and control is one of the most important requirements of socialist society, one of the objective laws governing it. Like the other objective laws of the development of socialist society it does not operate automatically but through the conscious and purposive activity of people. As the socialist economy grows, as its tasks expand and grow in complexity, the need for developing the democratic basis of economic activity increases and becomes more urgent.

Lenin emphatically warned against two dangers threatening the principle of democratic centralism. This is first of all a transformation of democratic centralism into bureaucratic centralism, and secondly a violation of centralism by all sorts of parochial or anarchic tendencies. Communist construction presupposes all-out development of the democratic basis of management and a simultaneous strengthening and perfection of centralised economic management by the state.

One of the most important laws of the socialist mode of production is that the creative activity of the masses is an enormous driving force in economic growth and progress. Socialism has released the energy of millions of people and the utilisation of this energy to the utmost largely decides the rate of economic development. At the same time the growing role of centralised economic management is one of the main laws of the socialist mode of production. Centralised management of the economy is a condition for its rational organisation and is one of the decisive advantages of socialism over capitalism.

The improvement in economic management and control is effected by the simultaneous development of both principles of democratic centralism: the democratisation of management and centralisation of guidance. A correct combination of these two principles is crusial for the scientific management of the economic construction of socialism and communism.

The improvement in economic management being carried out by the Communist Party and the Soviet Government is a further development of such time-tested Leninist principles of socialist management as democratic centralism, socialist cost accounting, the combination of moral and material stimuli to work and improve production. The Leninist principles of management express the objective economic laws of socialism. The improvement of the methods of socialist management signifies a more successful mastery of these laws and their more skilful utilisation in the interests of society.

At every stage of socialist and communist construction the Party fully considers the present position and maps out the regular tasks in accordance with the changing domestic and external situation. In this the Party is guided by Lenin's directives on the indissoluble link between economic and political tasks, on the unity of economic and political tasks in the process of socialist and communist construction.

REVISION QUESTIONS

1. What common features and differences are there between the two forms of socialist property?
2. How do the economic laws of socialism operate?
3. What is the essence of the scientific management of the socialist economy?
4. What is the essence of democratic centralism in economic management?

Chapter XI

PLANNED DEVELOPMENT OF THE SOCIALIST ECONOMY

1. PLANNED ECONOMY—SOCIALISM'S PRIME ADVANTAGE

The possibility and need for planned economic management under socialism

For economy as a whole to develop normally the development of all its parts must be co-ordinated. This means that definite types of products—coal and machinery, fabrics and footwear, grain and meat—must be produced in definite quantitative proportions. This is achieved through a definite distribution of the labour and means of production among the various branches.

As we saw above in capitalist economy the necessary proportions between the parts, the elements of social production, are established spontaneously. Under anarchy of production the necessary proportions are established as a result of innumerable fluctuations and deviations. This leads to an enormous destruction of the productive forces through competition, crises and unemployment.

The anarchy of production is engendered by the basic contradiction of capitalism—the contradiction between the social character of production and the private capitalist form of appropriation. Socialism abolishes this contradiction. In socialist society the public ownership of the means of production, and hence also of the results of production corresponds to the social character of production. Describing the general outlines of socialist society, Marx and Engels predicted that under socialism the anarchy of social production would be replaced by social production, organised according to plan, designed to satisfy the requirements of society as a whole and of its every member. Lenin emphasised that the socialist revolution faces the gigantic task of transforming the whole economic mechanism of the state into an efficient apparatus able to guide the work of hundreds of millions of people according to a single plan.

This means that socialism makes planned economic management both possible and necessary. Just as capitalism is inconceivable without anarchy of production, socialism is inconceivable without a planned development of the entire economy. Planned economic management is one of the main features of socialist economy. The co-operation between the socialist countries also has a planned nature.

The state economic plan ties up the production and distribution of output on a social scale into a single whole. The main indicators of state enterprises are endorsed by superior economic bodies. The collective farms work according to plans drawn up by their boards and endorsed by the general meeting of collective farmers. Not only industry, agriculture, transport, building organisations and trading enterprises, but also scientific institutions, cultural, educational and medical establishments all work according to plan. In socialist society the plan has the aim of ensuring the unity of purpose and will in the whole of economic and cultural development and the whole gigantic process of socialist and communist construction.

The planned nature of economic development is one of the decisive economic and social advantages socialism has over capitalism. The planned development of the socialist economy frees it from destructive competition, crises, unemployment and the other ills stemming from the anarchy of capitalist production. The planned economy enables socialism to attain much higher economic growth rates than under capitalism.

The law of the planned, proportionate development of the economy

Planned, proportionate development of the economy is an objective economic law of socialism. Applying this law, socialist society runs its economy ever more successfully according to plan.

The planned organisation of the economy is a new task, one taken up for the first time by socialist society. Under capitalism which is based on the private ownership of the means of production there is economic management only within the framework of individual enterprises, firms and concerns. The bourgeois state, especially in modern conditions, strives to introduce some elements of organisation in economic development, however, under capitalism the national economy as a whole remains unmanageable—it is left at the mercy of the spontaneous laws of the capitalist mode of production. The narrow framework of capitalist private ownership gives little opportunity for introducing planning in the development of the entire economy. Socialism is not constricted by these limits and opens up an unlimited scope for the most rational and effective organisation of the economy according to plan.

Increasing mastery and better application of the law of the planned, proportionate development of the economy is achieved by constantly improving economic planning. Planned management is called upon to ensure the smooth functioning of all economic links. To ensure the necessary proportions in the economy is a very complex problem. Accumulating practical experience, socialist society is successfully solving it.

However, because of the unprecedented scale of this problem and the difficulty of its solution some economic proportions may temporarily be disturbed. This makes it extremely important to discover the emergent disproportion as early as possible and to take effective measures to remedy it.

The proportions in the economy between the different elements are of an objective nature. At every stage they depend on the technological development, availability of labour resources, the level of labour productivity, on the one hand, and social requirements, on the other. Proportions cannot be established at will, the above factors must be taken into account.

This does not imply, however, that the proportions between the various links of the national economy are immutable. Technological progress, especially now that the scientific and technological revolution is in full swing, is changing the economic proportions.

The modern scientific and technological revolution dictates the need for the accelerated development of the most advanced and progressive branches and types of production. In the progressive branches the labour productivity is much higher. Capital investments in them justify themselves in a comparatively short time. For this reason

244

changes in the economic structure brought about by the intensive development of the progressive branches of production are vital in ensuring high and stable economic development rates.

The systematic improvement of the structure of social production is an extraordinarily important task for planned, proportionate economic development and for the creation of the material and technical basis of communism. But these structural changes must not interfere with the proportional development of the economy and must not cause disproportions.

"It is essential that the national economy develop on a strictly *proportionate* basis," the Programme of the CPSU says, "that economic disproportions are prevented in good time, ensuring sufficient economic reserves as a condition for stable high rates of economic development, uninterrupted operation of enterprises and continuous improvement of the people's well-being."

The law of labour economy

Planned economic development is unthinkable without thrifty economic management. The socialist economic system demands that there be thrifty economic management and does all it can to ensure this end. The need is governed by the aim of socialist production which is to satisfy social requirements. The possibility, on the other hand, is determined by the fact that socialism is free of such incurable ills of capitalism as the anarchy of production, destructive competition, economic crises, unemployment, etc. Socialism abolishes the causes responsible for the waste of the productive forces and makes it possible to use all social resources in the most rational and expedient way.

The classics of Marxism-Leninism emphasised the crucial principle of thrift under socialism. They considered this question in its indissoluble relation with the planned character of socialist production. Marx considered the economy of labour alongside with its planned distribution between the different branches of production an important law of the socialist mode of production.

Lenin always insisted on thrift; he said that money should be counted and that waste was intolerable in a socialist state. Like Marx, he linked thrifty economic

245

management with the planned guidance of the whole process of socialist construction.

Thrifty economic management is one of the most important features of planned economic development under socialism. Management disregarding thrift cannot be called planned management. Planned economic development is rational management, based on the most expedient and effective utilisation of all material, labour and financial resources and of the country's natural wealth. The achievement in the interests of society of maximum results with minimum expenditure is an immutable law of economic development in socialist society.

Economic planning on the basis of the conscious utilisation of the economic laws of socialism Planned economic management is called upon to ensure the rapid and steady growth of production for the ever fuller satisfaction of society's growing needs. It is based on the all-round utilisation of the economic laws of socialism, notably of the law of planned, proportionate development, determining the necessity of planned economy, and of the law of value, demanding that there be a correspondence between the expenditure and the results of production. At the same time planned economy is the form which is called upon to ensure the fullest possible application of all other economic laws of socialism.

Planning is at odds with any arbitrariness in the implementation of economic tasks. The scientific basis of plans is the most important condition for their success.

Economic planning is based on an accurate consideration of the objective conditions for the development of the economy, of its motive forces and trends. The more thoroughly objective conditions and the economic laws of socialism are considered in plans, the more successfully are they implemented. The socialist plan is based on scientifically established social requirements and an objective appraisal of the productive resources and reserves. It indicates the ways for the most effective development of the economy.

Tasks of the plan We have shown above that the supreme aim of socialism is the ever fuller satisfaction of the people's growing material and cultural requirements through the constant development and improvement of social production. The tasks of social-ist plans are naturally subordinated to this aim. At every stage planned economic management sets also more concrete tasks which are determined by the given situation.

Lenin described the GOELRO plan (State Plan for the Electrification of Russia) worked out in 1920, as a pro-gramme for the development of the whole economy on the basis of up-to-date technology—on the basis of electri-fication of the whole country.

The objectives of the initial Soviet five-year plans were to lay the foundation of the socialist economy, to ensure the technological re-equipment of the economy, the pre-dominance of socialist over capitalist elements in the country's economy and subsequently the complete elimina-tion of capitalist elements, to root out all exploitation of man by man and the causes responsible for it. At the same time the pre-war five-year plans were designed to strengthen the Soviet Union's economic and political independence and its defence potential in the face of the growing threat of imperialist armed attack. All these tasks were set and fulfilled in a definite sequence determined by historical conditions.

After the end of the Second World War the economic plans of the Soviet Union were aimed at the quickest rehabilitation of the war-devastated economy and at ensuring a further boost to socialist economy.

Main proportions in socialist economy

The planning of the socialist econ-omy must ensure the necessary quantitative relations between the individual parts and sectors of the economic organism.

The main proportions in the economy are those between its main sectors, i.e., between the development of industry and agriculture, between the growth of industrial and agri-cultural production and the work of transport. In industry itself an important role is assigned to the relation between the production of means of production and that of con-sumer articles. Between the separate sectors in each of the two departments there also exist definite proportions. The volume of construction, for instance, must be ensured by a corresponding output of building materials (cement, reinforced concrete, metal, etc.).

The mass of the output of industry and agriculture supplies the means for consumption and accumulation. The ratio between consumption and accumulation is one of the most important economic proportions, which in socialist society is established and maintained according to plan.

This ratio is inseparably linked with the proportion between the production of means of production and that of consumer articles. The output of the sectors producing consumer articles goes to satisfy the direct requirements of the people. The output of the sectors producing means of production goes to replenish the used up means of production and to expand productive capacities.

There must be a correspondence between production and realisation if the economy is to develop normally. The growing purchasing capacity of the population must be accompanied by a corresponding increase in the amount of goods being offered for sale. There must also be a definite ratio between the expenditure of the state and its revenue.

Definite proportions are essential not only in the structure of production but also in the utilisation of the labour resources.

Inter-district proportions are also of the utmost importance. Socialism ensures the rapid development of all economic regions of the country and a rational distribution of the productive forces. The comprehensive development of every region goes hand in hand with the specialisation of the region in accordance with its natural resources and a number of other factors. Specialisation evolves the need for the development of inter-district links which are becoming increasingly diversified.

Definite proportions exist not only between economic branches and enterprises but also within each individual enterprise. Thus, in an engineering works a definite ratio must be maintained between the work of the component and assembly shops. If the component shops fail to deliver the required parts, the assembly shop will be at a stand still. If the assembly shop fails to cope with its tasks, the manufactured components will be so much dead stock in the shops or stores, and the output of finished goods will stop.

National economic balances   Co-ordination of the separate parts of the plan on the basis of national economic balances is an important feature of socialist planning. Among the most important balances are the balance of the national income and of its utilisation; the balance of labour resources and of their utilisation, broken down according to economic districts; the balance of the population's monetary income and expenditure; the balance of financial resources, and the main material balances. A thorough, scientifically based system of balances is the main condition ensuring correct economic proportions and ties.

The balance of the national income and its utilisation illustrates the division of the national income into its main parts, that going to consumption and that going to accumulation. The balance of labour resources helps to establish labour requirements and the reserve of labour resources.

The balance of the monetary income and expenditure of the population takes into account all monetary incomes of the population—the wages of factory and office workers, incomes of collective farmers according to work-day units, pensions, grants and other incomes. The other side of this balance takes account of the sum of the prices of goods and services which can be sold to the population, the expenditure of the population on all sorts of payments. The balance of monetary income and expenditure is an important means of planning the money circulation. The state budget is the balance of state revenue and expenditure.

Chief among the material balances are the following: balances of the means of production—of electric power, fuel, metal, equipment, building materials, chemical products, paper. These balances help to co-ordinate the output of the extractive and manufacturing industries and to plan the development of the associate industries. The material balances include also the balances of consumer articles (industrial goods and foodstuffs). They are linked in turn with the balances of production and consumption of agricultural products.

In their totality, the balances embrace the whole economy and give a picture of the interrelations between all its principal elements. The balances ensure the establishment of correct proportions in the economy and help to disclose internal resources and reserves.

Optimisation of planning

To be realistic the plan must be well balanced. The failure to correlate all its elements results in disproportions and excessive strain, which makes it necessary to correct the plan in the course of its fulfilment. It should, however, be borne in mind that there can be a multitude of well-balanced and practically attainable variants of the plan.

This makes it extremely important to choose the best variant, the optimum plan. The rates and the proportions stipulated in the plans for economic development should be the optimum ones. This means that the plans should provide for the most effective utilisation of all potentialities and resources of socialist economy.

The rate of the national income growth (providing, of course, for the required level of the population's welfare and the full utilisation of the society's labour resources) serves as the general criterion for ascertaining that the plan has been drawn up in the optimum way. Diverse criteria can be applied for the separate branches—production growth, decrease in expenditure, etc.—their choice depending on the concrete situation.

A balanced plan is required to ensure high production growth rates, the most expedient economic proportions and the high quality of output, all of which should be achieved with a minimum outlay of social labour.

As the socialist economy grows and as the tasks it faces grow in complexity, the optimisation of planning becomes ever more important and demands that interdependence in the economy be based on highly accurate computations. The optimisation of planning is achieved through the application of mathematical methods. The modern development of mathematics and computing techniques makes it possible to compute optimal variants of the plan.

Modern electronic computing techniques enable us to make the vast number of computations needed for finding the best methods of solving economic problems in a very short time.

2. ORGANISATION AND METHODS OF ECONOMIC PLANNING

Compilation of the plan   The experience gained in socialist construction has made it possible to work out definite practical planning methods.

The plans for economic development are drawn up on the basis of directives endorsed by the Party and the Government. These directives determine the main political and economic tasks of the plan and the main quantitative targets for the various branches of the economy and economic districts of the country. They stipulate the volume and the direction of capital investments and the tasks in the field of technological progress and the improvement of the methods of economic management.

On the basis of the Party and Government directives the central planning bodies—the Gosplan (State Planning Committee) and the ministries—work out concrete draft plans and targets, relying on the great work in the compilation of plans being carried out by the enterprises, the basic links of the economy. The plans of enterprises are summarised in the plans for branches of economy. After the basic indicators in the plan have been endorsed by the superior economic body they become the basis for the activities of the enterprise.

The economic reform now in progress has reduced the plan indicators which have to be endorsed by the superior body to a minimum. All other indicators are worked out independently by the enterprise, taking due account of the concrete conditions in which the enterprise works and of its possibilities. The enterprise's annual plan co-ordinates the technological, economic and financial aspects of its activities. This plan is therefore called the technological output and financial plan. This is a programme determining all the production, technological and financial activities of the enterprise during the year. It includes the production programme, the plan for technological development, for material and technical supply, for labour and wages, for the cost of production, for financial operations, and for organisational and technological measures.

The production programme is the main link of the technical output and financial plan. This is the target for the production and realisation of the output. The production programme stipulates the volume of output, its assortment and quality.

The various departments of an enterprise are organically linked. Therefore all plan indicators must be tied up into a single whole. All sections of the plan, regulating the various activities of the enterprise are based on the same initial indicators. In the course of intrafactory planning the indicators in the enterprise's plan are broken down into targets for the enterprise's individual production sections, for its shops, departments and teams.

The plan of every enterprise provides for the receipt from other enterprises of definite kinds of raw materials, fuel, electric power, equipment. This aspect of the enterprise's activities is particularised in the economic contracts, regulating the interrelations of supplier and consumer enterprises. The contracts also stipulate the kinds of materials to be delivered, terms of delivery, the price of each material, and the terms of payment. The fulfilment of contracts is obligatory for both parties. Each side is held materially responsible in the case of violations of the contract.

The drawing up of the plan is only the beginning of planned economic management. The most important aspect of this management is to organise the efforts of the people to secure the fulfilment and overfulfilment of plans. While these efforts are applied new possibilities inherent in socialist economy are disclosed and the latent reserves of enterprises, branches and economic districts are mobilised.

Long-term and current planning

Socialist economic planning is based on the organic combination of long-term and current (annual) plans. At present the five-year plan is the principal form of scientific planning. It determines the prospects of the productive and economic activity of an enterprise for a period, which is sufficiently long for the fulfilment of major tasks concerned with the improvement of production and the increase of its effectiveness. The most important targets of the five-year plan are broken down into yearly targets. The targets are concretised and adjusted in the yearly plans in accordance with current changes in resources and requirements of society and with due account for the technological and economic progress.

Five-year plans are called upon to ensure a sound technological and economic basis for the tasks set before the economy as regards production growth, the wide introduction of scientific and technological achievements and progressive changes in the structure of social production. They enable the planner to give a correct appraisal of the economic effectiveness of measures extending over that period (for example, with regard to the development of new areas, the building of large power stations, factories, etc.).

Current plans, on the other hand, are necessary to ensure the fulfilment of concrete targets at the stipulated time, to unite the efforts of the people as a whole and those of individual collectives of working people in their work for the realisation of the immediate tasks of economic construction and to ensure a planned and rhythmical growth of production in all branches of economy.

Centralised state planning and the initiative of enterprises

The decisions of the 23rd Congress of the CPSU emphasise the need for a correct combination of centralised planning with the development of the economic initiative of enterprises. The Congress resolved that centralised planned economic management should concentrate in the first place on the improvement of the main economic proportions and the location of production, and on the complex development of economic districts. Planned management is to ensure high production rates and the supply of key products. It also is to provide for the implementation of a unified state policy in technological progress, capital investments, the remuneration of labour, prices, profits, financing and credit. Last but not least, there must be economic control over the effective utilisation of production assets, labour, material and natural resources.

Socialist planning presupposes active mass participation in working out plans and their implementation. Planned economic management does not exclude but presupposes the release of the creative initiative of the masses, of enterprises and collectives of the working people.

Lenin called the GOELRO plan a second Party programme. As distinct from the Party programme, which can be altered only at Party congresses, Lenin said, this second Party programme should be systematically improved, adjusted, developed and modified.

While the plan is being fulfilled the staff of enterprises work enthusiastically and creatively to disclose new potentialities for the growth of production and the improvement of output. It reveals the internal reserves and latent potentialities there are in enterprises, shops, sections, collective farms and teams. Important questions connected with the development of new areas, the utilisation of newly disclosed natural resources are put on the agenda; extensive tasks are advanced for introducing new equipment and technology and improving the organisation of production.

The national economic plan is not a collection of dead figures but a reflection of the live activity of the masses building socialism and communism. In the work for the fulfilment and overfulfilment of the plan, socialist emulation drives are launched between enterprises, teams and individual workers. The success of the plan depends on people.

Correct planning creates the conditions essential for the successful work of the enterprise, the fullest utilisation of its equipment, the prevention of idle time and fulfilling and overfulfilling the plan targets. It would be wrong, however, to think that the plan can be fulfilled automatically, without great efforts on the part of the whole population and without tenacious work in all the sectors of economic and cultural construction. It demands the mobilisation of all the efforts and creative abilities of the people.

Socialist planning implies the planned management of the whole economy. National economic plans assign top priority to general state interests. This makes it necessary to observe strict discipline in the implementation of the plan, to do away with all elements of parochialism and departmentalism which harm the interests of the economy as a whole.

Democratic centralism in economic development Planned organisation of socialist economy is based on the Leninist principle of democratic centralism. This principle provides full scope for the creative energy and initiative of the widest masses of the working people and combines it with the unity of will and purpose necessary for the normal operation of socialist enterprises and the economy as a whole.

As the socialist economy develops both centralised economic management and mass initiative grow in importance. The growth and expansion of democratic principles in planned socialist economy is an objective trend of the socialist system.

The democratic centralism in economic construction changes its forms as the economy develops. The improvement in the methods of planning and economic management simultaneously develops both principles of democratic centralism: the democratism in administration and the centralisation of planned management. The decisions of the 23rd Congress of the CPSU speak of the necessity to apply consistent efforts to achieve the all-out development of the democratic principles of administration and the simultaneous strengthening and improvement of centralised planned economic management.

The new system of economic management combines unified state planning with the work of enterprises on a basis of full cost accounting (on a self-supporting basis), and centralised management by branches of economy with extensive republican and local economic initiative, the principle of one-man management with the increase in the role of production collectives. The Party has censured the inadequate attention being given to economic methods in the planning and management of the economy, and the new system of management is therefore based on the combination of centralised planned guidance and the economic initiative of enterprises and their staffs and the strengthening of economic levers and material production stimuli.

Improvement in economic management is connected with a further development of its democratic basis and the wider participation of the masses in production management. The aim of the economic reform is to provide greater stimuli for production with the help of such economic levers as price, profit, bonuses and credit.

This ensures the further extension of the democratic principles of management, creates economic conditions for more extensive participation of the masses in the management of production and gives the people greater opportunities to influence the results of the economic performance of enterprises.

The combination of unified state planning with full cost accounting, and the extension of the rights and independence of enterprises, and of centralised management by branches of economy with broad local initiative, ensures the further extension of the democratic principles of management and creates the economic conditions for the wider participation of the masses in production management. The system of industrial management and planning based on the Leninist principle of democratic centralism satisfies the present-day requirements of Soviet economy in the best possible way.

The economic reforms being carried out in other socialist countries are also based on the Leninist principle of democratic centralism and on the recognition that this principle must be further developed in the new conditions.

Specifics of collective farm planning
Socialist agriculture is an integral part of the economy. It is closely linked with industry, construction, transport and trade. Collective farm production cannot therefore develop otherwise than according to plan.

The planned management of agriculture as a whole, including the commonly-owned economy of the collective farms, is based on a correct combination of centralised plan targets with the economic initiative of the collective farms in the utilisation of their internal reserves, in revealing the most expedient ways for the utilisation of their resources. Yet, the planning of collective farm production has a number of specific features. The collective farms draw up production development plans on the basis of assignment for the sale of definite agricultural products to the government, which are handed down to them from above. The system of establishing definite plans for the purchase of agricultural products for a number of years in advance and of submitting these to the collective farms ensures the conditions required for the correct management of the collective farm economy. Economically well-founded purchasing prices for agricultural products and mark-ups on prices for products sold over and above the plan targets make the collective farms and the farmers interested in better organisation of production and in raising its effectiveness. The production plans are worked out directly on the farms and take into account the material and human resources available to increase the volume of production, fulfil the plan for state purchases, raise the welfare of the collective farmers and expand production. Here great importance is attached to the correct utilisation of land, machines, equipment and production buildings, to endeavour to raise the labour productivity and to lower the cost of production, and also to the increase of material incentives to the collective farmers.

The state plan for the development of agriculture is a summary of the draft plans of the collective farms and state farms. It stipulates the sizes and directions of capital investments in agriculture, the supply of the collective farms and state farms with machines and equipment, land-improvement, the conditions for the crediting of agriculture, the development of direct links of collective farms and state farms with industry and trade.

Why plans must have a scientific basis

Planned economic management is based on a sound scientific foundation. The science of socialist planning is constantly developing and being enriched with new knowledge through everyday practice.

Economic planning determines the aims of economic development at every stage and also the means of achieving these aims. A scientific determination of the aims and means of economic activity demands accurate stock-taking of all available resources and requirements, all conditions for economic development and all known trends and those taking shape.

In the first stages of the development the Soviet economy produced a comparatively small number of mass products, such as coal, metal, cement, etc. In these conditions the determination of resources and requirements was a comparatively simple matter. But the enormous growth of socialist economy made this much more difficult. Socialist industry now produces a multitude of articles which few years ago did not even exist. The number of new products being evolved on the basis of scientific and technological progress is rapidly growing.

The stupendous economic growth complicates the tasks

of planned economic management enormously. It evolves the need for an improvement of planned economic management, for higher scientific standards in state planning. This applies first and foremost to the scientific validity of the planned rates for the growth of production and the national income and of the basic proportions in the economy. Plans are called upon to ensure the most effective utilisation of all potentialities and resources, to ensure rapid rates for the introduction of the latest achievements of science and technology into industry. This means that they should take into account the prospects offered by scientific and technological progress. The level achieved by the productive forces and the scale of the tasks facing the economy evolved the need for a radical improvement of planned economic management. This management must rely on a genuine scientific basis, on objective economic laws and take sober account of both social requirements and genuine possibilities.

The higher level of scientific planning and centralised economic management is secured alongside decisive strengthening of the economic methods of management and of the economic stimulation of industrial and agricultural production.

The rise in the level of scientific planning allots enormous tasks to the planning bodies. They must determine the optimum proportions for the development of the various branches and the best structure for the country's economy as a whole. They must find ways and means to raise the effectiveness of social production and find resources for the accelerated growth of the national income and the people's welfare.

The greater scientific, technological and economic validity of plans enhances their stability. Yet, they must be verified and adjusted in the course of their fulfilment in accordance with changing conditions.

Planned quotas Planned quotas (or norms) are of the greatest importance to the scientific validity of the plan.

Quotas regulate the utilisation of the material and labour resources and also the utilisation of finances. They are established for the expenditure of labour, materials, fuel, electricity per unit of output, and also for the utilisation of equipment, semi-finished products and for stocks of raw materials and fuel, etc.

Quotas cannot be established once and for all. They improve with economic development, technological progress, improvements in the organisation of labour and production. Particularly important is the improvement of the quotas for machinery and equipment utilisation, for example, the coefficient for the utilisation of the efficient volume of blast-furnaces, the yields of steel per square metre of the hearth of open-hearth furnaces, the number of operating hours of power stations, the yield of coal per combine, etc. The lowering of the quotas for labour and material expenditure per unit of output is also very important.

The experience of go-ahead workers opens up vast possibilities for the improvement of the quotas for the utilisation of machinery and equipment, for the economy of raw and other materials, the growth in labour productivity and the decrease of production costs. Socialist planning relies on the practice of advanced enterprises, progressive workers, engineers and technicians. Planned economic management pursues the aim of systematically introducing scientifically-based, progressive quotas in all branches of economy.

Progressive planned quotas for the utilisation of machinery and equipment, raw and other materials and also for technological methods and terms for the execution of work must be reflected in the plan. At present quotas are being worked out for the labour expenditure required for the production of a centner of agricultural output in different zones. The level achieved in advanced collective farms and state farms is to serve as the basis for these quotas.

The plan and rhythmical production

Planned economy ensures every opportunity for the rhythmical work of every enterprise. The constantly rhythmical operation of all enterprises is a condition for plan fulfilment.

Thus, an enterprise works rhythmically if it produces every decade 32 to 34 per cent of the planned monthly volume. Some enterprises, however, produce only 10 to 15 per cent of the monthly target in the first decade, and between 15 and 20 per cent in the second decade, which means that they have to produce 65 to 70 per cent in the last decade. This means that these enterprises work below capacity at the beginning and in the middle of the month, adopting storm-tactics at the end. Such organisation naturally does not contribute to the enterprise's performance.

The irregular output of production has a negative effect on the fulfilment of all plan assignments. Such work interferes with normal operating conditions, gives rise to disproportions in the utilisation of capacities in shops and departments. Workers stand idle and equipment is not used to capacity. The quality of production drops and the amount of rejects grows.

Work according to schedule ensures rhythmical production. Monthly output targets handed down to every section—shop, department, team—stipulate total volumes, broken down by decades, sometimes even by days. The schedule makes it possible to control the progress made in the fulfilment of the monthly target constantly and to take measures to remove obstacles and delays.

Planning and accounting

The system of economic accounting and statistics is a most important instrument of planning. Lenin said that socialism is accounting and that accounting is inconceivable without statistics. In the period of communist construction accounting becomes even more important.

In socialist society accounting and reporting are organically linked with the economic plan. Since the plan includes monetary and physical indicators, accounting is effected both in monetary and in physical form.

A smoothly functioning system of accounting and reporting makes it possible to control the progress made in the fulfilment of the whole plan and of its separate parts. It helps to disclose what interferes with its fulfilment and to outline measures to improve work. Data on the fulfilment of the plan provided by the system of accounting and reporting are indispensable for compiling the plan for the consecutive period.

The principal types of accounting in socialist economy are statistics and book-keeping.

Statistics are summary numerical data on the processes at work in the national economy and in its separate sectors.

Statistics ensure the systematic collection and grouping of accounting data, their unity and comparability. For this reason statistics serve as the organising and leading principle in the whole system of socialist accounting. Without statistics there can be no scientific economic management based on an understanding of the laws of the socialist mode of production.

Statistics put the finger on weak links in the development of the economy and warn well ahead of the danger of economic disproportions. The accuracy and opportuneness of statistical returns are of great importance to planned economy.

Book-keeping is the method of recording the daily movement of material and monetary means at every enterprise and institution. It is conducted in the form of a balance and gives a characteristic of the financial results of an enterprise's activity. The monetary indicators in book-keeping reflect all the aspects of the enterprise's performance, its successes in production and its shortcomings.

Book-keeping is a means of controlling the fulfilment of plans, the state and movement of the material values and money, placed by the state at the disposal of the enterprise. It must be exact and at the same time simple so as to be accessible to the broad mass of the working people. Good book-keeping organisation is an essential condition for the implementation of cost accounting battling against mismanagement and for successful plan fulfilment at every enterprise.

3. IMPROVEMENT OF PLANNING IN MODERN CONDITIONS

New system of planning and economic stimulation of production   The concrete forms of planned economic management develop and improve in keeping with changing conditions and the new tasks assigned to the economy. The improvement of the planned management of socialist economy is among the most important tasks of the economic reform now underway in the Soviet Union and in other socialist countries.

The economic reform being carried out in accordance with the decision of the September (1965) Plenum of the

Central Committee and the 23rd Congress of the CPSU consists of a system of measures aimed at improving the management of industry and planning, and at granting more economic incentives for industrial production. The economic reform proceeds from the leading role of centralised planned management in the development of Soviet economy. Its main purpose is to improve the system of planned management and management methods, to make them correspond to the wider tasks of communist construction, to develop the basic aspects and advantages of the socialist mode of production and to utilise them to the fullest extent.

The growth and development of socialist economy have evolved the objective need to improve the organisational forms of economic management on the basis of the Leninist principle of democratic centralism. This means that outmoded forms of management have to be replaced by new forms corresponding to the new requirements of the development of the productive forces and relations of production in socialist society.

The new system of management creates more favourable conditions for the rational utilisation of the country's gigantic productive forces, for the rapid growth of the national welfare, and for the complete utilisation of the advantages of the socialist system.

Industrial management on a branch principle

The Communist Party has made a deep analysis of the experience gained in the organisation of industrial management over the past few years and has found serious shortcomings stemming from the rejection of the branch principle. Even though at first the organisation of industrial management through Economic Councils did exhibit certain advantages, with the passing of time the shortcomings of this system came ever more strongly to the fore. Negative consequences followed the rejection of the branch principle.

The management of the branches of industry deteriorated, the unity of technological policy suffered and highly-skilled personnel dispersed. The many-layered system of management with a large number of bodies that evolved led to the wasteful duplication of efforts and to irresponsibility. Endless co-ordination of questions interfered with operational efficiency.

To remedy these shortcomings it was decided to reorganise the industrial management according to the branch principle: Union-Republican and all-Union ministries were organised for the various branches of industry.

This was not a simple return to the former ministries. The new ministries organise the management of the branches of industry in a new way by combining administrative methods with the all-out development of cost accounting methods and economic stimuli. This substantially expands the economic independence of enterprises and their associations, and further develops the Leninist principle of democratic centralism.

The national economic plan is to assign greater importance to the planning by branches, combining it correctly with the planning by republics and economic areas.

Extension of the rights and responsibilities of enterprises The new system of management substantially extends the economic independence and initiative of enterprises and their associations. Prior to the reform the work of enterprises was regimented by a large number of plan indicators. This restricted the independence and initiative of enterprises, lowered their responsibility for the effective organisation of production.

At present the number of plan indicators being handed down (endorsed) to the enterprise from above has been reduced. The enterprises receive only the following plan targets:

  total volume of output to be marketed,
  basic nomenclature,
  wage fund,
  sum total profits and level of profitability,
  payments to budget and budgetary allocations.

In addition to the above, the following indicators are handed down to enterprises: the total volume of centralised capital investments and targets for the commissioning of productive capacities and fixed assets; basic targets for the introduction of new equipment; volume of deliveries of materials and equipment.

All other indicators of the enterprise's economic activity,

including the number of employees, labour productivity, average wage and cost of production, are planned by every single enterprise independently, and are not subject to approval by superior organisations.

Excessive regimentation of the economic activities of enterprises is being eliminated. Enterprises are provided with the means they need for production development. The legal guarantees of the extended rights of enterprises have been laid down in the Statute of Socialist State Productive Enterprises. The enterprise is freed from unnecessary tutelage and is given the opportunity to solve its problems in the most expedient way in keeping with concrete production conditions.

The economic reform is being implemented gradually, as the conditions for the transition of the enterprises and branches of industry to the new conditions of management mature.

The new system of management grants wide operational and economic independence to the enterprise in looking for ways and means to fulfil plan targets, provides for the development of direct links between producer enterprises and consumers and between industrial enterprises and trading organisations. Developing the principle of democratic centralism in economic management, the Party is guided by Lenin's instructions on the need to extend the rights and the responsibility of enterprises in every possible way.

23rd Congress of the CPSU on the main tasks of the five-year economic development plan of the USSR for 1966-70 The five-year plan for 1966-70 worked out on the basis of the Directives of the 23rd Congress of the CPSU is a new important stage in the struggle of the Party and the entire Soviet people for the creation of the material and technical basis of communism and the further strengthening of the country's economic and defence potential.

The main task of the new five-year plan, as defined by the 23rd Congress of the CPSU, is to secure—through the utmost application of the achievements of science and technology, the industrial development of the whole of social production, and the enhancement of its efficiency and higher labour productivity—a considerable growth of industry and stable high rates of agricultural development, thereby achieving a substantial rise of living standards and fuller satisfaction of the material and cultural requirements of all Soviet people.

The tasks of the five-year plan are called upon to ensure the development of the material and technical basis and also to advance the living standard of the people. The increase in the volume of output will go hand in hand with profound qualitative changes in the economy. The growth of the productive forces will be paralleled by an improvement in socio-economic relations.

The targets of the five-year plan are called upon to ensure the technological re-equipment of all branches of social labour on a highly productive industrial basis. Owing to the consistent implementation of the Party's general line on the socialist industrialisation of the country the Soviet Union now has a powerful industrial base with a wide network of specialised engineering and instrument-building plants, which makes it possible to introduce industrial methods in all the branches of the economy.

Industrialisation was and continues to be the general line of Soviet economic development. But the framework of industrial development has extended enormously. In the first stages of the industrialisation the Party and the people faced the task of transforming the Soviet Union from an agrarian into an industrial country. This task was fulfilled through the extensive development of industry, the building of new factories, notably in heavy industry. At present industrial development consists in the intensification of production and raising its effectiveness in all economic branches and spheres.

Heavy industry plays the decisive role in the technical re-equipment of all branches of economy. Its leading branches—power engineering, machine-building, the chemical industry—are to be developed at a higher rate than industry as a whole. The development of these branches creates the material conditions for technological progress and for raising the labour productivity. A new feature in the industrial development of our country in the present five-year period is the rise of the technological level of the branches catering directly for the people's requirements: of agriculture, the food and light industries, trade and public catering, the services sector, transport, communications, and the transformation of the services sector into a mechanised branch of the economy. The provision of all branches with modern equipment will be a further step towards the creation of the material and technical basis of communism.

The five-year plan provides for higher growth rates of social production and of the national income. The aggregate social product will increase yearly by an average of more than 7 per cent as compared with the annual increment of just over 6 per cent during the preceding five-year period. The average yearly absolute increment of industrial output will comprise 22,000-23,000 million rubles as against 15,800 million rubles in the preceding five-year period. The volume of industrial output will grow during these five years by about 50 per cent, the agricultural output by 25 per cent.

The capital investments in the economy will amount to about 310,000 million rubles, i.e., will exceed those of the preceding five-year period by 50 per cent. This ensures the development of all branches of economy and all Union republics.

The main aim of socialist production is to satisfy the growing material and cultural requirements of the people to an ever fuller degree. The Directives for the 1966-70 five-year plan provide for a further substantial rise in the people's welfare on the basis of higher labour productivity, increased output of material wealth and the accelerated growth rate of the national income.

As a result of the fulfilment of the five-year plan much will be done to obliterate the essential distinctions between town and country, between labour by brain and labour by hand. The political and material basis of the alliance of the working class and the peasantry will grow even stronger. The fraternal union of peoples inhabiting our country will further consolidate. The economic ties of the Soviet Union with other socialist countries and the young sovereign countries will be further developed.

The methods of economic development and management worked out by the Party in recent years will be further developed in the current five-year period. A correct combination of scientifically based centralised planned management with the development of the economic initiative and independence of enterprises is an important condition for the successful fulfilment of the new five-year plan.

1. Why is planned economy essential under socialism and what are its advantages?
2. What is the role played by long-term and current plans in the development of socialist economy?
3. What is democratic centralism in economic development?
4. What is the principal content of the new system of planning and economic stimulation?

Chapter XII

SOCIALIST COMMODITY PRODUCTION

1. SPECIFICS OF COMMODITY PRODUCTION UNDER SOCIALISM

Planned nature of commodity-money relations The abolition of the private ownership of the means of production and the establishment of public ownership radically change the character of commodity production and the role of commodity-money relations.

In socialist society the absolute bulk of the output is produced at socialist enterprises. The predominant part of it is produced at state enterprises and therefore is the property of the people as a whole. A definite part is produced at the collective farms and comprises the public property of groups of working people. The output of socialist production embodies directly social labour, organised on a country-wide scale, and not the private labour of individual producers.

Therefore, commodity production under socialism is planned. It is free from the contradictions bred by the anarchy of production under the domination of the private ownership of the means of production. This is new, socialist commodity production.

The Programme of the CPSU points out that in communist construction full use must be made of the commodity-money relations in accordance with the new content they acquire in the socialist period. A major role is played by the utilisation of such instruments for economic development as cost accounting, money, price, production cost, profit, trade, credit, finances.

The product of socialist production is the bearer of new, socialist production relations between people. The commodity as a product of socialist production is, on the one hand, a use value, and on the other, a value.

In the socialist system of economy there is no contradiction between the use value and the value of the commodity, which under the domination of private property embraces in embryo all the antagonisms of the capitalist mode of production. This does not however mean that under socialism there are no contradictions between the use value and the value of the commodity. There are times when some products cannot be sold because of their low quality or their high price.

In perfecting the methods of planned economic management due account is taken of the fact that contradictions between the use value and value of the commodity produced in socialist countries are possible. When the gross output was the main indicator regulating an enterprise's activity, the enterprise sometimes fulfilled the plan by producing output which did not correspond to the existing demand. Under the new system of management one of the plan targets being handed down to the enterprise is the volume of output to be sold. This means that in order to fulfil the plan its output must correspond to social requirements. This removes the possibility of a glut—a result of the contradiction between the use value and the value of the commodity.

The magnitude of the commodity's value is determined not by the individual labour expenditure, not by the amount of labour actually spent on its production, but by the amount of labour socially necessary for its production and reproduction. At every stage of the development of socialist society each product embodies a definite amount of socially necessary labour, depending on the technological level, the organisation of production, and the level of labour productivity achieved at that stage.

In socialist economy we understand under compensation of expenditure the compensation of socially necessary expenditure. If, for example, the enterprise produces articles that are not wanted, the compensation it receives for its expenditure will directly decrease the total amount of society's material wealth. The same thing happens when an enterprise spends more labour and material resources on the production of its output than necessary under concrete production conditions.

Under capitalism enterprises, in which the individual expenditure of labour and materials is higher than the socially necessary one, are doomed to ruin and extinction. In socialist society such enterprises are in a planned way raised to the level of advanced enterprises by modernising their equipment, improving technology and organisation of labour and production, and by eliminating the causes responsible for the unproductive expenditure of labour and material resources.

Changed production conditions, the introduction of better equipment and technology and the growth of labour productivity change the amount of socially necessary labour embodied in a unit of output.

These objective factors are taken into account by society in the planned management of the economy when prices are fixed, labour is paid for, etc.

Production costs and their structure The value of a commodity is the social expenditure on its production. A distinction should be drawn between the value of a commodity and the costs of its production at a given enterprise.

The production costs are made up of the total expenditure a particular enterprise incurs on the production of a definite commodity.

The production costs of a commodity constitute only part of its value. They do not include the part of its value embodying the surplus labour. The direct expenditure of an enterprise on production of the commodity consists of a number of elements.

This is, first of all, the remuneration of the labour of workers at the enterprise in question, i.e., the wages.

Secondly, it includes the expenditure on raw and other materials and fuel.

Thirdly, it is the expenditure on the restoration of the fixed assets, i.e., of the means of labour used in production. To ensure the stable functioning of an enterprise the worn means of labour must be systematically renewed:

buildings and all installations and structures serving production must be repaired or substituted, machinery and equipment must be repaired or renewed, tools must be replaced and supplemented, and so on.

The sums spent on wages and to pay for raw and other materials and fuel are charged fully to the costs of the output produced during a given period. This does not apply however to the expenditure on the restoration and renewal of machinery, equipment and productive structures.

This expenditure cannot be fully charged to a definite single production process or to a definite part of the produced output. It is included in the cost of the total output produced with the help of these means of labour during the whole period of their service in proportional shares as deductions on depreciation.

Depreciation is the compensation for the wear of the fixed assets, which gradually transfer their value to the newly produced output. Depreciation deductions are part of the expenditure on the production of output and their size affects the production costs. The sum of depreciation deductions during the whole service life of the fixed assets must be sufficiently large to compensate for all the expenditure on the acquisition of these assets and on their partial restoration and modernisation.

In addition to the expenditure on wages, raw and other materials and the depreciation deductions production costs include also other expenditure connected with the organisation of production in the shops and in the enterprise as a whole. This is the wages of the administrative personnel and the engineers and other technical workers and also of the servicing personnel. This includes also the expenditure on the repair of various production buildings and structures, expenditure on the power equipment of the enterprise and on intra-factory transport. This group of expenditure is called the general factory and shop expenditure.

Finally the full production costs include also the expenditure on the sale of the output: expenditure on warehousing, packing, transportation, etc.

The ratio of the different components of the production costs is known as their structure. The production costs structure differs in the various branches of industry; it differs also in individual factories of a single branch, depending on their size, technical equipment, situation, etc.

In the extractive industry wages account for a large share of the production costs, since the objects of labour (coal, ore) are given by nature. These are labour-intensive branches. In the manufacturing industry, on the other hand, material expenditure accounts for the larger share of the production costs. These are material-intensive branches. In some branches of industry—the power-intensive industries—the expenditure on electric power (non-ferrous metallurgy, for example) is very high. Finally there are branches of industry in which the share of equipment depreciation is very high (in the oil industry, for example). These are branches in which the capital/product ratio is high. As regards the overall structure for the whole of Soviet industry in 1964, the production costs structure in industry was as follows: raw and other basic materials accounted for 63.6 per cent, auxiliary materials 4.6 per cent, fuel 3.2 per cent, power 2 per cent, depreciation 4.9 per cent, wages plus social insurance charges 18.4 per cent and other expenditure 3.3 per cent.

Raising the quality of output

One of the vital tasks of economic development at the present stage is to achieve a radical improvement in the quality of output. Modern technological progress calls for the constant improvement of machinery, machine tools and equipment. Outmoded types of equipment arrest the growth of production and put a brake on the rise in labour productivity. The branches producing means of labour must keep pace with the progress of science and technology, must produce output corresponding to the modern level of technological development. It is particularly important to lengthen the service life of machinery and to raise its reliability and precision.

Technological progress puts increasing demands on materials. Many modern industries require materials of high purity, great strength, etc.

The growth of the Soviet people's welfare puts ever greater demands on the quality of consumer goods. The consumer wants elegant clothes and footwear, modern furniture and so on.

Finally, in view of Soviet goods being placed on the world market, where they have to compete against the goods of the highly advanced capitalist countries, it is particularly essential for Soviet goods to be superior to foreign goods in quality.

The higher the quality of output, the more effective and productive is social labour. One of the main tasks of the present five-year period is to raise the quality of output so as to ensure all branches of the economy with better means of production (highly productive machinery, equipment and instruments, high-quality raw and other materials), and the population with a wide range of goods satisfying the growing demands of the Soviet people.

2. THE ROLE OF THE LAW OF VALUE IN PLANNED ECONOMY

Objective character of the law of value in socialist economy The planned management of the economy makes it necessary to commensurate and compare the expenditure on production with its results. The expenditure on production consists, first, of the expenditure of live labour and, secondly, of the expenditure of labour embodied in the form of means of production—raw materials, fuel, machinery and equipment. The effectiveness of social production is highest when each enterprise provides maximum results at minimum outlay. Only the comparison of the sum total of production expenditure with its result enables us to evaluate how this immutable law of socialist economic management is being observed by an enterprise.

Furthermore, under any social system the production of output in keeping with the various demands requires an expenditure of a definite amount of social labour. The need for the distribution of social labour in definite proportions cannot be ruled out by any social system. In all and every society the working time at the disposal of society is in one way or another distributed among the various branches of production.

The planned distribution of social labour and of the means of production among the individual branches and enterprises requires an accurate commensuration of the expenditure of labour and material means with the results of production. To compare the expenditure of an enterprise over a definite period of time with the mass of the output produced during that period both the expenditure and the results of production must be reduced to a common denominator. Only value and the economic categories based on it can be used as such a common denominator.

The following question may arise in this connection: cannot the expenditure and the results of production be compared directly in units of labour, for example, in working hours or days, without resorting to value categories such as price, production cost, etc.?

The answer to this question is no. Although socialist labour has a directly social character it is not homogeneous as regards its quality. In this respect it differs from labour under full communism. There still is a difference between physical and mental labour, between the labour of workers and collective farmers. The skills of different workers are also not identical. Different branches of the economy and individual enterprises differ as regards the mechanisation of labour in them.

In these conditions a comparison of the expenditure on production with its results can be based only on the law of value. Under capitalism the law of value operates blindly, spontaneously. In socialist economy it is used consciously by socialist society for the planned organisation of the economy.

Thus, the law of value is an objective economic law of the socialist mode of production. Economic methods of planned economic management and the economic stimulation of production are based on this objective law.

In the period of communist construction the full mastery of the law of value is a condition for the economic stimulation of production, thrifty management, the multiplication of social wealth and the advance of the people's welfare. Value categories give socialist society an objective yardstick gauging the effectiveness, expediency and rationality of any economic measure. They ensure the correct refunding of the expenditure of enterprises and economic branches. Value categories help to prepare the conditions for the transition to the highest phase of communism.

Communist society will be guided directly by the principle of labour economy in economic development without resorting to the expression of labour expenditure in terms of value. Then, with the transition to a single public communist form of property and to the communist system of distribution, commodity-money relations will become redundant and will fade out.

System of value relations under socialism For socialist economy to function normally there must be a definite system of interlinked value relations, including price and profit, wages and bonuses, trade, finances and credit, differential rent, interest, taxes, etc. The economic methods of planned management, the strengthening of which comprises the most important aspect of the new system of management, are based on that system of value relations. The economic reform aims at strengthening and developing cost accounting, enhancing the economic stimulation of production with the help of the system of the value categories of socialism.

Value categories of socialism have an entirely different socio-economic content from the analogous categories of capitalism.

Under the domination of private property price is a form of expression of the law of value which, in conditions of anarchy of production and destructive competition, operates spontaneously. In socialist economy price is one of the most important means of planned economic development, a form of the expression which the operation of the law of value assumes under public ownership of the means of production.

Under capitalism wages are the price of labour power the proletariat sells to the capitalist. In socialist economy wages are a form of remuneration of the labour of workers who are free from exploitation and are engaged in social production.

Under capitalism profit is the fruit of the exploitation of labour by capital, it embodies the surplus value created by the unpaid labour of the workers and appropriated by the class of the capitalist exploiters. In socialist economy profit is the yardstick determining the contribution made by each enterprise to the development of social production, and the multiplication of social wealth.

The character and role of all other value categories changes in the same way. Instead of being forms expressing capitalist relations of production, they all become forms expressing the production relations of socialism.

The system of socialist value relations, regulating the exchange of activities in socialist economy, serves as a basis for effective economic stimulation. In socialist society there is no objective basis for the emergence of contradictions between the interests of individual working people, the staffs of enterprises and the interests of society. However, such contradictions are not inevitable. And if they do occasionally arise, it is because the system of economic stimulation is at fault. This system is called upon to ensure conditions under which what is profitable for society is profitable also for the staff of enterprises and for each worker.

The unity of the plan and the law of value
The novelty of the commodity-money relations in socialist economy consists in the fact that they express socialist production relations, relations of the socialist production organised along planned lines. In socialist society the law of value differs radically from that law under capitalism both as regards content and form.

Under socialism every labouring man receives from society as much as he gives to society minus the share going to satisfy social requirements. The amount of labour he gives to society in one form is returned to him in another. This relates not only to individual workers but also to entire collectives, enterprises, branches. For an enterprise or branch to develop normally its expenditure must be refunded. If, for example, agriculture were not refunded its expenditure, it would not be able to advance. Material stimulation of production is based on the refund of expenditure.

This determines the fundamental features of socialist commodity production, of the law of value and of all the categories connected with that law under socialism.

First, in socialist economy the law of value is no longer a force operating spontaneously through endless price fluctuations. The socialist law of value cannot lead to anarchy of production and destructive crises.

Secondly, with the abolition of the exploitation of man by man, labour power stops being a commodity, an object that can be bought and sold. With the socialist reorganisation of agriculture land also stops being an object that can be bought and sold. Therefore, under socialism the law of value does not have the consequences it inevitably has under the domination of private property. It cannot give rise to capitalist relations with all the contradictions inherent in them. This is because in socialist society the means of production cannot turn into means of exploitation, into capital. Only articles of consumption can be bought and turned into personal property.

In this way in socialist society the law of value and the categories based on it—price, wages, profit, etc.—acquire a new content. They are economic categories of planned socialist economy, excluding the exploitation of man by man, anarchy of production, etc.

In the socialist economic system the law of value is not alien to the planned, proportional development of the economy but is indissolubly bound up with it. The law of value becomes an inalienable component of the whole system of objective economic laws of socialism. Scientific planning is based on an ever sounder understanding and application of these laws.

The unity of these laws, their indissoluble interconnection and interaction create the objective need for centralised planned economic management combined with the extensive operational and economic independence of the basic economic cells, of the socialist enterprises. This combination presupposes the all-round development and strengthening of the economic methods of planned management with the help of the system of socialist value categories, such as price and profit, wages and bonuses, credit and interest, trade and finance.

The practice of socialist construction, founded on the fundamental principles of Marxist-Leninist theory and on the creative experience of the popular masses, has evolved a system of economic methods, which in aggregate can be used to ensure rational business management. These methods are based on an organic combination of planned economic management with the conscious utilisation of the law of value.

The value categories of socialist commodity production are objective criteria for evaluating the performance of enterprises, their staff and every separate worker. They help solve the economic and technological problems constantly facing the economic bodies, industrial and agricultural enterprises, their associations and construction and design organisations. Economic methods regulate in the best possible way the relations between industry and agriculture, economic branches, enterprises, ensuring the refund of the socially necessary expenditure and the remuneration of labour in accordance with its quantity and quality.

The extensive utilisation of socialist value categories and economic stimuli is an important condition for improving the country's economic planning, ensuring the balance and effectiveness of economic plans, the correspondence between production, consumption and accumulation and correct proportions in the economy.

Price in socialist economy The price of a commodity produced in a socialist enterprise is a monetary form of its value. Having mastered the law of value the socialist state fixes prices on commodities proceeding from the socially necessary expenditure of labour on their production.

The Programme of the CPSU states that the system of prices should be constantly improved, that it should be brought in line with the tasks of communist construction, with technological progress, with the growth of production and consumption and cuts in production outlays. Prices must, to a growing extent, reflect the socially necessary expenditure of labour, ensure the return of production and circulation outlays and a certain profit for each normally working enterprise.

Hence, the price of a commodity is based on its value, i.e., on the sum total of socially necessary labour expended, the expenditure of the live and embodied labour needed for the production of the commodity.

Price serves first and foremost as a universal means of accounting in planned socialist commodity production. In addition the price category fulfils also a number of other functions. Prices are fixed to stimulate technological progress, expand production and steadily lower costs. Furthermore, prices are fixed so as to co-ordinate the consumer demand for definite commodities with the possibilities of increasing their output. That is why it is sometimes necessary to fix for some commodities prices which deviate from their value.

The price policy being conducted by the socialist state serves to promote the constant improvement of production techniques. Prices must promote the output of better kinds of equipment, machinery and instruments. At the same time they must become instrumental in making enterprises stop the production of outmoded types of products.

An important aspect of the price policy is that it promotes economy in the expenditure of scarce types of raw materials, the introduction of new materials and the transition to locally available fuel and raw materials. The price policy is a means of struggle against excessively distant and unrational freight transport. The relation of prices of individual commodities is fixed to stimulate the consumption of goods the output of which can be rapidly expanded (owing to the availability of raw materials, productive capacities, etc.).

The basic trend in price policy in the period of communist construction is to lower the prices in an economically rational way on the basis of the growth in the labour productivity and the reduction of production costs. An essential condition for the lowering of retail prices is a cut in the production and circulation costs per unit of output.

3. MONEY IN SOCIALIST ECONOMY

The functions of money in socialist society The operation of the law of value under socialism makes it necessary to have a monetary system. The value categories—price, production cost, wages, profit, etc. —are expressed in terms of money.

In the socialist economic system money expresses socialist production relations and serves as an important instrument of planned economic management. It fulfils a number of functions.

First, money serves as a measure of value. The value of the commodity—all socially necessary expenditure of live and embodied labour spent on its production—can be counted and expressed only in terms of money. The value of the commodity is expressed in a definite sum of money comprising its price. In this connection money is also a yardstick measuring prices: it serves to compare and to commensurate the prices of commodities.

In its function as a measure of value money serves as a means of public control over the measure of labour and the measure of consumption of the members of society. The labour of the members of society is measured in terms of money. The factory and office workers, and to a high degree also collective farmers, receive money for their work.

In its function as a measure of value money also serves as an instrument of cost accounting. The labour expenditure necessary for the production of commodities, the expenditure of raw and other materials and fuel, the wear of equipment, buildings, the expenditure on the management of production, freight transportation, the delivery of goods to the consumer through the trading network, etc., are all expressed in terms of money. The results of an enterprise's performance can be expressed most fully and in a most general way in terms of money.

Secondly, under socialism money serves as a means of circulation. The factory and office workers employed at state enterprises and institutions spend their wages on the purchase of goods. The collective farmers also buy goods for their money incomes. The sale and purchase of commodities is effected through the instrument of money.

As distinct from capitalism, under socialism money in its function of a means of circulation does not evolve contradictions and is not fraught with the threat of crises. In their bulk, the goods sold in socialist society are the product of direct, social labour. For this reason the sale of goods does not encounter the obstacles which under capitalism arise from the contradiction between the social character of production and the private capitalist form of appropriation.

If some commodities cannot be sold, if in certain cases we observe overstocking, this is due to the inferior quality of the goods, defects in the work of trading organisations, etc. Such defects are not rooted in the socialist economic system and are removed by the improvement in economic management.

Thirdly, in socialist society money serves as a means of payment. As a means of payment money is used to settle accounts between socialist enterprises, to pay wages to factory and office workers, taxes, lottery winnings, interest on state loans, etc. Under capitalism money in its function of a means of payment aggravates the contradiction inherent in the commodity and hence contributes to the maturing of economic crises. Socialist economy is free of these contradictions of capitalism. Socialist enterprises may delay the payment for goods and services only because of a failure to fulfil the production or construction plan, because of the inferior quality of the output, the excessive production cost or slowness of the circulation of material means. Such payment difficulties are overcome by improving the work of the enterprise and by increasing the responsibility of enterprises for the fulfilment of their contractual obligations.

Fourthly, in socialist society money fulfils the function of a means of socialist accumulation and saving. The mobilisation of the accumulations, forming in the whole economy, is also effected in the form of money. These means are used to expand socialist production, to strengthen the country's economic potential and to provide for the material and cultural needs of the working people.

Finally, money in a socialist state fulfils the function of world money. Thus, Soviet currency serves as a means of payment in the commodity exchange and other economic ties with the countries in the socialist system, and also with a number of countries outside that system. This role is also being played to a greater or smaller extent by the currencies of other socialist countries, which have extensive economic ties with the outer world.

The law of money circulation

Money must be stable if the socialist economy is to develop successfully. Therefore, the regulation of the money circulation is one of the principal tasks of planned economic management.

The stability of money in socialist society is ensured first and foremost by the enormous commodity stocks accumulated in the hands of the state and sold by it at fixed prices. The stability of money is ensured also by the crisis-free development of the economy, the planned organisation of labour on a social scale.

With the growth of the socialist economy the socialist monetary system becomes stronger. This can be seen from the example of the Soviet monetary system in the post-war period. Owing to the growth of the industrial and agricultural output the real incomes of the population have grown substantially.

In an economy, in which there are commodity-money relations, the amount of money needed for circulation is determined by the sum of the prices of commodities in circulation and the rate of the money turnover. The larger the sum of prices of the circulating commodities, the more money has to be in circulation. At the same time the faster the money turnover the less money is needed in circulation. This is the law of money circulation. A violation of this law, i.e., the issue of an excessive amount of money leads to a rise in prices. The amount of money in circulation can be reduced where accounts are settled by written orders.

One of the tasks of planned economic management is to ensure the correspondence between the mass of commodities being offered for sale and the amount of money in circulation. This correspondence is established through the credit and finance system of socialism, by increasing the production of commodities and expanding trade.

REVISION QUESTIONS

1. What are the specifics of socialist commodity production?
2. What is the role of the law of value in socialist economy?
3. What importance has the high quality of output for economic development?

Chapter XIII

COST ACCOUNTING AND PROFITABILITY

1. SOCIALIST PRODUCTIVE ENTERPRISE

The enterprise—the primary cell of the economy The socialist economic system embraces tens of thousands of state-owned enterprises in industry, construction, agriculture, transport and other branches of economy. In addition to state enterprises there are collective farm and co-operative enterprises, primarily collective farms, producing the absolute bulk of agricultural products.

An enterprise is a production unit and at the same time a technological unit. Every enterprise manufactures products of a definite kind, and has a corresponding productive apparatus and uses corresponding types of raw and other materials for this purpose. At the same time an enterprise is a socio-economic unit—a collective of people employed in the given cell of the economy.

An enterprise is the basic, primary cell of the economy. Its activities affect the whole of planned socialist economy. At present many enterprises are very large production units. There are branches in which a single big enterprise produces as much, or more, than was produced by the corresponding branch in the whole of pre-revolutionary Russia.

The state provides material and monetary resources to every enterprise: buildings, machinery, equipment, raw material stocks, fuel, etc. The enterprise sells the products it produces or procures and covers its expenditure out of the proceeds. A socialist enterprise acts in a legal capacity and as an economic unit and bears responsibility for the results of its activities. Its activity is based on a combination of centralised guidance with economic independence and its own initiative. Working in accordance with the plan on a cost accounting basis, it must achieve maximum results with a minimum expenditure of labour, material and financial resources. For this purpose the enterprise must use its productive capacities, internal reserves, the land at its disposal, and other natural resources to the maximum.

The enterprise must observe a strict regime of economy, introduce the latest achievements of science, technology, advanced experience, progressive quotas for the expenditure of raw and other materials, fuel and electric power; it must lower production costs and raise the profitability of production. The enterprise is able to achieve such results since it is granted with rights and is given every opportunity to display economic initiative.

A new and very important form of organisation of industry that has been advanced by practical requirements are branch associations working on a cost accounting basis. The setting up of such associations opens up extensive possibilities for specialisation, co-operation and concentration of production, promotes the rational utilisation of skilled personnel and better technological and economic management of the enterprises.

The state allots material and monetary means to the socialist enterprise working on a cost accounting basis. These means are the assets of the enterprise.

The enterprise uses its assets for the production of output. The finished output is realised, i.e., is sold for money to other production enterprises or to trading organisations. The enterprise uses the proceeds to pay for the expenditure needed to continue production. In this way the assets issued to the enterprise are in constant turnover.

The means of production at socialist enterprises form their productive assets. They are divided into fixed assets and the assets in turnover. The fixed assets embrace the means of labour, the assets in turnover—the objects of labour.

The fixed assets serve the production process over a number of production cycles. They transfer their value to the finished product piecemeal over a long period. They maintain their physical form during the whole production process.

The assets in turnover are completely used up in every production cycle. Accordingly they transfer their value to the finished products in full. During the production process they change their form and become new products, satisfying some social want.

The assets in turnover of an enterprise are made up, first, of the subjects of labour that have not yet entered the production process and, secondly, the subjects of labour that are already in the production process. In accordance with this division the assets in turnover consist of: 1) the production stocks (stocks of raw materials, fuel, etc.) and 2) of the work in progress.

In addition to the productive fixed assets the enterprise has also non-productive assets. These are the fixed assets consisting of the enterprise's houses, schools, clubs, hospitals, etc.

In addition to the productive assets every enterprise has definite assets on hand. These are the means of the enterprise serving in the sphere of circulation. They include finished but unsold output and the money resources of the enterprise designed for the payment of wages, the purchase of raw and other materials and for sundry payments.

The productive assets in turnover and the assets on hand form the circulating assets of the enterprise. Part of the circulating assets have been placed at the disposal of the enterprise by the state. These are the enterprise's own circulating assets. The other part consists of borrowed funds loaned to the enterprise by the bank.

All assets and means of the enterprise must be used in a clever, rational way if the enterprise it to work effectively. This means that the fixed assets—productive areas, buildings, equipment, machinery, lathes, etc.—must be used to the maximum. This presupposes also the economic expenditure of the circulating assets: the lowering of the expenditure of raw and other materials, fuel per unit of output, an acceleration of the turnover of the circulating assets by eliminating surplus and superfluous stocks and by accelerating the sale of the finished output.

The economic relations between society, the enterprise and every individual worker

Definite economic relations exist between society, the enterprise and every individual worker. Society grants the enterprise extensive rights and this imposes on the staff of the enterprise definite obligations to society, as represented by the socialist state.

The vital interests of all members of society coincide under socialism because the means of production are public property. All members of socialist society are keenly interested, first, in the existence and consolidation of the socialist social and political system and, secondly, in the growth and flourishing of socialist economy, for this is a precondition and at the same time the main guarantee of their growing welfare. It is thanks to this that public interest plays the leading role under socialism.

Society, each enterprise and every single labouring man pursue in the main identical interests. This does not mean however that their interests automatically coincide in every practical question and in every concrete case.

Socialist economy presupposes, first, the operational and economic independence of enterprises within definite limits and, hence, the need for an equivalent compensation for the efforts of their personnel. Socialist economy presupposes, secondly, observance of the principle of remuneration of workers in accordance with the amount and quality of labour expended by them for the benefit of society. Yet, these distinctive features make possible the emergence of differences between the interests of society, production collectives and individual working people, and it is therefore necessary to use rational methods of economic stimulation to ensure the required community of interests.

Contradictions between the direct economic interests of the enterprise and society as a whole emerge under socialism only if the system of economic stimulation is not used to a sufficient degree. With the development of socialist economy and the growth in the complexity of its tasks it becomes increasingly important to implement the Leninist principle of material incentives to the full. This principle presupposes a correct combination of the interests of individual working people, collectives of working people, enterprises and society as a whole. The possibility of a successful solution of this task is inherent in the socialist system, which is free of class antagonisms, because under socialism production benefits the people and its growth leads to a rise in their welfare. Production for the sake of the ever fuller and all-round satisfaction of the requirements of society as a whole and of its every member is the cornerstone of economic development under socialism and communism.

The plan targets and the criteria for the evaluation of the enterprise's performance are designed to make the enterprises interested in producing the commodities needed by the economy and to use methods which are most expedient from a national economic standpoint. Economic stimuli are used to achieve this effect.

The essence of cost accounting and its tasks We saw above that the achievement in the interests of society of maximum results with a minimum outlay is an immutable law of economic development under socialism. Cost accounting is the most important instrument for ensuring thrift at socialist enterprises.

Cost accounting is a method of planned management of socialist enterprises based on a comparison of their expenditure and the results of production in value (money) terms.

Cost accounting presupposes constant commensuration of the expenditure of the enterprise and the results of its activities. Every enterprise working on a cost accounting basis draws up an independent balance sheet, accurately reflecting its income and expenditure, its profits and losses. It has a current account in the State Bank and disposes of the sums on that account in accordance with the existing rules. The enterprise enters into economic contracts with other enterprises, institutions and organisations and is responsible for their fulfilment. It has the right to obtain credits to supplement its own resources.

Thus, cost accounting is a definite form of relations between the socialist state and the enterprises and also between individual enterprises. This form of relations is designed to ensure the most expedient and rational utilisation of the assets issued to the enterprise by the state.

The consistent observance of the cost accounting principle helps to reveal all the resources and potentialities of the enterprise and to make the fullest use of them. Cost accounting is designed to ensure that the labour expenditure on the production of every commodity is reduced to the minimum socially necessary level. It helps systematically to lower the socially necessary expenditure of labour.

Cost accounting is indissolubly linked with the regime of economy for it presupposes a rational and prudent expenditure of labour, material and money resources, the avoidance of losses and unproductive expenditure in all branches of economy.

Cost accounting presupposes the responsibility of every enterprise (of its administration) for the utilisation of its assets and the results of the enterprise's performance. It requires that there be strict order at the enterprise, a strict accounting of all the enterprise's material and monetary resources and strict control over their expenditure.

Under socialism all working people are vitally interested in prudent and expedient business management at every single enterprise and also on a national scale. The more effectively business is conducted, the more output is obtained with the same labour and material expenditure, the fuller can the requirements of society as a whole and of its every member be satisfied.

In addition to this general interest, cost accounting creates a direct material interest of the staff of every enterprise in the fulfilment and overfulfilment of the plan, in achieving maximum results with minimum outlay. This aim is achieved through the application of the system of economic stimulation of production, based on cost accounting.

Intrafactory cost accounting

The success of the national economic plan is decided by the enterprises, while the success of the plan at every enterprise is decided in its shops, production departments, teams, at every place of work.

Cost accounting could not be complete if it embraced only the economic links between enterprises. To be complete cost accounting must embrace also the relations within the enterprise, between its parts—the shops, departments, teams. Intrafactory cost accounting, as applied within the shop, department, team, serves this purpose. It consists in comparing the expenditure on production with its results in every one of these sections of the enterprise. Intrafactory (shop) cost accounting is an integral part of the system of economic stimulation of production. In connection with the introduction of the new system of management, the further development of intrafactory cost accounting has become even more important.

The introduction of intrafactory cost accounting presupposes first of all that plan targets be handed down to every production section. The fulfilment and overfulfilment of the plan targets is encouraged by issuing bonuses to the workers of the shop, department and team in question.

Cost accounting and economic laws of socialism Socialist cost accounting is based on the utilisation of the objective economic laws of socialism, notably the law of labour economy, the law of planned, proportionate development and the law of value.

Cost accounting has the purpose of ensuring the thrifty conduct of business at every enterprise in accordance with the law of labour economy. Furthermore, cost accounting has the purpose of directing the whole activity of the enterprise so as to enable it to fulfil its plan targets in the most successful way. Thirdly, cost accounting is based on the full utilisation of the law of value.

The new economic system of management means a transition to economic methods of management in the national economy, to the economic stimulation of enterprises on the basis of full cost accounting, providing for the thorough, economically well-founded commensuration of expenditure with results on a national scale and in every enterprise. The economic methods of management and socialist cost accounting presuppose the management of business activities with the help of a system of value categories, such as price, profit, wages and bonuses, credit and interest, rent and charges for the use of productive assets.

2. BASIC PRINCIPLES OF COST ACCOUNTING

Profitability of production and ways to raise it Cost accounting is one of the most typical features of socialist economic management. However, while administrative methods of economic management predominated, it had a more or less formal character. The new system of management requires the introduction of genuine cost accounting in all the activities of the enterprise. The skill of accurately comparing the expenditure and results of production, establishing the effectiveness of capital investments, the relative profitability of definite technological processes and the use of definite types of raw and other materials, in short, the taking of rational economic decisions in matters large and small determines in the final count the results of the people's labour and hence also the advance in their living standard.

Cost accounting aims at ensuring the profitable operation of enterprises. Every enterprise operating on a cost accounting basis must not only cover its expenditure out of its proceeds but must also yield a certain profit.

Already in the first years of socialist construction Lenin emphasised the need for strict cost accounting and for the profitable operation of enterprises. After the transition to the new economic policy Lenin said that trusts and enterprises working on a cost accounting basis had been founded exactly for the purpose of making them fully responsible for operation without losses and that their transition to cost accounting was connected with the urgent need to raise labour productivity and to ensure that every enterprise work without loss and make a definite profit.

The profitability of production is raised through the better utilisation of all resources at the disposal of the enterprise, the liquidation of all losses, the thorough financial control of all the aspects of the enterprise's business activity, by lowering production costs and ensuring the high quality of its output. The Programme of the CPSU states that it is essential to strengthen cost accounting in every way, to lower the costs and to raise the profitability of production.

To strengthen and develop genuine cost accounting, and hence to raise profitability, the following measures have to be taken. First, conditions must be created in which the enterprise is independently able to solve questions connected with the improvement of production and in which it is interested in the optimum use of its assets, in increasing its output and raising its profits. Secondly, it is essential to strengthen the cost accounting principle in the relations between enterprises, to ensure the strict observance of their obligations of deliveries and to increase their material responsibility for the fulfilment of their obligations. Thirdly, cost accounting must make every enterprise, every shop and department interested not only in fulfilling its targets, but also in improving the overall results of the enterprise's operation, in working out and fulfilling higher plan targets, in the better utilisation of internal resources with a view to increasing the profitability of production.

Extended economic independence of enterprises The new system of management provides for a decisive extension of the operational and economic independence of enterprises. The enterprise is given far wider rights in the organisation of production and in all other spheres of economic activity.

The rights and duties of the enterprise are laid down in the Statute of the Socialist State Industrial Enterprise, confirmed by the USSR Council of Ministers and put into force in October 1965. The Statute is in full conformance with the new system of planning and economic stimulation of production and in accordance with the decisions of the September (1965) Plenary Meeting of the Central Committee of the CPSU and the 23rd Congress of the CPSU.

The Statute of the Socialist State Industrial Enterprise contains the general principles regulating the enterprise's activities, gives an outline of its managerial structure, its production and economic activities, its rights in planning, capital construction and major repairs, in the improvement of the production equipment and technology, in obtaining materials and equipment and in marketing its output, in the field of finance, labour and wages. Substantially extending the rights, economic initiative and independence of enterprises, the Statute is in full conformance with the new tasks facing not only enterprises in industry but also in construction, agriculture, transport and communications.

As we have said above, the extension of the economic independence of enterprises involves first and foremost a substantial decrease in the number of plan indicators, regulating the operation of the enterprises, being endorsed by superior organisations. All other indicators are worked out by the enterprise independently and the personnel participates in production planning on a much wider scale than it did before.

The production plans are considered by the superior economic bodies with the participation of the enterprises. Once approved, plans are changed only in exceptional cases. When targets are changed amendments must simultaneously be made in all interlinked plan indicators and also in the accounts of the enterprise with the budget.

The personnel of the enterprises, provided there are sufficient internal resources, is entitled to increase its programme without special permission, to accept orders and enter into contracts with other enterprises, on the condition, of course, that this does not interfere with the fulfilment of the state target. An enterprise is allowed to manufacture output over and above the plan target, if it is able to ensure the sale of the surplus.

The personnel of the enterprise is interested in the profitable performance of the enterprise as a whole since the general results of its activity determine the formation and the size of the incentives funds, which finance the bonuses being paid to workers, engineers and technicians and the administrative personnel in addition to wages and also the measures to improve the way of life of the staff of the given enterprise, and to expand production.

Cost accounting and price fixing

The introduction of genuine cost accounting calls for the improvement of the price fixing system.

In socialist economy prices play a major role. First of all the price is the common denominator with the help of which all the expenditure on production is compounded and compared with the results of production. The price system is the focus in which gather all the threads of the planned management of the national economy. The price co-ordinates the whole complex aggregate of relations within the individual branches and those between the different economic branches. Prices reflect the expenditures and results in the economy as a whole and in every single enterprise. The cost of production depends on the prices of raw and other materials, tariffs for electric power and transport operations, while the profit at the given cost level depends on the price of the output being produced by the enterprise.

The price on industrial output expresses either the relation between state enterprises operating on a cost accounting basis (wholesale prices) or the relation between the state and individual members of socialist society in the sphere of the distribution of consumer articles (retail prices). The relations between the state and the collective farms are expressed in the purchasing prices for collective farm products.

The Programme of the CPSU points out that prices must to a growing extent reflect the socially necessary expenditure of labour, ensure the return of production and distribution outlays and a certain profit for each enterprise normally operating.

The price of a commodity is based on its average branch production costs. But the price cannot be equal to the costs. The costs include only part of the socially necessary expenditure on the production of that commodity, namely, the expenditure on raw and other materials, the depreciation of the fixed assets and the wages paid out. But the commodities produced embody also the surplus labour of the workers in socialist economy, and its value is not included in the production costs. Thus, the costs do not exhaust all the socially necessary expenditure on the production of the commodity and therefore do not ensure profit and accumulations.

The price of the commodities, embodying the whole sum of the socially necessary expenditure on its production, is made up of the average branch cost of the commodities plus a definite profit. The sum of the profit included in the prices of all commodities produced by society is equal to the value of the whole product of the surplus labour expended in social production. The sum of prices of all commodities produced by the socialist economy is equal to the sum of their values.

The cost of production reflects the labour/product and material/product ratio of the production of the commodity while the profit must express also the assets/product ratio. Output, the production of which requires high capital investments from society (i.e., a large expenditure of the fixed and circulating productive assets), cost it more than output, the production of which requires smaller capital investments. Society is therefore naturally concerned with the assets/product ratio in the various industries. It follows, that generally the price of the commodities produced must contain a definite share of pure profit in addition to the costs, the size of that share depending on the assets/product ratio of the commodities.

The new system of management is indissolubly linked with a decisive increase in the role of profit as a criterion for the evaluation of the performance of the enterprise, its production staff and its administration. Formerly the enterprise's performance was evaluated according to numerous plan indicators which were handed down from above; now that the number of these indicators has been decreased, the main criteria in the evaluation of its performances are the volume of commodities sold, the sum total of profits and the level of profitability.

To maintain the necessary proportionality in the economy every enterprise must fulfil definite targets as regards the amount of output it sells and the basic nomenclature of its output. Providing these targets are fulfilled, the following are regarded as the general criteria of the enterprise's performance—profit as the difference between the total outlay on production and the proceeds from the sale of the finished output and the level of profitability (hereinafter called simply profitability) as the ratio of the sum total of profits to the sum total of productive assets.

There are close links between the indicators for the volume of marketed output, the sum total profits and the profitability. The target for the marketing of output is designed to establish closer links between production and consumption. The profit and profitability indicators enable us to evaluate the effectiveness of production, the contribution made by every enterprise to the sum total resources of socialist society.

The volume of marketed output characterises the results of production, but in itself does not provide any information as to the outlay on production. The sum total of the expenditure on production is expressed by the production costs, but this indicator, which is extremely important to the technical, output and financial plan, does not enable us to make an estimate of the results of production. While the lowering of costs per unit of output is extremely important, it is but one way of increasing the resources of society, the growth of the volume of produced and sold output, and the improvement of its quality being other ways towards achieving this end.

294

The profit indicator is important because it reflects all aspects of the enterprise's production activities. Every improvement in its work—the economy of raw materials, the better utilisation of equipment, a rise in labour productivity, etc.—result in an increase of the total profits, while deteriorating performance decreases profits. Profits grow through an increase of the proceeds as a result of an expansion of production and through the decrease of outlay, as a result of lowering production costs. Therefore, profit is the most general criterion for the evaluation of an enterprise's economic performance.

The profitability indicator also plays a very important role. It characterises the effectivenes of production, which is the higher, the greater is the profit per ruble of productive assets.

Ruble control One of the most important principles of socialist cost accounting is the ruble control (financial control) of the enterprise's activity.

All the money resources of the enterprises—the proceeds from the sale of their output, bank credits and budget finance—are charged to the account of the enterprise in the State Bank.

The enterprises settle mutual accounts and those with institutions and organisations and also with the financial system by written order. Cash is drawn from the account to pay wages and certain other overheads. In exceptional cases the account may be debited without the agreement of the management: this happens generally only to enterprises which fail to pay their debts on time and thus violate the financial discipline essential to ensure the all-round fulfilment of the plan.

The enterprise's account is, as it were, the cashier since all its income and expenditure passes through it. The money being paid into the account accurately reflects the fulfilment of the plan indicators for the production and sale of output. The state of the account and the financial statements and balances give the bank a picture of the progress made in the fulfilment of the plan. Whenever necessary, the bank gives opportune warning to the enterprise's superior economic bodies about its financial position and suggests that measures be taken to improve its work. In this way the bank exercises financial control over the activities of every enterprise.

This control is based on the enterprise's financial dependence on the results of its activities and on the fulfilment of its contractual obligations with other enterprises—consumers and suppliers. The better the enterprise works, the more economically it uses raw and other materials, fuel, money resources and the quicker the turnover of the enterprise's assets the better is its financial position.

But the financial position even of an excellently operating enterprise may be unsatisfactory if the buyer of its output fails to pay on time, or if the suppliers do not supply it regularly with raw and other materials, fuel, etc., or supply it with materials of inferior quality. This explains the need for the mutual control of enterprises and economic organisations.

Incentive funds of enterprises
The greater role being played by profit in the economic stimulation of enterprises is linked with the formation of incentive funds at enterprises. Deductions are made from the profits of the enterprise to form the material incentive funds, the fund for social and cultural measures and housing construction, and the production development fund. Deductions to these funds are regulated by quotas fixed for a number of years in advance. The sizes of these funds depend on the growth in the volume of marketed output, the profit and the profitability stipulated in the plan. The size of the emolument paid for the overfulfilment of the plan is smaller than that paid for the fulfilment of the plan, which makes the enterprise interested in assuming higher plan targets.

The material incentive fund finances workers' bonuses. Bonuses are paid not only for high production indicators during the year but also as lump sum rewards at the end of the year, depending on the results of the enterprise's activities for that period.

The fund for social and cultural measures and housing construction is used to satisfy the urgent needs of the enterprise's staff. It finances housing construction and social development, the repair of the enterprise's housing facilities, the improvement of welfare and medical services for its staff, pays for medicines at medical and anti-epidemic establishments, accommodations at rest homes and sanatoriums and lump sum grants to workers.

The production development fund is used to finance measures connected with commissioning new equipment, for the modernisation of operating equipment and the expansion of production.

The incentive funds of enterprises are used to pay material rewards to workers, not only for successes in the work done by them personally but also for the economically effective work of the enterprise as a whole. This not only helps to rouse the material interest of the working people but is also instrumental in promoting their consideration for the interests of the enterprise as a whole and attaches them to their enterprise.

The new system of management makes it possible to realise to the full the workers' material interest in the growth and profitability of production, the improvement of labour organisation, raising the quality of output and increasing the yield of the productive assets. The system of material stimulation of enterprises is called upon to make enterprises, their staffs and their managers materially interested in mobilising all reserves, in using all resources to raise the level of production and thereby to increase their contribution to the public wealth.

Introduction of full cost accounting
The 23rd Congress of the CPSU emphasised that it was important to implement the Leninist principles of cost accounting consistently. It stressed that it was essential consistently to extend the rights and economic independence of enterprises, to develop their initiative, notably by providing material stimuli for the achievement of high production results by the collectives of enterprises in the interests of society and by raising the material responsibility of enterprises for the fulfilment of their obligations arising from the plan and their contracts.

The Directives of the 23rd Congress for the five-year plan make it incumbent to introduce genuine cost accounting in all the branches of the economy. The introduction of full cost accounting is called upon to strengthen the interest of the staffs of enterprises and of individual workers in improving the performance of enterprises, expanding production, increasing the profitability of enterprises, raising the quality of output and in the utilisation of the productive assets to an optimal degree. The implementation of genuine cost accounting calls for a deep, expert analysis of the economic activities of individual enterprises and of whole industries and economic districts. All measures boosting the effectiveness of the people's labour assume enormous importance.

These measures include the most effective channelling of capital investments, the most expedient methods for utilising all the resources available in industry and agriculture. Lenin's appeal for economy means that the enterprises must tighten the strings of the public purse and avoid all unnecessary expenditure. This also means that constant care should be taken to develop each industry and each enterprise in the most productive direction.

Specific features of cost accounting in collective farms

Cost accounting serves as the basis of a rational management not only in state enterprises but also in collective farms.

In collective farms, like at state enterprises, thrifty management presupposes that accurate and strict accounts be kept of all expenditure on production and of the results of production, and that the two be accurately compared. Every collective farm must be conducted on strict cost accounting principles.

The criterion of a collective farm's performance is the quantity, quality and cost of the products it produces, or, to be more exact, the labour expenditure on the production of a unit of output. The computation of the production costs of the collective farm output attaches certain specific features. These specifics stem from the fact that in the collective farms a definite part of the output is used in natural form for the further production on the same farm (seed, cattle), while a part of it is distributed among the members of the artel according to work-day units.

Like in state enterprises, the general economic results of the activities of collective farms are determined by the ratio of the expenditure on production to the results of production. This makes the collective farm interested in systematically lowering expenditure of social labour and material means on the production per unit of agricultural output and in a simultaneous growth of the farm's volume of output. Thus they have to lower the value and cost per unit of output, which can be achieved through the all-round utilisation of the productive resources and labour power, the consistent observance of the socialist principle of labour remuneration, a thrifty attitude towards the wealth of the collective farm, and the multiplication of the collective farms commonly-owned property.

To obtain the best possible results the soil must be used rationally for the production of the most valuable crops. Considering the vast territory of the Soviet Union and the diverse natural conditions there can be no uniform farming system for all areas. There can be no tailor-made patterns, and agricultural experts and practical workers must have the final say as to what crops should be cultivated. Rational farming includes also land improvement, the extensive use of fertilisers, improvement and cultivation of wasteland, the reclamation of swamps, irrigation, the building of water reservoirs, and the introduction of correct crop rotation.

The rational utilisation of the means of production demands that equipment be used skilfully and that comprehensive mechanisation of production be introduced. This makes it necessary to supply the collective farms and state farms with more and better equipment and improve the designs of farming equipment. Particularly important is technological progress, which helps to produce highly productive machinery, the utilisation of which enables the farms to carry out a larger volume of work with fewer machines.

The comprehensive utilisation of the labour resources of collective farms is achieved through the widest possible participation of all able-bodied collective farmers in the work of the artel. The complete utilisation of the labour force in the collective farms can be ensured only through a consistent implementation of the socialist principle of remuneration according to the quantity and quality of work done, through the eradication of all egalitarianism and the transition to the most progressive forms of labour remuneration.

Rational management also implies the opportune servicing of machinery and implements, care for the collective farm buildings and structures, thrifty expenditure of raw and other materials, and care for cattle. It is also essential to prevent write-ups of work-day units, to do away with overstaffing in the administrative apparatus of the collective farm, and systematically to lower administrative expenditure. A constant struggle must be conducted to do away with losses in all the sectors and stages of the collective farm production, to safeguard collective farm property and to improve the system of accounting.

The most important way of raising the output of agricultural products is to intensify agriculture consistently on the basis of mechanisation, electrification and chemicalisation of production, and to extensively develop amelioration in zones where unfavourable natural conditions prevail.

The expansion of agricultural production and the lowering of costs lead to a steady rise in the incomes of the collective farms and collective farmers, and at the same time make it possible to lower retail prices on these products, thereby raising the living standard of the Soviet people.

Differential rent

The nationalisation of the land removed the conditions for the formation of absolute rent. This does not, however, apply to differential rent.

Some tracts of land carry with them certain qualities such as advantage of climate, soil fertility, closeness to markets, etc., which provide the additional incomes forming the differential rent.

Collective farms on more fertile land spend less labour per unit of output than do collective farms on less fertile land. Equal expenditure on labour and equal level of mechanisation, if the farming system is the same, will enable collective farms located on better land to produce more than collective farms on worse lands.

Differential rent emerges also as a result of the varying distances of collective farms from railway stations, docks, collecting centres, towns and other points for the disposal of agricultural products. The collective farms located nearer these points spend less labour and funds on the transportation of products. As a result the value per unit of output is lower in these collective farms than it is in those located at a greater distance from these points.

The economic policy of the Soviet state with respect to differential rent proceeds from the premise that the excess income received from the natural fertility of better plots and also from the vicinity of sales markets should be used for public needs.

This principle is practically implemented mainly by fixing differential purchasing prices for agricultural products according to the various zones of the country, differing as regards the conditions for agricultural production. Part of the differential rent is kept by the collective farms and serves as a source of expanding production and improving the way of life of the collective farmers.

The Programme of the CPSU aims at creating equal economic conditions for raising the incomes of collective farms operating under unequal natural and economic conditions in different zones, and also within the same zones, so as to be able more consistently to implement the principle of equal pay for equal work in all collective farms.

3. RAISING THE EFFECTIVENESS OF SOCIAL PRODUCTION

Main ways of raising the effectiveness of social production The new system of management and the introduction of genuine cost accounting aim at ensuring a steady increase in the effectiveness of production. The effectiveness of social production covers the whole range of processes determining the growth of production at a minimum of social expenditure. The main factors for raising the effectiveness of social production are all the elements which under the obtaining conditions help to multiply the results of production. These factors include the rise in labour productivity, economy of raw and other materials, the improvement of the quality of output and notably the increase of the volume of output per unit of the productive assets—the assets/product ratio.

The Soviet economy has an economic potential enabling it to ensure a steady increase in the effectiveness of social production. However, in the last years of the seven-year plan period the rate at which the effectiveness of social production was growing began to drop. Growth rates of production and labour productivity suffered the same setback. Productive assets and capital investments were used less effectively. In a number of branches new enterprises were not commissioned in time, and many of those that were did not reach rated capacity. As a result the growth rate of the national income did not reach the level projected in the seven-year plan.

The increase in the effectiveness of social production is one of the prime tasks of the current five-year plan. The Directives of the 23rd Congress of the CPSU for the five-year plan emphasise the need for raising the effectiveness of production on the basis of technological progress, the improvement in the organisation of labour and production, the utilisation of productive assets and capital investments, and the quality of output and the implementation of a strict regime of economy.

The need to increase the accumulations required for capital investments and at the same time to raise the people's living standard demands that there be an all-out increase in the effectiveness of social production, strict economy of live and embodied labour, a systematic increase in the yields from capital investments and the fixed productive assets.

To raise the effectiveness of social production it is necessary to abolish such shortcomings as the scattering of capital investments and the ensuing extension of the period required to build new projects and to master new capacities, machinery and equipment, to prevent the immobilisation of funds through laying in excessive stocks of raw and other materials, to avoid a growth in the volume of work in progress and to fight all wastefulness of live and embodied labour. In other words, there must be a maximum mobilisation of the resources and reserves of socialist economy and the fullest possible utilisation of the advantages and potentialities of the socialist system of economy.

To achieve this aim it is essential, first, to improve the utilisation of productive capacities steadily, to increase the yield per ruble invested in productive assets and, secondly, systematically to lower the per unit expenditure of labour and materials.

The increase in the effectiveness of social production plays a decisive role in ensuring the rapid growth of the people's welfare. In socialist society the fund of social consumption grows the quicker, the higher is the productivity of social labour, the higher the yield per ruble of productive assets, the more output is manufactured from every ton of raw and other materials. This makes the working class, the collective farmers and intelligentsia vitally interested in raising the effectiveness of social production.

The new system of economic management has an enormous role to play in achieving this aim. The granting of wide economic initiative to the enterprises promotes a considerable rise in the quality and quantity of production, and helps to utilise latent reserves and the resources of socialist economy to the maximum.

The economic reform promotes the better utilisation of productive assets

The new system of economic management is aimed at mobilising the internal reserves of Soviet economy to the fullest extent. The greater economic stimulation of production creates favourable conditions for implementing a regime of economy, which means a rational and thrifty expenditure of the labour, material and money resources, the elimination of losses and unproductive expenditure in all branches of the economy.

To raise the effectiveness of social production it is necessary first and foremost to ensure the more efficient use of the productive assets.

Under the new system enterprises are given wide autonomy in the utilisation of the fixed assets and assets in turnover. A larger share of the profits goes to replenish the productive fixed assets, and the share of the depreciation deductions remaining at the disposal of the enterprises has been raised. This promotes the rational use of funds meant for repairs and the modernisation of equipment and helps to channel capital investments to the decisive sectors of production. Furthermore, enterprises are now entitled to sell equipment, materials and other assets they do not need.

This raises the responsibility of the enterprise for the rational use of its productive assets. Under conditions of full cost accounting the effectiveness of the utilisation of the raw and other materials and of the equipment decides the size of the profit and the level of profitability of the enterprise and, hence, the size of the incentive funds. This makes the staff interested in a strict regime of economy and in progressive quotas for the expenditure of raw and other materials, fuel and electric power.

Payment for the use of productive assets The new system of management provides for the introduction of a charge for the use of productive assets in the form of a deduction from the profits to the budget, the size of the deduction depending on the value of the fixed and circulating assets on the balance sheet of the enterprise.

The productive assets are the fundamental basis of the national wealth. Their quantitative and qualitative growth is the main condition for raising the productivity of social labour and for increasing the national income. Naturally, placing a share of its wealth at the disposal of an enterprise and its staff, society expects them to contribute to the national wealth. Part of these contributions are paid as the charge for the use of assets.

The free allocation of assets ran counter to the principles underlying planned socialist commodity production. It gave a distorted picture of the enterprise's performance and failed to take into account such important aspects of the enterprise's activities as the degree to which the productive assets were utilised. Neglect of this important factor makes it impossible to appraise the enterprise's full expenditure on the production of output. The placing of the productive assets at the disposal of enterprises free of charge did not stimulate their utilisation to the maximum.

The introduction of the charge for the use of productive assets aims at making the enterprise interested in expanding its output and in increasing not only the sum total of profits but also the profitability, i.e., the size of the profit as related to the value of the productive assets. The charge for the use of the productive assets is fixed at a size that enables any enterprise functioning normally to keep a definite sum of the profit (after it has paid the charge) for making up the incentive funds and covering its planned expenditure.

The charge for the use of assets is not a deduction of profits to the budget over and above the payments made before this charge was introduced. It has become the main channel through which the bulk of the enterprise's payment to the state budget is made. This charge will gradually diminish the role of other payments, notably that of the turnover tax. The quotas for the payment of the charges for the use of assets will be fixed for a number of years in advance so that enterprises using their assets in the most economic way will obtain greater profits to make up incentive funds.

Ways for the better utilisation of technology and productive capacities

Technological progress holds a key position among the measures to raise the effectiveness of social production. The material and technical basis of communism is being constructed at a time when a grandiose scientific and technological revolution is in progress. Socialist economy is well equipped to march in the front ranks of the scientific and technological revolution and to take advantage of its results in the quickest possible way. Socialism ensures favourable conditions for the development of all branches of sciences. The socialist countries always set great story by training scientific personnel and assign considerable sums to building and equipping scientific research institutes. The Soviet Union leads the world in many key branches of science.

At the present time the need for accelerated technological progress is specially urgent. It is important to instal perfect and productive types of equipment, machines and lathes and to improve technology urgently. The tasks of creating the material and technical basis of communism insistently demand the enhancement of the role of science and especially the rapid introduction of its achievements in all spheres of material production. Successes of science and technology decide the growth of the Soviet people's welfare and the rate at which they advance towards communism. The latest achievements of science and technology must be implemented speedily in industry, agriculture, transport and communications, and all must be done to ensure the steady growth of the country's productive apparatus on the most perfect technical basis and to obtain greater results from its utilisation.

As the amount of technical equipment in industrial and agricultural production grows naturally there is an increase in the share of the expenditure on the maintenance and restoration of machinery, lathes and other equipment.

This means that there is a rise in the share of depreciation in production costs. At the same time, however, there is also an increase in labour productivity and, hence, in the amount of output being produced by a worker per hour or per day. While there is a general increase in the size of the depreciation deductions, while their share in the costs of production as a whole increases, their share in the costs of the production of every single unit of output decreases.

Socialism has an enormous advantage over capitalism in the way it rationally utilises productive capacities—machines, equipment, etc. In socialist economy, where there are no crises of overproduction and where the rapidly growing commodity stocks always find a sufficiently wide market, the productive apparatus does not suffer from enforced underemployment.

The socialist system of economy ensures every condition for the fullest utilisation of productive capacities. The task of every enterprise is to utilise its equipment to the fullest and mobilise all reserves of its productive capacities.

The Decisions of the 23rd Congress of the CPSU oblige the industrial enterprises to improve the utilisation of equipment, to raise its productivity and thus to achieve an increase in output, and raise the level of profitability on every ruble of productive assets. In the current five-year plan the production of operating enterprises will be systematically increased by removing bottlenecks, intensifying production processes, improving technology, raising the coefficient of exchangeability and doing away with the time equipment stands idle. The five-year period also aims at improving quality and lowering the cost of major equipment repairs.

Economic use of raw and other materials, fuel and electric power

An essential condition for the rise in the effectiveness of social production is economic use of raw and other materials, fuel and electric power. The task is to lower systematically the material/product and the power/product ratio per unit of output, i.e., the amount of materials and power spent on their production.

To save raw and other materials and electric power means to use them to the best advantage. This means also that production waste must be systematically lowered, that there must be no rejects, and no losses due to careless storage of materials. This also means that only products of high quality must be produced, for the production of inferior products is tantamount to wasting valuable materials. Of great significance is the introduction of progressive expenditure quotas for raw and other materials, fuel and electric power per unit of output. The quotas must be technically based and correspond to the modern level of advanced technology and production organisation.

The experience of advanced collectives and innovators of production opens up considerable reserves for an economy of material resources. There are such reserves in industry and agriculture, construction and transport, trade, research and design and government institutions. In many cases the expenditure of raw materials and fuel per unit of output is still very high. Some machines are extremely heavy. In machine-tool building, for example, a ton of metal produces only an average of 400-500 kilogrammes of finished products. Every year more than 4 million tons of metal go into shavings in machine-building.

The rise in quality and the improvement of the assortment of metals, outlined in the directives on the five-year plan are tantamount to the production of an additional 5 million tons of rolled metal in 1970.

The decisions of the 23rd Congress of the CPSU emphasise the need to work out and introduce highly effective technological processes—physico-chemical, electrophysical, electronic and others. The present five-year plan sets important tasks as regards the better utilisation of raw and other materials and fuel. It is expected to lower the expenditure of ferrous rolled metal in machine-building and metal-working by about 20-25 per cent, to save steel in the production of rolled metal, to substitute non-ferrous metals with cheaper materials and bimetals on a wider scale. This has been devised to lower the rate of fuel expenditure in industry during the five-year period by no less than 8-10 per cent, including in the production of electric power by 11-14 per cent, and the rate of expenditure of electric power by 6-8 per cent. The decisions also emphasise the need for an increase in the output of finished products from the same amount of raw materials, for a fuller use of secondary fuel and power resources, secondary raw and other materials.

The struggle for economy and thrift

A thrifty attitude towards every expenditure of labour—live or embodied in the form of material means of production—is the duty of every socialist enterprise. This aim is achieved by constantly combatting unproductive expenditure, and rectifying all sorts of surplus in production and the strengthening of state financial discipline.

Planned economy has immense prospects for the saving of expenditure connected with the realisation and sale of output. The planned distribution of the country's productive forces affords every opportunity for a considerable cut in transport expenditure.

Socialist management means a decisive struggle against losses and unnecessary expenditure and simultaneous concern for the lightening of labour and the improvement of its conditions. Thus, taking care to avoid losses of electric power does not mean the economising on electric power at all cost or lowering its consumption in every case. On the contrary, a rational utilisation of electric power can and must be combined with a growth in the power available to labour and with improvement of its conditions, for example, the better illumination of productive premises, better ventilation, etc.

The struggle for economy is justly considered a national task in socialist society. The competition for thrift and economy is embodied in thoroughly worked out organisational and technical measures and concrete socialist obligations. To disclose and use reserves it is necessary to introduce the latest equipment and technology, to spread progressive experience, scientific organisation of labour and production. Thrift is often exhibited in small things: picking up and using a nut, a part, a bit of metal that would otherwise be thrown away, mending an air or steam leak, or switching off an electric lamp when it is no longer needed. Economy in things large and small is the duty of all Soviet labouring people.

Thrift must be rational. There must not be "economy" that harms the quality, reliability and endurance of products or the proper maintenance of equipment. The output of low quality products is an extremely dangerous form of waste.

1. What is the essence of cost accounting?
2. What are the best ways for the fullest utilisation of the productive assets of an enterprise?
3. What is the role of profit and profitability in socialist economy?

Chapter XIV

SOCIALIST ORGANISATION OF SOCIAL LABOUR

1. MAIN FEATURES OF SOCIALIST LABOUR ORGANISATION

Socialism—the highest form of the organisation of social labour

A definite organisation of social labour is typical of every mode of production. "Chattel slavery" under feudalism relied on the discipline enforced by the whip, on the extreme poverty and oppression of the working people being exploited by a handful of landowners. The capitalist organisation of social labour relies on the discipline of hunger, whereby the mass of the working people are nothing but hired slaves exploited by a handful of capitalists. The communist organisation of social labour, socialism being the first step in this direction, relies on the free and conscious discipline of the working people themselves who have torn themselves free of the landowners and capitalists, and it will rely on it to an even greater extent as socialist society advances towards communism.

The working class's seizure of power represents and implements a higher type of social labour organisation. Lenin considered this source of power as an earnest of the inevitable complete triumph of communism. The higher type of social labour organisation evolves a higher labour productivity in comparison with capitalism. The labour productivity is the main, the most important condition for the victory of the new, higher social system.

Liquidation of exploitation and of the commodity nature of labour power

The socialist organisation of social labour proceeds from the emancipation of labour from the fetters of exploitation. Socialism is a great change from forced labour for the exploiters, who ruled for millennia, to labour for one's self, for the good of all society. Besides, it is labour using all the achievements of up-to-date technology and culture.

The liquidation of exploitation of man by man has put an end to the division of society into antagonistic classes with irreconcilable, opposing interests. At enterprises, which are the property of the whole people, all workers are hired by the state. This form of hire expresses not relations between different classes, but relations between individual working people and society as a whole. In socialist society there is not and cannot be two classes, one of which sells its labour power to the other. Thus, working power has stopped being a commodity. It is no longer an object that can be bought and sold. The working class uses its labour power at enterprises which it owns jointly with all the people.

Wiping out exploitation and unemployment has also eliminated the conditions which under capitalism inevitably give rise to competition among the working people. The production relations of socialism are relations of friendly emulation and co-operation and mutual support in labour.

Necessary and surplus labour
Now that the sale and purchase of labour power in socialist society is no longer possible, the labour process has changed—it is no longer a process of the production of surplus value for the capitalists. Unearned, exploiting incomes have been abolished together with the exploiting classes, the receivers of these incomes.

Before the emergence of Marxism some utopian socialists asserted that socialism must implement the "right to the full labour product". Later petty-bourgeois theoreticians attempted to reduce the whole content of socialism to this right. However, in actual fact, the abolition of exploitation of man by man does not at all mean that every worker can receive the full product of his labour.

The labour of the members of socialist society includes, first of all, the necessary labour, the product of which goes to satisfy the direct requirements of the working people for food, clothes, housing, cultural benefits, and secondly, the surplus labour, the product of which goes to satisfy social needs and requirements.

The surplus labour, as labour over and above the amount necessary to satisfy the direct requirements of the working people, must exist in any form of society. Without surplus labour and surplus product there could be no further development of the productive forces, and hence, no social progress.

In socialist society surplus product is essential first and foremost for the purpose of accumulation. It is through the accumulation of a definite part of the surplus product that the socialist countries have carried out and continue to carry on their sweeping building programmes. Secondly, part of the surplus product serves to maintain the administrative apparatus, covers expenditure on education and public health, and also ensures the defence potential of the socialist state. Thirdly, a definite share of the surplus product is needed to maintain the incapacitated members of society——old people, the ill, and children. Fourthly, a part of the surplus product goes to form reserves, the contingency fund needed to cope with natural calamities and possible miscalculations in planning.

In socialist society the surplus product is not appropriated by the class of owners but goes to all the working people, and only to them. The surplus product is placed at the disposal of society as a whole and is used for the satisfaction of all social needs and requirements. Hence, under socialism there is no antagonism between the surplus and the necessary labour: both the necessary labour and the surplus labour are labour for one's own benefit and for that of society.

In socialist society the development of the productive forces and the growth of the productivity of social labour lead to an increase in the size of both the surplus product going to the needs of society as a whole and also of the fund for the satisfaction of the working people's direct needs.

The right to work The socialist organisation of social labour guarantees the right to work. The dream of generations of working people of a social order under which there would be no unemployment and no economic crises, which in capitalist society periodically destroy huge masses of the fruits of labour and throw colossal material wealth down the drain, has come true for the first time in history. This absurdity in the capitalist system has been destroyed by planned socialist economy once and for all.

In socialist society the young generation enters life without any fear of the future, it does not know the threat of being left by the board of life, of being "surplus people", "surplus mouths to feed".

The right to work cannot be realised under capitalism. It recognises quite a different "right"—the "right to other people's labour", which only the exploiters enjoy. The exploitation of the wage worker is based on the threat of hunger, which relentlessly pursues the proletariat. Therefore the "right to other people's labour" for the capitalist inevitably means the absence of the right to work for the working class.

Socialism, destroying the exploiters' "right to other people's labour", implements the right to work for all working people, i.e., the right to receive guaranteed work with payment for it in accordance with its quantity and quality. The right to work is ensured by the socialist organisation of planned economy, the steady growth of its productive forces, the elimination of the possibility of crises and the abolition of unemployment.

The implementation of the right to work is achieved by the rapid development of the productive apparatus of socialist society. In a number of countries there was mass unemployment and a huge agrarian overpopulation before the socialist revolution. This was the case in Russia, Poland and some other countries. Millions of people from these countries were forced to emigrate in search of work.

In the Soviet Union unemployment was wiped out in the early thirties. The first large successes of socialist industrialisation drew enormous masses of workers into production. At the same time the collectivisation of agriculture, pulling up kulak exploitation by the roots, abolished the sources of poverty in the countryside.

The liberation of the working class from the scourge of unemployment is a legitimate result of the liquidation of the contradiction between the social character of production and the private capitalist form of appropriation, upon which the inevitability of crisis and unemployment under capitalism depends. Therefore the socialist system of economy has not only abolished unemployment but also its roots.

	The socialist organisation of social
Universal and	labour makes labour universal and
obligatory labour	obligatory.

The right to work simultaneously implies the duty to work honestly and conscientiously for the benefit of society. Socialism abolishes the parasitical classes which do not participate in social labour. By abolishing unemployment and crises it cuts the working people free of forced idleness.

Under these conditions it would be inconceivable for a certain part of society, for some of its able-bodied members, to go scot free of social labour. Nobody can delegate his share in the social labour, since such labour is a natural condition of human existence. All able-bodied members of society are obliged to work, to do a definite amount of work for the good of all of society, and all labouring people have the right to free time for rest and recreation, for cultural improvement, etc. At the same time labour stops being a means of enslaving man but liberates him, promoting the development of the individual.

The universal and obligatory nature of labour under socialism is expressed in the principle "He who does not work, neither shall he eat". Lenin emphasised that this was the prime, chief principle of socialism, the ineradicable source of its strength, the earnest of its ultimate victory. It embodies the hopes and aspirations of many generations of working people and exploited people and their striving for a just and rational social system.

The replacement of forced labour for the exploiter by free labour for one's own benefit, for the whole of society, releases in the people an enormous upsurge of creative energy and labour enthusiasm. But, this substitution cannot be effected without a resolute attack on the vestiges of capitalism in the minds of the backward sections of the working people.

There are still people in socialist society who strive to live at the expense of society, without giving it anything in return. This makes it necessary to fight idlers, persons who shirk socially useful labour, against the remnants of parasitical elements, working for the strict observance of the principle "He who does not work, neither shall he eat".

The universal and obligatory labour is an integral feature of both socialism and communism.

Communist society, the Programme of the CPSU says, which is based on highly organised production and on advanced technology, changes the character of labour but does not free the members of society from it. Communist society is not and never will be a society of anarchy, idleness and inactivity. Every able-bodied person will participate in social labour and ensure the constant growth of the material and spiritual wealth of society.

Socialist methods of stimulating labour

The most important feature of the socialist organisation of social labour is the evolution of new stimuli to work.

Every social system has its special methods to induce people to work, to draw them into productive activity. Direct coercion under slavery and feudalism and the threat of starvation under capitalism make the working people labour for their exploiters.

Socialism has rooted out the methods of inducing people to work used under capitalism: the threat of starvation for the majority, the craving for profits for the minority. The abolition of exploitation has radically changed the conditions and the methods used to induce people to work. It, therefore, became inevitable to work out new, unprecedented methods for inducing people to work.

One of the many lies spread by the bourgeoisie about socialism is that socialism destroys all stimuli to work. For a long time now the lackeys of the bourgeoisie have maintained that the abolition of private property will lead to universal idleness. Then, Marx and Engels answered them in the *Manifesto of the Communist Party*, bourgeois society ought long ago to have slumped through sheer idleness, for those of its members who work acquire nothing, while those who acquire something do not work.

The defenders of capitalism assert that under socialism, which has eradicated the opportunity to profit at the expense of other people's labour, there can be no stimuli to work. In saying this they attempt to gloss over the fact that under the domination of private property the bulk of the people are propertyless labouring toilers, while the opportunity of making a profit is practically enjoyed only by a handful of exploiters.

The experience of the economic development of the Soviet Union and other socialist countries has demonstrated that with the abolition of capitalism the people's labour far from being corroded by idleness, acquires new properties which are inconceivable in any exploiting society. Socialism evolves new, and much more effective methods for ensuring the participation of the people in the labour process.

Capitalism uses methods for inducing people which have been worked out for centuries. The elaboration of all sorts of intricate methods for pumping as much work as possible out of the hired slaves of capital continues to this day. Naturally, the elaboration of new socialist methods for inducing people to work is no simple matter, but one requiring a lot of patient and painstaking work.

With the abolition of exploitation all the fruits of labour go to society and are used to benefit the working people themselves. This is the root of people's keen interest in the results of production inconceivable under capitalism. Under socialism the connection between the labour expended and its remuneration must be felt by every worker. This is achieved by implementing the socialist principle: "From each according to his ability, to each according to his work".

This formula is rich in content. It presupposes, first, the obligation of all members of society to work to the best of their ability, and secondly, the right of every labouring man to receive from society a reward in accordance with the quantity and quality of his work.

Socialism abolishes the discrepancy between the rights and duties existing under capitalism and under any other exploiting system. In bourgeois society all rights are enjoyed by a negligible minority of society—the owners of the means of production—while all the duties are assumed by the enormous bulk of the population deprived of these means. In socialist society all able-bodied members of society have equal access to the means of production, which are public socialist property. Under these conditions everybody works for one's own benefit and for that of society. When a man works for himself he naturally works to the best of his ability.

Socialist labour discipline
The socialist organisation of social labour calls for strict discipline in the labour process, for an orderly and efficient organisation of production.

The fall of capitalism inevitably leads to the break-up of capitalist labour discipline based on the threat of hunger and on the economic enslavement of the working people. But large-scale social production is inconceivable without strict labour discipline. Lenin therefore emphasised that labour discipline is the pivot upon which economic development under socialism hinges.

Socialist labour discipline differs radically from all preceding types of labour discipline both as regards its essence and the way in which it is created and maintained. This is a higher type of labour discipline than that of capitalism. It is the conscious discipline of workers who have thrown off the yoke of the exploiters. The setting up and maintaining socialist labour discipline is the sacred cause of all working people.

The education of socialist labour discipline is one of the main forms of the proletarian class struggle after the seizure of state power. Lenin said that the development of a new labour discipline, of new forms of social links between people and new forms and methods to induce people to work is a job that will take years and decades. He considered it a grateful and noble task.

While changing the psychology of all working people on the basis of large-scale socialist production, while educating in them the discipline of joint comradely labour, the working class also re-educates itself. In its endeavours to strengthen labour discipline socialist society through its state resorts to methods of persuasion and coercion directed against idlers and loafers, who strive to get as much as possible from society while giving it as little as possible in return.

Strict labour discipline is essential also in communist society. Communist production is distinguished by its high organisation and efficiency. Under communism it is not coercion but the understanding by all working people of their civic duties that ensures discipline and organisation.

2. PRODUCTIVITY OF SOCIAL LABOUR

Steady rise of labour productivity— an essential law of socialism

The socialist organisation of social labour is designed to achieve labour productivity higher than that under capitalism so as to satisfy the growing requirements of socialist society and its members.

The socialist system ultimately triumphs over the outmoded capitalist system thanks to its higher labour productivity. Capitalism attained a labour productivity feudalism never could have achieved. Socialism creates a much higher labour productivity than capitalism.

It achieves this by freeing the productive forces of society previously fettered by exploitation, by releasing the creative energy and initiative of the working masses.

The growth of the labour productivity is expressed in the decrease of the total live and embodied labour contained in a unit of output. The share of the live labour decreases at a more rapid rate than the share of the past, embodied labour. The rise in labour productivity is achieved by replacing manual labour by mechanised labour, old or outmoded machinery by new and more up-to-date machinery.

Another condition that is essential for the labour productivity to grow is the constant improvement of the organisation of labour and production. In addition to technological progress, Lenin considered the stricter labour discipline of the working people, the improvement of their skills, the greater intensity and better organisation of labour important conditions for the rise in labour productivity.

Under capitalism the growth in labour productivity means an intensification of the exploitation of the working class, a growth of unemployment, a worsening of the working people's conditions. The anarchy of capitalist production, competition, crises result in a senseless waste of natural resources, labour power and the products of social labour. Marx points out that for this reason the significance of the law of increasing labour productivity has a conditional nature under capitalism. This explains the unstable nature of the labour productivity growth under capitalism.

Under socialism, however, the law of increasing labour productivity has an unconditional nature. Socialism ensures more favourable conditions for developing and utilising the achievements of science and technology in the interests of society as a whole. The universal and obligatory nature of labour ensures full, systematic utilisation of the live labour resources at the society's disposal. The absence of anarchy of production, competition and crises makes it possible to use the natural resources and the means of production in a planned and rational way on a national economic scale.

The development of socialist economy is linked with all people striving to ensure the constant growth of labour productivity in all branches of economy. The growing welfare of socialist society is based on the rise in labour productivity.

Factors promoting the growth of labour productivity The interests of communist construction demand a systematic rise in the productivity of social labour. The growth of labour productivity decreases the amount of labour expended on the production per unit of output.

Labour productivity is a very inclusive term. It is based on the individual output of the worker in the basic production processes. This output can be computed in tons, metres, pieces of articles produced within the working hour, day, week or month by a worker engaged in production or, if the products are heterogeneous, in monetary terms (in stable prices).

However, the individual output of the worker in the basic production processes does not give a clear idea of the movement of the labour productivity in the enterprise as a whole. The growth in the individual output in the basic production processes does not necessarily lead to a growth in the labour productivity in the enterprise as a whole, in fact, it may even be attended by a drop in productivity. This happens when the higher productivity of individual workers is attended by an increase in the number of auxiliary workers, when the non-productive labour expenditure grows, when the administrative apparatus is inflated, etc. Conversely, if the growth in the output of the worker is attended by a decrease in the administrative apparatus and the number of auxiliary workers, by the elimination of unproductive labour expenditure, the output per the worker grows quicker than the individual output of the worker in the main production processes.

The level of the productivity per worker also fails to provide a full picture of the movement of the productivity of social labour as a whole. A correct, economically well founded choice of the direction in which individual enterprises, industrial branches and economic areas are to be developed is crucial to the rise of the productivity of social labour. In other words, the rise in the productivity of social labour is due to a rise in the effectiveness of social production.

Under socialism the struggle for the systematic growth of labour productivity is waged with methods that differ fundamentally from those used under capitalism.

In capitalist society the growth of the labour productivity is achieved largely by raising the labour intensity, i.e., by overdriving the worker. In socialist society the growth of labour productivity is achieved mainly by improving equipment, introducing more productive machinery, machine-tools and production methods that facilitate work and raise its productivity and improving the labour and production organisation.

The most important way of raising labour productivity is continuous and rapid technological progress, the modernisation of equipment and technology, better production organisation. Modern equipment and technology attaches particular importance to scientific labour and production organisation and the full utilisation of labour time: the abolition of stoppages, the fight against unproductive expenditure (losses) of labour time.

One of the basic factors promoting the growth of labour productivity is the improvement of skills. Modern scientific and technological progress demands a steady growth in the cultural and technological level of the personnel employed in the economy. The introduction into production of new, more perfect and productive equipment gives the desired effect only if it is operated and used by skilled workers in all sections of the socialist economy.

In socialist economy the share of wages in the production costs drops constantly owing to the rise in labour productivity. However, lowering the share of the expenditure on wages in production costs is not accompanied by a drop in wages but by a steady growth of the wage fund as a whole and hence also of the absolute size of the wages being drawn by individual workers. The vast advantages of the socialist system can be seen from the fact that under that system the economy of live labour goes hand in hand with the steady growth in the working people's welfare.

In the Soviet Union the labour productivity in industry has grown by more than 11-fold between 1928 and 1964 despite the substantial shortening of the working day.

The Soviet Union's high labour productivity growth rate rapidly reduces the gap still existing between the labour productivity levels of the USSR and the USA. In 1913 the labour productivity in Russian industry was about 11 per cent of that of the USA, at present Soviet labour productivity is 40 to 50 per cent of the American.

During the construction of communism the growth of the productivity of social labour is a major prerequisite for the creation of an abundance of material wealth required for the transition to the communist principle of distribution according to requirements.

The 23rd Party Congress on the acceleration of scientific and technological progress The Directives of the 23rd Congress of the CPSU for five-year plan emphasise the need for an acceleration of scientific and technological progress through the extensive development of research and the rapid introduction of its results in production. The acceleration of scientific and technological progress is an essential condition for the fulfilment of the five-year plan.

The five-year plan provides for massive research in all spheres of science, ensuring technological progress: in theoretical and applied mathematics, nuclear physics and other branches of physical science, chemistry, biology, geology, medicine and in the social sciences. To raise the effectiveness of research and to accelerate the introduction of its findings into production it is intended to concentrate the scientific personnel and material resources in solving the basic problems of science and technology thereby ensuring the greatest economic effect.

In accelerating technological progress utmost importance is attached to the rapid development of the most progressive sectors of machine- and instrument-building, supplying the economy with modern means of labour, and to the systematic mastery of the production of output technologically new and better, and also to the improvement of the quality of output in all branches of the economy.

A distinctive feature of the current five-year plan is the course on the rapid re-equipment of the whole economy, the progressive change of its structure and the timely replacement of outdated output by new, better products. These measures will accelerate scientific and technological progress.

The rise in the technological level of production on the basis of the development and introduction of new equipment and progressive technology, the extensive utilisation of comprehensive mechanisation and automation, increased specialisation and combination of production are to be the principal factors ensuring the growth of labour productivity.

Development of specialisation and co-operation of production and their economic effectiveness The spread of progressive methods peculiar to large-scale production and promoting the onward march of scientific and technological progress are crucial in ensuring the steady rise in the productivity of social labour. Among these methods are the specialisation and co-operation of enterprises, mass production and combination of production.

Specialisation means that the production of homogeneous articles is concentrated at definite enterprises. This is one of the forms of the social division of labour.

The progress of technology steadily increases the number of independent industries. The production of separate types of output is concentrated at definite enterprises. Specialisation makes for a deeper division of labour between enterprises and also within them, between shops and departments. It makes it possible to apply highly productive equipment, improve machinery and mechanisms and the technology of production. At the same time specialisation helps the workers and engineering personnel to acquire skill by training and practice.

There are three basic types of specialisation. First, there is the break-down of the production of heterogeneous articles so that each factory specialises on the production of definite articles (for example, factories for producing cars). Secondly, there is a break-down of production so that each factory produces parts of the finished product—specialisation in components (special factories for producing automobile parts—engines, bodies, piston rings). And finally there is the specialisation in the separate operations or stages of the technological process—the technological or stage specialisation (foundries, forging and pressing works, etc.).

The growth of the specialisation increases the interdependence of branches and enterprises. This promotes co-operation, i.e., the establishment of long-term production links between enterprises and branches jointly producing definite kinds of products. Co-operation requires a higher level of planning and organisation than do ordinary supplier-consumer relations between enterprises.

The socialist system of economy opens up the possibility of developing specialisation and co-operation of production on a scale unattainable under capitalism. The domination of public ownership of the means of production and planned economic development and the absence of economic crises help to develop production on the basis of an extensive division of labour.

The specialisation and co-operation of enterprises create a basis for mass production. Mass production saves labour and material resources. An increase in the scale of production opens up the possibility of using automated equipment, production lines, assembly conveyors, which greatly increase the labour productivity.

Under the new five-year plan the level of specialisation is to be raised, especially spare parts, machine units and components are to be produced more extensively at specialised factories. This will help to rationalise equipment repairs on which about 10,000 million rubles a year are spent.

Combination of production

The combination of production is another factor promoting a rise in the productivity of social labour. Combination means the concentration of interconnected production processes in a single enterprise.

At first glance combination is the opposite of specialisation, but actually it is directly linked with it. These are but different methods of concentrating production, affording in definite conditions great economic benefits.

There are three basic forms of combination. First, there

is combination based on uniting consecutive processing stages. An example of this is the iron and steel combines. They combine all stages of metallurgical production, from the extraction of iron ore down to the production of rolled metal. They also burn coke needed for metallurgical production. This form of combination is also widely used in the textile industry. Secondly, there is combination based on the complex utilisation of raw materials. This form of combination is most extensive in the chemical industry processing organic raw materials (coal, oil), complex ores of non-ferrous metals, and in the processing of agricultural products in food industry enterprises. Thirdly, there is combination based on the utilisation of by-products. This is widely practised in wood-working enterprises, which also process sawdust and shavings.

Thus, combination is extensive in the branches where the processing of raw materials passes through several stages, comprising a single cycle, and in branches where production is based on the complex utilisation of raw materials and fuel.

Several factors account for the economic effectiveness of combination. This is first of all dependent on the attendant improvement in the equipment and technology of production. Furthermore, economy is yielded by eliminating unproductive expenditure on the transportation of products, since a large part of the raw materials, and semi-finished goods is processed within enterprises practising combination. Also very profitable is the complex utilisation of resources, and equipment and production structures too are used in a more rational way.

At large iron and steel combines (producing millions of tons of metal) about 40 million tons of raw materials, semi-manufactures, waste and other freight have to be transported every year. If the open-hearth, blast furnace, rolling mill and other production sectors were scattered among separate factories, the expenditure on transportation would be extremely high.

In a number of branches technological progress promotes the spread of combination. Take for example the building industry. House-building combines, based on extensive mechanisation, considerably reduce construction periods and reduce expenditure.

The complex utilisation of raw materials makes for the greater effectiveness of production. Thus, there still are many wood-working factories in the USSR which obtain a yield of finished articles per cubic metre of wood that is only one-third to one-fifth of that obtained at factories applying modern wood-processing methods and equipment. The complete utilisation of raw materials is a large reserve for a growth of labour productivity in industry.

Socialist emulation, its role in economic development and the communist education of the working people Socialist emulation plays a major role in raising the productivity of social labour. The bourgeoisie and its defenders assert that only competition makes every producer reveal all his abilities to the full. Actually, however, competition brutally suppresses the abilities of the working people. Deceit, fraud, the ruin of the masses and the enrichment of a handful of exploiters are all part and parcel of competition.

Socialist emulation has for the first time afforded full scope to the development of the innumerable abilities and talents which the bourgeois system warped and strangled. Competition is the struggle of everybody against everybody else, while socialist emulation is the comradely co-operation of the working people, their joint struggle for their common advance. Competition expresses the disunity and hostility of producers, socialist emulation expresses universal collaboration of people in a friendly collective.

Socialist emulation in all its forms is a wide movement of the working people based on the principle—catch up with the best, help those lagging behind, attain a general advance of production. The working people launch emulation campaigns for the fulfilment and overfulfilment of plans, for an increase in labour productivity, for the improvement of the quality of output and the lowering of costs and the economy of raw and other materials, fuel, and electric power. Emulation campaigns clearly demonstrate the new, conscientious attitude of the workers towards production and labour for the benefit of society. Work for the sake of universal welfare is the main content of communist labour.

Socialist emulation releases the labour activity and initiative of the masses that is characteristic only of socialism.

It accelerates the development of technology and helps to improve production organisation and to scrap outdated and advance progressive labour productivity standards. In the Soviet Union and other socialist countries socialist emulation has truly become a cause of all people and is having enormous impact on the whole course of economic development.

Socialist emulation is founded on the enormous educational and organising force of example. For the first time under socialism the force of example encourages mass action and serves as a means of improving production and as the motive force of social progress. Lenin considered that the organisation of socialist emulation must be based on the following principles: wide publicity, comparability of results, dissemination of progressive experience, material and moral stimuli to work.

In bourgeois society every improvement of the labour process is introduced only as a result of competitive struggle. The improvement of production in one factory poses a threat for the factories competing with it. Every innovation is kept secret and is the "commercial secret" of the factory applying it. The production process remains a process alien to the masses.

In socialist society, where the working people are vitally interested in the improvement of production, the initiative of go-ahead workers meets with keen response. It stimulates the creative initiative of the masses, evokes a spirit of comradely emulation and serves as a mighty instrument working for their joint progress.

The movement of shock-workers became widespread during the initial five-year plan periods in the USSR, later a movement of innovators of production was started. During the Great Patriotic War of the Soviet people the emulation campaigns of the working people in the rear contributed greatly to victory. In the postwar period they helped quickly to rehabilitate the war-devastated economy.

The movement of teams and shock-workers of communist labour began to gain ground at the time preceding the Soviet seven-year plan. The participants in the movement set themselves extensive tasks—to inculcate in themselves a conscientious, creative attitude towards their work, substantially to raise labour productivity, to become highly cultured people, constantly to raise their ideological and political level and to help their comrades in their work and life. Their slogan is: learn to work and live as Communists.

The further spread of socialist emulation, which has become a live expression of the revolutionary initiative among the masses and one of the basic forms of their participation in communist construction, is vital for the successful implementation of the current five-year plan and the advance of Soviet society along the road to communism.

Targets for the increase in labour productivity of the new five-year plan

The five-year plan provides for the growth of labour productivity at an accelerated rate. The average yearly rates for the growth of labour productivity per worker are to reach 6 per cent in industry as against 4.6 per cent between 1961 and 1965, 6.6 per cent in construction as against 5.3 per cent, about 7 per cent in the public sector of agriculture as against 3.7 per cent. During the current five-year period the labour productivity in industry is to grow by 33 to 35 per cent. In construction by 35 to 40 per cent, in state farms and collective farms by 40 to 45 per cent.

The acceleration of the labour productivity growth rate is to be achieved on the basis of accelerated scientific and technological progress and the extensive introduction of scientific and technological achievements into production, the development of specialisation of production and scientific labour organisation, the rise in skills and the intensification of economic stimuli.

One of the most important indices of the degree to which labour is equipped technically is the electrical power available per worker. During the five-year plan this index will rise 1.5 times in industry and 3 times in agriculture.

Growth of the cultural level and technological knowledge of the working people and of their skills

The systematic growth of the cultural level and technological knowledge of the working people has an enormous role to play in raising labour productivity. Scientific and technological progress is indissolubly linked with the improvement of the skills of workers, engineers and technicians. The socialist system creates perfect conditions for all working people to improve their general and technical education.

Technological advance and the rise of the cultural level and technological knowledge of the broad mass of the working people gradually eliminate the distinctions between physical and mental labour. The educational level of the working class and the collective farmers grows every year. In 1939 there were 123 people with higher and secondary (complete and incomplete) education per 1,000 people employed in the economy, in 1959, 433, in 1965, 522. As a result of the spread of secondary general and specialised education the bulk of the young people joining production now have an eight-year education, and a substantial part joins production after completing the 9th and 10th forms of secondary school.

At many enterprises equipped with progressive equipment up to one-third of the workers have a complete secondary education (10 and 11 forms). The number of collective farmers which have no special professions is also rapidly shrinking, while the number of operators, specialised farm workers and other skilled personnel having a general education and special training is rapidly growing.

The number of engineers and technicians is systematically increasing, and their skill is growing.

3. SCIENTIFIC PRODUCTION AND LABOUR ORGANISATION

Importance of correct production and labour organisation for raising the productivity of labour and improving labour conditions At the dawn of socialist construction Lenin emphasised the need to introduce scientific production and labour organisation. He considered that in socialist conditions scientific labour organisation is a mighty factor not only in raising labour productivity but also in facilitating labour in every way.

The scientific organisation of production and labour is particularly important in present-day conditions. The improvement of labour and production organisation is one of the main conditions for raising the effectiveness of production. Technological progress, the re-equipment of enterprises, and the introduction of better technological processes have assigned high priority to the radical improvement of labour organisation on genuinely scientific principles.

Soviet industry has become a world leader as regards the technological level of production and the qualifications of its workers and specialists. However, many enterprises still lag behind in production organisation, which has the purpose of merging the equipment and the people handling it in a single production process. This makes the introduction in all enterprises of a scientific production and labour organisation, corresponding to the requirements of modern scientific and technological progress, a most urgent economic task.

Experience of progressive enterprises, shops and departments in introducing scientific labour organisation The concrete forms of scientific labour organisation depend on the specifics of production. However, all advanced enterprises have certain features in common. The improvement of labour organisation is combined with the introduction of new technology, automation and mechanisation of basic and secondary operations. The systematic decrease in the labour intensiveness of production serves as the basis for the revision of output quotas. Along with the introduction of scientific labour organisation in production processes, measures are taken to improve the production management fundamentally, to mechanise administrative work, and systematically to raise the skills of engineers, technicians, factory and office workers. The improvement of labour organisation yields the best results when it takes into account the specifics and needs of production.

Indicative in this respect is the experience of the Gorky Motor Works. Since the transportation and warehousing were the major bottlenecks in that factory, it was important first of all to reduce the freight flow, to mechanise warehousing and transportation. Appreciable success has been achieved in this field. On an average from 20 to 44 per cent of the total labour force in factories in this branch of industry is engaged in transportation, warehousing and materials handling, while at the Gorky Motor Works these operations are handled by only 15 per cent of its staff. An independent department for the organisation of production and management has been set up at the works and is engaged in working out a system for rating the labour of office workers, engineers and technicians.

The Urals Chemical Machine-building Works considered it essential to work out plans for scientific labour organisation at every bench, to introduce progressive working methods and a more effective system of remuneration. A penetrating analysis of the work of the enterprise revealed that only an improvement in production organisation would make it possible to attain a higher labour productivity, profitability and economic operation. The programme drawn up for the improvement of production organisation provided for the preparation of production, the planning of production within the works and the material supply of its shops and departments, greater efficiency in management and the introduction of more rational working methods for workers, engineers and technicians.

The experience of the Urals Chemical Machine-building Works, the Gorky Motor Works and of a number of other enterprises, which initiated the movement for scientific labour organisation, attracted country-wide attention. Laboratories for the introduction of scientific labour organisation are being set up at many enterprises and plans and schedules are being worked out. Engineers, technicians and workers participate in their work and the measures already taken have had tangible results.

REVISION QUESTIONS

1. What are the advantages of socialist labour organisation?
2. What significance has the growth of labour productivity for the triumph of communism?
3. How is labour productivity increased?
4. What are the benefits of scientific production and labour organisation?

Chapter XV

DISTRIBUTION ACCORDING TO LABOUR AND SOCIAL CONSUMPTION FUNDS

1. DISTRIBUTION ACCORDING TO LABOUR—AN ECONOMIC LAW OF SOCIALISM

Social control over the measure of labour and measure of consumption The implementation of the principle "From each according to his ability, to each according to his work" means that society must take account of and control the measure of labour and the measure of consumption of every worker. Lenin considered this a most vital condition for the success of socialist construction. Such accounting and control is needed for a number of objective reasons.

First, society does not as yet have an abundance of products to ensure the full and all-sided satisfaction of the rapidly growing requirements of all members of society.

Secondly, labour has not yet become the prime vital necessity of man; hence, it is necessary to ensure material incentives to induce every worker to work for the common good with maximum productivity.

Thirdly, there still are appreciable distinctions between town and country, between mental and physical labour. Therefore, the labour of individual workers differs not only in quantity but also in quality.

The exploiting system has left a deep residium in the minds of people and throughout the socialist epoch a struggle is waged against capitalist vestiges. For instance, the backward portion of the working people strives to give society as little as possible and to get from it as much as possible, a condition nurtured by ages of forced labour. The social control of the measure of labour and the measure of consumption is an extremely important factor in the struggle for a new, socialist attitude towards labour.

This form of social inducement to work has nothing to

do with the methods of coercion to work applied under capitalism. Under that system the exploiter class uses the threat of hunger to make the exploited classes work. Under socialism society as a whole exercises an influence on its members by controlling the measure of labour and the measure of consumption of every worker: the share of the social product received by every worker is made to depend on the extent to which he participates in the labour of society.

The distribution of material wealth depends on the social mode of production. Under socialism distribution is effected according to labour.

The distribution according to the quantity and quality of labour serves as a powerful stimulus to raise the labour productivity, to advance the economy and the people's welfare. It induces the working people to raise their skills, take an interest in the improvement of the labour organisation, and take an active part in promoting technological progress. The distribution according to labour thus promotes the rapid development of the productive forces in every way.

The distribution according to labour is therefore an objective economic law of socialism. Socialist society, mastering this law, applies it as the basis for the remuneration of labour in all spheres of human activity. The distribution according to labour is closely linked with the whole system of socialist management in the Soviet Union and other socialist countries.

Enemies of socialism, striving to discredit socialism in the eyes of uninformed people, depict the principle of material incentives as a concession to capitalist methods. This is a slander against socialism. The principle of distribution according to labour has nothing whatsoever to do with the capitalist striving for profits. A chasm divides the socialist principle of higher pay for more effective work from the capitalist striving for profits.

Remuneration according to labour shows millions of working people the indissoluble connection which exists between the results of labour and the people's material welfare in socialist society. The distribution according to the quantity and quality of labour is thus a powerful means of educating new, conscious, socialist labour discipline, a feeling of being part of a collective and is a factor strengthening the relations of co-operation and comradely mutual assistance, which are a distinctive feature of socialist production relations.

The distribution according to labour ensures the direct material interest of the working people in the results of their labour. It shows millions of working people that it is necessary to work well in order to live well. Material incentives spur on the advanced workers and raise the mass of the workers to the level of the advanced.

Remuneration according to labour makes for the correct combination of the personal and public interests of the working people and for the subordination of personal interests to those of society as a whole. The system of material incentives is based on Leninist principles of planned, economic business management, the introduction of cost accounting, the elimination of all mismanagement and waste. Strengthening cost accounting and economic management is inconceivable without the material interest of every worker in the results of his labour, without the interest of the staffs of factories, shops, departments and teams in their joint performance.

Combination of the economic interests of society, of staffs of enterprises and individual workers
Fundamental, irreconcilable contradictions of class and group interests are typical of all exploiting societies. In capitalist society these interests are particularly antagonistic. Bourgeois ideologists consider it one of their central tasks to camouflage the antagonism of interests under capitalism. The anti-scientific theories of bourgeois pseudo-scientists about the harmony of interests in capitalist society have nothing to do with reality and the facts nail these lies at every step.

There can be no irreconcilable interests in socialist society, since all working people are interested in a flourishing socialist economy. This, however, does not exclude the necessity of skilfully combining the direct material interest of the enterprise's staff and individual working people with those of society as a whole.

The essential aim of economic stimulation is to ensure that the interests of workers' collectives and every worker and those of society as a whole match. The greater economic stimuli granted to production are to resolve the contradictions arising or likely to arise between the interests of society, enterprises and individual working people.

The economic way of resolving these contradictions presupposes the full and knowledgeable utilisation of the whole system of value categories: such indices as realisation of output, profit and profitability, payment for the use of productive assets, deductions from the enterprises' profits to special funds, wages, bonuses, etc. The correct utilisation of these and other economic instruments helps to achieve a unity between the interests of society, of workers' collectives at enterprises and of individual working people.

Combination of material and moral stimuli to work

In the early years of Soviet power Lenin wrote that socialism and communism must not be built on enthusiasm alone, but with the help of the enthusiasm, born of the great revolution, on personal interest, on cost accounting. Lenin's behest shows that there must be a correct combination of material and moral stimuli to work.

The practice of socialist construction confirms that without the material interest of workers in the results of their labour the productive forces of the country cannot be raised, socialist economy cannot be created and scores of millions of people cannot be led towards communism. At the same time socialism evolves ever more powerful and effective moral stimuli to work. The fundamentally different position the working people hold in society is a source of moral stimuli. It induces the working people to work better and more productively for the benefit of society. In addition to material stimuli the social approval shown for the work people do for society is becoming an enormous driving force of social progress.

Lenin pointed out that personal interest is instrumental in raising production. He attached enormous importance to material stimuli, to ensuring the material interest of workers and production staffs in good, successful work for the benefit of society. He regarded material incentives for good work as an effective factor influencing economic advance, and a powerful lever of progress in economic development, supplementing the moral stimuli to work evolved by the socialist system.

The correct combination of material and moral stimuli to work is a great creative force in the struggle for communism. The further we advance towards communism the greater will become the importance of moral stimuli to work, the social approval of the results of labour and the feeling of responsibility of every member of society for the cause of the whole people.

The greater incentives granted to enterprises the further development of the principle of material stimulation are called upon to ensure a correct combination of material and moral stimuli to work. It has been observed that in some cases the essential unity between the two is lacking. The unity of the material interest and moral stimuli is vastly important not only economically, but also for the development of a truly communist attitude towards labour and for the education of the builders of communist society.

Material incentives should be organised so as to strengthen the moral stimuli to work. The whole system of the accounting of labour and of its results must evoke a desire to work better, more productively, to further social interests, to exhibit care for the people's wealth, to economise labour and material resources.

In the course of socialist and communist construction moral and material stimuli to work enhance each other and aim at a single goal. The ideological and educational work directed at developing moral stimuli to work and sharpening the material interest of the working people in developing production are indissolubly interlinked. Any counterpositioning of moral and material stimuli will inevitably harm communist construction.

The harm of wage-levelling At the dawn of capitalism, when the bourgeoisie fought feudalism, it used the equality slogan to draw the popular masses over to its side. But under the guise of formal equality bourgeois rule conceals the greatest inequality between the exploiter and the exploited, the rich and the poor.

The working class counters the formal equality of bourgeois society with the demand for genuine equality. The real content of this demand for equality, Marx and Engels explained, is the destruction of classes.

Having abolished exploitation, socialism eliminates class inequality. This does not mean, however, that socialism levels everybody's consumption and everybody's personal tastes and requirements.

The distribution according to the quantity and quality of labour is attended by a struggle against petty-bourgeois levelling. The levelling of the remuneration of labour irrespective of the quantity and quality of labour expended, qualification, productivity and conscientiousness is incompatible with socialism. Levelling is at odds with the material stimulation of those who work well, it blunts the material interest of workers in improving production, the growth of labour productivity and improving their skills.

Distribution according to labour and communist construction

The distribution according to labour plays an enormous role in the creation of the material and spiritual prerequisites of the higher phase of communism. This method of distribution is essential to ensure the most rapid development of the productive forces of socialist society.

The building of communism must rely on the principle of material interest. During the whole period of communist construction remuneration according to labour remains the main source for satisfying the working people's material and cultural requirements. At the same time as communism draws closer, the Programme of the CPSU says, personal requirements will be satisfied to an ever greater extent from social consumption funds, and the rate of their growth will outstrip that of the individual remuneration according to labour. The transition to communist distribution according to requirements will be completed only when the socialist principle of distribution according to labour exhausts itself completely, i.e., when there will be an abundance of material and cultural wealth and labour will become a vital necessity for all members of society.

The dialectics of life are such that the implementation of the principle of distribution according to labour creates the conditions for implementing the communist principle of distribution according to requirements. No wall divides the two forms of distribution, just as no wall divides the two stages of communist society.

2. WAGES AT STATE ENTERPRISES

Basic principles of the organisation of wages at socialist enterprises Under socialism labour is remunerated in keeping with the law of the distribution according to the quantity and quality of work done. Having taken cognisance of this law socialist society constantly utilises it to improve the forms and methods of labour remuneration.

Factory and office workers employed at state-owned socialist enterprises are paid wages. Under socialism wages express the relation between society as a whole, as represented by the state, and the individual factory and office workers, the labour of which is assessed according to its quantity and quality.

The wages of the whole working class are the share of the national income that goes to cover the individual consumption of the factory and office workers and is distributed according to labour. Wages are paid in cash.

In socialist society there is no room for the operation of the market laws of value of labour power, which determine the wage level under capitalism. There is no struggle between the working class and the capitalists for the size of the wages, since there is no capitalist class. There is no competition between workers. The working class, through its state bodies, determines the size of wages in a planned way in the interests of society as a whole.

The wage level is fixed so as to ensure that alongside the steady rise in the working people's welfare, the share of the surplus product left to society should suffice to cover all its needs. The wage policy is called upon to ensure the material interest of factory and office workers, specialists, and managers of state enterprises in the results of their labour.

At the present time the main objective of the wage policy is to steadily raise the wages as a stimulant in the fulfilment of the most important production tasks of the current five-year plan. The systematic increase of wages will be combined with the provision of greater incentives to those workers who contribute a greater share to the development and improvement of production. The remuneration of labour must be organised so that every worker and technician should know by how much his wage will grow if he improves the indicators of his work, what share he personally will receive from the additional income of the enterprise.

In socialist society the size of wages depends mainly on the level of labour productivity. Labour productivity must grow quicker than wages. This is a condition that guarantees society sufficient means to satisfy its growing requirements and accumulate and expand production.

Skilled workers receive more pay than unskilled workers. This is in keeping with the socialist law of distribution according to the quantity and quality of labour: skilled labour is labour of a higher quality, labour creating a higher value. The higher reward of skilled labour stimulates the self-improvement of workers and prompts them to raise their skills.

Workers employed in arduous jobs, and also workers with leading professions (for example, combine operators—in coal mining; kiln operators, steel smelters, rolling mill operators—in metallurgy) also receive higher wages. In the new five-year plan period more advantages will be given to those working in arduous or harmful conditions, on underground and more exacting jobs.

The wage policy takes account also of the specifics of the various regions of the country, their natural and climatic conditions, the degree to which the areas are economically developed and the obtaining retail prices.

Rating of work The organisation of wages in accordance with the economic law of the distribution according to labour presupposes a correct rating of work and a rational grading system.

To pay a worker in accordance with the quantity and quality of his labour we must preliminarily establish how much labour is needed to fulfil each job. This is achieved through technical rating—the establishment of time quotas or output quotas (or standards). The constant improvement of technical rating is one of the main tasks of economic development.

The time standard is a definition of all time expenditure needed to fulfil a definite job. The output standard is the determination of the number or the volume of output, or number of parts, or operations the worker must fulfil within a certain time—an hour, a working day or a month. The output standard is determined by dividing the working hour (or the working day, or total number of working hours per month) by the time standard for the production of a unit of output.

The time standard is used predominantly in individual or batch production and output standards—in mass production.

The conditions obtaining at the enterprise are taken into account when output standards are established, at the same time, however, due account is taken also of available reserves: the opportunities for the better utilisation of equipment and the improvement of technology. Organisational and technical measures are outlined to ensure the application of the most productive methods for the fulfilment of every job. In this way technically justified standards are established.

The technological equipment of socialist industry grows constantly. Production methods and labour organisation are improved, a great number of measures are implemented to improve production. All this enables the workers to raise their output without an increase in labour expenditure. Standards are therefore revised as technological and organisational improvements are introduced into production. To prevent an unfounded revision of standards and to ensure the participation of the enterprise staffs in this matter all revisions of standards must be approved by the factory's trade union organisation.

The standards must always correspond to the level of equipment, technology and production organisation. Only in that case are they able to fulfil their organisational role in production.

The remuneration of the workers is based on the grading system. The principal elements of this system are the schedules of grades, the basic rate, and the skill-grading handbook.

The schedules of grades determine the payment for work according to how complicated or difficult it is. All jobs are divided into a definite number of groups or grades.

The basic rates determine the amount of payment for the fulfilment of the fixed output standard. The basic rate in Grade 1 serves to determine rates in the upward grades. The wage rates of other skill-categories are determined by multiplying the rate of Grade 1 by the coefficient for the skill-category of the grade in question.

The skill-grading handbook contains the characteristics of the jobs performed at the enterprise. It serves as the basis for determining the worker's qualifications and for placing him in a definite grade in the schedule of grades.

Forms and systems of wages

At state-owned socialist enterprises two basic forms of wages are used —piece-rates and time-rates. Each of these forms can be individual or group (collective).

The piece-rate, under which the worker's earnings depend directly on the amount of output, the parts or operations he produces, is more widespread. More than two-thirds of the workers employed in Soviet industry are paid according to piece-rate systems. Piece-rates stimulate the raising of workers' skills, better equipment utilisation, the struggle against losses of working time, stoppages and organisational hitches in production.

Under the individual direct piece-rate system the worker is paid a definite piece-rate price for each unit of output. Piece-rates are fixed in accordance with the grade and time or output standard.

In some cases the progressive piece-rate system is applied, according to which every unit produced over and above the basic quota is paid for at a progressively increasing rate. This system cannot be applied on a mass scale or constantly, because under it a worker's wages can grow quicker than his labour productivity. In certain cases, however, when bottlenecks must be urgently abolished, it may be in the interest of the enterprise to apply progressive piece-rates.

Time-rates are also applied in industry. Under this system the worker is paid on the basis of time actually worked.

About one-third of the workers in Soviet industry work under this system.

Time-rates are used where it is impossible accurately to determine the output of the workers, as for example in repair work. It is used to pay repair workers, adjusters, crane operators, electricians, etc. Time-rates are used also on some sections of automated production, where the worker is engaged mainly in the adjustment, repair and maintenance of machinery. The time plus bonus system is successfully used at enterprises and in sectors equipped with strictly-regimented (automatic) machinery and working conditions.

Improvements in the organisation of wages

All forms of labour remuneration are being improved as the productive forces of socialist society develop, and as more equipment becomes available to labour. Within the past few years measures have been taken to reform the wages of factory and office workers. Unified grades have been introduced in the various branches of production. New basic rates, schedules of grades and salaries were introduced in the branches of production, irrespective of the departmental subordination of enterprises. As a result the number of the schedules of grades has been reduced from about 2,000 to 10, the number of basic rates for Grade 1 from several thousand to 30, the number of scales of salaries from 700 to about 30-35. Thus a firm basis has been created for the extensive introduction of unified standards in the various branches of the economy. The share of technically based output standards has grown in the basic industries.

The wage reform has abolished the excessive differentiation in the remuneration of the labour of different categories of workers, which had arisen after the Second World War. During the seven-year plan period the minimum wage of factory and office workers and the wage rates and salaries of workers in the low and medium income bracket have been raised. The remuneration of the labour of workers in industries directly catering for the population—workers in education, public health, culture, trade and housing and utilities has also been raised. In the current five-year period the minimum wage in the economy has been raised again and is now sixty rubles a month.

Material incentives fund

The new system of management creates conditions under which the opportunities of the enterprises to raise wages will depend mainly on the growth of production and the improvement of the quality of output, on an increase in profits and a rise of the profitability. While the basic rates and salaries of the factory and office workers will continue to grow in a centralised way, enterprises will in addition to the wage fund have a material incentives fund to reward workers for individual achievements which is geared to the performance of the enterprise as a whole.

The economic reform is a fundamental change from former conditions when far too little material incentives were provided to enterprise's staffs to improve the general results of their work. Before the reform enterprises had only very limited means at their disposal to stimulate the factory and office workers from finances created by the enterprise itself. About a half of the factories did not have a fund formed from profits. And even at factories which did have such a fund it was very small and the sums allotted to incentives were negligible. As a rule bonuses and other rewards were paid not out of profits but out of the wage fund. The increase in profits and the growth of the profitability of production did not exert a direct influence on the size of the workers' wages.

With the transition to the new system of planning and economic stimulation, the material incentives fund is being created out of deductions from the enterprise's profits. This fund pays for the bonuses of factory and office workers for good work during the year and also for lump sum awards at the end of the year. Deductions to the material incentives fund are made according to quotas stipulated for a number of years ahead, and the size of the fund depends on the growth in the output sold or on the profits and profitability envisaged in the plan. The rewards for the overfulfilment of the plan will be relatively smaller than those for the fulfilment of the plan indicators to make the enterprise interested in assuming higher plan targets and in mobilising all its reserves for their fulfilment.

The material incentives fund will also grow with an increase in the share of new output and also as a result of additional incomes received by the enterprise from mark-ups on the price in connection with improvements in the quality of output. This makes enterprises interested in mastering the production of new output and in up-grading the quality of output. The creation of the enterprise's fund for socio-cultural measures and housing construction further extends its sphere of granting material incentives to its workers. The means in this fund supplement centralised resources for the building of housing, maintenance of children's institutions and pioneer camps, and for the better organisation of rest homes and sanatoriums.

The economic reform thus makes it possible to put the share of the enterprise's profits used to raise the material interest of the workers in the results of production to better use. Profit becomes an important internal resource of the enterprise for the material stimulation of the factory and office workers. This creates conditions for increasing the material interest of workers in the general results of the enterprise's activities, for enhancing the interest of all working people in the growth of production, organising labour in a better way and raising the quantitative and qualitative indicators of the enterprise's performance.

The formation of material incentives funds at enterprises will enhance the collective interest of all workers in improving the general results of the enterprise's performance. The rise in the share of bonuses and lump sum rewards in the wages of factory and office workers, envisaged in the new five-year plan, will help better to combine the interests of every worker with those of the whole staff and of society as a whole. With the introduction of the new system of stimulation, the bonus systems, which take into account the labour productivity, the quality of work and individual and collective production results will gradually extend to workers of all categories.

3. PAYMENT FOR WORK IN COLLECTIVE FARMS

Specifics of the payment for work in collective farms The working class and the collective farmers receive their incomes for their collective labour at socialist enterprises according to the socialist principle "From each according to his ability, to each according to his work". There is, however, a difference in the methods by which work is paid for at state enterprises and at collective farms.

At state enterprises factory and office workers receive wages of a size fixed by the state. In collective farms the farmers are paid out of the incomes of the collective economy and the size of the payments is determined by the members of the relevant collective farm. The increase in the incomes of the collective farm resulting from the growth of output and the lowering of outlay on production increases the welfare of the artel members.

The piece-rate is the main form used for the remuneration of labour in collective farms. The board of the collective farm works out and the general meeting of the collective farm members approves the output quotas and rates for every job in keeping with the conditions at the given farm, with the skill required for the relevant job and with its complexity and arduousness.

The greater mechanisation of agricultural production, the growing skills of the collective farmers, and better labour organisation make it necessary to revise the output quotas and wage rates at collective farms systematically and to fix more suitable ones. This ensures a constant rise in the labour productivity, increases accumulations for the extended reproduction of the collective economy and advances the collective farmers' material welfare. The improvement of the relations within the collective farms makes it necessary for the rating, organisation and remuneration of labour in collective farms to draw nearer to the level and forms at state enterprises.

For a long time collective farmers were paid exclusively according to the system of workday units. The workday unit was the common measure for the heterogeneous kinds of labour in the collective farm.

Under the workday unit system the income of every farmer from his work in the collective farm depends on the number of workday units earned and on the growth of the farm's income. The number of workday units depends on the amount of work done by every member of the farm. But the size of the workday unit, i.e., the amount of products and money the farmer is paid per workday unit is determined by the work of the whole artel, by the state of its economy and by its incomes.

Under the system of remuneration according to workday units the farmers receive for each workday unit a part of the collective farm's output in kind and a certain share of the collective farm's money incomes in cash. The collective farmers sell part of the products they receive according to workday units, and also part of those they produce on their personal subsidiary plots on the market.

The workday unit replaced the system of egalitarian distribution according to "mouths to feed". Therefore the remuneration of the collective farmers according to workday units was a major triumph of the socialist principle of distribution according to labour. But the workday unit in itself does not take into account the qualitative aspect of the labour of separate teams. The further development of the collective farms made it necessary to introduce an additional reward for quality—for high yields in crop farming and high productivity in animal farming.

Under the workday unit system the collective farmers received their whole income at the end of the year and predominantly in kind. Later monthly advances in cash were introduced. With the further advance of the collective farm economy and the growth of commodity-money relations the artels made a transition to the remuneration of the labour in cash according to fixed quotas and rates. Under this system a definite part of the farm's agricultural output is distributed among the collective farmers on account of their earnings in kind in amounts laid down by the general meeting of the artel members.

Increase in the incomes of collective farms and farmers

In accordance with the decisions of the March (1965) Plenary Meeting of the Central Committee and the 23rd Congress of the CPSU the Party and the Government are implementing a wide set of measures aimed at raising the incomes of collective farms and farmers from their work in the collective farm.

Stable plans containing yearly targets have been fixed for the purchase of agricultural products for a number of years in advance—six years for grain and five years for other products. In fulfilling the plan for state purchases, the collective farms have been afforded the opportunity to plan production independently, to specialise their economy so as to derive maximum economic benefits on the basis of advanced agricultural techniques. At the same time the former purchasing plans were reduced, while purchasing prices were substantially raised so that agricultural production has become profitable in all farms operating normally. If there is a surplus of crops over and above the plan targets, the collective farms can sell them at prices that are higher than those for the planned output. This is an additional incentive to increase output.

Changes in the methods of planning and the increase in the purchasing prices for agricultural products create conditions for raising the material interest of the collective farmers in the growth of the collective farm economy. The collective farms are able to set aside larger sums for payment to farmers. The proviso of the Programme of the CPSU that every collective farm increase the incomes of the farmers from the commonly-owned economy and raise their living standard in accordance with the rise in their labour productivity is being realised in this manner.

Vital to the growth of the incomes of the collective farms and of the farmers from the commonly-owned economy is the assistance being given by the state to the development and strengthening of the material and technical basis of agriculture. The five-year plan provides for a growth of state capital investments in agriculture by about 100 per cent. A total of 41,000 million rubles have been assigned to the construction of productive capacities and the acquisition of equipment during the five-year period. During that period an additional 1,790,000 tractors, 1,100,000 lorries and 550,000 combine harvesters will be supplied to collective farms. The supply of mineral fertilisers will also be increased with every passing year. The electrification of collective farms and state farms is assuming a wider scale. The substantial increase in the delivery of new equipment, mineral fertilisers, power and the simultaneous growth of the material interest of the workers in agriculture is to ensure a high development rate in agriculture. The growth in the production of foodstuffs and industrial raw materials will help fuller to satisfy the country's requirements. The use of chemical fertilisers, the mechanisation and electrification of agriculture will make it possible to raise the labour productivity and gradually to raise the index of machinery available to labour and the organisation of labour in agriculture to the level in industry.

The economic growth of the collective farms is the foundation ensuring the advance of the collective farmers' welfare and guaranteeing that the level of their remuneration will draw closer to the level of the remuneration of the factory and office workers.

Introduction of a guaranteed remuneration of labour in collective farms

The introduction of guaranteed payments in collective farms is crucial in strengthening the economic position of the collective farms and to the improvement in the living conditions of the rural population.

The methods by which the incomes in collective farms were formerly distributed often led to vacillations in the size of the remuneration of the collective farmers' labour. In many collective farms there were no permanent payments for work done. In this connection the Party and the Government recommended that the collective farms introduce guaranteed payments to the collective farmers on the basis of the wage-rates used in state farms for corresponding work. The output quotas introduced take into account the concrete conditions at the farm, and are based on the quotas in collective farms.

The introduction of guaranteed monthly remuneration of labour in collective farms has become possible thanks to the development of the collective farm economy. In 1965 the incomes of the collective farms from sales of output increased by more than 2,500 million rubles over the 1964 figure, and about 50 per cent of that sum went to raise the incomes of the farmers. The number of farms with a low level of remuneration has quickly shrunk. Conditions have been created to make the few remaining ones financially sound.

The introduction of guaranteed monthly payments to collective farmers is a fundamental improvement of the whole system of distribution of collective farm incomes. Formerly, the fund of payments to collective farmers was formed from the income which remained after allotments had been made to the non-distributable and social funds. Now, however, before the collective farm's income is distributed, funds are set aside for payments for the collective

347

farmers' labour. It has also been recommended to set aside a definite part of the collected gross harvest of grain and other products to guarantee the collective farmers' income in kind. The collective farmers may receive these products on account of their guaranteed pay in accordance with the procedure laid down by the general meeting of the artel members.

The introduction of guaranteed remuneration of labour for collective farmers and the further increase in the size of that remuneration are carried out on the basis of the growth of production and the rise in the labour productivity in collective farms, the strict observance of the regime of economy and the constant concern for the advance of the collective farm economy. This is a major step in fulfilling one of the main tasks of the five-year plan: a closer approximation of the living standards in town and country.

4. SOCIAL CONSUMPTION FUNDS

Importance of social consumption funds to the rise in the people's living standard Alongside the growth of the working people's incomes through the remuneration of labour, the growth of the social consumption funds is vital in advancing the people's welfare. These funds finance the expenditure of the state on education, health services, pension benefits, the maintenance of children in children's institutions, and in future will finance the transition to free communal services, etc. The social consumption funds play an enormous role in satisfying the social and cultural requirements of the people in socialist society. The social consumption funds are particularly important to families with many children.

Free education, health services, the absence of unemployment and many other advantages of socialism have long since been part of the everyday life of the Soviet people. These benefits are an irrevocable achievement of the Soviet people, who have left the capitalist countries far behind in this respect. These benefits are paid for by the social consumption funds, which have grown at a particularly rapid rate in the postwar period. The grants and privileges paid out of these funds to the population have grown from 4,600 million rubles in 1940 to 41,500 million rubles in 1965.

The growth of the social consumption funds exerts an appreciable influence on the advance of the people's living standard. This can be seen from the following. The average monthly wages of factory and office workers have grown from 78 rubles in 1958 to 95 rubles in 1965, while considering the grants and privileges they have received from the social consumption funds, the incomes of factory and office workers have grown from 104 to 128 rubles during that period. In 1965 state pensions were introduced for collective farmers. The number of people drawing state pensions has grown from 20 million to 32 million. Close on 17 million flats and individual houses have been built in town and country, the increment being equal to two-fifths of the total housing facilities that were available at the beginning of the seven-year plan period.

Types of social consumption funds While the remuneration according to the quantity and quality of work done will remain the basic source of satisfying the people's requirements, during the whole period of communist construction, there will be at the same time a steady growth of the social consumption funds. This does not undermine the material interest of the working people in the results of their labour, but promotes the solution of a number of important socio-economic problems in a communist way.

Among them are, first, the maintenance of the up-and-coming generation. Soviet society is now on its way to assuming all expenditure connected with this task.

Second, the rise in the educational level of the population and the development of culture and science. This includes the state expenditure on the building of schools, universities, research institutes, theatres, cinemas, etc.

Third, the safeguarding of the people's health. This includes the vast sphere of medical services, the organisation of rest and treatment.

Fourth, the improvement of the people's living conditions. This includes the solution of the housing problem, supplying the population with well-appointed houses, communal services, etc.

Fifth, the care of society for its incapacitated members. This includes old age and disability pensions.

The growth of the social consumption funds considerably mitigates the inequality as regards property, which is inevitable in socialist society, since under it the remuneration according to the quantity and quality of work done remains an objective necessity.

5. MAIN WAYS FOR THE FURTHER ADVANCE OF THE PEOPLE'S LIVING STANDARD

Indicators of the people's living standard The living standard of the people cannot be characterised by any single indicator, but only by a whole set of indicators characterising the various sides of the people's labour and life.

One of the main indicators of the material welfare of a people is the size of the working people's real income. The size of the real incomes depends on three factors: first, on the size of the money incomes, secondly, on the level of the prices of consumer goods and services, and thirdly, on the size of social consumption funds. The higher the real incomes of the population the greater is the per capita consumption.

At the same time the working conditions of workers and peasants are also enormously important to the people's living standard. They include the length of the working day and paid vacations, the degree of mechanisation of labour, the degree of its intensity, the arduousness and harmfulness of labour, its safety and many other factors. In comparing the living standards in countries with different social systems it is necessary to take into account the employment index, which depends on whether there is unemployment in the country and on its size and for the rural population on whether there is an overpopulation and on its size. An important aspect of the working people's living standard is the structure of their expenditure (family budget), the relation of the expenditures on the satisfaction of different sorts of requirements.

Housing, health services, the longevity of the people, and the cultural facilities at their disposal, are another factor determining the standard of living.

The growth of the socialist economy is indissolubly linked with the enormous facilitation of labour. In Soviet industry technological progress has led to the disappearance of many professions, connected with hard physical labour, while the rapid development of science and technology leads to a further facilitation of labour. The hard labour of the individual farmer, who tilled the land with outmoded implements, has disappeared once and for all from agriculture.

During the years of Soviet power the average duration of the working day in industry has decreased from 9.9 hours in 1913 to 6.93 hours in 1964, i.e., by 2.97 hours. It should be remembered that in tsarist Russia the working day often reached 12 to 14 hours. Today the actual working week in the U.S.S.R. is approximately 40 hours. The working day has been decreased while wages have remained at the same level or have been raised. The collective farmer works today 33 per cent less time than individual farmers did. All intensive work in the collective farms is done with the help of tractor-drawn implements or self-propelled farm machinery.

The growth of the population's real incomes systematically increases popular consumption. The volume of the retail trade turnover of state and co-operative trading enterprises, including public catering establishments, has grown in 1965 by 336 per cent over the 1940 volume, the sale of foodstuffs by 260 per cent, non-foodstuffs by 467 per cent.

In pre-revolutionary Russia the working people's housing conditions were extremely inadequate. In the Soviet Union gigantic housing construction is underway. Between 1918 and 1965, 1,190.9 million square metres of direct use living space were built, of which 556.5 million square metres were built between 1959 and 1965. At the same time the share of rent in the family budget has decreased substantially. In pre-revolutionary Russia rents swallowed an average of 20 per cent of the working family's budget, often as much as 33 per cent. At present the expenditure on rent and communal services averages 4 to 5 per cent of the working family's budget.

A striking indication of the Soviet people's growing welfare is the fact that their longevity has almost doubled, as compared with pre-revolutionary times.

In socialist society the people's material welfare grows with the expansion of social production, the development of the productive forces, the rise in labour productivity and the increase in the effectiveness of social production. This regularity is conditioned by the main aim of socialist production, which is the ever fuller satisfaction of the working people's growing requirements.

The systematic rise of the people's living standard is an economic law of socialism. Like other economic laws, this law does not operate automatically. Persistent, selfless labour, the growth of its productivity, the improvement of its organisation, the struggle against all unproductive expenditure and losses are conditions for the systematic growth of the Soviet people's material welfare.

The only source ensuring the rise of the people's living standard is the mass of material wealth being created by their labour. In socialist society the working people know: to produce more today, means to possess more tomorrow.

Rise in the people's welfare under the five-year plan

The five-year plan for economic development between 1966 and 1970 opens up wide prospects for the further advance of the people's welfare. The growth of the working people's living standard is the main economic and political task of the five-year period. A system of well-considered and scientifically based measures serves to accomplish this task which will affect all aspects of economic and cultural development.

In the present five-year period the Communist Party is steering a consistent course towards accelerating growth rates in the people's welfare, one of its chief tasks. The Directives of the 23rd Congress of the CPSU say: "In view of the fact that the main purpose of socialist production is to satisfy the growing material and cultural needs of the people, a further substantial improvement in living standards shall be ensured in the next five years by means of greater labour productivity, by increasing the output of material values and accelerating the growth rate of the national income."

The further advance of the people's welfare will be achieved by a series of measures, including:

first, the rise in the wages of factory and office workers,

and of the incomes of collective farmers from the socialised economy;

second, the growth of the social consumption funds;

third, the expansion of consumer goods production;

fourth, the further expansion of housing construction;

fifth, a considerable improvement in the communal and cultural services rendered to the urban and rural population.

Growth of the remuneration of labour in the new five-year period

The higher remuneration of labour will be decisive in raising the welfare of the people. It is the primary stimulus for the development of production and at the same time the main source of the working people's higher incomes. For this reason the increase in the remuneration of labour will remain the chief means of raising the people's living standard during the period of communist construction.

The new five-year plan provides for a considerable growth of this main source of the population's income. The average monthly wages of factory and office workers will grow by 20 per cent during the period. By the end of the five-year period the average monthly wage will be 115 rubles. Taking into account the grants and privileges from the social consumption funds, the average wage of factory and office workers will reach about 155 rubles. The incomes of the collective farmers from the collective economy will grow by an average of 35-40 per cent. As a result the fund for the remuneration of the labour of factory and office workers and collective farmers will grow by about 40 per cent during the five-year period.

In addition to wage increases the abolition and reduction of taxes on the wages of some categories of factory, office and other workers will continue. The gradual introduction of guaranteed monthly payments for the work of collective farmers, taking into account the wages of state farm workers doing identical jobs and output quotas, will also greatly contribute to the advance of the collective farmers' welfare. The incomes of the collective farmers from the collective economy will grow on the basis of a rise in labour productivity and the better use of the labour resources of the collective farms throughout the year. Another source for a growth of the income of the rural population are the personal subsidiary plots of the collective farmers.

Growth of social consumption funds in the new five-year period

The five-year plan envisages an increase in the money grants and privileges afforded to the population at the expense of social consumption funds by no less than 40 per cent. These funds are to finance social insurance measures, pensions, students' and other grants, paid vacations, free tuition and free medical services, the provision of accommodations in sanatoriums and rest homes free of charge or on cut-rate terms, the maintenance of kindergartens and crèches and other socio-cultural services.

Under the five-year plan the minimum size of the old-age pensions of factory and office workers and collective farmers has been raised, and collective farmers receive pensions now on the same conditions as factory and office workers. The payment of temporary disability grants to all working people has also been improved.

The development of education and medical services is a major factor determining the people's material and cultural standard. The five-year plan envisages completing, in the main, the introduction of universal secondary education, greatly increasing the number of students in secondary specialised and higher educational institutions and also in vocational schools. The network of state children's institutions is to be extended so as to satisfy in the main the urban population's need for them and to fulfil the rural population's requirements to a high degree. The five-year plan provides for a considerable improvement of the medical services in town and country. This is to be achieved through the extensive building of hospitals and other medical establishments, increasing the medical industry output through measures serving to further improve the treatment in sanatoriums and facilities in rest homes.

Growth of consumption

The increase in the people's incomes during the current five-year plan period will be attended by a further growth of consumption.

The five-year plan provides for a considerable increase in the population's consumption of foodstuffs and industrial goods. The sale of consumer goods by state and co-operatives will grow by no less than 40 per cent. At the same time the range and quality of consumer goods is to improve.

The five-year plan provides for an improvement of the structure of the family diets. There is to be an increase in the per capita consumption of meat and meat products by 20 to 25 per cent, milk and dairy products by 15 to 18 per cent, sugar by about 25 per cent, vegetables and melons by 35 to 40 per cent, vegetable oils by 40 to 46 per cent, fruit and grapes by 45 to 50 per cent and fish and fish products by 50 to 60 per cent.

Sales of fabrics, clothes and knitwear are to grow by 40 per cent, those of knitwear by more than 90 per cent.

A major role is assigned to the improvement of trading methods, to greater consideration for the consumer demand, the adjustment of the assortment of goods in keeping with the tastes and wishes of consumers, the widespread introduction of higher trading standards and the improvement of the quality of consumer goods.

The real incomes of the population will grow also through retail price cuts on some foodstuffs and industrial goods, notably children's goods. The price cuts will be based on the growth of consumer goods production and will be effected as the necessary commodity resources accumulate.

The role of the services sector in raising the people's living standard grows as the productive forces develop and the welfare of the population advances. In the current five-year period this sector will expand substantially. During this period the real per capita income is to grow by about 30 per cent, the volume of the retail trade by 43.5 per cent and the turnover of public catering establishments by about 50 per cent, the volume of services to the population by about 150 per cent. The five-year plan envisages transforming the service industry into a large, technically well-equipped sector of the economy which is to provide better services in less time.

Housing   Housing is a cardinal social problem. During the years of Soviet power much has been done to solve the housing problem. Yet, much still remains to be done.

The five-year plan envisages a further extension of housing construction. During the five-year period 400 million square metres of housing space are to be built in towns, urban settlements and state farms at the expense of state capital investments and co-operative funds. In addition factory and office workers will build with the help of state credits individual houses of a total floor-space of over 80 million square metres. In rural areas the population and collective farms will build 2-2.5 million houses. The total volume of housing construction will grow by 30 per cent. All this is a long step towards solving the housing problem.

Enterprises being transferred to the new conditions of planning and economic stimulation are accumulating funds for socio-cultural measures and housing construction. This will expand the building of houses. Factory and office workers and collective farmers building individual houses from their private means or with state credits are rendered extensive assistance.

The fulfilment of the housing construction programme envisaged in the five-year plan will improve housing conditions for some 65 million people as compared with 54 million in the preceding five years. But even this enormous programme will not fully solve the housing problem. The extent to which the population is provided with housing is an indicator of the people's living standard that depends not only on the current national income but also on the level of accumulated wealth, since housing facilities are created over decades. The growth of the national wealth of socialist society is an earnest of the successful solution of this vital problem.

Approximation of the income levels

The rise in the material welfare in socialist society, which is advancing along the road to communism, is attended by a gradual decrease in the difference between high and comparatively low incomes.

The development of the productive forces of society and technological progress raise the cultural and technological level of the working people. A steadily growing number of unskilled factory and office workers are acquiring skills. The rise in skills and the increase in labour productivity go hand in hand with a consistent decrease in the pay differential. As the welfare of the whole population grows the wages of people in the low income brackets will rise and the difference between the incomes of workers and peasants will gradually diminish.

The decrease of the pay differential however should not be regarded in the light of an egalitarian distribution. It is based on the approximation of the levels of qualification and labour productivity. The approximation of the income levels is therefore not at odds with the principle of the material interest of the working people in better work but, on the contrary, promotes this principle.

The new five-year plan sets the task of radically improving the material conditions of low-paid working people. This refers to unskilled factory and office workers and junior service personnel. Extensive mechanisation of auxiliary work and of all sorts of accounting techniques as well as the automation of production will ease the need for unskilled labour. Many of unskilled workers will raise their skills and obtain better paid jobs.

The targets of the five-year plan provide for measures aimed at the consistent approximation of the way of life in rural and urban areas, at overcoming the socio-economic and cultural distinctions between town and country and cementing the alliance between the working class and the peasantry. During the five-year period the general educational and cultural and technological level of the masses will rise substantially, and the essential distinctions between manual and physical labour will decrease. The substantial growth of the people's welfare provided for by the five-year plan can be achieved only if the effectiveness of social production is consistently raised. The success depends on the efforts of all Soviet people, on their initiative and on their truly business-like attitude towards their duties.

REVISION QUESTIONS

1. What is the meaning of the socialist principle "From each according to his ability, to each according to his work"?
2. What interdependence is there between the growth of labour productivity and the growth of wages?
3. What are the social consumption funds and what is their role in the real incomes of the working people?
4. What are the tasks of the five-year plan with respect to the growth of the Soviet people's material welfare?

Chapter XVI

SOCIALIST REPRODUCTION AND CIRCULATION PROCESSES

1. SOCIALIST REPRODUCTION

Specifics of socialist reproduction Under socialism, the most progressive social system, reproduction is of the extended type. Extended socialist reproduction embraces three interlinked processes.

First, the reproduction of socialist production relations, which are steadily improving in the course of extended reproduction.

Second, the reproduction of the social product, which is effected on a growing scale with every passing year.

Third, the reproduction of the labour force, in the course of which the skills and the culture of the working people grow, as does also the productivity of their labour.

As we saw above, under capitalism too there is extended reproduction. However, socialist economy grows at a rate unattainable by capitalism. Socialism is free of crises of overproduction, which under capitalism periodically interrupt the course of reproduction. Socialism is also free of uneven development, which is one of the unconditional laws of capitalism. These advantages make the steady and rapid growth of production in all economic spheres a regularity of socialist extended reproduction.

Socialism is free of the contradictions of the capitalist system, under which the accumulation of wealth on one pole of society inevitably goes hand in hand with a growth of insecurity on the other pole. Under socialism, the wealth, multiplying with the development of the productive forces, is public property. It is not destroyed and wasted at the whim of the capitalists, or through the operation of the destructive forces of anarchy of production and competition.

The systematic increase of the social wealth under socialism goes hand in hand with the steady rise of the material and cultural level of the working people. Extended socialist reproduction means, on the one hand, a growth of public wealth, and, on the other, a rise in the material and cultural level of the working people.

Reproduction of socialist relations Following the triumph of socialism the development of the productive forces in all economic spheres proceeds in conditions of the undivided rule of the socialist system of economy. While the reproduction of capitalist relations inevitably leads to the growth and exacerbation of the contradictions typical of those relations, the reproduction of socialist relations leads to the systematic elimination of contradictions and to the eradication of the vestiges of capitalism in the economy and the consciousness of the people.

Socialist production relations are constantly improving in the course of extended reproduction. The new system of planning and economic stimulation of production is an important stage in their improvement.

The material and spiritual prerequisites for the highest phase of communism mature gradually during the whole period of communist construction.

The progress in all aspects of socialist production relations logically leads to the gradual elimination of the distinctions between town and country, between the classes and social groups of socialist society. It brings the growth and consolidation of communist principles in the relations between workers, peasants and intellectuals and leads to classless communist society.

The targets of the current five-year plan combine in an organic unity the development of the material and technical basis and the rise in the standard of living; the quantitative growth in the output and the further radical qualitative changes in the economy; the enhancement of the productive forces and the improvement of social and economic relations.

The fulfilment of the five-year plan will be a long stride towards the solution of important social and economic problems. It will gradually eliminate the essential distinctions between town and country and between physical and mental labour. It will further consolidate the political foundation and material basis of the alliance between the working class and the peasantry. The fraternal union of the peoples inhabiting the Soviet Union will be further cemented. The economic links of the Soviet Union with the fraternal socialist countries and the developing countries will grow even firmer.

Gross social product The gross social product comprises all the goods resulting from the economic production over a definite period of, say, a year.

Under socialism the bulk of the social product is the property of the whole people and some of it is the property of individual collectives of working people. The growth of the social product is the most general indicator of the development of all sectors of social production. The high economic development rates under socialism are reflected in the rapid growth of the social product. In 1965 the gross social product of the Soviet Union grew by 5.64 times, as compared with 1940. In 1965, it amounted to 62 per cent of the gross social product of the USA.

All branches of the economy engaged in production, transportation and the storage of material wealth participate in the creation of the social product. The ratio of the individual branches in the sum total of the social product is known as the branch structure of production. In 1964 the structure of the Soviet gross social product was as follows: industry accounted for 64.1 per cent of the sum total, construction for 9.5 per cent, agriculture for 16.4 per cent, transport and communications for 4.1 per cent, trade, procurements, material and technical supplies and so on— for 5.9 per cent.

The five-year plan for 1966-70 envisages high growth rates for the social product. It will grow every year by an average of more than 7 per cent, as compared with the annual increment of slightly over 6 per cent during the preceding 5 years. The average yearly increment of industrial output will comprise 22,000-23,000 million rubles, as against 15,800 million rubles in the past five-year period. The volume of industrial output is to increase during that period by about 50 per cent and agricultural output by 25 per cent.

Physical and value form of social product   The annual social product of socialist society is identified in natural (physical) and value form. As regards its natural form all the mass of the social product is divided into two major parts. This is first of all the means of production which are designed to re-enter the production process and, secondly, the articles of consumption, which are designed for the individual and joint satisfaction of the requirements of the members of society.

In their turn, the means of production are divided into two parts. One part are the fixed assets of the economy: buildings, equipment, the rolling stock of railways, agricultural machinery, etc. The other part are the assets in turnover: raw materials and semi-manufactures, fuel and electric power.

The growth of the fixed assets and assets in turnover extends the sphere of socialist labour, increases the wealth of all of society, facilitates labour, increases its productivity, and raises the material and cultural level of the working masses.

The means of production, or the productive fixed assets and assets in turnover, comprise the main part of socialist society's national wealth. The other part of the material wealth does not participate in production directly. It consists of housing facilities and the buildings and structures for social and cultural purposes: theatres, museums, clubs, schools, parks, etc., all of which form the non-productive assets of the economy.

In its value form the social product is the sum total of values produced by all sectors of the economy. This sum includes first, the value of the expended means of production and, second, the added value, created by the labour of workers, collective farmers and intelligentsia in all spheres of material production. The first of these two parts reimburses the used up means of production, the second is placed at the disposal of society for the satisfaction of all its requirements. This second part is the national income of socialist society, which will be dealt with further in the book.

Planned economy aims at adjusting the separate parts of the economy in a ratio that would ensure the correspondence of the structure of the social product (as regards its material form) with the social designation of its separate parts in the process of reproduction. This is the most important aspect of the task of ensuring proportionality in the process of extended socialist reproduction.

The normal course of socialist reproduction makes it necessary to realise the product of all branches without obstruction and without delay. This shows how important is the role played in socialist society by the market, i.e., by the aggregate of conditions for the realisation of commodities. The socialist market is a market organised according to plan. Socialist enterprises realise their goods, the products of socialist production, on this market. A constant check of market conditions, of the changes taking place on it and changes in the consumer demand is one of the basic tasks of the planned management of socialist economy.

Replacement of the means of production A definite mass of means of production—machinery, raw materials and fuel—are expended to manufacture the social product. To enable the unobstructed and continuous renewal of production on an unchanged scale, this mass of means of production must be replaced out of the annual social product.

Let us assume that 125,000 metal-working lathes and 450 million tons of coal have been consumed. In that case an equal amount of lathes and coal must be deducted from the annual product of society and returned to the fixed assets and assets in turnover in the economy to compensate it for the expended means of production.

The compensation of the expended means of production must be ensured also in value (money) form. Let us assume that means of production to the value of 100,000 million rubles were spent during the year. This means that society must be able to replace means of production for the same sum. In socialist society the renewal of the material productive assets is effected in a planned and organised manner.

Priority growth of the means of production Extended socialist reproduction presupposes definite quantitative relations between the branches of economy, notably between the production of means of production and the production of articles of consumption.

We have learned above that capitalist extended reproduction demands that the sum of the essential and the surplus product of Department I should be of a greater value than the fixed capital of Department II. This quantitative relation must also be established in socialist society, with the difference, however, that here it is not a question of fixed capital but of the fixed productive assets and the assets of turnover.

In other words, the priority growth of the production of means of production over the production of consumer articles is a law of extended socialist reproduction.

This does not mean, however, that the relation between the growth rates for the two groups remains unchanged at all stages of socialist and communist construction. In the Soviet Union, in the first decisive stages of the industrialisation drive, when it was necessary to set up a powerful basis for heavy industry as quickly as possible there had to be a considerable difference between the development rates of the two groups of industry. Between 1929 and 1940 the production of means of production grew at an average yearly rate that was close on 70 per cent higher than the growth rate of the production of consumer articles. Once a powerful economic potential had been created and the productive forces had developed to a high degree it became possible substantially to increase the growth of the branches of social production serving to satisfy the direct needs of the population. The success achieved in the development of heavy industry now makes it possible to channel considerably more resources to the development of the branches producing consumer goods.

Approximation of the growth rates of the production of means of production and the production of consumer articles The five-year plan provides for a decisive improvement of the proportions between industry and agriculture, and within industry—between the branches producing means of production (Group A) and those producing consumer goods (Group B).

In the post-war period agriculture faced difficult tasks, their solution was complicated by mistakes in the management of collective farm development. The result was a certain lag in the development of agriculture, which was unable fully to satisfy the requirements of the population and industry. During the seven-year plan period the output of industry grew by 84 per cent, that of agriculture by only 14 per cent. The lag in agricultural development was one of the main reasons responsible for the emergence of the disproportion between the production of means of production and the production of consumer goods, which had an unfavourable effect on the growth of the consumption fund in the country's national income.

The Party adopted an extensive programme of urgent measures to develop agricultural production, designed to boost this important branch of economy. The elimination of the disproportion between the development of agriculture and industry and a rise in agricultural production is one of the key tasks of the five-year plan for 1966-70. The fulfilment of this task is to be achieved through the supply of powerful equipment to agriculture, the substantial increase in the procurement and purchasing prices for all sorts of agricultural products (introduced in 1965), through the drawing up of stable procurement plans, through the material stimulation and removing obstacles, which stifled the initiative of the collective farmers, state farm workers, agronomists, operators, chairmen of collective farms and directors of state farms.

A major task of the five-year plan is to improve the proportions within industry and the relation in the development of its two groups of branches. The priority growth of the branches producing means of production was and continues to be an essential condition for the successful fulfilment of the tasks of building the material and technical basis of communism, a condition for continued technological progress and for raising the technological level of production throughout the economy. At the same time it is important to stop the branches producing consumer goods from lagging behind too far.

The five-year plan for 1966-70 envisages the approximation of the growth rates of the production of means of production and the production of consumer articles. The development of the food and light industries is to be accelerated and they are to be supplied with most up-to-date equipment. In the preceding five-year period production in Group A increased by 58 per cent and in Group B by 36 per cent, in the current five-year period the increase is to be correspondingly 49-52 per cent and 43-46 per cent. In the preceding five-year period the growth of production in the branches producing means of production outstripped the growth of the branches producing consumer goods by more than 50 per cent. In the current five-year period the difference will be only 10-12 per cent. This will be made possible, in particular, by the acceleration of the growth rate of the production of consumer goods in all branches of industry, including also the branches of heavy industry.

The accelerated growth of the production of consumer goods is an essential condition for the further successful development of the whole economy, since only this growth is able to actuate material stimuli for the upswing of productional surge forward.

Reproduction of the labour force Extended socialist reproduction would be inconceivable without a constant growth in the numbers of the working class and the systematic rise in the cultural and professional level of the workers.

Socialism has put an end to the method of replenishing the labour force which plays a decisive role under capitalism: workers thrown out of jobs by machines, ruined small commodity producers in town and country, and the reserve army of unemployed. The main source of replenishing the labour force under socialism is natural population growth. Furthermore, industry is absorbing the surplus labour force forming in agriculture as a result of the mechanisation of production. Finally the freeing of women from domestic labour makes it possible to draw them into the production process.

The numbers of the working class have grown considerably during the years of Soviet power. At the same time workers' skills are being rapidly raised in an organised way. In socialist society skilled personnel is trained according to plan in the wide network of educational institutions and also through on-the-job training.

The rapid growth and improvement of production in the course of communist construction changes the occupational structure. The introduction of new labour-saving equipment first of all abolishes the jobs of those engaged in auxiliary work. The decrease in the administrative and managerial apparatus, the further mechanisation of agriculture, the freeing of many women from domestic work are the sources making it possible to enlarge the number of people engaged in industry and other branches of the economy. At the same time the extensive development of the health services, education and culture requires a rapid increase in the number of workers engaged in these sectors.

This growth is conditioned by the need to enlarge the social consumption funds and to expand education and the public utilities in every way. In socialist society the expansion of the non-productive sphere ensures the fuller satisfaction of the working people's requirements, the improvement of their living and working conditions.

The changes in the utilisation of the social labour resources place high demands on the mass education and retraining of workers, and also on the planned redistribution of the labour force. In this it is strictly necessary to observe the principle of full voluntariness and material interest and to provide cultural facilities and social amenities in new regions.

2. NATIONAL INCOME

Growth of the national income in socialist economy

The national income is the gross social product minus the part going to compensate for the expended means of production. In other words the national income is all the added value created by society in the current year. Under socialism the whole national income is placed at the disposal of society and upon its growth the successes of socialist economy and the growth of the people's wealth depend.

Just like the gross social product, the national income of socialist society is expressed in natural (physical) and value (money) form.

In its physical form the national income of socialist society includes, first, the mass of the consumer goods produced during the year, and secondly, the mass of the added means of production, remaining after part of it has been used to compensate for those used up during the year, or, in other words, the means of production designed for the further expansion of production.

In its value (monetary) form the national income of socialist society is the whole mass of values produced by both the necessary labour and the surplus labour of the workers, collective farmers and intelligentsia in the sphere of material production. These values are designed to satisfy the personal and public requirements of the members of society and cover state needs and the expansion of production.

The main two sources contributing to the growth of the national income are the increase in the number of workers employed in the various branches of material production and the rise in labour productivity.

The growth of employment is rather limited and, moreover, a considerable part of the increment in the number of employed workers is accounted for by the non-productive sphere, notably by education and the health services. Therefore, the rise in labour productivity is the main source contributing to the growth of the national income.

Under socialism the rapid expansion of industry, agriculture and the other branches of economy ensures a national income growth rate that is unattainable under capitalism. The following data characterise the growth rate of the absolute size of the national income of the USSR. Taking the national income of the country for 1913 as 100, it was 75 in 1917, 119 in 1928, 611 in 1940. If we take the national income of the USSR for 1940 as 100, it was 83 in 1945, 164 in 1950, 435 in 1960 and 593 in 1965.

The new five-year plan provides for a growth of the national income by 38-41 per cent. It is to grow by an average 7 per cent a year, as compared with the average yearly growth of 6 per cent during the preceding five-year period. The acceleration of the national income growth rate in the current five-year period will be achieved through an increase in labour productivity and the effectiveness of social production. The more effectively the productive resources are used, i.e., the greater is the assets/product ratio, the more economically raw and other materials are used, and the higher the labour productivity, the higher are also the national income growth rates.

The new five-year plan creates all necessary conditions for an acceleration of the national income growth rate. Among them is the expansion and improvement of the productive apparatus. During the five-year period the fixed productive assets of the economy will grow by more than 50 per cent, including by 60 per cent in industry and by 90 per cent in agriculture. The new system of management is designed to ensure a rise in the effectiveness of social production. This creates the conditions for achieving the high national income growth rate envisaged in the five-year plan.

Distribution of the national income. Consumption and accumulation funds

The national income is the mass of the means—in physical and monetary form—socialist society has at its disposal for the satisfaction of its various requirements.

The requirements of socialist society can be divided into four basic groups. First, the remuneration of workers, collective farmers and the intelligentsia in accordance with the economic law of distribution according to labour. Second, the requirements of the population, which are satisfied at the expense of social funds, including the expenditure on the development of education, science, culture, public health, the improvement of the working people's living conditions, the payment of old-age and disability pensions, state assistance to mothers with many children and to single mothers, etc. Third, the expenditure on the maintenance of the central and local bodies of the state apparatus, and on defence. Fourth, the expenditure on the expansion of production and the nonproductive funds of the economy, and on the creation of reserve funds.

In accordance with these main requirements of socialist society the national income is divided into two basic funds: the accumulation and the consumption funds. The first three groups of requirements are paid for from the consumption fund, the fourth from the accumulation fund. For many years now in the Soviet Union the consumption fund accounts for about 75 per cent of the national income, the accumulation fund—for 25 per cent. The rise in the effectiveness of social production increases socialist accumulations and the working people's welfare.

In socialist society the growth of the national income is an essential condition for a rise in the people's standard of living. In the socialist countries the per capita national income grows at a much quicker rate than it does in the capitalist countries.

Under capitalism the lion's share of the national income is being parasitically wasted by the exploiting classes, while the material conditions of the working people do not depend on its growth. Under socialism there is a direct connection between the growth of the national income and the rise in the people's welfare: the higher the national income the greater is the people's welfare.

The growth of the national income during the present five-year period will make it possible to raise the wages of factory, office and other workers by an average of 20 per cent, the incomes of the collective farmers from their common economy by an average of 35 to 40 per cent. The share of bonuses and lump sum rewards in incomes will grow substantially and this will ensure an even fuller coincidence of the interests of every working-man with the interests of the production's collective and those of society as a whole. The money grants and privileges being granted to the population out of the social consumption funds will grow by no less than 40 per cent. As a result the real per capita incomes of the working people will grow by an average of 30 per cent.

Owing to the growth of the national income the consumption will increase during the current five-year period by 36-39 per cent over that in the preceding five-year period.

The average yearly increment of the consumption fund will be 11,000 million rubles, as compared with 6,500 million rubles in the preceding five-year period.

Socialist accumulation

Socialist accumulation is an essential condition of extended socialist reproduction. Accumulation means that a definite share of the national income is systematically used to expand the productive assets of society, to build new enterprises and to expand, modernise and reconstruct existing ones.

Socialist accumulation differs radically from capitalist

accumulation as regards its sources, the methods by which it is effected and its social consequences.

First, the source of socialist accumulation is the surplus labour of working people who are free of exploitation and work for themselves and their society, while the accumulation of capital is effected at the expense of the surplus value the capitalists squeeze out of the workers they exploit.

Second, socialist accumulation is carried out in a planned way with the aim of multiplying the social wealth and raising the people's welfare, while the accumulation of capital proceeds in a random way, in the course of competition and with the aim of increasing capitalist profits.

Third, socialist accumulation increases public property, while the accumulation of capital increases capitalist private property.

Socialist accumulation is essential to raise the working people's welfare, while the accumulation of capital makes the working people's existence even more insecure. Socialist accumulation strengthens the socialist economic system, ensures crisis-free economic development and the right to work for all citizens, while the accumulation of capital exacerbates the antagonistic contradictions of capitalism and leads to unemployment and crises.

First and foremost, socialist accumulation ensures the rapid and steady growth of the country's productive assets. The fixed productive assets of the USSR grew in 1965 by 400 per cent over the 1940 figure, those in industry by more than 600 per cent. In 1908 there were only 75,000 metal-cutting lathes and 18,000 forging presses in Russia. At the beginning of 1965 the Soviet Union had 2,760,000 metal-cutting lathes (36.8 times more than in 1908) and 580,000 forging presses (32.2 times more than in 1908).

The five-year plan for 1966-70 provides for a considerable share of the increment of output to be produced by capacities made operative during the five-year period.

Extended reproduction and capital construction

Capital investments create the material basis for extended reproduction. They finance the construction programme of the economic plan.

Under the five-year plan for 1966-70 the capital investments in the Soviet economy will amount to about 310,000 million rubles, i.e., will exceed those of the preceding five years by about 50 per cent. This will ensure the development of all branches of economy and all Union Republics, accelerate the growth of vital branches and remove the disproportions between and within branches that evolved during the past few years.

Hundreds of factories, mines and power stations, new towns and settlements, state farms and collective farm premises, irrigation systems and power transmission lines, millions of new flats and houses, thousands of schools, kindergartens, crèches and hospitals will all be built under the current five-year plan.

Under the new system of economic management extended socialist reproduction proceeds not only on the basis of centralised capital investments but also through the expansion, improvement and modernisation of production financed by the production development funds forming at enterprises from depreciation deductions and profits. This will enable the basic cells of the economy—the enterprises —to make a substantial contribution to the planned, balanced development of socialist economy and to improve its structure by introducing more progressive and prospective production methods.

The improvement of planning and economic stimulation of capital construction is to ensure a cut in the time needed for the completion of projects, improve the quality and lower the cost of construction. The rapid commissioning of productive capacities, paralleled by the high quality of construction, should become the main indicator in planning and the evaluation of the activities of building organisations.

The key task of the five-year plan is to accelerate construction and improve its quality and raise the effectiveness of capital investments. This makes it necessary to do away with the scattering of capital investments among numerous projects since this retards construction and freezes investments, delays the commissioning of capacities and thereby inflicts heavy damage on the economy.

3. CIRCULATION PROCESSES IN SOCIALIST ECONOMY

Specifics of the circulation processes under socialism

The circulation processes are a major and important aspect of socialist reproduction. These include: first, the circulation of goods —the trade turnover and the material and technical supply of all branches of the economy, second, the whole sphere of finance and credit relations, and third, the money circulation.

Based on public property, circulation processes are planned in the socialist economic system. They do not aim at ensuring private capitalist profits but at satisfying the people's requirements and ensuring uninterrupted socialist production and reproduction. Circulation is effected through the agency of industrial and trading enterprises and by groups of working people, collective farms, co-operatives under state supervision and also by the collective farmers selling the products of their labour.

The bulk of the means of production accounting for a considerable share of the social product is covered by the material and technical supply system. The uninterrupted supply of means of production—equipment and raw materials, fuel, power, etc.—is a crucial condition for the normal course of socialist reproduction. The new system of economic management affords wide scope for improving material and technical supply. Direct links between supplier and consumer enterprises are being extensively developed. In the new five-year period the task has been set to decisively improve the system of material and technical supply and to prepare the transition to the planned distribution of equipment, raw materials and semi-manufactures through wholesale trade.

Forms of trade and its tasks

In socialist economy not only production but also the trade develops according to plan. Planning accounts for the most important part of the trade turnover, namely the whole sphere of trade conducted by the state and by co-operatives. Trade is an indissoluble component of planned socialist economy.

There are three basic forms of trade in the Soviet Union: state, co-operative and collective farm trade.

The two giants in the trade turnover are state and co-operative trade. These two forms of Soviet trade rely on socialist production in industry and agriculture. The whole marketable output of state enterprises and a considerable share of the foodstuffs, produced by the collective farms, are sold through state and co-operative trade. They comprise the bulk of the commodities used for personal consumption. The retail prices for goods handled by state and co-operative trading establishments are fixed by the state in a planned way.

Alongside state and co-operative trade, there is collective-farm trade. The existence of this type of trade is conditioned by the nature of collective farm co-operative property—the collective farms dispose of their output as they see fit.

Collective-farm trade plays a noticeable role in supplying towns and industrial settlements with vegetables, potatoes, meat, dairy products and so on and thus expands the circulation of commodities between town and country.

On collective farm markets goods are sold by the collective farms, which realise part of the output of their socialised economy, and by individual collective farmers, who sell part of the products they have received according to work-day units and part of the products grown on their subsidiary plots. The prices on the collective farm markets are regulated by supply and demand. As state and co-operative trade improve, the prices of the collective-farm market drop under the influence of the planned prices of state and co-operative trade.

Trade is a means of balancing production and consumption, a means of studying the growing and changing demand. Socialist trade is required to make a thorough study of the consumer demand and to systematically induce the relevant enterprises and industries to satisfy this demand to the maximum as regards the assortment of goods, their quantity and quality. The systematic improvement of the work of trading organisations, the elimination of the shortcomings in their work is a condition for the unobstructed course of socialist reproduction and for the further advance of the working people's welfare. The inefficient work of trading organisations weakens the material interest of the working people in raising the productivity of their labour.

Flexibility and manoeuvrability are conditions for the

efficient work of trading organisations. Thus, for example, even though the volume of output of a definite commodity may be sufficient, incorrect planning and distribution of the commodity among the regions and districts of the country, a distribution that does not take into account their specifics, may and sometimes does lead to interruptions in supplying consumers. The mobilisation of local commodity resources, the utilisation of local potentialities to expand the commodity stocks entering the trade turnover is a major task of trade.

It is only by expanding trade and improving the work of trading organisations that the complex communist apparatus for distribution according to requirements can be created.

Monopoly of foreign trade
The domestic market of the socialist countries is protected against attempts of economic aggression from the capitalist countries by the monopoly barrier of foreign trade. All trade transactions with foreign countries are the exclusive right of the socialist state and of its bodies.

The foreign trade of the Soviet Union, a most important form of economic contact between the USSR and other countries, is a state monopoly. The monopoly of foreign trade thwarted from the very start all world capitalist attempts to establish an alliance with capitalist elements in the country. It enabled socialist society to subordinate foreign trade contacts to the interests of socialist construction.

The monopoly of foreign trade played an important role in carrying out the socialist industrialisation of the country and the collectivisation of agriculture. The development of foreign trade was made to serve the fulfilment of economic plans. In the initial period of the reconstruction the USSR imported a large amount of machinery and machine-tools, which were used to equip emergent socialist industry.

Foreign trade plays an important role in the economy of all socialist countries. It serves first of all as a means of developing and expanding the trade between the countries of the world socialist economic system. It serves at the same time as a means of developing economic contacts between the socialist and the industrial capitalist and young developing countries.

The socialist countries strive to use foreign trade extensively to accelerate economic development to the maximum.

Finances of socialist society

The socialist state must possess definite resources to satisfy its various needs. The principal revenue (income) of the socialist state are the incomes of state-owned enterprises and economic organisations.

Out of its proceeds from the sale of output every state enterprise first of all covers its expenditures, which in aggregate comprise the production costs. The gross proceeds minus the production costs form the net income (profit) of the enterprise. Its size depends on the quantity and quality of the output sold, the level of the production costs and the relation between the costs and the prices at which the output is sold.

The money incomes of the enterprise provide it with the monetary resources essential for it to operate. A definite part of the monetary income of the enterprises goes to the general state fund of resources for the utilisation by other enterprises and to cover other state expenditure.

The incomes of state enterprises and economic organisations are used to satisfy the state's general needs, partly directly and partly through the general state fund of monetary resources. A definite part of the incomes of collective farms and co-operative enterprises is also channelled to the general state fund of monetary resources.

The free money resources of collective farms and co-operative enterprises, organisations and the population at large may also be placed in that fund at a definite interest, and be used to satisfy the general requirements of the state.

This redistribution of the money resources mobilises part of the incomes, accumulations and savings of enterprises, institutions, organisations and the population and transfers the means thus collected to other enterprises, institutions and organisations. This redistribution provides an opportunity to exercise financial control over the activities of enterprises. All these operations are the functions of the financial system, which embraces the state budget, the banks, state insurance bodies and savings banks.

State budget   The state budget is the main link
of the socialist financial system.
The state budget of a socialist country is closely tied up
with the whole economy, for it concentrates the bulk of the
country's financial means, and allocates the sums needed
to satisfy the bulk of the state's requirements.

The state budget of the USSR is the basic financial
plan of the state. It takes the form of a balance of the
revenue and expenditure during the fiscal year, and is approved by the session of the Supreme Soviet of the USSR.

The USSR state budget is the fund of resources at the
direct disposal of the state as represented by its central
and local organs of power. The mainspring of the resources
in the budget are the incomes of the socialist economy. At
present they consist mainly of the deductions from the
profits of state enterprises and economic organisations and
of the turnover tax paid by them. As the enterprises are
being transferred to the new system of planning and
economic stimulation, the charge for the use of assets will
become the main channel through which the payments of
enterprises will enter the budget.

The deductions from profits depend on the efficacy and
the financial results of the activities of every enterprise.
The turnover tax is paid into the state budget as the commodities are realised. When the charge for the assets becomes the main part of the state budget revenue, the role
of other payments, including that of the turnover tax, will
grow correspondingly less important.

Redistributing the funds entering the budget, the state
strengthens the economic might of the USSR. A growing
share of the state budget expenditure is directed to education
and public health, the development of science and culture,
and to social security.

In the USSR state social insurance covers all factory and
office workers, and no deduction is made from the wages
of the insured. Social insurance is handled by the trade
unions, the mass organisation of the factory and office workers.

The system of state property and personal insurance and
the state savings banks, in which the savings and temporary
free money resources of the population are concentrated
are closely linked with the budget.

Credit in socialist economy In socialist society the credit system draws temporarily idle money resources into the economic turnover and satisfies the temporary need for cash. This determines the specifics of the credit methods of redistributing money resources as compared with the financial and budgetary methods, which have to do mainly with incomes and accumulations.

Credit is a method of mobilising funds, the attendant condition being that these funds are returnable at the first request. To provide these funds temporarily free money resources are attracted into the accounts and deposits at credit establishments. Temporarily free moneys, belonging to definite enterprises, institutions and organisations in accounts and on deposits are channelled into the economic turnover by placing them for a definite time at the disposal of other organisations, who are obliged to return them when that period expires. A definite interest is paid for the loan of these funds. In socialist economy interest is not the price of loan capital (for there is no such category as loan capital) but is a payment for the services of the bank.

Free money resources in the accounts and on the deposits of credit institutions make it possible to use settlements by book entries extensively. These book entries help to accelerate the turnover of money and material resources. They also help to regulate the money circulation, make it possible to establish effective control over the money turnover.

Credit serves the economic turnover of enterprises in all phases of production and circulation of commodities. This applies to the loan of funds for the payment of raw materials, fuel, semi-manufactures and other materials for production and the supply of cash for the payment of wages to the factory and office workers.

The USSR State Bank is the main institute for short-term crediting and settlements in the economy, the cash and issuing centre of the country and also the agency for settlements of accounts with foreign countries. The money resources providing for the movement of the assets in turnover and the assets on hand are concentrated there. The State Bank is the agency through which all the settlements are made of accounts between enterprises, institutions and organisations. It also handles the accounts of the state budget with the national economy and payments to the budget. Money streams into the State Bank and from it enters circulation.

The money system of socialism
In the socialist countries the money system is a component of planned socialist economy.

In the Soviet Union money enters the circulation through the State Bank. Giving loans to economic organisations and enterprises in accordance with the progress made by them in the fulfilment of their plans, the State Bank satisfies the requirement for money in circulation.

As production and the trade turnover expand, larger sums of money circulate. This is because the loans issued by the bank increase, as do also the payments made by the bank on behalf and by order of economic organisations. During periods when there is a seasonal contraction of the trade turnover the need of economic organisations for money resources decreases, loans are paid off, money is returned to the bank, and the money supply in circulation shrinks. Thus, the money circulation is closely connected with the credit operations of the bank.

It is to no less degree linked with its clearing operations. We have mentioned above that the bulk of the settlements between enterprises, institutions and organisations in the socialist economy is effected by book entry: the organisations issue written orders to the bank instructing it to pay a definite sum. Upon receipt of the order the bank debits the organisation issuing the order and credits that to which the order is made out.

Cash is needed mainly to pay for wages, the procurement of agricultural products, and small bills. Accordingly, the bulk of the money being paid out by the State Bank goes to pay for wages and procuring agricultural products.

In addition the State Bank regularly receives cash as sundry payments into the budget, deposits in savings banks, etc. The State Bank supplies cash for paying pensions, grants, insurance, etc. The money at the bank is in constant movement flowing both in and out.

The money circulation is regulated in the USSR in keeping with the cash plan of the State Bank. The cash plan takes into account all cash receipts by the bank and all expected cash payments to be made by it during the period covered by the plan. The cash plan is drawn up on the basis of the retail trade turnover plans, the plan for the number of factory and office workers, the wage fund and other indicators of the economic plan determining the size of cash receipts and payments.

For socialist economy to develop successfully, money must be stable. The regulation of the money circulation is one of the key tasks of planned economic management. The stability of money in socialist economy is ensured by the enormous commodity stocks which are concentrated in the hands of the state and are placed by it on the market at fixed prices.

State financial discipline and the regime of economy

The financial and credit system plays a very important role in socialist economy. Its normal functioning is a condition for the uninterrupted growth of socialist reproduction. The strict observance of state financial discipline and the regime of economy are essential for the financial and credit system to function normally.

State financial discipline demands all enterprises to fulfil their obligation to the state accurately and punctually, that they meet their contractual obligations vis-à-vis other enterprises and organisations accurately and that they make their payments when due and deliver goods and pay for deliveries on time. Care must constantly be taken to avoid all unnecessary expenditure and to prevent rejects and losses in production and trade. It is also vital to combat the immobilisation of financial means and material values working for the acceleration of the circulation of assets in turnover.

All measures directed towards thrifty and efficient management strengthen socialist economy as a whole and its financial system in particular.

REVISION QUESTIONS

1. What is the essence of socialist reproduction?
2. What makes the national income grow?
3. What are the functions of the financial system in socialist economy?

Chapter XVII

WORLD SOCIALIST ECONOMIC SYSTEM

1. FORMATION OF THE WORLD SOCIALIST SYSTEM

Emergence and development of the world socialist system The triumph of socialism in the Soviet Union led to the emergence alongside the capitalist economic system of the socialist economic system. However, for close on three decades the Soviet Union remained the only socialist country.

With the victory of the socialist revolution in a large group of European and Asian countries socialism went beyond the boundaries of a single country and became a world system. The world socialist economic system emerged and began to consolidate. The formation and strengthening of the world socialist system substantially changed the relation of forces between socialism and capitalism throughout the world. This is the greatest achievement of the international communist and working-class movement, a new historic triumph of Marxism-Leninism, a vivid demonstration of the irresistible progress of mankind towards socialism. More than a thousand million people live in the countries of the world socialist system. This is more than one-third of the world population.

The world socialist community is a powerful stronghold of the world's progressive forces. There is no power in the world that could restore capitalism in the countries that have fallen away from the capitalist system.

The transformation of socialism into a world system has strikingly demonstrated capitalism's historical doom. It ushered in a new stage in the struggle between the two social systems, the struggle that has become the principal feature of the general crisis of capitalism. The main contradiction of our time, the contradiction between growing socialism and moribund capitalism, has gone on to a higher stage.

The formation of the world socialist system is the main result of society's progressive development today. The main distinguishing feature of our times is that the world socialist system is becoming the decisive factor in the development of mankind. This is the result of the logical course of history at the present stage of human development.

The world socialist system is a social, economic and political community of free, sovereign peoples advancing towards socialism and communism, united by their community of interests and aims and the close bonds of international socialist solidarity. The socialist countries have an economic basis of the same type—public property of the means of production; a state system of the same type—people's power headed by the working class; a single ideology—Marxism-Leninism; common interests in defending their revolutionary gains and their national independence against imperialist encroachments; and a single supreme goal—communism.

All this creates an objective basis for stable and friendly relations between the socialist countries. Characteristic features of these relations are full equality, respect for independence and sovereignty, mutual advantage and fraternal mutual assistance. In the world socialist community no country has or can have special rights or privileges. New forms of interstate relations are steadily improving as the world socialist system develops.

New stage in the development of the world socialist system

As a result of the deep qualitative changes that have taken place in the socialist countries and in the relations between them, the world socialist system has entered a new stage in its development.

The advent of this stage is determined by the following basic factors. The Soviet Union has entered the stage of communist construction. In most socialist countries multisectoral economy has been abolished and the foundation of socialism has been completed. The fraternal co-operation and mutual assistance between the socialist countries has developed comprehensively.

The socio-economic possibilities for restoring capitalism have been eliminated in all socialist countries. The growing might of the world socialist system guarantees that their political and social and economic achievements will be safeguarded.

The share of industrial output grows in all socialist countries. Industrial development is the trend underlying the economic development of the world socialist system. The co-operation of agriculture has been completed in most socialist countries.

Changes in the class structure of society have stemmed from the deep revolutionary transformations. The alliance between the working class and the peasantry has consolidated. The economic basis of the exploitation of man by man has been wiped out, the socio-economic and political unity of the people is gaining ground.

The soaring economy in the socialist countries has considerably raised the living standard of the working people. The systematic growth of the people's material welfare in the socialist countries is a convincing proof of the decisive superiority of socialism over capitalism.

The world socialist system, in spite of its youth, has already amassed enormous experience which is of the greatest significance in determining the ways of mankind's further development. Now it is not only the experience of a single country but also that of a big group of countries that has proved the inevitability of the replacement of the capitalist system by the socialist system and has shown the decisive privileges of socialism. The new system has ensured high growth rates of productive forces, the steady rise of the working people's living standard, freedom from exploitation and extensive social and political rights of the individual.

Fundamental distinctions between the world socialist and world capitalist systems

The world socialist economic system emerged and develops in quite a different way from the world capitalist system.

Capitalism became a world system because it drew more and more countries into the whirlpool of the world capitalist market and spread the relations of capitalist exploitation across the globe. At the same time the relations between countries were to an ever growing extent ruled by the principle of domination and subordination. The growth of economic ties in the world capitalist system proceeded through some countries financially subjugating others and the colonial enslavement of hundreds of millions of people by a few imperialist powers.

Socialism became a world system owing to the abolition of the relations of capitalist exploitation in a number of countries, as a result of establishing new relations between them, relations of friendly co-operation and fraternal mutual assistance. Socialism has appeared on the world scene as a consolidated community of countries, the mutual relations of which are based on the principle of socialist internationalism.

As opposed to capitalism, socialism does not divide but unites peoples, establishes between them close relations based on full equality, comradely co-operation and mutual assistance. The extensive co-operation of the socialist countries strengthens the general economic basis of world socialism. All socialist countries contribute their share to developing and strengthening the world socialist system. The existence of the Soviet Union, its experience, its assistance considerably facilitate the building of socialism in the countries of the world socialist community.

The world socialist system embodies new, unprecedented international relations in the political, economic and cultural spheres. These relations are a result of the character of the production relations of socialism and are based on the economic laws of socialism.

In the world capitalist system the law of the uneven development of individual countries is responsible for deepening the chasm between the highly developed and less developed, the rich and the poor countries. In the world socialist system the law of planned, proportionate development, the fraternal, mutual assistance of countries accounts for the steady growth of the economies of all countries in that system, and this naturally leads to approximating their levels of economic development.

In the world capitalist system the growth of production in individual countries aggravates the contradictions and intensifies the competitive struggle between them. In the world socialist system the economic growth of every country boosts and strengthens the system as a whole.

The economy of the world capitalist system develops slowly, going through a series of crises and shocks. The world socialist economic system grows at a rapid and stable rate, owing to the steady economic advance of all socialist countries.

The world socialist system is a community of socialist countries in which the individual national economies are interlinked by comprehensive economic relations. The economic co-operation of the fraternal countries and the international socialist division of labour make it possible to use to the full the advantages of the world socialist economic system for developing the productive forces of each socialist country and for economically strengthening the world socialist system.

The relation of forces between socialism and capitalism is constantly changing to the detriment of capitalism and the advantage of socialism. The socialist system is becoming a factor determining the course of world development in the interests of peace and social progress to an ever greater extent.

The unity and cohesion of the socialist countries —an earnest of the victories of socialism

The world socialist system is not a simple sum of the countries in that system. It is a fundamentally new phenomenon in the life of mankind that multiplies the power of socialism. Already in 1920 Lenin brilliantly predicted the need for considering the tendency towards the creation of a single world-wide economy, regulated under a general plan by the proletariat of all nations, a tendency clearly displayed already under capitalism and which undoubtedly might be further developed and fully consummated under socialism.

This tendency was reflected in the world socialist system, which is a forerunner of socialist economy on a world scale. The fraternal co-operation of equal peoples, united in a single family by the principles of socialist internationalism grows and consolidates within the world socialist system.

The presence in the world today of the mighty socialist community is the main condition for the triumph of socialism and communism in individual countries. One of the most important factors contributing to the strength and invincibility of the world socialist system is the steady consolidation of the fraternal socialist countries politically and economically.

Blazing the trail to communism for the first time in history, the Soviet Union facilitates and accelerates the movement towards communism for the whole socialist community. Communist construction in the USSR strengthens the economic might and defence potential of the entire world socialist system. It creates ever more favourable possibilities for deepening the economic and cultural co-operation of the USSR with other socialist countries, for giving these countries assistance and support. Thus communist construction in the USSR falls in with the vital interests of all socialist countries.

The Communist Party of the Soviet Union, the fraternal Marxist-Leninist parties of the other socialist countries proceed from the need to cement the unity of the world socialist system.

2. THE ECONOMIC CO-OPERATION AND MUTUAL ASSISTANCE OF THE SOCIALIST COUNTRIES

Socialist international division of labour The development of the world socialist system evolves a new type of international division of labour.

Formerly there was only the capitalist division of labour between countries, which was based on the exploitation of weak countries by powerful predators. Now the socialist international division of labour is forming. It develops in the course of the extensive economic, scientific and technological co-operation of the socialist countries.

The socialist international division of labour is based on principles of voluntariness and full equality. It takes into account the specifics of every country in the world socialist system, their natural wealth and the skills of the personnel in those countries. This division of labour is to ensure the expedient development of the socialist countries' productive forces. It is a factor serving to accelerate the economic and cultural surge forward of every socialist country and of the world socialist system as a whole.

The international socialist division of labour helps to raise the effectiveness of social production and to accelerate scientific and technological progress. In this way it helps to attain high rates of growth of the economies and of the working people's welfare in all socialist countries.

The systematic deepening of the international socialist division of labour plays an ever greater role in ensuring the economies of individual countries with essential equipment and raw materials and their populations with consumer goods. It promotes the correct location of the productive forces on a scale embracing the entire world socialist system, the establishment of the essential proportions in the economy of every single country and the formation in it of a rational complex of interlinked and mutually supplementing branches. Achieving the most effective utilisation of common labour and material resources serves to accelerate the growth of the productive forces.

The decisions of the 23rd Congress of the CPSU regard the further development of the economic ties of the Soviet Union with the socialist countries and the utilisation of the international socialist division of labour on the basis of Leninist principles of proletarian internationalism and fraternal mutual assistance in the interests of strengthening the world socialist system as one of the most important tasks of the economic plan for 1966-70.

The development of the international socialist division of labour promotes the conscious rational economic management that socialism substitutes for the anarchy of capitalist production. This multiplies the power of every socialist country and of the world socialist community as a whole.

Role of economic co-operation between socialist countries The economic co-operation between the countries of the world socialist system grows and assumes more perfect forms as that system expands and consolidates.

In the first stage of the system's existence the economic co-operation was mainly based on bilateral foreign trade and the exchange of scientific and technological information. Granting credits of some countries to others was also practised.

With the further growth of the world socialist system new forms of economic co-operation evolved. The Council for Mutual Economic Assistance set up in 1949 began to play an ever greater role. The Council works out recommendations for the development of the economic, scientific and technological co-operation between the fraternal countries, looks for new forms of such co-operation. The Directives of the 23rd Congress of the CPSU on the five-year plan for 1966-70 speak of the need to develop new rational forms of economic co-operation between the CMEA member-countries in the spheres of industry, transport, trade, credit and financial links and international currency settlements.

The economic co-operation and fraternal mutual assistance of the socialist countries are of the greatest importance to the successful fulfilment of the economic development plans, to the upswing of science and technology and the steady advance of the peoples' living standards. Thanks to the comprehensive economic co-operation with and fraternal mutual assistance by the Soviet Union and of the socialist countries among themselves, the European socialist countries have in an historically brief span developed a domestic coal and metallurgical basis, many branches of the extractive industry, a power industry, and created a number of new branches of engineering and the chemical industry. The scale of production has grown in the socialist community and dozens of new branches have evolved and the mass production of thousands of new industrial products has been taken up.

The economic co-operation of the socialist countries is a powerful factor adding to the strength of socialism in the economic competition with capitalism. The further upswing of the world socialist economy is being achieved by the combination of their efforts in developing the economy of every socialist country and their joint efforts to strengthen and expand their economic co-operation and mutual assistance.

Main forms of the economic co-operation between socialist countries Among the most important forms of economic co-operation between the socialist countries is mutual trade, specialisation and co-operation of production, scientific and technological co-operation, joint organisation of vitally important industries.

The strengthening of the economic ties between the socialist countries is expressed in the growth of their trade turnover. At present the socialist countries account for about 70 per cent of the Soviet Union's foreign trade turnover. Over 95 per cent of the necessary equipment and machinery needed by the socialist countries is either produced at home or received as a result of the exchange within the socialist system.

The five-year plan provides for a further growth of the trade with the socialist countries. The tasks of the five-year plan in the sphere of foreign economic ties include the increase in the trade turnover between the USSR and other socialist countries, the implementation of co-ordinated measures to improve further the structure of exports and imports, and raising the economic effectiveness of foreign trade on this basis. The 23rd Party Congress noted that the co-operation with other socialist countries will help to fulfil the tasks of the five-year plan. It is expected to purchase in these countries over a thousand sets of equipment for enterprises and shops of the chemical, light, food and other branches of industry. Deliveries from the socialist countries will fill 48 per cent of the Soviet Union's requirements for marine transport vessels, 40 per cent of the need for main-line and industrial electric locomotives, 36 per cent of the needed railway coaches, etc. It is planned to purchase in the socialist countries a large amount of consumer goods: ready-made garments, knitwear, footwear, fabrics, food and chemical industry products. At the same time Soviet deliveries will fill the principal requirements of the socialist countries for many types of equipment and machinery, solid and liquid fuel, metallurgical raw materials and metals, cotton, timber, cellulose and paper and many other commodities.

Wider co-operation and specialisation in industry holds an important place in the economic collaboration of the socialist countries. Socialist specialisation and co-operation of production develop on the basis of the full observance of the interests of every participant. Specialisation and co-operation of production make it possible better to utilise the natural wealth and to develop the economy of every country to greater advantage, expanding at rapid rates the industries favoured by the conditions obtaining in the relevant country. This promotes the most rational utilisation of productive capacities and skilled personnel, raises the technical level and the scale of production and helps to organise line and large-series production.

At present the fraternal countries face the task of further developing economically effective and stable specialisation and co-operation, notably in engineering, the chemical industry, ferrous metallurgy and electronics.

In agriculture the economic co-operation between the socialist countries and the development of the division of labour among them makes it possible to use the economic and natural conditions and the experience and traditions of the population of every country most effectively. In this way they achieve an increase in the output of agricultural products for internal consumption and for exports. The mutual co-ordination of the different sectors of agriculture, taking into account the natural conditions and requirements of the socialist countries, leads to a better supply of the population with foodstuffs and of industry with agricultural raw materials. All this helps to raise the living standard of the peoples in the socialist countries.

Vital to the acceleration of technological progress in the socialist countries is the scientific and technological co-operation between them. The co-ordination of the efforts of the socialist countries in the field of theoretical and applied research and designing is becoming an important means of ensuring the rational utilisation of the resources of the world socialist system. The expansion of scientific and technological co-operation with other socialist countries goes hand in hand with an improvement of its methods, the development of the exchange of information on scientific and technological achievements, and of licences.

The existence of the world socialist system enables socialist countries to solve complex economic tasks jointly. Thus the economic co-operation of socialist countries promotes the growth of the coal and engineering industries in Poland, the aluminium industry in Hungary, some sectors of engineering in Czechoslovakia and the German Democratic Republic. Soviet iron ore, Polish and Czechoslovakian coke play an important role in developing metallurgy in the fraternal countries. Deliveries of machinery and equipment from the Soviet Union, Poland, Czechoslovakia and the GDR help other socialist countries carry out their industrialisation programmes.

A symbol of the economic co-operation between the

socialist countries is the construction of the giant Druzhba Oil Pipeline, which links the Soviet Union, Poland, the GDR, Czechoslovakia and Hungary. Oil from the Volga is carried by it to the banks of the Oder, Vistula and Danube. The delivery of oil along the pipeline costs only a fraction of the railway costs. Each country using the pipeline contributed its share to building this giant structure.

Approximation of the levels of economic development of the socialist countries The existence of the world socialist system, the development of economic co-operation between the socialist countries and of the international socialist division of labour —all this has created the real possibility of eliminating the gap in economic and cultural development between the individual countries which they inherited from capitalism.

The interstate relations of socialism are built on full equality of big and small countries. The mutual assistance and transference of experience, notably the mutual exchange of scientific and technological achievements, and the co-operation in the development of natural wealth ensure the approximation of the development levels of the countries in the world socialist system.

The planned levelling of the economic development of the socialist countries is promoted by the fact that the countries, which lagged behind in economic respects under capitalism, advance particularly rapidly, notably in industrial development. Thanks to this the share of these countries in important types of industrial output in the world socialist system as a whole is rapidly growing.

Within the framework of the world socialist system the formerly backward countries have in a short span of time drawn considerably close to the level of the developed socialist countries, the stronger supporting the weaker. But the degree in the development of the productive forces in the socialist countries is as yet not the same. The rise and levelling of the general economic level of the socialist countries is being achieved notably through the complete utilisation by every country of its domestic resources, the improvement of the forms and methods of economic management, the consistent application of the Leninist principles and methods of socialist management and the effective utilisation of the advantages of the world socialist system.

3. ECONOMIC COMPETITION OF THE TWO WORLD ECONOMIC SYSTEMS

Principle of peaceful coexistence between the two systems and economic competition The simultaneous existence of two opposing social systems is an indisputable historical fact, an objective inevitability of the modern epoch. The transition from capitalism to socialism extends over a long period of history. During that period socialist states live side by side with capitalist states. The question arises what should be the relations between countries with different social systems.

The socialist countries consistently follow the Leninist principle of peaceful coexistence between countries with different social systems. This principle proceeds from the assumption that the peoples in every country must themselves choose their social system. Marxism-Leninism holds that every country makes the transition from capitalism to socialism only when the objective and subjective preconditions for such a transition have matured in it. Lenin emphasised that Marxism had always denied the "pushing on" of revolutions, for they develop as the class contradictions giving birth to the revolution mature.

At the same time it is obvious that the principle of peaceful coexistence is inapplicable to relations between oppressors and oppressed, that there can be no peaceful coexistence in the class struggle within the capitalist countries and in the national liberation struggle in the colonies and dependent countries, between socialist and bourgeois ideology.

The principle of peaceful coexistence between countries with different social systems involves the possibility and need for the development of normal economic relations between the countries in question. The socialist countries therefore stand for the development of economic ties with the countries of the capitalist system on a mutually advantageous basis, without discrimination and without a restriction of the rights of either party.

The coexistence between the two systems presupposes the peaceful economic competition between them. The competition between the two systems embraces not only the economy but also other aspects of social life. But the economy is the main arena in which competition between the socialist and capitalist systems proceeds.

Two main stages in the development of the economic competition between the two systems In the course of its development the economic competition between the two systems passed through two principal stages. The first stage covers the period when the Soviet Union was the only socialist country in the world and had to compete against the whole capitalist world on its own. The second stage began when socialism went beyond a single country and the world socialist system emerged, when competition between socialism and capitalism became competition between the two world systems.

The socialist system of economy that has asserted itself in the USSR demonstrated the irrefutable supremacy of socialism even in the first stages of the competition with capitalism. At the second stage the vast expansion of the geographical and economic scale of the competition between the two world systems gave this competition a number of important new features. The advantages and successes of socialism in the economic competition with capitalism were thrown into bold relief. Now it is not only the economic victories of the Soviet Union but also the successes of economic construction in all countries of the socialist community, the new type of relations between them, that demonstrate the gigantic possibilities for the rapid upswing of the productive forces that are inherent in the socialist economic system.

With the emergence of the world socialist system the constant change in the relation of forces to the detriment of capitalism and in favour of socialism is becoming more and more clearly evident.

The economic growth of the world socialist system shows that socialism is a higher form of society as compared with capitalism. While modern capitalism with its outmoded relations of production arrests the development of the modern productive forces, the socialist system and socialist production relations promote their development.

In the conditions of the competition and struggle between the two social systems the constant increment of the material forces of socialism is of extreme international importance. It is essential for the rapid achievement and consolidation of the victory over imperialism in all fields of social life—the economic, political, scientific and technological.

Economic growth rates

The successes of socialism in economic competition with capitalism and the inevitable triumph of socialism in this competition is based on the fact that socialism ensures growth rates of the productive forces unattainable under capitalism.

The high rates of economic development is a general regularity in the countries progressing along the socialist road. In 1965 the industrial output of the socialist countries was almost ten times greater than the total produced there in 1937. During the same period the output of the capitalist countries grew only by 240 per cent. In 1965 the socialist countries raised their industrial output by 410 per cent over the 1950 level, while the capitalist countries increased their respective output by only 120 per cent. As a result of the high growth rates the share of the socialist countries in the total world industrial output is rapidly growing. The share of the socialist countries in the world industrial output was less than 3 per cent in 1917, less than 10 per cent in 1937, about 20 per cent in 1950, about 27 per cent in 1955 and about 38 per cent in 1965. The Soviet Union alone now accounts for close on 20 per cent of the total world industrial output. In 1965 the industrial output of the socialist countries reached about 67 per cent of the total industrial output of the developed capitalist countries.

The results of the competition between the USSR and the USA are no less indicative in this respect. In the twenty years from 1945 to 1965 the industrial output of the USSR has grown 760 per cent, that of the USA—100 per cent. The average yearly growth rate of industrial output was between 1946 and 1965 in the USSR—11.4 per cent, in the USA—3.6 per cent. The volume of industrial output in pre-revolutionary Russia was one-eighth of the US volume. In 1950 Soviet industry produced less than 30 per cent of US output. In 1965 Soviet industrial output reached more than 65 per cent of the US level.

The Soviet Union consistently strengthens its positions in the economic competition with the main capitalist countries. Events have demonstrated that the continuous expansion of production at high and stable rates is a regularity of socialist economy, an indisputable advantage of socialism over capitalism.

The fulfilment of the five-year plan for 1966-70 will further raise the economic potential of the Soviet Union, which will mean a further shift in the relation of forces between socialism and capitalism in the world in favour of socialism.

Economic aid to developing countries

In the course of economic competition between the two world social systems an ever increasing role is being played by the rapidly expanding comprehensive economic co-operation of the socialist countries with the young sovereign countries that have risen on the ruins of the colonial empires.

The existence of the world socialist system and the weakening of imperialism opens up before the peoples of these countries prospects of national revival, the liquidation of age-old backwardness and poverty, and the achievement of economic independence. Of enormous importance to the developing countries is the fact that socialism has taken the lead in economic development rates and has outstripped capitalism in a number of key fields of scientific and technological progress. Thanks to this, the former monopoly of the highly developed capitalist countries in the supply of means of production, aid, loans, credits, etc., has become a thing of the past.

The former colonies and dependent countries, which have achieved political independence as a result of a long and persistent struggle, are obtaining ever increasing economic assistance and all-sided support from the socialist states. This aid is vital in solving the urgent problems they are facing in connection with overcoming the grim heritage of the colonial system.

The assistance being given to the developing countries by the Soviet Union and other socialist countries has no political or military strings attached to it. Socialist countries in their economic contacts with the newly free people do not strive for any privileges. The co-operation on mutually advantageous terms between the socialist countries and the peoples who have embarked on the road of independent development is rapidly progressing on this basis.

The countries of the world socialist system supply the young developing countries with the necessary equipment and other commodities, grant them credits for the purchase of equipment and the payment of technical assistance on easy terms.

The Soviet Union as a leading industrial power, renders the developing countries comprehensive assistance in setting up the economic basis of their independence, in developing their industry and raising their national economies, which are necessary conditions for advancing the living standard of their populations.

Soviet economic and technological assistance embraces the construction of hundreds of industrial and agricultural enterprises and other objects in the young countries.

The five-year plan provides for the expansion of economic co-operation with the developing countries by strengthening trade ties and rendering them economic and technological assistance in reinforcing the independence of their national economies.

To the developing countries the friendly relations with the Soviet Union and other socialist states are a decisive factor in strengthening their freedom and independence and in their development along the road of social progress. As distinct from the imperialist powers, which are frantically attempting to subjugate the peoples once again, the countries of the world socialist system support the great process of liberation of peoples from colonial slavery, discerning here one of the main preconditions for the decline of capitalist exploitation.

REVISION QUESTIONS

1. What are the advantages of the world socialist system over the world capitalist system?
2. What are the main forms of the economic co-operation between the socialist countries?
3. What is the meaning of the economic competition between the two world systems?

Chapter XVIII

FROM SOCIALISM TO COMMUNISM

1. TWO PHASES OF COMMUNISM

General features and specifics of socialism and communism
Socialist and communist teachings were for a long time no more than utopias. The champions of these teachings argued which of the two principles was better: "From each according to his ability, to each according to his needs", or "From each according to his ability, to each according to his work". These arguments could not be fruitful because they did not rest on a scientific basis.

Only the founders of Marxism, having transformed socialism from a utopia into a science discovered the genuine relations between socialism and communism. They showed that society comes to communism not through the discovery of the best principle but as a result of objective laws of development.

Socialism emerges and develops on the basis of elements prepared by capitalism. After the abolition of exploitation of man by man society has to be guided for some time by the principle "From each according to his ability, to each according to his work". But this is not the end of its development. It progresses to a system under which society will be able to implement the principle "From each according to his ability, to each according to his needs".

The founders of Marxism disclosed the scientific difference between socialism and communism. They showed that these are two stages, two consecutive phases, two steps in the economic maturity of communist society: socialism is the lower stage, communism the higher. There is no wall between the two. Socialism in the course of its development logically grows into communism.

Socialism is the first, or lower, phase of communist society. The word "communism" can be used to describe this formation because the means of production are publicly owned. But it is not full communism. In the first phase communism is not yet economically mature and not yet free of the traditions or residium of capitalism. Socialism grows on the basis inherited from capitalism. Socialism effects gigantic historic transformations, yet, nonetheless, it still has the birthmarks of the old society, from the womb of which it emerged.

Socialist society as the first phase of communism is characterised, first, by the fact that the means of production are no longer privately owned but are public property, and, secondly, by the fact that each worker is remunerated by society in accordance with the quantity and quality of the labour he spends on social production.

Socialism, having smashed the exploitation of man by man, has rooted out age-old social injustice.

Socialism makes all members equal as regards the ownership of the means of production. Owing to this, conditions arise for the first time in the history of mankind in which the growth of the productive forces and the multiplication of the social wealth benefits all members of society. The experience of the Soviet Union and of all socialist countries has demonstrated that in socialist society the expansion of production unavoidably leads to the steady growth of the people's welfare and living standard. Thus socialism creates a sound basis for the people's fortune.

Under the socialist system all able-bodied members of society work and are remunerated by society for their work in accordance with its quantity and quality. But not all people are the same. Some are stronger, others weaker, some are married, others single, some have more children, others less. Therefore the socialist rule: equal pay for equal labour —does not as yet ensure full equality, full justice. Such full justice is achieved only at the higher phase of communism, when the principle "From each according to his ability, to each according to his needs" is implemented.

While the socialist law of distribution according to labour is in operation, there will inevitably exist a certain inequality among the members of society. These vestiges of inequality are fully eliminated under communism, with the transition from the distribution according to labour to the distribution according to requirements.

The building of communism will bring full social equality of all members of society. High labour productivity on the basis of rapid scientific and technological progress will create an abundance of material and spiritual wealth, which will open up the possibility of effecting the great principle of communism "From each according to his ability, to each according to his needs". The aim of communist production consists in ensuring the steady progress of society, in providing each member of society with the material and cultural benefits in accordance with his growing requirements, his individual demands and tastes.

When we speak of the satisfaction of the requirements of people, we do not have in mind their whims, but the sane requirements of cultured people.

At the present level of the development of the social productive forces the requirements of people for means of subsistence are not unlimited. People cannot eat more than is required without damaging their health. At the same time people have requirements which naturally grow with the development of the productive forces. For example, the enormous expansion of the production of polymer materials, synthetic fibres, plastics, etc., evolves the requirement for new and more comfortable and elegant clothes and footwear produced from these materials. The development of television gives birth to the requirement for TV sets. The building of ever more comfortable and well-appointed houses puts greater pressure on housing.

Under communism there will be a particularly rapid growth of the social requirements of people—requirements for the joint upbringing of children, for providing services and amenities, cultural recreation and the joint utilisation of the treasures of human culture. The growth in the requirements will in turn serve as a stimulus for the uninterrupted and soaring growth of society's productive forces.

The building of communist society is the ultimate aim of the revolutionary struggle of the working class, the supreme goal of the Marxist-Leninist Party.

With the completion of the building of socialism in the Soviet Union it embarked on a new stage of its historical development, the stage of the building of the higher phase of communism. Now the building of communism has become the immediate practical task of the Soviet people.

In the Programme of the CPSU communism is characterised as a classless social system with a single public ownership of the means of production, full social equality between all members of society, where the all-round development of people will go hand in hand with the development of the productive forces on the basis of constantly developing science and technology, where all sources of public wealth will be abundant and the great principle "From each according to his ability, to each according to his requirements" will be implemented. Communism is a highly organised society of free and conscious labouring people, in which there will be social self-government, where labour for the good of society will become a prime vital requirement, a comprehended need, where the abilities of each will be used to the greatest benefit of the people. The slogan of the Communist Party—"All for the benefit of man, for the good of man" will be fully implemented.

The growing of socialism into communism

Pointing out that from capitalism mankind can pass directly only to socialism, Lenin emphasised that the Communist Party looks further ahead, that socialism must inevitably gradually grow into communism. He pointed out that in beginning socialist transformations we must clearly picture the aim to which these transformations will ultimately lead. This aim is the creation of communist society.

The growing of socialism into communism is a natural process. Communism can develop only where socialism has firmly asserted itself. The transition to communism is effected through the steady growth, development and strengthening of the foundations of socialist society. The flourishing of the socialist system creates all preconditions essential for the gradual transition to the highest phase of communism. This transition is effected in the order and at the rate at which its preconditions accumulate and develop.

For communism to be built there must be the following conditions: a high level of the productive forces of socialist society, an advance of the people's welfare, an improvement of the production relations and a growth in the consciousness, the ideological and political level of all members of society. These conditions are created through building the material and technical basis of communism, the formation of communist social relations, the education of the New Man. All these conditions are indissolubly interlinked.

The chief condition ensuring the abundance of material and spiritual wealth for the people is the creation of the material basis of communism.

On the threshold of the socialist revolution, Lenin wrote that the political differences between the first, or lower, and the higher phase of communism would as time passed probably become enormous. At the same time he emphasised that only socialism will usher in the rapid, genuine advance in all spheres of social life, in which the masses will participate, the bulk of the population, and finally the whole population. This unusually rapid advance in all spheres of life is already taking place in the countries of the world socialist system.

The period of building communism in the Soviet Union is characterised by a powerful growth of the economy and culture, the maturing of all conditions for the achievement of full communism. The active and conscious participation of millions and millions of people in the building of communist society opens up the possibility for the accelerated growing over of socialism into communism. A key condition for this growing over is the high development of material production and the rapid development of the productive forces.

Highest form of social organisation

Communism is the highest form of social organisation. It is a society that has achieved enormous mastery over the forces of nature. It will have powerful productive forces unprecedented in history before. The gigantic growth of production creates an abundance of material and spiritual wealth necessary for the full satisfaction of the people's rapidly growing requirements.

Communism puts an end to the division of society into classes. The socio-economic distinctions and the differences in the way of life between the urban and the rural population will fade away. The countryside will rise to the level of the town as regards the development of the productive forces, the character of labour, the forms of production relations, the degree of welfare, culture and the way of life of the population. There will be an organic fusion of physical and mental labour. The people engaged in physical labour will in cultural and technological respects rise to the level of the workers of mental labour. As a result the intelligentsia will stop being a separate social layer.

Communism is the highest stage of the planned organisation of all of social economy. It ensures the most effective and most rational utilisation of the material wealth and of the labour resources for the satisfaction of the growing requirements of the members of society.

The unprecedented development of the technology of production and the enormous cultural advance of the people in communist society will change the nature of labour. Labour will no longer be only a means of livelihood and will become the prime vital requirement of man.

As distinct from all other preceding socio-economic formations communist society is built through the conscious activity of the popular masses, headed by the Marxist-Leninist Party. The Party directs the whole work of the builders of communism, lends it a planned, organised, and scientific nature. The Communist Party fulfils this role as the vanguard of the whole Soviet people, a vanguard that is strong by virtue of its close links with the broadest masses of the working people, its powerful weapon, Marxism-Leninism, the most progressive scientific theory, and its mastery of the laws of social development.

2. CREATION OF THE MATERIAL AND TECHNICAL BASIS OF COMMUNISM

The main economic task of the Party and people
The building of the material and technical basis of communism is the main economic task of the Party and the people. The Programme of the CPSU points out that the building of the material and technical basis of communism means complete electrification of the country and perfection on this basis of the techniques, technologies, and organisation of social production in all the fields of the national economy; comprehensive mechanisation of production operations and a growing degree of their automation; widespread use of chemistry in the national economy;

vigorous development of new, economically effective branches of production, new types of power and new materials; all-round and rational utilisation of natural, material and labour resources; organic fusion of science and production, and rapid scientific and technical progress; a high cultural and technical level for the working people; and substantial superiority over the more developed capitalist countries in labour productivity, which constitutes the most important prerequisite for the victory of the communist system.

In aggregate these main tasks characterise the scientifically based plan for the comprehensive development of the productive forces of socialist society.

The material basis of communism grows out of the material and technical basis of socialism through its rapid development, consolidation and comprehensive improvement. But this is not only a quantitative growth, it is at the same time a leap made in the course of the development of the social productive forces, a transition to a new quality.

The transition from socialism to communism is a continuous process. This means that building the material and technical basis of communism is also a continuous process.

Creating the material and technical basis of communism is the main economic task of the Party and the Soviet people throughout the whole period of building communist society. The relations of production improve in step with the successes in developing the productive forces of socialism. Such features of communism as more efficient organisation, the improvement of economic management become ever more apparent. The rapid development of the productive forces and the improvement of the production relations of socialism raise the productivity of social labour and the effectiveness of social production. The material welfare and cultural level of the people constantly grows on this basis.

The task of the creation of the material and technical basis of communism is being accomplished in the Soviet Union at a time when mankind is entering the period of the greatest ever scientific and technical revolution. This revolution is a logical outcome of the whole preceding development of science and technology. It is linked with har-

nessing nuclear energy, the conquest of space, the development of chemistry, the automation of production and other
enormous achievements of science and technology.

Only socialism is able to use the fruits of scientific and
technological revolution in the interests of society. This
revolution opens up unlimited prospects for the further
extension of the power of man over nature. It marks a
qualitatively new stage in the development of the productive forces of society.

It is common knowledge that the productive forces are
the aggregate means of production and human labour
power. The means of production in turn embrace the means
of labour and the objects of labour.

Modern means of labour are first and foremost machines.
The growth of a large-scale machine industry presupposes
the development of power sources, the perfection of the
instruments of labour and the objects of labour.

Main trends of technological progress
Accordingly, we can distinguish
three basic trends in technological
progress in the present period.
This is first, the revolution in
power sources. It is connected above of all with the complete
electrification of the country, the peaceful utilisation of
atomic energy, and in future, the possibility of utilising thermonuclear energy.

Second, it is the revolution in the field of the instruments
of labour. It is connected with the automation of production
leading to the creation of automatic machines systems.

Third, it is the revolution in the field of the objects of
labour. It is linked with the rapid development of the chemical industry. Of particular importance is the production
of synthetic polymer materials with preliminarily determined properties.

These main directions of present-day technological progress point to the enormous leap in the development of the
productive forces. There is now the possibility of freeing the
production process from the confines in which it was constrained up to the present.

As a result of the present scientific and technological
revolution the progress of production will no longer depend
on natural conditions which until recently were more or less
insuperable. Among these conditions were first of all the

limited power resources (mineral fuel and hydro-power resources). These are furthermore the limits of man's natural senses (his limited eyesight, hearing, etc.). These are finally the limited objects of labour found in a ready form in nature.

The utilisation of atomic and especially of thermonuclear energy for peaceful purposes opens up practically inexhaustible power sources. Automation, tending to become the main means for managing production processes, opens up the possibility for the unlimited growth of labour productivity. At the same time it serves as a condition for the organisation of new productions based on the utilisation of super-high temperatures, pressures and speeds. Chemistry, many of whose products were still recently considered substitutes, now supplies new materials that are indispensable for technological progress.

The material and technical basis of communism will be an aggregate of automatic systems of self-regulating machines in all spheres of production, using ever new materials and operated by electricity and atomic power, and in future by thermonuclear power. Such a material and technical basis will be able to develop at an unprecedented rate, ensuring a gigantic growth of social wealth while substantially reducing working time and radically changing the nature of labour, which will become a creative activity in all its forms.

Crucial to the creation of the material and technical basis of communism are the outstanding successes of Soviet science at present in the forefront of space research, nuclear physics, mathematics, electronics, radio engineering, metallurgy, rocketry, aircraft construction and many other fields of creative endeavour.

The new five-year plan is an important stage in the struggle of the Party and the Soviet people for the creation of the material and technical basis of communism and the further strengthening of the economic and defence potential of the Soviet Union. The main directions of the five-year plan reflect the basic trends of the modern scientific and technical revolution, outstanding discoveries in the field of physics, chemistry, mathematics, cybernetics, biology and the other sciences. The main tasks of the five-year plan are part of a scientifically planned programme for developing the productive forces of Soviet society and perfecting socialist production relations, drawing them closer to those of communism.

Complete electrification of the country
Electrification of the country is the backbone of the material and technical basis of communism. Lenin pointed out that communism is the Soviet power plus the electrification of the whole country.

Electrification plays the leading role in the development of all branches of the economy, in the development of the country along the road to technological progress. The priority growth of the production of electric power is the most important condition for the rapid rise in industrial and agricultural production. Cheap electric power will promote the rapid development of the power-intensive industries. Mass electrification will leave its imprint on transport, agriculture and the way of life of the urban and rural population.

Lenin's idea of the electrification of the whole country is decisive for the new five-year plan. The production of electric power will grow in the five years by about 70 per cent, while the general volume of industrial output will grow by 47 to 50 per cent. The plan provides for the building of large thermal power and hydroelectric power stations. The single power grid in the European part of the USSR will be completed. Construction is to be started of high-voltage lines to transmit the electric power from the eastern parts of the country to the European part of the USSR.

The further tasks for the development of the material and technical basis of communism will demand an even more rapid growth of the power industry. This growth will be ensured by the extensive utilisation, in addition to the old sources of power, of new sources of power—atomic and nuclear power.

In the field of the peaceful uses of atomic energy the Soviet Union already holds leading positions in the world. The first commercial atomic power station in the world was built and commissioned in the Soviet Union in 1954. The *Lenin,* the first atomic ice-breaker was also built in the Soviet Union. A number of other atomic power stations have been built since.

The growth of the atomic power industry makes it possible to solve two major tasks simultaneously. First, the electric power being supplied by atomic power stations will eventually be much cheaper than any other power. Secondly, the growth of the atomic power industry will save coal, oil and gas for utilisation as raw materials for the chemical industry.

The control of nuclear synthesis reaction tenders vast prospects for the development of the power basis of production. The solution of the problem of controlling thermonuclear reactions has been placed on the agenda of Soviet science. Among its tasks is also the discovery of methods for the direct transformation of thermal, nuclear, solar and chemical energy into electric power. The solution of this task will supply Soviet society with inexhaustible power reserves.

Comprehensive mechanisation and automation of production

The creation of the material and technical basis of communism presupposes comprehensive mechanisation and automation of production. This is the general trend of technological progress, one of the decisive factors for rapid economic growth, the main condition for a steep rise in labour productivity.

The mechanisation of the labour-intensive branches is effected even while the material and technical basis of socialism is being built. At first, however, mechanisation embraces only basic production processes, while in a number of other production processes, notably the auxiliary ones, use is still made of manual work of low productivity.

In creating the material and technical basis of communism the task of comprehensive mechanisation, embracing all stages of production, is a pressing one. Comprehensive mechanisation provides the greatest effect: it leads to the elimination of manual labour in the basic and auxiliary processes (the transportation of raw materials, fuel and finished articles, finishing, packing, etc.).

The automation of production is the natural continuation and completion of comprehensive mechanisation. At the same time it introduces a qualitatively new stage in technological progress. Under mechanisation the control of the technological process, and also of separate machines and operations is still man's work. Under automation these functions, embracing also regulation and supervision, are all machine work. Under full, comprehensive automation, machines control other machines.

The modern development of science and technology, especially of electronics and calculating techniques, makes it possible to create computing systems able to fulfil the most complicated tasks of automatic production control, many functions in research work, plan computations, and computations in accounting, statistics and management.

These systems not only replace human labour in the field of control, regulation and management of production processes but do this work much better than people. They operate with a speed and accuracy man can never attain. Furthermore they work in conditions in which people are unable to work, for example in harmful ambient conditions, owing to high temperatures and pressures, radioactivity, etc. Many modern industries would be inconceivable without automation. Such is the peaceful use of atomic energy, a number of chemical industries, etc.

Automation first embraces separate production operations and processes. Automatic lathes appear, then automatic lines, incorporating a series of lathes. But the trend of development is comprehensive automation, which means the automation not only of the basic production processes but also of auxiliary operations.

In the Soviet Union there are already many fully automated factories, where automation is closely linked with telemechanics, making it possible to control production processes at a distance. About 50 per cent of all district hydroelectric power stations are controlled from co-ordinator's points of the power grid by telemechanics or from the basic power stations in the chain. For example, the Rybinsk station is controlled from the co-ordinator's switchboard located at a distance of 300 kilometres, the Tsymlyansk station from a distance of over 100 kilometres.

The operating conditions of fully automated electric power stations are controlled by automatic devices, which switch separate units on and off as the need arises. In case of trouble they switch off the damaged unit and cut in the stand-by unit and at the same time send an immediate signal to the central distribution switchboard.

The possibilities of telemechanics are really inexhaustible. Proof of this were the world-acclaimed successes of the Soviet Union in discovering the mysteries of space and the historic flights of Soviet cosmonauts. These achievements are admired by people all over the world.

Automation penetrates not only industry but also agriculture.

Modern technical means are called upon to play an increasing role in managing the national economy. The use of electronic computers in combination with means of communications, passing on information from enterprises, will help to improve the operational management of industry, construction and transport. Electronic computer techniques are able to make various engineering, economic, financial computations, to automate accounting. The introduction of these techniques into the system of management will have an enormous economic effect.

Improved technology is linked with the spread of more progressive forms of the organisation of production. This means a further development of specialisation and co-operation of enterprises, the growth of combination of production and the introduction of mass production. At the same time the improvement of the organisational forms of production creates more favourable conditions for further rapid progress in the field of equipment and technology.

Chemistry in the economy The creation of the material and technical basis of communism presupposes a wide introduction of chemistry into the economy. The utilisation of highly effective materials being produced by the chemical industry, the utilisation of chemical methods will play an ever increasing role in production.

The rapid development of chemistry, its introduction into industry and everyday life are characteristic features of modern technical progress. Marx foresaw that with the development of science and technology, with the mastery of chemical methods and reactions, mechanical technology would to an ever greater extent give way to chemical technology , which would help to obtain an enormous economy of labour.

The utilisation of chemical methods reveals new useful properties in things and helps to use raw materials in the most comprehensive, i.e., in the most useful way. The introduction of chemistry into technology, the utilisation of synthetic materials give an enormous effect in many branches of the national economy.

The achievements of modern chemistry have considerably extended the possibilities of the growth of the national wealth. The successes of modern chemistry of organic synthesis have shown the practical possibility of obtaining a great many new products, more perfect and cheap means of production and consumer goods. These are various plastics, textile fibres, new kinds of glass, synthetic fuels, fats, pharmaceutical preparations. It is not a question of substituting materials found in nature, but of new products which are far superior to the former types of raw materials as regards their various properties and the possibility of their utilisation in production.

Chemistry produces materials of great purity, which are needed for building large atomic power stations and for portable semi-conductor radio sets. Therefore, the development of chemistry is an essential condition, without which there can be no further development of engineering, rocketry, radio-electronics, atomic production, light and other industries.

The use of polymer materials makes the economy of labour readily practicable. In the near future the industry of synthetic materials will begin to compete with metallurgy both as regards the volume of output and the diversity of the application of its products. It is common knowledge that the working of metals requires more people and more labour than their smelting. The replacement of ferrous metals by polymer materials is economically advantageous to an enormous extent.

Marx pointed out that chemistry forms the direct scientific basis of agriculture. The achievement of abundance of consumer goods presupposes the extensive chemicalisation of agriculture.

The rapid development of the chemical industry demands that complex mechanisation and automation of production processes be introduced. Modern chemical lightning-speed processes cannot be regulated and controlled without automatic devices. The automation of production processes, that opens up a wide scope for increasing labour productivity, in all industries, in the chemical industry is dictated by the prevailing conditions of production.

In this way, chemistry is a powerful spur to technological progress, called upon to accelerate the creation of the material and technical basis of communism.

The new five-year plan provides for high development rates in the chemical industry. Particularly rapid will be the growth of the production of mineral fertilisers, chemical fibres, plastics, synthetic resins, synthetic rubber and other products of organic synthesis, detergents and household articles. In five years the output of mineral fertilisers is to increase from 31.3 million to 62-65 million tons a year, of plastics and synthetic resins from 821,000 to 2,100,000-2,300,000 tons, of chemical fibre from 407,000 to 780,000-830,000 tons. The production of synthetic materials for the manufacture of fabrics, knitwear and artificial fur will be considerably expanded.

Science as a direct productive force
In creating the material and technical basis of communism an enormous role is played by the further growth of the role of science in economic development. Modern technological progress is based on the successes of the natural and technical sciences. The achievements of advanced science, developing in close contact with the practice of communist construction, are being ever more extensively applied in production techniques.

Science is becoming the decisive factor in the development of the productive forces. Scientific and technological progress opens up the possibility for the most effective utilisation of the wealth and the forces of nature in the interests of the people, finds new kinds of energy, creates new kinds of materials and works out methods for influencing climatic conditions, and mastering space.

Human development advances ever increasing demands on the scale, subjects, level and rate of research in physics, mathematics, chemistry, mechanics, and many other applied sciences. The greatest technological achievements of the present age are a result of the indissoluble unity of science, technology and industry. Technological discoveries embody the results of extensive scientific and technological research. At the same time the introduction of these discoveries into practice demands the presence of a relevant highly industrial basis.

The socialist system ensures the most favourable conditions for fruitful scientific work. A ramified network of research institutes has been set up in the Soviet Union and has been fitted out with the latest equipment. The Soviet Government invests considerable funds in the development of research institutes, experimental stations, pivot plants and design bureaus. The Soviet Union has achieved outstanding scientific and technical triumphs and has become the world leader in a number of important fields of knowledge. Soviet science has made an enormous contribution to technological progress in all fields of the economy.

To create the material and technical basis of communism science must develop at an even more rapid rate. In the process of the building of that basis, science, as predicted by Marx, becomes to an ever greater degree a direct productive force. Production gradually becomes the technological application of modern science.

The acceleration of scientific and technological progress presumes the extensive development of scientific research, the rapid utilisation of its results in production and the utilisation of inventions. Science plays an enormous role in the growth of the productivity of social labour, and in raising the effectiveness of production. The development of science and the rapid introduction of its results in the economy strengthen socialism's positions in the economic competition between the two systems.

The road to a single communist property As was mentioned above communism is a classless social system with a single ownership of the means of production belonging to the whole people. In the process of communist construction the two forms of socialist property will gradually draw closer together and ultimately fuse into a single communist one. The formation of a single communist property is effected through the growth, strengthening and improvement both of state property (that of the whole people) and of collective farm cooperative property.

In socialist society the property of the whole people is the basis of the livelihood of the whole population, including the collective farmers. At the same time the development and strengthening of the collective farm system lead to the emergence and strengthening of the features that are typical of the property of the whole people.

The merger of collective farm-co-operative property and the property of the whole people will proceed not as a result of the liquidation of the former but through a rise in the level of its socialisation with the assistance of the socialist state. Collective farm property does not put a brake on the development of the productive forces of socialist society towards communism, towards the creation of its material and technical basis, but promotes this process in every way.

The road leading to the rapprochement of the two forms of property is at the same time the road leading millions of peasants towards communism. The rapprochement of the two forms of socialist property and the transformation of the agricultural labour of the collective farmers into a variant of industrial labour will mean that the distinctions between workers and peasants will gradually fade away. This will put an end to the socio-economic and cultural distinctions between town and country. It will be one of the most important results of communist construction.

Throughout the period of communist construction a classless communist society of free and conscious labouring people is being created.

The fading away of the distinctions between the classes is a gradual and lengthy process. It leads to an ever greater social homogeneity. The liquidation of all class distinctions will be completed with the building of a full communist society.

The growing of socialist labour into communist labour In explaining the difference between the two phases of communist society, Lenin pointed out that socialism presupposes social labour combined with strict accounting, control and supervision on the part of the organised vanguard, the progressive part of the working people, and defining the measure of labour and its remuneration. Communism is a system in which people are used to carry out their social obligations without a special apparatus of coercion, in which work, free of charge, for the common good becomes universal.

The gigantic, unprecedented growth of the productive

forces serves as a basis for building communism. The creation of the material and technical basis of communism radically changes the conditions of labour. Comprehensive mechanisation and automation of production serves as the material basis for the gradual growth of socialist labour into communist labour.

New equipment and technology of production is a firm foundation for the enormous rise in the cultural and technical level of the working people, for the gradual drawing closer of physical and mental labour, and eventually for the complete fading away of the distinctions between them. At the same time the growth in the cultural level of the working people, the rise of their technical knowledge under socialism serves as a powerful driving force further accelerating technological progress.

The development of new technology will be used for a radical improvement and lightening of labour conditions for Soviet people, cuts in working hours and the improvement of amenities, the elimination of hard physical labour and later of all unskilled labour.

During the period of communist construction labour becomes the prime vital necessity of man. This transformation is logical and is a natural result of the radical transformations which mark the building of communism. It embraces both the material sphere and the spiritual life of society and is being prepared by the whole course of the development of socialist production relations, the process of their transformation into communist production relations.

The enormous successes in the development of the productive forces and production relations will create a sound basis for the transformation of labour into the prime vital necessity of man. On this basis a truly communist attitude towards labour will develop in all members of society. The enormous work of the communist education of the working people—through the best examples of labour and management of the public economy—will not fail to bear fruit. Labour will no longer be only a means of subsistence but will become a truly creative activity, a source of joy.

Everybody will voluntarily and consciously participate in production to create the wealth for himself and for the welfare of society. Owing to the changed nature of labour and to the abundance of equipment, and also to the high level of consciousness, there will develop an internal requirement in people to work according to their inclinations for the good of society. People will not be able to live without participating in creative, constructive labour, just as they are unable to live without air. Labour according to ability will become a habit, the prime vital necessity of man.

Communist education of the working people Building communist society includes, in addition to the development of the productive forces and the improvement in the production relations, the education of the New Man—the builder of communism. The education of all working people in the spirit of devotion to communism, the education of a communist attitude towards labour and towards the social economy, the final extinction of the remnants of bourgeois attitudes and morals is one of the most important conditions for the successful struggle for communism. Of special importance is the communist education of the young—the future builders of communist society.

The moulding of the New Man, as pointed out in the Programme of the CPSU, proceeds as the working people actively participate in communist construction and as communist principles in economic and social life develop through the educational activities of the Party, the state and mass organisations. All means of ideological work— the press and radio, the cinema and TV—are called upon to play an important role in the communist education of the working people. Of great importance in working out a communist world outlook are science and the arts. Marxism-Leninism, as an integral and harmonious system of philosophical, economic and socio-political views, serves as a basis for the formation of a scientific world outlook in all the working people of Soviet society.

Thus, in addition to the material conditions for the implementation of the higher phase of communism there must be definite mental preconditions, which involve the education of the New Man, fit to be a member of communist society. In the process of building communism the significance of the communist education of the working masses increases immeasurably, since they are the main productive force of society, since they are the builders of communist society.

REVISION QUESTIONS

1. What are the common features and differences between the two phases of communism?
2. What are the main directions for the creation of the material and technical basis of communism?
3. What is the essence of the communist education of the working people?

REQUEST TO READERS

Progress Publishers would be glad to have your opinion of this book, its translation and design and any suggestions you may have for future publications.

Please send your comments to 21, Zubovsky Boulevard, Moscow, USSR